Managing Knowledge

The Open University Business School

The Open University Business School offers a three-tier ladder of opportunity for managers at different stages of their careers: the Professional Certificate in Management; the Professional Diploma in Management; and the Master of Business Administration.

This book is an MBA Course Reader for the Managing Knowledge course (B823) at the Open University Business School. Opinions expressed in this Reader are not necessarily those of the Course Team or of The Open University.

Further information on Open University Business School courses and qualifications may be obtained from The Open University Business School, PO Box 197, Walton Hall, Milton Keynes, MK7 6BJ, United Kingdom; OUBS Information Line: tel: +44 (0) 8700 100311.

Alternatively, much useful course information can be obtained from the Open University Business School's website at www.oubs.open.ac.uk.

Managing Knowledge:
An Essential Reader

Second Edition

Edited by Stephen Little and Tim Ray

 The Open University   in association with    SAGE Publications

London ● Thousand Oaks ● New Delhi

First published 2002
Second edition published 2005

SAGE Publications Ltd
1 Oliver's Yard
55 City Road
London EC1Y 1SP

SAGE Publications Inc.
2455 Teller Road
Thousand Oaks, California 91320

SAGE Publications India Pvt Ltd
B-42, Panchsheel Enclave
Post Box 4109
New Delhi 110 017

British Library Cataloguing in Publication data

A catalogue record for this book is available
from the British Library

ISBN 1 4129 1240 7
ISBN 1 4129 1241 5 (pbk)

Library of Congress Control Number: 2005925396

Typeset by C&M Digitals (P) Ltd., Chennai, India
Printed in Great Britain by The Cromwell Press Ltd, Trowbridge, Wiltshire
Printed on paper from sustainable resources

Contents

Preface   vii

Acknowledgements   ix

1   Making Sense of Managing Knowledge   1
    Tim Ray

PART 1:   KEY CONCEPTS   21

2   SECI, *Ba* and Leadership: A Unified Model of
    Dynamic Knowledge Creation   23
    I. Nonaka, R. Toyama and N. Konno

3   Bridging Epistemologies: The Generative Dance between
    Organizational Knowledge and Organizational Knowing   51
    S.D.N. Cook and J.S Brown

4   What is Organizational Knowledge?   85
    Haridimos Tsoukas and Efi Vladimirou

5   Do We Really Understand Tacit Knowledge?   107
    Haridimos Tsoukas

6   An Overview: What's New and Important about
    Knowledge Management? Building New Bridges
    between Managers and Academics   127
    J.-C. Spender

CONTENTS

PART II: KNOWING IN PRACTICE   155

 7 Deep Smarts   157
     Dorothy Leonard and Walter Swap

 8 Organizational and Occupational Commitment:
    Knowledge Workers in Large Corporations   171
     May Yeuk-Mui Tam, Marek Korczynski and Stephen J. Frenkel

 9 Human Resource Policies for Knowledge Work   199
     John Storey

10 Knowledge Management Initiatives: Learning from Failure   221
     John Storey and Elizabeth Barnett

11 IC Valuation and Measurement: Classifying the State of the Art   239
     Daniel Andriessen

12 Managing Knowledge and Innovation Across Boundaries   255
     Paul Quintas

13 The Human Resource Architecture: Toward a Theory
    of Human Capital Allocation and Development   273
     David P. Lepak and Scott A. Snell

14 HR's Role in Building Relationship Networks   299
     Mark L. Lengnick-Hall and Cynthia A. Lengnick-Hall

PART III: REVISING THE AGENDA   317

15 Tacit Knowing, Communication and Power:
    Lessons from Japan?   319
     Tim Ray and Stewart Clegg

Index   349

Preface

This collection combines specially written contributions, from leading figures in the field of managing knowledge, with essential readings that frame the evolution of the topic and illustrate its relevance to managers, academics and others who are interested in 'knowing how to make a difference'. It is the second edition of a book designed to support the Open University Business School's MBA course, Managing Knowledge (course code B823), which was launched in 1999 – with some 850 students graduating from its first presentation.

When preparations for the Managing Knowledge course began in the mid-1990s, links between knowledge, knowing and MBA programmes represented uncharted waters. A decade later, the subject has soared to prominence and new questions are being asked about what might lie over the horizon. Throughout this process, the Open University Business School's Managing Knowledge Course Team has participated in a range of research and teaching activities in the UK and across the globe. The course is regularly updated to accommodate new ideas and fresh thinking, with a substantially revised and updated version being launched in November 2005. Particular attention has been paid to factors such as developments in Japan and implications arising from increased interconnection between local and global practices.

Chapters that have been produced for this volume include contributions from Stewart Clegg, who is Professor and Director of ICAN RESEARCH (Innovative Collaborations, Alliance, and Networks Research), University of Sydney, Australia, and J.C. Spender, who is based in New York and is a Visiting Professor at the Open University Business School. J.C. Spender was formerly Dean of the School of Business and Technology FIT/SUNY in New York and is now researching, consulting, writing and teaching 'Strategy and Knowledge Management' around the world. There are also original chapters from members of the Open University Business School team who established and developed the Managing Knowledge course. Paul Quintas, who is Professor of Knowledge Management, has written about managing knowledge across boundaries, while John Storey, who is Professor of Human Resource Management, has contributed a chapter entitled 'Human Resource Policies for Knowledge Work'. He is also co-author of an award-winning paper, reproduced here as a chapter, about learning from knowledge management projects that fail.

The Open University Business School specializes in supporting distance learning for managers. Managing Knowledge benefits from this tradition and has proved to be popular among students. It can be studied alone or as part of the school's MBA programme. Face-to-face tutorials, day schools and online activities help the student to progress through a total of nine interactive teaching texts or 'course units'. Those who enrol in one of the school's courses join more than 25,000 fellow students in 37 countries. There is also an active MBA Alumni Association with some 8500 members. If you would like to study Managing Knowledge or receive further information about Open University Business School courses, please visit our website at http://www.oubs.open.ac.uk, or telephone +44 (0) 8700 100311.

Special thanks in producing this reader are owed to Kiren Shoman at SAGE Publications and our colleagues at The Open University, especially the Managing Knowledge Course Team, Pam Cook, Gill Gowans and Shirley Eley.

Stephen Little and Tim Ray
March 2005

Acknowledgements

Grateful acknowledgement is made to the following sources for permission to reproduce material in this book.

1   Figure 1.1, The structure of DNA, reprinted from J.D. Watson and F.H.C. Crick (1953) 'Molecular structure of Nucleic Acids', *Nature*, 171: 737–8. © Macmillan Publishers Ltd. Republished with permission.

2   *SECI, Ba and Leadership: A Unified Model of Dynamic Knowledge Creation*
    I. Nonaka, R. Toyama and N. Konno (2000) *Long Range Planning*, 33(1): 5–34.
    © 2000, with permission from Elsevier.

3   *Bridging Epistemologies: The Generative Dance between*
    Organizational Knowledge and Organizational Knowing
    S.D.N. Cook and J.S. Brown (1999) *Organization Science*, 10(4): 381–400.
    Reproduced by kind permission of the Institute for Operations Research
    and the Management Sciences, INFORMS (www.informs.org) and
    the authors.

4   *What is Organizational Knowledge?*
    H. Tsoukas and E. Vladimirou (2001) *Journal of Management*
    Studies, 38(7): 973–93. © Blackwell Publishers 2001.

5   *Do We Really Understand Tacit Knowledge?*
    H. Tsoukas (2003) in M. Easterby-Smith and M.A. Lyles (eds) *The Blackwell*
    Handbook of Organizational Knowledge Management, pp. 410–27. Oxford:
    Blackwell. Reproduced by permission of Blackwell Publishing.

7   *Deep Smarts*
    Dorothy Leonard and Walter Swap (2004) *Harvard Business Review*,
    September Issue: 88–97. © 2004 by the Harvard Business School
    Publishing Corporation; all rights reserved.

ACKNOWLEDGEMENTS

8 *Organizational and Occupational Commitment: Knowledge Workers in Large Corporations*
M.Y.-Mui Tam, M. Korczynski and S. Frenkel (2002) *Journal of Management Studies*, 39(6): 775–801. Reproduced by permission of Blackwell Publishing.

10 *Knowledge Management Initiatives: Learning from Failure*
J. Storey and E. Barnett (2000) *Journal of Knowledge Management*, 4(2): 145–56. © MCB University Press. Republished with permission, Emerald Group Publishing Ltd (www.emeraldinsight.com).

11 *IC Valuation and Measurement: Classifying the State of the Art*
Daniel Andriessen (2004) *Journal of Intellectual Capital*, 5(2): 230–42. © Emerald Group Publishing Ltd. Republished with permission, Emerald Group Publishing Ltd (www.emeraldinsight.com).

13 *The Human Resource Architecture: Toward a Theory of Human Capital Allocation and Development*
D.P. Lepak and S.A. Snell (1999) *Academy of Management Review*, 24(1): 31–48. © 1999 by Academy of Management. Reproduced with permission of Academy of Management in the format of Other Book via Copyright Clearance Center.

14 *HR's Role in Building Relationship Networks*
M.L. Lengnick-Hall and C.A. Lengnick-Hall (2003) *Academy of Management Executive*, 17(4): 53–63. © 2003 by Academy of Management. Reproduced with permission of Academy of Management in the format of Other Book via Copyright Clearance Center.

Making Sense of Managing Knowledge

Tim Ray

In the late-1990s, many people were taken aback by the rapid diffusion of knowledge management (KM) initiatives. Burgeoning markets for new trade journals have encouraged knowledge-related titles (*Knowledge Management, KM World, KM Review, The Journal of Knowledge Management, The Journal of Knowledge Management Practice* and *The Journal of Intellectual Capital*). Major consulting firms have KM specialists and new KM marketing organizations. Pressure to follow the KM fashion has been an important influence on information technology expenditure and has given rise to new job titles, such as 'Chief Knowledge Officer'. The recent explosion in the academic literature seeking to make sense of the KM terrain and its messages for practitioners has matured into handbooks (Choo and Bontis, 2002; Easterby-Smith and Lyles, 2003; Holsapple, 2003). So how does this collection of original chapters and readings fit into an already crowded picture?

KM has become important, not least of all, because important people have taken it seriously and allocated big budgets to projects that attempt to 'manage' knowledge. Yet, there are signs that the achievements of such initiatives often fall short of expectations. Amid rapidly growing interest in KM, John Storey and Elizabeth Barnett won the *Journal of Knowledge Management's* 'Best Paper of the Year Award' with a perceptive assessment entitled 'Knowledge Management Initiatives: Learning from Failure' (reproduced in this volume as Chapter 10). When John Seely Brown and Paul Duguid sought to challenge some of the extravagant claims made in the name of information, they felt that publication of their book *The Social Life of Information* in March 2000, at the height of the dot.com boom, was a case of unfortunate timing. A year later, the dot.com bubble had burst, while interest in the book surpassed the authors' anticipations, as they noted in the preface to the second edition (Brown and Duguid, 2002: ix–x).

Notwithstanding the KM hype, Brown and Duguid appeared to echo the *Economist* magazine's judgement that the term is merely a 'buzzword': another light-weight managerial fad:

> *Certainly much about knowledge's recent rise to prominence has the appearance of fad-dishness and evangelism. Look in much of the management literature of the late 1990s*

and you could easily believe that faltering business plans need only embrace knowledge to be saved. While it's often hard to tell what this embracing involves, buying more information technology seems a key indulgence. (Brown and Duguid, 2002: 118)

To the extent that KM offers 'information' (in the form of so-called 'explicit knowledge'), it adds a new dimension to the dramatic advances in Information Communication Technologies (ICTs) that have transcended traditional boundaries between organizations and nations. Access to cyberspace provides previously unimaginable amounts of information but, as the philosopher Ludwig Wittgenstein (1889–1951) demonstrated in his *Philosophical Investigations* (2001), no amount of information can account for its own interpretation. Each interpretation would itself require an interpretation, implying a regress into infinite explanation. Access to information is not the same as the capacity to render that information meaningful. Nor is information about doing something the same as knowing how to do that thing in practice (Ryle, 2000: 26–60; Tsoukas and Mylonopoulos, 2004: 6). Although enthusiasm for measuring intangible assets and accounting for Intellectual Capital (IC) rocketed in the 1990s, as Daniel Andriessen (2004a, 2004b) explains in Chapter 11, 'IC Valuation and Measurement: Classifying the State of the Art', there is considerable disagreement about 'how to measure what' and the extent to which such measurements might be regarded as useful.

One of the problems to be faced when making sense of *managing knowledge* stems from the sheer breadth and diversity of interests that have identified with management and business knowledge. Suddenly, many well-established areas of study have appeared eager to demonstrate their knowledge credentials. Moreover, unlike easily forgotten management fashions, knowledge and knowing are important subjects in their own right.

Whereas a national flag or a tombstone might *denote* a great country or the life of a great person, the objects themselves (as pieces of cloth or stone) are of rather less intrinsic interest (Polanyi and Prosch, 1977: 72); their significance lies in the integration of a vast range of subsidiary details. Flags and tombstones from an era that has been lost to history fail to integrate emotions in the way that they might once have done. In the fast-changing and fickle world of management fashion, the symbolism of fads such as business process reengineering, quality circles and management by objectives seems to have become associated with past eras. In contrast, the knowledge fashion is double-edged: it combines the capacity to integrate thoroughly positive connotations associated with the word 'knowledge' (the fashion element of its brand image) with an intrinsically interesting subject that has fascinated history's brightest minds – a side of the blade that is less likely to become blunt. In this respect, J.C. Spender's specially written contribution to this reader (Chapter 6, An Overview: What's New and Important about Knowledge Management? Building New Bridges between Managers and Academics) is worthy of special mention being an attempt to integrate the practice and conceptual edges.

On occasions, KM might be seen as being a high-profile accessory to the managerial tool kit: a new solution of the type that is often presented with PowerPoint slides, designer mineral water and fashionable mints in imitation cut-glass containers.

And failure to pay sufficient attention to know-how embedded in established practices can create problems. As Storey and Barnett's study of KM failure (Chapter 10) notes, even the generous provision of organizational resources and an apparent commitment from top management is not necessarily sufficient to overcome the power embodied in established practices. In an additional chapter especially written for this volume (Chapter 9, 'Human Resource Policies for Knowledge Work'), John Storey explains how Human Resources Management is often expected to facilitate KM, while at the same time being intertwined with the very processes that it is trying to shape.

Meanwhile, the philosophical dimensions of knowledge and knowing are serious subjects that are deeply embedded in human practice. Myths and legends are the stuff of history. Stories are an essential part of sensemaking and communication: they exploit information about history or events in other places to make sense of the here-and-now and speculate on imagined futures. Metaphors and analogies provide powerful tools for explaining one thing in terms of another. Indeed, storytelling techniques are becoming an increasingly popular part of the management and business literature (Brown et al., 2005; Denning, 2001). Even though scientific stories are told according to strict rules, they are still stories that can be used to make a case and influence people. In all their various forms, stories are a valuable device for soliciting the intelligent cooperation of others and stimulating creativity – along with the emotional force of factors such as love, fear or money. Ultimately, effective management is about aligning the capacity to imagine a difference with knowing how to make a difference: the practice of power. But how does the new and fashionable KM paradigm relate to these long-standing questions?

The sections that follow introduce some key themes in the evolution of recent interest in management and business knowledge. Although problems with the practical implementation of KM often stem from misunderstandings that fuel overly optimistic expectations, these disappointments should not distract from the substantial insights that can be achieved by developing a better appreciation of how knowledge relates to the active process of 'doing things' in practice. Such issues frame the arrangement of this book, which is explained at the end of the chapter.

The Seeds of Misunderstanding

As Chapter 15 ('Tacit Knowing, Communication and Power: Lessons from Japan?') argues, the KM paradigm appears to blend at least two areas of misunderstanding: (a) Michael Polanyi's concept of tacit knowing; (b) and the assumption that practices situated in Japan's company-as-family workplace organizations can be divorced from their institutional context and used as a guide for managing knowledge in other contexts. The connection between these themes arises from the colossal influence of Nonaka and Takeuchi's (1995) book, *The Knowledge-Creating*

Company: How Japanese Companies Create the Dynamics of Innovation. The book was written specifically for the Anglophone market. Veteran management guru, Peter Drucker, has described it as a 'classic' (Takeuchi and Nonaka, 2004: ix). And its success has helped to propel Michael Polanyi's work on tacit knowing into the managerial mainstream.

Michael Polanyi (1891–1976) was born in Budapest, gained degrees in medicine and the physical sciences, before achieving recognition as an outstanding chemist, first in Germany, where his work included scientific exchanges with Einstein, and later in Britain (as an aside, his son, John, was joint winner of the 1986 Nobel Prize for Chemistry). In the later decades of his life, Polanyi turned to philosophy, publishing his magnum opus *Personal Knowledge* in 1958, after nine years devoted almost exclusively to its preparation (Polanyi, 1974: ix). Notwithstanding prevailing expectations that 'true knowledge' should be deemed objective and impersonal, he demonstrated that *Personal Knowledge* was not a contradiction in terms.

Polanyi's philosophical work developed the idea that there was an inexpressible tacit coefficient that enabled every thought and action. For example, we can recognize our friend's face from one in a thousand or, indeed, one in a million. The tacit integration of subsidiary information 'clues' is achieved in an instant – it is an instantaneous 'gestalt' perception in which, what we perceive as an organized whole, is greater than the sum of its parts. When we watch a movie, we see the flow of moving pictures, as opposed to individual frames of film. Similarly, we integrate information clues to recognize our friend in an instant, but we cannot say which clues we attended to, nor how we integrated them. We know 'how to do it in practice', but we cannot articulate what it is that we know: *'we can know more than we can tell'* (Polanyi, 1983: 4, italics in the original). After the event, we might attempt to construct an explanation of how the information clues could have been related to each other; but this is merely speculation and per force historical. If we were to give such an account to a stranger, we might not be confident that he or she would be able to pick out our friend instantaneously and unambiguously from a face among a thousand or a million candidates. Yet, a central theme of Nonaka and Takeuchi's (1995) model of knowledge creation turns on the claim that tacit knowledge can be converted into explicit knowledge (information) and moved from one context to another.

As the chief editor of the prestigious journal, *Organisation Studies*, Haridimos Tsoukas (2003; reproduced here as Chapter 5) has pointed out Nonaka and Takeuchi's (1995) book has been instrumental in the institutionalized misunderstanding of 'tacit knowledge' in management studies:

> *Ever since Nonaka and Takeuchi (1995) have published their influential* The Knowledge-Creating Company, *it is nearly impossible to find a publication on organizational knowledge and knowledge management that does not make a reference to, or use the term 'tacit knowledge.' And quite rightly so: as common experience can verify, the knowledge people use in organizations is so practical and deeply familiar to them that when people are asked to describe how they do what they do, they often find it hard to express it in words ...*

> *... My argument will be that popular as the term 'tacit knowledge' may have become in management studies, it has, on the whole, been misunderstood. (Tsoukas, 2003: 412)*

Tsoukas (2003 and ch. 4) goes on to explain that tacit knowing is essential to every thought and action, but it cannot be converted into information (so-called 'explicit knowledge') and 'managed'. If you tell me something, I might learn, yet your knowledge will not be diminished or 'converted' into something else. The capability to know is possessed by people: short of brain transplant, it stays with the knowing subject.

The Danish science writer Tor Nørretranders (1999: 125) suggests that human sense perceptions deliver more than 11 million bits of information per second (at least 10 million bits of which come from the eyes) but consciousness can only process 40 bits of information per second – at best. Moreover, consciousness comes some time after sense perceptions are delivered to the brain. Drivers can brake as much as 0.5 seconds before they are conscious of seeing the child run in front of the car. Fortunately, from the point of view of accident statistics, they can act in advance of consciousness. They do not have to wait for tacit–explicit knowledge-conversion. Parallel processing enables our brains to leap to conclusions before we are consciously aware of what the problem might be.

Malcolm Gladwell (2005) has popularized the concept of 'knowing more than we can tell' in his recent book, *Blink: The Power of Thinking without Thinking*. This highlights the importance of what psychologists call 'adaptive unconsciousness' Gladwell (2005: 11) – people can take a look and, in a blink experience emotions, intuitions and hunches that race ahead of conscious thought. In a similar vein, Guy Claxton's (2005) *The Wayward Mind: An Intimate History of the Unconscious*, begins by marvelling at his mind's capacity to exercise a 'mind of its own':

> *It wanders off while I'm trying to concentrate. It refuses to stop churning over the day while I'm trying to get to sleep. At night it creates movies that range from the exceedingly tedious to the embarrassingly bizarre. It comes up with tunes and phrases that I didn't intend, and often didn't want. It tells me that someone has come into the room when I've got headphones on and my eyes shut and I'm miles away – and often it's right. It forgets well-known names at crucial moments. It feels hurt or angry out of all proportion. It is a royal pain in the ass sometimes. But apparently it's the only mind I've got. (Claxton, 2005: vii)*

The capacity of the tacit dimension to act as an unseen 'mental butler' is an integral but unknowable part of every thought and action. It's not possible to observe yourself thinking, or 'see' the mental processes that enable and constrain thoughts and actions, any more than you can expect to leave your body and meet yourself as an object. Much of the time the mental butler might be a loyal servant – but not always, as Claxton points out. There are occasions when consciousness is accompanied by regret; for example, when you realize that emotions have overruled your intentions.

Metaphorically speaking, the tacit dimension might be represented as a 'tool of knowing' in the way that spectacles represent a 'tool of seeing'. And, as Polanyi commented, you cannot use your spectacles to scrutinize your spectacles (Polanyi and Prosch, 1977: 37). We can only point to the tacit dimension because of the fact that we can self-evidently do whatever it is that we do and think whatever it is that we think. On this account, tacit knowledge is unknowable in any abstract sense – 'We must be forever unable to give it an explicit specification' (Polanyi and Prosch, 1977: 62) – but its existence is implied by our ability to 'do things' in practice.

Learning from Japan?

At the height of Japan's miracle economic growth, many Westerners were eager to learn the secrets of its success. However, in contrast to the other G7 economies, Japan's traditional values owe almost nothing to Mediterranean origins – and the lack of common reference points can mask misunderstandings.

As Chapter 15 ('Tacit Knowing, Communication and Power: Lessons from Japan?') explains, the assumption that Japan's workplace organizations are roughly similar to the Western counterparts overlooks, among other things, the processes by which Japanese organizations have emerged in tandem with power relationships mediated by Japanese institutions. Nobel Laureate Douglass North (1990) has famously defined institutions as the 'rules of the game'. Throughout history, institutions have created order and reduced uncertainty in exchange: they enable and constrain what can and cannot happen in any given context (North, 1991: 97). For North, institutions comprise informal constraints (sanctions, customs, traditions and codes of conduct) and formal rules (constitutions, laws and property rights). He argues that they exist on a continuum, which stretches from the informal to the formal. Thus, economic development and the change from less to more complex societies represent a unidirectional move (albeit lengthy and uneven) from unwritten customs and traditions to written laws that underpin specialization and the division of labour (North, 1990: 46). However, the implication that economic progress is a march towards liberal individualism, impersonal transactions and the logic of Anglo-Saxon market-rational capitalism, misses the point that no rule can account for its own interpretation.

The reflexively automatic practice of power, mediated by highly aligned tacit knowing among insiders, in any tightly bounded collective, shapes what can and cannot happen in ways that are not even apparent to the insiders themselves. Here-and-now gestalt tacit integrations that guide behaviour cannot be articulated – yet, they shape what does and does not happen. Etiquette guides for visitors to Japan outline the rules of play for almost every social occasion, but they cannot account for how Japanese people themselves think and act *in situ*.

In Japan, employee loyalty, long working hours and work-before-family attitudes are not so much an achievement of coercive corporate rules, but a reflection of the way that organizations are embedded in Japan's wider social order. Sustaining obligations to the group in Japan's group-oriented society, and *esprit de corps* that is generated by repeat transactions, reinforce the status quo: group affiliation and appropriate introductions are essential to getting things done and ostracism (*mura-hachibu*) can have serious consequences. Within the organization, close community relationships reduce the marginal cost of information transfer, enabling insiders to retaliate against and ostracize those who break their code. Insiders (us) are differentiated from outsiders (them) and develop high levels of *esprit de corps* that facilitate breathtaking levels of coordination and flexibility. Meanwhile, the organization, as a collective entity, is fixed in web of repeat transactions with other organizations (such as regular suppliers and customers). Organizational insiders have a clear sense of 'the way that things should be done around here'. This relies on a facilitative and disciplinary power that operates through obligations arising from being a member of Japanese society in general, and any given company as family workplace organization, in particular. Many organizational practices are facilitated by expectations that are deeply embedded in Japanese society.

Foreigners who go to work in a Japanese organization might stumble over even the most basic rules of play and never come close to thinking and acting in the manner of an insider. Although they might take comfort in legal frameworks and formal rules that appear broadly similar to those found in Japan's Western counterparts, disciplinary authority turns on the power mediated by highly aligned tacit knowing among members of the relevant collective – whether it be Japanese society in general or a specifically organizational matter. Belonging to a Japanese organization involves demonstrating commitment to the organizational cause through voluntary overtime, not going home before the boss and after-hours socializing: one should 'be there' (even in the absence of essential work) to lend emotional support to one's colleagues. And holidays should be short. Consider the case of the foreign employee (FE), in discussion with his division chief (DC) in a Japanese organization. The FE wanted to take his full entitlement of three weeks holiday all in one go.

FE: I have three weeks' holiday and I should like to take them.
DC: Japanese people do not take so many holidays in one go
FE: But I'm entitled ...
DC: Sit down, have some green tea, have some rice crackers ...
FE: Thank you. [Accepting the green tea and a rice cracker]
DC: Why didn't you take all the rice crackers?
FE: Well, I didn't want to appear greedy ...
DC: And so it is with holidays! We offer you these holidays as a gesture. Only a foreigner would fail to see that it's greedy to take them all! What would your colleagues think?

Eventually, the story had a happy ending: the division chief learned that the employee had to return to his home country to sort out affairs after a family bereavement and sent him on an expenses-paid business trip to that country with no apparent work to do. The spirit of friendly paternalism can be warm and embracing; but only if the principle of commitment to the organization is observed. On this point, the Japanese American Dorinne Kondo's (1990) ethnographic study of life in a small family-owned Japanese factory offers some fascinating insights into the practice of facilitative and disciplinary power.

Nonaka's Model of Organizational Knowledge Creation

Nonaka, who had studied in the United States, was struck by the American respect for information processing of the type developed by Nobel Laureate, Herbert Simon. He felt that Simon's model of 'organizations as information-processing machines' overemphasized the logical aspects of human reasoning (see Nonaka and Takeuchi, 1995: 37–9). As Nonaka and his colleagues (2000; reproduced here as Chapter 2) argue, Japanese organizations are able to include care, love, security, energy, passion and tension among their organizational assets: such values spring naturally from close community relationships associated with being part of the organizational 'family'. But how do you communicate these taken-for-granted aspects of life inside a Japanese organization to outsiders who expect that there will be formal rules and levers that can be pulled to control cause and effect relationships? Western social science places considerable emphasis on the 'scientific' and finding causal mechanisms for all phenomena – yet, if insiders themselves are unclear about why and how they 'do what they do', what authority would outsiders have for making such judgements?

Whereas Polanyi insisted that the tacit dimension was, by its very nature, inexpressible, Nonaka's concept of knowledge-conversion turns on the idea that, given sufficient effort, aspects of the tacit dimension could be converted into information (which he called 'explicit knowledge') and communicated around the organization if it is first: 'converted into words or numbers that anyone can understand' (Nonaka and Takeuchi, 1995: 9). Thus, the tacit knowing that enables practice is objectified: knowledge becomes a transferable commodity and communication is presented as if it were a form of conveyance. For Nonaka, the challenge is to: 'express the inexpressible' (Takeuchi and Nonaka, 2004: 36). As a grand gesture, this is not without theatrical impact. Nonaka offered the Anglophone management world a new type of rice cracker and the Western appetite for new fashions seems to have relished the opportunity to consume everything on offer: oriental oracular mystique appeared to inspire Western managers to pursue new dreams with big budgets. Yet, Japan itself seems remarkably immune to the craze for KM crackers. Takeuchi[1] has, for example, noted that there has not been any sign of a Western-style KM boom in Japan.

The emotional glue or *esprit de corps* that binds insiders together in Japan's company-as-family organizations generates group-level knowledge of the type that

Cook and Brown (1999; reproduced here as Chapter 3) argue is qualitatively different to individual knowledge. For example, the collective dimension of a particular language is qualitatively different to what a particular person might have said in that language. Medical knowledge about a disease is different from the individual doctor's diagnosis that a particular patient is suffering from that disease. Similarly, tacit knowing possessed by a group is distinct from the tacit knowing of each individual member. Thus, the collective tacit knowing possessed by a football team that plays together regularly cannot be reduced to the individual skills of its members; individual players who move to another team can take their individual skills with them, but not their previous team's *esprit de corps*.

In a book first published in 1959, Edith Penrose (1995: 78) touched on something similar in her conception of a 'free resource', which is knowledge learned by one firm that is not immediately available to other firms. This collective capacity to know cannot be traded, but it has value in the services that it can render to insiders. Once this collective know-how has been mastered, it can be reused at no extra cost. Indeed, far from being consumed by its use, the resource is strengthened in the process. In this respect, Penrose pioneered a dynamic resource-based view of the firm that proved to be well ahead of its time – although renewed interest in her work prompted publication of a second edition in 1995. The cover carried a warm endorsement from Nonaka, although he appears to differ with Penrose on the individual-collective issue.

Nonaka adopts the view that 'knowledge is created only by individuals' (Nonaka and Takeuchi, 1995: 239). Accordingly, the individual – collective distinction is presented as a continuum. In a graphical representation of their famous knowledge-creating 'spiral' Nonaka and Takeuchi (1995: 72–3) plot tacit–explicit knowledge conversion (on the y-axis) against an ontological continuum (the x-axis) that stretches from the individual to the collective, passing through group, organization and inter-organizational boundaries. The creative individual's original idea is modified and expanded in the process of being repeatedly converted into 'explicit knowledge' and reinterpreted by an expanding community of interaction. Ultimately, it is speculated, such a process might render the secrets of Japanese knowledge-creation 'universal' (Nonaka and Takeuchi, 1995: 246). But is it reasonable to assume that only an individual can create knowledge? And can that creative individual's 'explicit knowledge' eventually become 'universal'? Does this 'universal' refer to 'universal truth' or merely information that is circulated widely? For example, in the manner of a sensationalist headline that whizzes around international media even though it has no basis in 'truth'. What is the intended relationship between information, 'explicit knowledge' and 'truth'?

Whereas occidental philosophy has tended to treat the subject and object as discontinuous entities ('true knowledge' has to be independent of the knowing subject and represent a knowable reality 'out there' in a more or less veridical fashion), tacit–explicit knowledge-conversion has provided (if unwittingly) scope to blend the two. Tacit knowing could be converted into 'explicit knowledge' (information) and combined with objective knowledge (also expressed as information) and 'managed'. Thus, knowledge-conversion implies that it is possible to be subjective and objective at the same time. As Nonaka et al. (2000: 7/Chapter 2) put it: 'we adopt the traditional definition of knowledge as "justified true belief". However, our focus is on the "justified" rather then the "true" aspect of belief'. Thus, the Western expectation that knowledge has something to do with objectively determined 'truth' is blurred to accommodate other forms of information – yet, this is not merely mundane-sounding information, but re-branded as 'explicit knowledge'.

Albert Einstein famously observed that: 'Knowledge is experience. Everything else is just information'. Thus, experience is afforded a centre-of-stage role. In contrast, Nonaka's concept of tacit–explicit knowledge-conversion provides a device for separating 'knowledge' from knowing subjects by converting their capacity to know into information or 'explicit knowledge'. However, this road leads to abstraction. It abstracts information from the here-and-now processes by which people think and act in any given context. For Michael Polanyi (1969: 195), all of knowledge is either tacit or rooted in tacit knowledge, hence: 'The ideal of a strictly explicit knowledge is indeed self-contradictory; deprived of their tacit coefficients, all spoken words, all formulae, all maps and graphs, are strictly meaningless ... The false ideal of a strictly explicit knowledge was pursued with the greatest zeal in the twentieth century by modern positivism.'

In Western cultures, science has been equated with an attempt to reveal eternal 'truth' that transcends human experience. However, as Ernst von Glasersfeld (2002) and other radical constructivists have argued (see Chapters 6 and 15), unless we claim some form of direct mystical revelation of an eternal truth (such as a message from the gods) all of human knowing – including scientific information about a supposedly independent reality – is constructed. And to the extent that these constructions are articulated, they are represented as *information*.

Consider, for example, the race to decode the human genome. These advances build on the development of knowledge about the structure of deoxyribonucleic acid (DNA) that was published in the top-ranking scientific journal *Nature* in 1953, by James Watson and Francis Crick, who went on to win the 1962 Nobel Prize for Medicine. The entire paper – it only covers about a page – is reproduced in Figure 1. In some respects, it might be seen as one of the 20th century's most important scientific breakthroughs: but is the paper knowledge, information or something else? To Watson and Crick's peers and rivals, the publication was a potent and highly meaningful symbol of the knowledge that had been mastered. In KM terms, its cogent presentation might be a textbook example of 'explicit knowledge' – but what does this knowledge mean to you? For those who possess the capacity to read the paper in a meaningful manner, it might be of great interest. It might also be of interest to those who are curious to note how the style of academic publishing has changed over the last half-century. However, those who lack the necessary background knowledge could struggle to make sense of the information contained in the paper. And even if the paper was explained, for example, with hypertext annotations, these annotations could not explain themselves without recourse to more annotations. Meaning can only be generated in the mind of the knowing subject. Someone who has never seen the artifacts of today's society might struggle to differentiate a scientific paper from a railway timetable or wallpaper.

No. 4356   April 25, 1953   NATURE   737

equipment, and to Dr. G. E. R. Deacon and the captain and officers of R.R.S. *Discovery II* for their part in making the observations.

[1] Young, F. B., Gerrard, H., and Jevons, W., *Phil. Mag.*, **40**, 149 (1920).

[2] Longuet-Higgins, M. S., *Mon. Not. Roy. Astro. Soc., Geophys. Supp.*, **5**, 285 (1949).

[3] Von Arx, W. S., Woods Hole Papers in Phys. Oceanog. Meteor., **11** (3) (1950).

[4] Ekman, V. W., *Arkiv. Mat. Astron. Fysik. (Stockholm)*, **2** (11) (1905).

MOLECULAR STRUCTURE OF NUCLEIC ACIDS

A Structure for Deoxyribose Nucleic Acid

WE wish to suggest a structure for the salt of deoxyribose nucleic acid (D.N.A.). This structure has novel features which are of considerable biological interest.

A structure for nucleic acid has already been proposed by Pauling and Corey[1]. They kindly made their manuscript available to us in advance of publication. Their model consists of three intertwined chains, with the phosphates near the fibre axis, and the bases on the outside. In our opinion, this structure is unsatisfactory for two reasons: (1) We believe that the material which gives the X-ray diagrams is the salt, not the free acid. Without the acidic hydrogen atoms it is not clear what forces would hold the structure together, especially as the negatively charged phosphates near the axis will repel each other. (2) Some of the van der Waals distances appear to be too small.

Another three-chain structure has also been suggested by Fraser (in the press). In his model the phosphates are on the outside and the bases on the inside, linked together by hydrogen bonds. This structure as described is rather ill-defined, and for this reason we shall not comment on it.

We wish to put forward a radically different structure for the salt of deoxyribose nucleic acid. This structure has two helical chains each coiled round the same axis (see diagram). We have made the usual chemical assumptions, namely, that each chain consists of phosphate di-ester groups joining β-D-deoxyribofuranose residues with 3', 5' linkages. The two chains (but not their bases) are related by a dyad perpendicular to the fibre axis. Both chains follow right-handed helices, but owing to the dyad the sequences of the atoms in the two chains run in opposite directions. Each chain loosely resembles Furberg's[2] model No. 1; that is, the bases are on the inside of the helix and the phosphates on the outside. The configuration of the sugar and the atoms near it is close to Furberg's

This figure is purely diagrammatic. The two ribbons symbolize the two phosphate—sugar chains, and the horizontal rods the pairs of bases holding the chains together. The vertical line marks the fibre axis

'standard configuration', the sugar being roughly perpendicular to the attached base. There is a residue on each chain every 3.4 A. in the *z*-direction. We have assumed an angle of 36° between adjacent residues in the same chain, so that the structure repeats after 10 residues on each chain, that is, after 34 A. The distance of a phosphorus atom from the fibre axis is 10 A. As the phosphates are on the outside, cations have easy access to them.

The structure is an open one, and its water content is rather high. At lower water contents we would expect the bases to tilt so that the structure could become more compact.

The novel feature of the structure is the manner in which the two chains are held together by the purine and pyrimidine bases. The planes of the bases are perpendicular to the fibre axis. They are joined together in pairs, a single base from one chain being hydrogen-bonded to a single base from the other chain, so that the two lie side by side with identical *z*-co-ordinates. One of the pair must be a purine and the other a pyrimidine for bonding to occur. The hydrogen bonds are made as follows: purine position 1 to pyrimidine position 1; purine position 6 to pyrimidine position 6.

If it is assumed that the bases only occur in the structure in the most plausible tautomeric forms (that is, with the keto rather than the enol configurations) it is found that only specific pairs of bases can bond together. These pairs are: adenine (purine) with thymine (pyrimidine), and guanine (purine) with cytosine (pyrimidine).

In other words, if an adenine forms one member of a pair, on either chain, then on these assumptions the other member must be thymine; similarly for guanine and cytosine. The sequence of bases on a single chain does not appear to be restricted in any way. However, if only specific pairs of bases can be formed, it follows that if the sequence of bases on one chain is given, then the sequence on the other chain is automatically determined.

It has been found experimentally[3,4] that the ratio of the amounts of adenine to thymine, and the ratio of guanine to cytosine, are always very close to unity for deoxyribose nucleic acid.

It is probably impossible to build this structure with a ribose sugar in place of the deoxyribose, as the extra oxygen atom would make too close a van der Waals contact.

The previously published X-ray data[5,6] on deoxyribose nucleic acid are insufficient for a rigorous test of our structure. So far as we can tell, it is roughly compatible with the experimental data, but it must be regarded as unproved until it has been checked against more exact results. Some of these are given in the following communications. We were not aware of the details of the results presented there when we devised our structure, which rests mainly though not entirely on published experimental data and stereo-chemical arguments.

It has not escaped our notice that the specific pairing we have postulated immediately suggests a possible copying mechanism for the genetic material.

Full details of the structure, including the conditions assumed in building it, together with a set of co-ordinates for the atoms, will be published elsewhere.

We are much indebted to Dr. Jerry Donohue for constant advice and criticism, especially on inter-atomic distances. We have also been stimulated by a knowledge of the general nature of the unpublished experimental results and ideas of Dr. M. H. F. Wilkins, Dr. R. E. Franklin and their co-workers

(Continued)

at King's College, London. One of us (J. D. W.) has been aided by a fellowship from the National Foundation for Infantile Paralysis.

J. D. WATSON
F. H. C. CRICK

Medical Research Council Unit for the
   Study of the Molecular Structure of
      Biological Systems,
   Cavendish Laboratory, Cambridge.
       April 2.

[1] Pauling, L., and Corey, R. B., *Nature*, **171**, 346 (1953); *Proc. U.S. Nat. Acad. Sci.*, **39**, 84 (1953).

[2] Furberg, S., *Acta Chem. Scand.*, **6**, 634 (1952).

[3] Chargaff, E., for references see Zamenhof, S., Brawerman, G., and Chargaff, E., *Biochim. et Biophys. Acta*, **9**, 402 (1952).

[4] Wyatt, G. R., *J. Gen. Physiol.*, **36**, 201 (1952).

[5] Astbury, W. T., Symp. Soc. Exp. Biol. 1, Nucleic Acid, 66 (Camb. Univ. Press, 1947).

[6] Wilkins, M. H. F., and Randall, J. T., *Biochim. et Biophys. Acta*, **10**, 192 (1953).

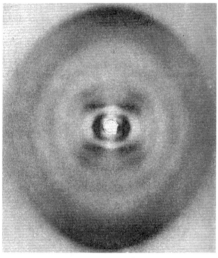

Fibre diagram of deoxypentose nucleic acid from *B. coli*. Fibre axis vertical

Figure 1.1   The structure of DNA

Cook and Brown's Generative Dance

Amid the surge of interest generated by Nonaka and Takeuchi's (1995) path-breaking work, Scott Cook and John Seely Brown's (1999/Chapter 3) *Bridging Epistemologies: The Generative Dance between Organizational Knowledge and Organizational Knowing* offered arguments for reinterpreting Nonaka's insights in a way that shifted the spotlight of attention towards the active process of 'knowing as action'. Cook and Brown retained Nonaka's distinction between tacit knowledge and explicit knowledge, but insisted that it was not possible, under any circumstances, to convert one into the other.

They also insisted that not every aspect of what is known by a group can be usefully or meaningfully reduced to the actions of an individual. For example, the English language is possessed, as a tool that is held-in-common by English language speakers, irrespective of whether you tell me what you did last night. If my bus breaks down and has to be towed off the highway, it will not change the collective dimension of the Highway Code. Conversation and the conventions associated with road traffic regulations are group-level 'tools' that enable communication, safer highways and other factors that contribute to knowing as action. Clearly, this group-level issue is important in enabling what you can and cannot do. If you travel from Britain to France, the institutional 'rules of the game' change – and failure to adapt can have consequences. Yet, when people move from one organization to another, they might fail to notice that they are using the wrong language and 'driving' on the wrong side of the road (for example, by asking to take their holidays in ways that offend against the prevailing rules of play).

In Cook and Brown's 'generative dance', all four types of knowledge (tacit and explicit, possessed by individuals and groups), 'mutually enable' the active process of knowing as action. However, if tacit knowing is unknowable in any objective sense, is it viable to insist that it comes in two types? Can groups reproduce the unknowable gestalt tacit integrations, which are associated with individual experience, in a synchronized manner? Arguably, all that we can do is point to the collective experience (for example, the moment when everybody broke into spontaneous laughter) and infer that tacit knowing among members of the group was in some way aligned. When we are in the company of close friends, we might act and think as if there is an unambiguous alignment of tacit knowing: but there is always scope for the occasional surprise.

In Polanyi's approach, tacit knowing is reflexively automatic: you cannot consciously turn it off (anymore than Polanyi could scrutinize his spectacles through his spectacles). People are no more conscious of tacit knowing than a healthy person is conscious of his or her bones. Yet, aspects of Cook and Brown's argument reflect a distinctly transitive flavour. Take, for example, their comments about riding a bicycle:

> *If you ride around using your tacit knowledge as an aid to discovering which way you turn [to keep upright], when you ultimately acquire the explicit knowledge you still possess the tacit knowledge, and you still use it in keeping upright. (Cook and Brown, 1999: 385/Chapter 3)*

In the above excerpt, tacit knowledge becomes the object of the transitive verb 'to use'. So, where is Cook and Brown's 'you'? Where is the person-behind-the-person wielding the individual tacit knowledge and group-level tacit knowledge 'tools'? Who is this meta-person who can apparently scrutinize his or her spectacles through his or her spectacles?

Nested and Overlapping Collectives

Social learning, working and innovating of the type that takes place within Japan's company-as-family workplace organizations is evident in the Western concept of communities of practice. For example, one of its pioneers, Etienne Wenger (2003: 80) has written about a *shared repertoire* of communal resources – language routines, artifacts, tools, stories and so on – that emerge from practice and are possessed by practitioners as tools of practice.

> *Communities of practice are groups of people who share a concern, a set of problems, or a passion about a topic, and who deepen their knowledge and expertise in this area*

by interacting on an ongoing basis. Engineers who design a certain kind of electronic circuit called phase-lock loops find it useful to compare designs regularly and to discuss the intricacies of their esoteric specialty. Soccer moms and dads take advantage of game times to share tips and insights about the subtle art of parenting. Artists congregate in cafés and studios to debate the merits of a new style or technique. Gang members learn to survive on the street and deal with an unfriendly world. Frontline managers running manufacturing operations get a chance to commiserate, to learn about upcoming technologies, and to foresee shifts in the winds of power. (Wenger et al., 2002: 4)

In the course of daily life, people are simultaneously members of many nested and overlapping collectives. As Wenger (2003, p. 91) has pointed out, you do not cease to be a parent because you go to work; you do not cease to be a nurse because you step out of the hospital – the responsibilities of childcare exist in parallel with work and other responsibilities. Even so, some collectives are more important than others. And power, mediated by prevailing institutional rules of practice, has a profound effect on the way that collectives, situated in different institutional contexts, operate and achieve insider–outsider distinctions. For example, Japan's institutional rules of practice militate against 'horizontal' collaboration and self-organizing communities of practice – as Nonaka et al. (2000/Chapter 2) imply:

However, the knowledge creating process is not confined within the boundaries of a single company. The market, where the knowledge held by companies interacts with that held by customers, is also a place for knowledge creation. It is also possible for groups of companies to create knowledge. If we further raise the level of analysis, we arrive at a discussion of how so-called national systems of innovation can be built. For the immediate future, it will be important to examine how companies, government and universities can work together to make knowledge creation possible. (Nonaka et al., 2000: 30/Chapter 2)

Practice within Japan's tightly bounded company-as-family workplace organizations is a matter for insiders; self-organizing horizontal networking by individuals lacks legitimacy. However, in the US, UK and other societies, institutional rules of practice legitimize liberal individualism, employee mobility and a labour market for specialists. Accordingly, responses to the question that Haridimos Tsoukas and Efi Vladimirou (2001; reproduced here as Chapter 4) pose, in 'What Is Organizational Knowledge?', might vary considerably according to power relationships that are mediated by the prevailing institutional rules of practice.

In the US, UK and other leading Western economies, traditional professions (such as law and medicine) and organizational professions (for example, managers and administrators) are being complemented by the rise of so-called knowledge workers. As May, Korczynski and Frenkel (2002; reproduced here as Chapter 8) point out, new occupations such as financial and management consultants, information technology analysts, project engineers and computer technologists are often assumed to be free agents who can create special 'market niches' for themselves. However, these workers might be more intimately connected with their organizations than is commonly assumed: knowledge-based perspectives provide a potentially valuable tool for revising simplistic assumptions about alliances, networks and partnerships.

The boundaries of Western organizations tend to be ambiguous and attempts to work out who is allied with whom on what issue can reveal tensions between formal statements about what lies in the organization's interests and individual ambitions. In an original chapter produced for this volume, Paul Quintas has addressed the challenging topic of 'Managing Knowledge and Innovation across Boundaries' (Chapter 12). This is an important theme that highlights issues in the two subsequent chapters.

In Chapter 13, 'The Human Resource Architecture: Toward a Theory of Human Capital Allocation and Development', David Lepak and Scott Snell assess four modes of soliciting the intelligent cooperation of employees: home-grown internal development (in the manner of a Japanese company); acquisition of key personnel on the labour market; contracting out specific tasks; and alliances. The viability of each mode depends on generating intelligent cooperation of knowers (the people who possess the capacity to do what your organization believes it wants done) and each carries its own costs and benefits. Effective communication and cooperation depend on social processes. Yet, the importance of the social dimension only becomes apparent when somebody does something that offends against the institutional rules of practice. The social dimension is a vital, but frequently under-acknowledged, tool of effective management. On this account, Mark Lengnick-Hall and Cynthia Lengnick-Hall's 'HR's Role in Building Relationship Networks' (2003; reproduced here as Chapter 14) is of particular interest. It explains how HR professionals can orchestrate six types of relationship that enable the pursuit of competitive advantage. Effective communication depends on alignment of tacit knowing: the capacity to read information signals in a similar way. Building effective relationships is a vital part of coming to appreciate what other people know and the extent to which their knowledge might be of interest to you.

Can you Tell Me How to be Smart?

Dorothy Leonard and Walter Swap sound as they are a smart couple: they are respected US academics – she is a professor at Harvard Business School, while he holds a chair at Tufts University – and they are married to each other. Moreover, they have written a book *Deep Smarts: How to Cultivate and Transfer Enduring Business Wisdom* (Leonard and Swap, 2004a) and an article in *Harvard Business Review* (2004b; reproduced here as Chapter 7) that deal with the problem of transferring business expertise to other people. What they call 'deep smarts' (a deeply smart insight), is not the sort of thing that can be transferred in a series of PowerPoint slides or by downloading data:

When a person sizes up a complex situation and comes to a rapid decision that proves to be not just good but brilliant, you think 'That was smart.' After you've watched him do this a few times, you realize you're in the presence of something special. It's not raw brainpower, though that helps. It's not emotional intelligence, either, though that too is often involved. It's deep smarts, the stuff that produces that mysterious quality, good judgement. (Leonard and Swap, 2004: 88)

To be sure, it's hard to argue against the importance of good judgement: but how is this mysterious quality to be nurtured and managed with regard to organizational and other activities? An instruction manual that merely says, 'Work out what good judgement is and be sure to apply it at all times' would not be much help. Calls to identify and use 'best practices', or managerial edicts to ensure that employees always aspire to 'best practices', can be irritating. Moreover, these bland slogans often dodge the tricky question of how to define 'best' in concrete, measurable terms. What sense is a manager to make of a trusted colleague who suddenly fails to meet expectations? Is it reasonable to assume that he or she is simply having a bad day or does the problem run deeper? Have that person's circumstances changed (for example, as a result of non-work commitments), or is there some change in the nature of the job that undermines the value of yesterday's 'best practice'? A person might be doing his or her best in changed conditions that require new or different practices and fresh thinking. Without a clear understanding of the person and the various contexts that shape his or her capabilities, aspirations and problems, it is difficult to make an informed judgement.

A part of the manager's problem is that what Leonard and Swap call 'deep smarts' – the capacity to act and think in a wise and insightful manner – are difficult to imagine in the abstract: you have to be familiar with the context in which a particular person was being smart. To the uninitiated spectator, skilled practice enabled by 'deep knowledge' can be more or less indistinguishable from mediocre or downright poor performance. A casual or uninformed glance might not be sufficient to differentiate between the skilled action of the expert and the lucky guess of a novice. Even the most well-intentioned or heroic attempt to 'rise to the occasion' might, if it is taken out of context, come across as a bungled, last-minute scramble. Separating 'snapshots' of actions from their appropriate context can seriously misrepresent what those snapshots meant to people at that particular time and place. What appears to be smart today might turn out to be less impressive tomorrow, and vice versa.

Intuition, hunch and 'gut feeling' all represent the type of knowledge – born from experience – that might help people to 'read' the signs and respond appropriately. For example, an experienced doctor's 'inspired guess' can be a lot more useful than the novice's 'hard information' – even if the latter is supplied in huge quantities. As insiders come to know 'what is what' in a particular context, they develop a 'sixth sense' of what might happen next and, in normal circumstances, are rarely surprised. In contrast, novices who have only grasped part of the picture might be entirely confident until a 'killer fact', which they have hitherto overlooked, forces them to reassess their position.

In an effective example of what KM might miss, Flyvbjerg illustrates how focusing on the rules of practice can conflict with the skilled execution of practices based on those rules:

> *Some years ago in the USA, an experiment was conducted on a group of paramedics. Video films were made of six persons administering cardiopulmonary resuscitation (CPR) to victims of acute heart failure. Five of the six were inexperienced trainees just learning CPR, while the sixth was a paramedic with long experience in emergency life-saving techniques. The films were shown to three groups of subjects: paramedics with practical experience, students being trained in this field, and instructors in life-saving techniques. Each subject was asked the following question: 'Who of the six persons shown in the films would you choose to resuscitate you if you were the victim of such an accident?' Among the group of experienced paramedics, 90 percent chose the one experienced paramedic from the films. The students chose 'correctly' in only 50 percent of the cases. Finally, and perhaps surprisingly, the instructors in resuscitation had poorer results than either the experienced paramedics or the students, choosing the experienced paramedic in only 30 percent of the cases.*
>
> *What form of rationality led the instructors to achieve such a poor performance? And what mechanisms lay behind the experienced paramedics' well-developed ability to choose correctly? (Flyvbjerg, 2001: 10)*

Flyvbjerg makes the point that the experienced paramedics are 'experts' who have a familiarity with the task in hand. Competent practice involves tacit knowing: one practitioner can recognize the expertise of another without being able to say exactly what it is that he or she is recognizing. Practice cannot be reduced to rules and undue attention to rules can distract from the 'flow' of competent performance. For example, people who become preoccupied with why it is not possible to detect individual frames in the movie that they are watching, might be distracted from subtle nuances of plot.

The Readings

The remainder of this book is divided into two principal sections: Part 1: Key Concepts and Part 2: Knowing in Practice. Part 3, entitled Revising the Agenda, comprises an extended chapter that reprises the Japan theme that underpinned Ikujiro Nonaka's influential work on tacit–explicit knowledge-conversion. Chapter 15 'Tacit Knowing, Communication and Power: Lessons from Japan?' emphasizes potential insights that might be gained by paying appropriate attention to Michael Polanyi's original work on tacit knowing and considers how these might be related to communication, meaning and the practice of power. It concludes that the KM agenda has embraced some unfortunate misunderstandings of the type that have been outlined above. Arguably, more account should be taken of how the capacity to 'know how to do things' and imagine a difference is aligned with the power to make a difference.

Broadly speaking, the readings in Part 1 reflect two distinct themes in the development of management and business knowledge. First, Japanese propositions – advanced by Nonaka and his colleagues – that 'tacit knowledge' could be converted into 'explicit knowledge' and communicated from one context to another (Chapter 2). If this were the case, experience of 'how to do things in a particular context' (practical know-how, judgement, intuition, gut feelings, and so on) could be converted into 'explicit knowledge' and managed. However, a second theme, which embraces conceptual aspects of knowing-in-practice, is evident in Chapters 3–6; albeit with different twists that reflect the evolution of debates since the late-1990s.

The readings in Part 2 reflect different aspects of the human dimension to managing people who know things. Throughout human history, knowing how to do things and change things has been intertwined with the practice of power. However, the advent of the bureaucratic organization and expectations that social science should be 'scientific' or 'as objective as possible' have tended to overshadow the crucial issue of knowing how to make a difference. Take, for example, the economic theory of perfect competition: there are a large number of buyers and sellers, everybody knows everything about everyone else and there is only one price – nobody can change anything. As McNulty (1968: 640) has argued, the perfection of this model of competition is achieved by separating competition from the verb 'to compete'. KM has enjoyed some success in establishing a preference for the noun 'knowledge' as opposed to the verb 'to know' But should this be regarded as progress?

Note

1 See Takeuchi, H. (1998) 'Beyond knowledge management: lessons from Japan', published on www.sveiby.com/articles/LessonsJapan.htm.

References

Andriessen, D. (2004a) 'IC valuation and measurement: classifying the state of the art', *Journal of Intellectual Capital*, 5(2): 230–42.

Andriessen, D. (2004b) *Making Sense of Intellectual Capital: Designing a Method for the Valuation of Intangibles*. Burlington MA: Butterworth-Heinemann.

Brown, J.S. and Duguid, P. (2002) *The Social Life of Information*. Boston, MA: Harvard Business School Press.

Brown, J.S., Denning, S., Groh, K. and Prusak, L. (2005) *Storytelling in Organizations: Why Storytelling is Transforming 21st Century Organizations and Management*. Burlington MA, Elsevier, Butterworth-Heinemann.

Choo, C.W. and Bontis, N. (eds) (2002) *The Strategic Management of Intellectual Capital and Organizational Knowledge*. New York: Oxford University Press.

Claxton, G. (2005) *The Wayward Mind: An Intimate History of the Unconscious*. London: Little, Brown.

Cook, S.D. and Brown, J.S. (1999) 'Bridging epistemologies: the generative dance between organizational knowledge and organizational knowing', *Organization Science*, 10(4): 381–400.

Denning, S. (2001) *The Springboard: How Storytelling Ignites Action in Knowledge-Era Organizations*. Woburn, MA: Butterworth-Heinemann.

Easterby-Smith, M. and Lyles, M.A. (eds) (2003) *The Blackwell Handbook of Organizational Learning and Knowledge Management*. Malden, MA: Blackwell.

Flyvbjerg, B. (2001) *Making Social Science Matter: Why Social Inquiry Fails and How It Can Succeed Again*. Cambridge, Cambridge University Press.

Gladwell, M. (2005) *Blink: The Power of Thinking without Thinking*. New York, Little, Brown.

Glasersfeld, E. von (2002) *Radical Constructivism: A Way of Knowing and Learning*. London: RoutledgeFalmer. [Originally published 1995.]

Holsapple, C.W. (ed.) (2003) *Handbook on Knowledge Management*. Berlin: Springer-Verlag.

Kondo, D. (1990) *Crafting Selves: Power, Gender, and Discourses of Identity in a Japanese Workplace*. Chicago, IL: University of Chicago Press.

Leonard, D. and Swap, W. (2004a) *Deep Smarts: How to Cultivate and Transfer Enduring Business Wisdom*. Boston, MA, Harvard Business School Press.

Leonard, D. and Swap, W. (2004b) 'Deep Smarts', *Harvard Business Review*, September: 88–97.

Lengnick-Hall, M. and Lengnick-Hall, C. (2003) 'HR's role in building relationship networks', *Academy of Management Review*, 17(4): 53–63.

Lepak, D.P. and Snell, S.A. (1999) 'The human resource architecture: Toward a theory of human capital allocation and development', *Academy of Management Review*, 24(1): 31–48.

May, T.Y.-M., Korczynski, M. and Frenkel, S. (2002) 'Organizational and occupational commitment: knowledge workers in large corporations', *Journal of Management Studies*, 39(6): 775–801.

McNulty, P. (1968) 'Economic theory and the meaning of competition', *Quarterly Journal of Economics*, 82(4): 639–56.

Nonaka, I. and Takeuchi, H. (1995) *The Knowledge-Creating Company: How Japanese Companies Create the Dynamics of Innovation*. Oxford, Oxford University Press.

Nonaka, I., Toyama, R. and Konno, N. (2000) 'SECI, *Ba* and leadership: a unified model of dynamic knowledge creation', *Long Range Planning*, 33(1): 5–34.

Nørretranders, T. (1999) *The User Illusion: Cutting Consciousness Down to Size*. London: Penguin Books. [Originally published in Danish as *Maerk verden* by Gyldedendalske Boghandel, 1991.]

North, D. (1990) *Institutions, Institutional Change and Economic Performance*. Cambridge, Cambridge University Press.

North, D. (1991) 'Institutions', *Journal of Economic Perspectives*, 5(1): 97–112.

Penrose, E.T. (1995) *Theory of the Growth of the Firm*. Oxford, Oxford University Press. [Originally published in 1959.]

Polanyi, M. (1969) 'Sense-giving and sense-reading', in M. Greene (ed.) *Essays by Michael Polanyi*. Chicago, IL: University of Chicago Press, pp. 181–207.

Polanyi, M. (1974) *Personal Knowledge: Towards a Post-Critical Philosophy*. Chicago, IL: University of Chicago Press. [Originally published 1958.]

Polanyi, M. (1983) *The Tacit Dimension*. Gloucester, MA: Peter Smith. [Originally published by Doubleday, 1966.]

Polanyi, M. and Prosch, H. (1977) *Meaning*. Chicago, IL: University of Chicago Press. [Originally published 1975.]

Ryle, G. (2000) *The Concept of Mind*. London: Penguin Books. [Originally published by Hutchinson, 1949.]

Takeuchi, H. and Nonaka, I. (2004) *Hitotsubashi on Knowledge Management*. Singapore City: Singapore: John Wiley and Sons.

Tsoukas, H. (2003) 'Do we really understand tacit knowledge?', in M. Easterby-Smith and M.A. Lyles (eds) *The Blackwell Handbook of Organizational Learning and Knowledge Management*. Oxford: Blackwell. pp. 410–27.

Tsoukas, H. and Mylonopoulos, N. (eds) (2004) *Organizations and Knowledge Systems: Knowledge, Learning and Dynamic Capabilities*. Basingstoke: Palgrave, Macmillan.

Tsoukas, H. and Vladimirou, E. (2001) 'What is organizational knowledge?', *Journal of Management Studies*, 38(7): 973–93.

Wenger, E. (2003) 'Communities of practice and social learning systems', in D. Nicolini, S. Gherardi and D. Yanow (eds) *Knowing in Organizations: A Practice-Based Approach*. New York: M.E. Sharpe, pp. 76–99.

Wenger, E., McDermott, R. and Snyder, W.M. (2002) *Cultivating Communities of Practice: A Guide to Managing Knowledge*. Boston, MA: Harvard Business School Press.

Wittgenstein, L. (2001) *Philosophical Investigations*. Oxford: Blackwell. [Originally published 1953.]

PART I: KEY CONCEPTS

2

SECI, *Ba* and Leadership: A Unified Model of Dynamic Knowledge Creation

I. Nonaka, R. Toyama and N. Konno

As Alvin Toffler said, we are now living in a 'knowledge-based society', where knowledge is the source of the highest quality power.[1] In a world where markets, products, technologies, competitors, regulations and even societies change rapidly, continuous innovation and the knowledge that enables such innovation have become important sources of sustainable competitive advantage. Hence, management scholars today consider knowledge and the capability to create and utilize knowledge to be the most important source of a firm's sustainable competitive advantage.[2] The *raison d'être* of a firm is to continuously create knowledge. Yet, in spite of all the talk about 'knowledge-based management' and in spite of the recognition of the need for a new knowledge-based theory that differs 'in some fundamental way'[3] from the existing economics and organizational theory, there is very little understanding of how organizations actually create and manage knowledge.

This is partly because we lack a general understanding of knowledge and the knowledge-creating process. The 'knowledge management' that academics and business people talk about often means just 'information management'. In the long tradition of Western management, the organization has been viewed as an information processing machine that takes and processes information from the environment to solve a problem and adapts to the environment based on a given goal. This static and passive view of the organization fails to capture the dynamic process of knowledge creation.

Instead of merely solving problems, organizations create and define problems, develop and apply new knowledge to solve the problems, and then further develop new knowledge through the action of problem solving. The organization is not merely an information processing machine, but an entity that creates knowledge through action and interaction.[4] It interacts with its environment, and reshapes the environment and even itself through the process of knowledge creation. Hence, the most important aspect of understanding a firm's capability concerning knowledge is the dynamic capability to continuously create new knowledge out of existing firm-specific capabilities, rather than the stock of knowledge (such as a particular technology) that a firm possesses at one point in time.[5]

Source: I. Nonaka, R. Toyama and N. Konno (2000) '*SECI*, Ba *and leadership: a unified model of dynamic knowledge creation*', *Long Range Planning*, 33(1): 5–34, Edited version.

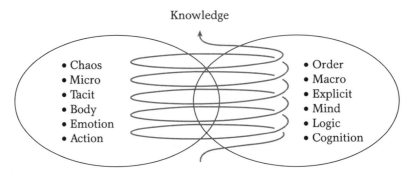

Figure 2.1 Knowledge created through a spiral

With this view of an organization as an entity that creates knowledge continuously, we need to re-examine our theories of the firm, in terms of how it is organized and managed, how it interacts with its environment and how its members interact with each other. Our goal in this chapter is to understand the dynamic process in which an organization creates, maintains and exploits knowledge. The following sections discuss basic concepts related to the organizational knowledge-creating process, how such a process is managed, and how one can lead such a knowledge-creating process. Knowledge is created in the spiral that goes through two seemingly antithetical concepts such as order and chaos, micro and macro, part and whole, mind and body, tacit and explicit, self and other, deduction and induction, and creativity and control. We argue that the key in leading the knowledge-creating process is dialectical thinking, which transcends and synthesizes such contradictions (see Figure 2.1).

What Is Knowledge?

In our theory of the knowledge-creating process, we adopt the traditional definition of knowledge as 'justified true belief. However, our focus is on the 'justified' rather than the 'true' aspect of belief. In traditional Western epistemology (the theory of knowledge), 'truthfulness' is the essential attribute of knowledge. It is the absolute, static and non-human view of knowledge. This view, however, fails to address the relative, dynamic and humanistic dimensions of knowledge.

Knowledge is dynamic, since it is created in social interactions among individuals and organizations. Knowledge is context-specific, as it depends on a particular time and space.[6] Without being put into a context, it is just information, not knowledge. For example, '1234 ABC Street' is just information. Without context, it does not mean anything. However, when put into a context, it becomes knowledge: 'My friend David lives at 1234 ABC Street, which is next to the library.' Knowledge is also humanistic, as it is essentially related to human action. Knowledge has the active and subjective nature represented by such terms as 'commitment' and 'belief' that is deeply rooted in individuals' value systems. Information becomes knowledge when it is interpreted by individuals and given a context and anchored in the beliefs and commitments of individuals. Hence, knowledge is relational: such things as 'truth', 'goodness' and 'beauty' are in the eye of the beholder. As Alfred North Whitehead stated, 'there are no whole truths; all truths are half-truths'.[7] In this study, we consider knowledge to be 'a dynamic human process of justifying personal belief toward the "truth"'.[8]

There are two types of knowledge: explicit knowledge and tacit knowledge. Explicit knowledge can be expressed in formal and systematic language and shared in the form of data, scientific formulae, specifications, manuals and suchlike. It can be processed, transmitted and stored relatively easily. In contrast, tacit knowledge is highly personal and hard to formalize. Subjective insights, intuitions and hunches fall into this category of knowledge. Tacit knowledge is deeply rooted in action, procedures, routines, commitment, ideals, values and emotions.[9] It 'indwells' in a comprehensive cognizance of the human mind and body.[10] It is difficult to communicate tacit knowledge to others, since it is an analogue process that requires a kind of 'simultaneous processing'.

Western epistemology has traditionally viewed knowledge as explicit. However, to understand the true nature of knowledge and knowledge creation, we need to recognize that tacit and explicit knowledge are complementary, and that both types of knowledge are essential to knowledge creation. Explicit knowledge without tacit insight quickly loses its meaning. Written speech is possible only after internal speech is well developed.[11] Knowledge is created through interactions between tacit and explicit knowledge, rather than from tacit or explicit knowledge alone.

The Knowledge-Creating Process

Knowledge creation is a continuous, self-transcending process through which one transcends the boundary of the old self into a new self by acquiring a new context, a new view of the world, and new knowledge. In short, it is a journey *'from* being to becoming'.[12] One also transcends the boundary between self and other, as knowledge is created through the interactions among individuals or between individuals and their environment. In knowledge creation, micro and macro interact with each other, and changes occur at both the micro and the macro level: an individual (micro) influences and is influenced by the environment (macro) with which he or she interacts.

In order to understand how organizations create knowledge dynamically, we propose a model of knowledge creation consisting of three elements: (1) the socialization, externalization, combination, internalization (SECI) process – the process of knowledge creation through conversion between tacit and explicit knowledge; (2) *ba* – the shared context for knowledge creation; and (3) knowledge assets – the inputs, outputs, and moderator of the knowledge-creating process. The three elements

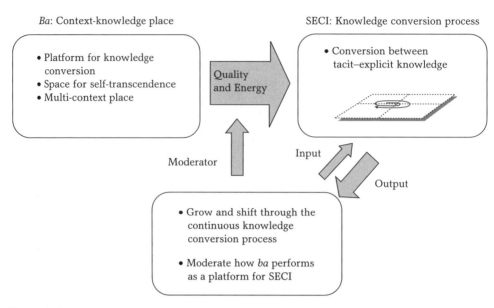

Figure 2.2 Three elements of the knowledge-creating process

of knowledge creation have to interact with each other to form the knowledge spiral that creates knowledge (see Figure 2.2). In the following sections, we discuss each of these three elements.

The SECI Process: Four Modes of Knowledge Conversion

An organization creates knowledge through the interactions between explicit and tacit knowledge. We call the interaction between the two types of knowledge 'knowledge conversion'. Through the conversion process, tacit and explicit knowledge expands in both quality and quantity.[13] There are four modes of knowledge conversion. They are: 1 socialization (from tacit knowledge to tacit knowledge); 2 externalization (from tacit knowledge to explicit knowledge); 3 combination (from explicit knowledge to explicit knowledge); and 4 internalization (from explicit knowledge to tacit knowledge).

Socialization Socialization is the process of converting new tacit knowledge through shared experiences. Since tacit knowledge is difficult to formalize and often time- and space-specific, tacit knowledge can be acquired only through shared experience, such as spending time together or living in the same environment. Socialization typically occurs in a traditional apprenticeship; where apprentices learn the tacit knowledge needed in their craft through hands-on experience, rather than from written manuals or textbooks. Socialization may also occur in informal social meetings outside of the workplace, where tacit knowledge such as world views, mental models and mutual trust can be created and shared. Socialization also occurs beyond organizational boundaries. Firms often acquire and take advantage of the tacit knowledge embedded in customers or suppliers by interacting with them.

Externalization Externalization is the process of articulating tacit knowledge into explicit knowledge. When tacit knowledge is made explicit, knowledge is crystallized, thus allowing it to be shared by others, and it becomes the basis of new knowledge. Concept creation in new product development is an example of this conversion process. Another example is a quality control circle, which allows employees to make improvements on the manufacturing process by articulating the tacit knowledge accumulated on the shop floor over years on the job. The successful conversion of tacit knowledge into explicit knowledge depends on the sequential use of metaphor, analogy and model.

Combination Combination is the process of converting explicit knowledge into more complex and systematic sets of explicit knowledge. Explicit knowledge is collected from inside or outside the organization and then combined, edited or processed to form new knowledge. The new explicit knowledge is then disseminated among the members of the organization. Creative use of computerized communication networks and large-scale databases can facilitate this mode of knowledge conversion. When the comptroller of a company collects information from throughout the organization and puts it together in a context to make a financial report, that report is new knowledge in the sense that it synthesizes knowledge from many different sources in one context. The combination mode of knowledge conversion can also include the 'breakdown' of concepts. Breaking down a concept such as a corporate vision into operationalized business or product concepts also creates systemic, explicit knowledge.

Internalization Internalization is the process of embodying explicit knowledge into tacit knowledge. Through internalization, explicit knowledge created is shared throughout an organization and converted into tacit knowledge by individuals. Internalization is closely related to 'learning by doing'. Explicit knowledge, such as the product concepts or the manufacturing procedures, has to be actualized through action and practice. For example, training programmes can help trainees to understand an organization and themselves. By reading documents or manuals about their jobs and the organization, and by reflecting upon them, trainees can internalize the explicit knowledge written in such documents to enrich their tacit knowledge base. Explicit knowledge can also be embodied through simulations or experiments that trigger learning by doing.

When knowledge is internalized to become part of individuals' tacit knowledge bases in the form of shared mental models or technical know-how, it becomes a valuable asset. This tacit knowledge accumulated at the individual level can then set off a new spiral of knowledge creation when it is shared with others through socialization.

The following lists summarize the factors that characterize the four knowledge conversion modes.[14]

Socialization – from tacit to tacit:

- Tacit knowledge accumulation: managers gather information from sales and production sites, share experiences with suppliers and customers, and engage in dialogue with competitors.
- Extra-firm social information collection (wandering outside): managers engage in bodily experience through management by wandering about, and get ideas for corporate strategy from daily social life, interaction with external experts and informal meetings with competitors outside the firm.
- Intrafirm social information collection (wandering inside): managers find new strategies and market opportunities by wandering inside the firm.
- Transfer of tacit knowledge: managers create a work environment that allows peers to understand craftsmanship and expertise through practice and demonstrations by a master.

Externalization – from tacit to explicit:

- Managers facilitate creative and essential dialogue, the use of 'abductive thinking', the use of metaphors in dialogue for concept creation, and the involvement of the industrial designers in project teams.

Combination – from explicit to explicit:

- Acquisition and integration: managers are engaged in planning strategies and operations, assembling internal and external data by using published literature, computer simulation and forecasting.
- Synthesis and processing: managers build and create manuals, documents and databases on products and services and build up material by gathering management figures or technical information from all over the company.
- Dissemination: managers engage in the planning and implementation of presentations to transmit newly created concepts.

Internalization – from explicit to tacit:

- Personal experience; real world knowledge acquisition: managers engage in 'enactive liaising' activities with functional departments through cross-functional development teams and overlapping product development. They search for and share new values and thoughts, and share and try to understand management visions and values through communication with fellow members of the organization.
- Simulation and experimentation; virtual world knowledge acquisition: managers engage in facilitating prototyping and benchmarking and facilitate a challenging spirit within the organization. Managers form teams as a model and conduct experiments and share results with the entire department.

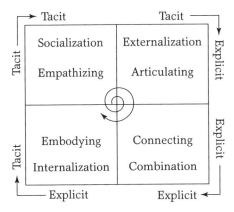

Figure 2.3 The SECI process

As stated above, knowledge creation is a continuous process of dynamic interactions between tacit and explicit knowledge. Such interactions are shaped by shifts between different modes of knowledge conversion, not just through one mode of interaction. Knowledge created through each of the four modes of knowledge conversion interacts in the spiral of knowledge creation. Figure 2.3 shows the four modes of knowledge conversion and the evolving spiral movement of knowledge through the SECI process.

It is important to note that the movement through the four modes of knowledge conversion forms a *spiral*, not a circle. In the spiral of knowledge creation, the interaction between tacit and explicit knowledge is amplified through the four modes of knowledge conversion. The spiral becomes larger in scale as it moves up through the ontological levels. Knowledge created through the SECI process can trigger a new spiral of knowledge creation, expanding horizontally and vertically across organizations. It is a dynamic process, starting at the individual level and expanding as it moves through communities of interaction that transcend sectional, departmental, divisional and even organizational boundaries. Organizational knowledge creation is a never-ending process that upgrades itself continuously.

This interactive spiral process takes place both intra- and inter-organizationally. Knowledge is transferred beyond organizational boundaries, and knowledge from different organizations interacts to create new knowledge.[15] Through dynamic interaction, knowledge created by the organization can trigger the mobilization of knowledge held by outside constituents such as consumers, affiliated companies, universities or distributors. For example, an innovative manufacturing process may bring about changes in the suppliers' manufacturing process, which in turn triggers a new round of product and process innovation at the organization. Another example is the articulation of tacit knowledge possessed by customers that they themselves have not been able to articulate. A product works as the trigger to elicit tacit knowledge when customers give meaning to the product by purchasing,

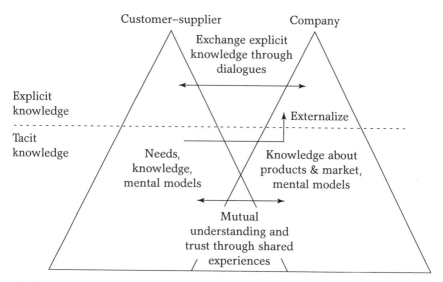

Figure 2.4 Creating knowledge with outside constituents

adapting, using or not purchasing it. Their actions are then reflected in the innovation process of the organization, and a new spiral of organizational knowledge creation starts again. Figure 2.4 shows how the organization interacts with outside constituents to create knowledge.

It should also be noted that knowledge creation is a self-transcending process, in which one reaches out beyond the boundaries of one's own existence.[16] In knowledge creation, one transcends the boundary between self and other, inside and outside, past and present. In socialization, self-transcendence is fundamental because tacit knowledge can only be shared through direct experiences, which go beyond individuals.[17] For example, in the socialization process people empathize with their colleagues and customers, which diminishes barriers between individuals. In externalization, an individual transcends the inner and outer boundaries of the self by committing to the group and becoming one with the group. Here, the sum of the individuals' intentions and ideas fuse and become integrated with the group's mental world. In combination, new knowledge generated through externalization transcends the group in analogue or digital signals. In internalization, individuals access the knowledge realm of the group and the entire organization. This again requires self-transcendence, as one has to find oneself in a larger entity.

Ba: Shared Context in Motion for Knowledge Creation

Knowledge needs a context in which to be created. Contrary to the Cartesian view of knowledge, which emphasizes the absolute and context-free nature of knowledge, the knowledge-creating process is necessarily context-specific in terms of who participates and how they participate. Knowledge needs a physical context to be created: 'there is no creation without place'.[18] *Ba* (which roughly means 'place') offers such a context. Based on a concept that was originally proposed by the Japanese philosopher Kitaro Nishida[19] and was further developed by Shimizu,[20] *ba* is here defined as a shared context in which knowledge is shared, created and utilized. In knowledge creation, generation and regeneration of *ba* is the key, as *ba* provides the energy, quality and place to perform the individual conversions and to move along the knowledge spiral.[21]

In knowledge creation, one cannot be free from context. Social, cultural and historical contexts are important for individuals, as such contexts provide the basis for one to interpret information to create meanings. As Friedrich Nietzsche argued, 'there are no facts, only interpretations'. *Ba* is a place where information is interpreted to become knowledge.

Ba does not necessarily mean a physical space. The Japanese word *ba* means not just a physical space, but a specific time and space. *Ba* is a time–space nexus, or as Heidegger expressed it, a locationality that simultaneously includes space and time. It is a concept that unifies physical space such as an office space, virtual space such as email, and mental space such as shared ideals.

The key concept in understanding *ba* is 'interaction'. Some of the research on knowledge creation focuses mainly on individuals, based on the assumption that individuals are the primary driving forces of creation. For example, quoting Simon's 'All learning takes place inside individual human heads', Grant claims that knowledge creation is an individual activity and that the primary role of firms is to apply existing knowledge.[22] However, such an argument is based on a view of knowledge and human beings as static and inhuman. As stated above, knowledge creation is a dynamic human process that transcends existing boundaries. Knowledge is created through the interactions among individuals or between individuals and their environments, rather than by an individual operating alone. *Ba* is the context shared by those who interact with each other, and through such interactions, those who participate in *ba* and the context itself evolve through self-transcendence to create knowledge (see Figure 2.5). Participants of *ba* cannot be mere onlookers. Instead, they are committed to *ba* through action and interaction.

Ba has a complex and ever-changing nature. *Ba* sets a boundary for interactions among individuals, and yet its boundary is open. As there are endless possibilities to one's own contexts, a certain boundary is required for a meaningful shared context to emerge. Yet *ba* is still an open place where participants with their own contexts can come and go, and the shared context (*ba*) can continuously evolve. By providing a shared context in motion, *ba* sets binding conditions for the participants by limiting the way in which the participants view the world. And yet it provides participants with higher viewpoints than their own.

Ba lets participants share time and space, and yet it transcends time and space. In knowledge creation, especially in socialization and externalization, it is important for participants to share time and space. A close physical interaction is important in sharing the context and forming a common language among participants. Also,

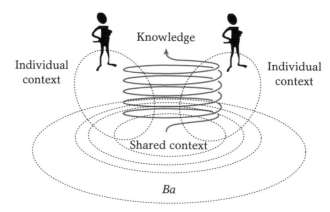

Figure 2.5 *Ba* as shared context in motion

since knowledge is intangible, unbounded and dynamic and cannot be stocked, *ba* works as the platform of knowledge creation by collecting the applied knowledge of the area into a certain time and space and integrating it. However, as *ba* can be a mental or virtual place as well as a physical place, it does not have to be bound to a certain space and time.

The concept of *ba* seemingly has some similarities to the concept of 'communities of practice'.[23] Based on the apprenticeship model, the concept of communities of practice argues that members of a community learn through participating in the community of practice and gradually memorizing jobs. However, there are important differences between the concepts of communities of practice and *ba*. While a community of practice is a living place where the members learn knowledge that is embedded in the community, *ba* is a living place where new knowledge is created. While learning occurs in any community of practice, *ba* needs energy to become an active *ba* where knowledge is created. The boundary of a community of practice is *firmly* set by the task, culture and history of the community. Consistency and continuity are important for a community of practice, as it needs an identity. In contrast, the boundary of *ba* is fluid and can be changed quickly as it is set by the participants. Instead of being constrained by history, *ba* has a 'here and now' quality. It is constantly moving; it is created, functions and disappears according to need. *Ba* constantly changes, as the contexts of participants or the membership of *ba* change. In a community of practice, changes mainly take place at the micro (individual) level, as new participants learn to be full participants. In *ba*, changes take place at both the micro- and the macro-level, as participants change both themselves and *ba* itself. While the membership of a community of practice is fairly stable, and it takes time for a new participant to learn about the community to become a full participant, the membership of *ba* is not fixed; participants come and go. Whereas members of a community of practice belong to the community, participants of *ba* relate to the *ba*.

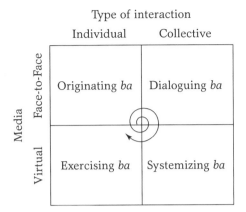

Figure 2.6 Four Types of *ba*

There are four types of *ba:* that is, originating *ba,* dialoguing *ba,* systemizing *ba* and exercising *ba,* which are defined by two dimensions of interactions (see Figure 2.6). One dimension is the type of interaction, that is, whether the interaction takes place individually or collectively. The other dimension is the media used in such interactions, that is, whether the interaction is through face-to-face contact or virtual media such as books, manuals, memos, emails or teleconferences. Each *ba* offers a context for a specific step in the knowledge-creating process, though the respective relationships between each single *ba* and conversion modes are by no means exclusive. Building, maintaining and utilizing *ba* is important to facilitate organizational knowledge creation. Hence, one has to understand the different characteristics of *ba* and how they interact with each other. The following sections describe the characteristics of each *ba.*

Originating *Ba* Originating *ba* is defined by individual and face-to-face interactions. It is a place where individuals share experiences, feelings, emotions and mental models. It mainly offers a context for socialization, since an individual face-to-face interaction is the only way to capture the full range of physical senses and psycho-emotional reactions, such as ease or discomfort, which are important elements in sharing tacit knowledge. Originating *ba* is an existential place in the sense that it is the world where an individual transcends the boundary between self and others, by sympathizing or empathizing with others. From originating *ba* emerge care, love, trust and commitment, which form the basis for knowledge conversion among individuals.

Dialoguing *Ba* Dialoguing *ba* is defined by collective and face-to-face interactions. It is the place where individuals' mental models and skills are shared, converted into common terms, and articulated as concepts. Hence, dialoguing *ba* mainly offers a context for externalization. Individuals' tacit knowledge is shared and articulated through dialogues among participants. The articulated knowledge is also brought back into each individual, and further articulation occurs through self-reflection. Dialoguing *ba* is more consciously constructed than originating *ba*. Selecting individuals with the right mix of specific knowledge and capabilities is the key to managing knowledge creation in dialoguing *ba*.

Systemizing *Ba* Systemizing *ba* is defined by collective and virtual interactions. Systemizing *ba* mainly offers a context for the combination of existing explicit knowledge, as explicit knowledge can be relatively easily transmitted to a large number of people in written form. Information technology, through such things as online networks, groupware, documentation and databanks, offers a virtual collaborative environment for the creation of systemizing *ba*. Today, many organizations use such things as electronic mailing lists and news groups through which participants can exchange necessary information or answer each other's questions to collect and disseminate knowledge and information effectively and efficiently.

Exercising *Ba* Exercising *ba* is defined by individual and virtual interactions. It mainly offers a context for internalization. Here, individuals embody explicit knowledge that is communicated through virtual media, such as written manuals or simulation programs. Exercising *ba* synthesizes the transcendence and reflection through action, while dialoguing *ba* achieves this through thought.

Let us illustrate how a firm utilizes various *ba* with the example of Seven-Eleven Japan, the most profitable convenience store franchiser in Japan. The success of Seven-Eleven Japan stems from its management of knowledge creation through creating and managing various *ba*.

Seven-Eleven Japan uses the shop floors of the 7000 stores around Japan as originating *ba*, where store employees accumulate tacit knowledge about customers' needs through face-to-face interactions with customers. Long-term experiences in dealing with customers give store employees unique knowledge of and insight into the local market and customers. They often say that they can just 'see' or 'feel' how well certain items will sell in their stores, although they cannot explain why.

To promote the use of its stores as originating *ba*, Seven-Eleven Japan gives its employees extensive on-the-job training (OJT) on the shop floor. Every new recruit is required to work at Seven-Eleven stores in various functions for about two years to accumulate experiences in dealing directly with customers, and in actually managing Seven-Eleven stores. Another instrument to create originating *ba* is 'Burabura Shain' (Walking around Employee), who has the task of wandering around and socializing with customers in stores to discover new knowledge in the field.

The tacit knowledge about the customers is then converted into explicit knowledge in the form of 'hypotheses' about market needs. Since local employees are the ones who hold tacit knowledge about their local markets, Seven-Eleven Japan lets them build their own hypotheses about the sales of particular items by giving store employees the responsibility to order items. For example, a local worker can order more beer, based on the knowledge that the local community is having a festival.

To facilitate hypothesis building, Seven-Eleven Japan actively builds and utilizes dialoguing *ba,* where the tacit knowledge of local employees is externalized into explicit knowledge in the form of hypotheses through dialogue with others. Several employees are responsible for ordering merchandise instead of just one manager. Each employee is responsible for certain merchandise categories, and through dialogues with others who are responsible for other categories they can build hypotheses that better fit changing market needs.

Another instrument to facilitate hypothesis building is the use of field counsellors, who visit the stores regularly to engage in dialogues with the owners and employees of local stores, and give them advice in placing orders and managing stores so that owners and employees can articulate their tacit knowledge well. If a field counsellor notices a unique hypothesis, such as a new way to display merchandise at one store, he or she takes note and shares that hypothesis with other stores.

The hypotheses built at shop floor level are shared throughout the company through various dialoguing *ba.* Field counsellors report on the knowledge built at the stores they are responsible for to their zone managers, who then disseminate knowledge acquired from one field counsellor to other field counsellors. Zone managers from across Japan meet at the headquarters in Tokyo every week, where success stories and problems at local stores are shared with Seven-Eleven's top management and other zone managers. Field counsellors also have meetings every week, where field counsellors and staff members from the headquarters, including the top management, share knowledge.

The cost of maintaining such *ba* is not small. To hold such meetings in Tokyo every week, it has been estimated that Seven-Eleven Japan spends about US$18 million per year on travelling, lodging, and so on. However, Seven-Eleven Japan emphasizes the importance of face-to-face interaction.

The hypotheses built at dialoguing *ba* are tested by the actual sales data that are collected, analysed and utilized through a state-of-the-art information system. The information system works as systemizing *ba,* where explicit knowledge in the form of sales data is compiled, shared and utilized by the headquarters and local stores.

The explicit knowledge compiled at systemizing *ba* is immediately fed back to stores through the information system so that they can build new hypotheses that suit the reality of the market better. Utilizing point-of-sales data and its analysis, store employees test their hypotheses about the market everyday at their local store, which works as exercising *ba.* In exercising *ba,* knowledge created and compiled in systemizing *ba* is justified by being compared with the reality of the world, and the gap between the knowledge and the reality then triggers a new cycle of knowledge creation.

The Plurality of *Ba*   *Ba* exists at many ontological levels and these levels may be connected to form a greater *ba.* Individuals form the *ba* of teams, which in turn form the *ba* of organization. Then, the market environment becomes the *ba* for the organization. As stated above, *ba* is a concept that transcends the boundary between micro and macro. The organic interactions among these different levels of *ba* can amplify the knowledge-creating process.

As *ba* often acts as an autonomous, self-sufficient unit that can be connected with other *ba* to expand knowledge, it seems to work in a similar way to a modular system or organization, in which independently designed modules are assembled and integrated together to work as a whole system. However, there are important differences between a modular organization and *ba*. Knowledge, especially tacit knowledge, cannot be assembled in the way in which various modular parts are assembled into a product. In a modular system, information is partitioned into visible design rules in a precise, unambiguous and complete way. 'Fully specified and standardized component interfaces' make the later integration of modules possible.[24] However, relationships among *ba* are not necessarily known a priori. Unlike the interfaces between modules, the relationships among *ba* are not predetermined and clear.

The coherence among *ba* is achieved through organic interactions among *ba* based on the knowledge vision, rather than through a mechanistic concentration in which the centre dominates. In organizational knowledge creation, neither micro nor macro dominates. Rather, both interact with each other to evolve into a higher self. The 'interfaces' among *ba* also evolve along with *ba* themselves. And the interactive organic coherence of various *ba* and individuals that participate in *ba* has to be supported by trustful sharing of knowledge and continuous exchanges between all the units involved to create and strengthen the relationships.

For example, Maekawa Seisakusho, a Japanese industrial freezer manufacturer, consists of 80 'independent companies' that operate as autonomous and self-sufficient *ba*. These companies interact with each other organically to form Maekawa as a coherent organization. Some of the independent companies share office space and work closely together. Individual employees of the different independent companies often spend time together and form informal relationships, out of which a new project or even a new independent company can be created. When they encounter problems too large to deal with alone, several independent companies form a group to work on the problem together. Such interactions among independent companies are voluntarily created and managed, not by a plan or order from the headquarters.

Knowledge Assets

At the base of knowledge-creating processes are knowledge assets. We define assets as 'firm-specific resources that are indispensable to create values for the firm'. Knowledge assets are the inputs, outputs and moderating factors of the knowledge-creating process. For example, trust among organizational members is created as an output of the knowledge-creating process, and at the same time it moderates how *ba* functions as a platform for the knowledge-creating process.

Although knowledge is considered to be one of the most important assets for a firm to create a sustainable competitive advantage today, we do not yet have an effective system and tools for evaluating and managing knowledge assets. Although

Experiential knowledge assets	Conceptual knowledge assets
Tacit knowledge shared through common experiences	Explicit knowledge articulated through images, symbols and language
• Skills and know-how of individuals • Care, love, trust and security • Energy, passion and tension	• Product concepts • Design • Brand equity
Routine knowledge assets	Systemic knowledge assets
Tacit knowledge routinized and embedded in actions and practices	Systemized and packaged explicit knowledge
• Know-how in daily operations • Organizational routines • Organizational culture	• Documents, specifications, manuals • Database • Patents and licences

Figure 2.7   Four categories of knowledge asset

a variety of measures have been proposed,[25] existing accounting systems are inadequate for capturing the value of knowledge assets, due to the tacit nature of knowledge. Knowledge assets must be built and used internally in order for their full value to be realized, as they cannot be readily bought and sold. We need to build a system to evaluate and manage the knowledge assets of a firm more effectively. Another difficulty in measuring knowledge assets is that they are dynamic. Knowledge assets are both inputs and outputs of the organization's knowledge-creating activities, and hence they are constantly evolving. Taking a snapshot of the knowledge assets that the organization owns at one point in time is never enough to evaluate and manage the knowledge assets properly.

To understand how knowledge assets are created, acquired and exploited, we propose to categorize knowledge assets into four types: experiential; conceptual; systemic; and routine (see Figure 2.7).

Experiential Knowledge Assets   Experiential knowledge assets consist of the shared tacit knowledge that is built through shared hands-on experience among the members of the organization, and between the members of the organization and its customers, suppliers and affiliated firms. Skills and know-how that are acquired and accumulated by individuals through experiences at work are examples of experiential knowledge assets. Other examples of such knowledge assets include emotional knowledge, such as care, love and trust, physical knowledge such as facial expressions and gestures, energetic knowledge such as senses of existence, enthusiasm and tension, and rhythmic knowledge such as improvisation and entrainment.

Because they are tacit, experiential knowledge assets are difficult to grasp, evaluate or trade. Firms have to build their own knowledge assets through their own experiences. Their tacit nature is what makes experiential knowledge assets the firm-specific, difficult-to-imitate resources that give a sustainable competitive advantage to a firm.

Conceptual Knowledge Assets Conceptual knowledge assets consist of explicit knowledge articulated through images, symbols and language. They are the assets based on the concepts held by customers and members of the organization. Brand equity, which is perceived by customers, and concepts or designs, which are perceived by the members of the organization, are examples of conceptual knowledge assets. Since they have tangible forms, conceptual knowledge assets are easier to grasp than experiential knowledge assets, though it is still difficult to grasp what customers and organizational members perceive.

Systemic Knowledge Assets Systemic knowledge assets consist of systematized and packaged explicit knowledge, such as explicitly stated technologies, product specifications, manuals, and documented and packaged information about customers and suppliers. Legally protected intellectual properties such as licences and patents also fall into this category. A characteristic of systemic knowledge assets is that they can be transferred relatively easily. This is the most 'visible' type of knowledge asset, and current knowledge management focuses primarily on managing systemic knowledge assets, such as intellectual property rights.

Routine Knowledge Assets Routine knowledge assets consist of the tacit knowledge that is routinized and embedded in the actions and practices of the organization. Know-how, organizational culture and organizational routines for carrying out the day-to-day business of the organization are examples of routine knowledge assets. Through continuous exercises, certain patterns of thinking and action are reinforced and shared among organizational members. Sharing the background to and 'stories' about the company also helps members to form routine knowledge. A characteristic of routine knowledge assets is that they are practical.

Mapping Knowledge Assets These four types of knowledge asset form the basis of the knowledge-creating process. To manage knowledge creation and exploitation effectively, a company has to 'map' its stocks of knowledge assets. However, cataloguing the existing knowledge is not enough. As stated above, knowledge assets are dynamic, and new knowledge assets can be created from existing knowledge assets.

Leading the Knowledge-creating Process

In the previous section, we presented a model of the organizational knowledge-creating process consisting of three elements: SECI, *ba* and knowledge assets. Using its existing knowledge assets, an organization creates new knowledge through the SECI process that takes place in *ba*. The knowledge created then becomes part of

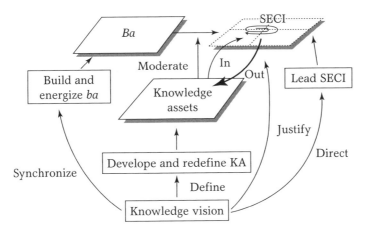

Figure 2.8 Leading the knowledge-creating process

the knowledge assets of the organization, which become the basis for a new spiral of knowledge creation. We now turn our attention to how such a knowledge-creating process can be managed.

The knowledge-creating process cannot be managed in the traditional sense of 'management', which concentrates on controlling the flow of information.[26] Managers can, however, lead the organization to actively and dynamically create knowledge by providing certain conditions. In this section, we discuss the roles of top and middle managers in leading a dynamic knowledge-creating process. Especially crucial to this process is the role of knowledge producers, that is, middle managers who are at the intersection of the vertical and horizontal flows of information in the company and actively interact with others to create knowledge by participating in and leading _ba_. In knowledge creation, 'distributed leadership' as seen in 'middle-up-down' management[27] is the key, as it cannot be 'managed' with traditional top-down leadership.

Top and middle management take a leadership role by 'reading' the situation, as well as leading it, in working on all three elements of the knowledge-creating process. Leaders provide the knowledge vision, develop and promote sharing of knowledge assets, create and energize _ba_, and enable and promote the continuous spiral of knowledge creation (see Figure 2.8). Especially important is the knowledge vision, which affects all three layers of the knowledge-creating process.

Providing the Knowledge Vision

In order to create knowledge dynamically and continuously, an organization needs a vision that synchronizes the entire organization. It is top management's role to articulate the knowledge vision and communicate it throughout (and outside) the company. The knowledge vision defines what kind of knowledge the company should create in what domain. The knowledge vision gives a direction to the knowledge-creating process, and the knowledge created by it, by asking such fundamental questions as 'What are we?', 'What should we create?', 'How can we do it?', 'Why are we doing this?' and 'Where are we going?' In short, it determines how the organization and its knowledge base evolve over the long term. Since knowledge is unbounded, any form of new knowledge can be created regardless of the existing business structure of the company. Therefore, it is important for top management to articulate a knowledge vision that transcends the boundaries of existing products, divisions, organizations and markets.

The knowledge vision also defines the value system that evaluates, justifies and determines the quality of the knowledge the company creates. The aesthetic value of higher aspiration sets a boundary to the expansion of knowledge creation. Together with organizational norms, routines and skills, value system determines what kinds of knowledge are to be needed, created and retained.[28] It also fosters the spontaneous commitment of those who are involved in knowledge creation. To create knowledge, organizations should foster their members' commitment by formulating an organizational intention, as commitment underlies the human knowledge-creating activity.[29]

Serving as a bridge between the visionary ideals of those at the top and the chaotic reality of the front line, the middle then has to break down the values and visions created by the top into concepts and images that guide the knowledge-creating process with vitality and direction. Middle managers work as knowledge producers to remake reality, or 'produce new knowledge', according to the company's vision.

Developing and Promoting the Sharing of Knowledge Assets

Based on the knowledge vision of the company, top management has to facilitate dynamic knowledge creation by taking a leading role in managing the three elements of the knowledge-creating process. First, top management has to develop and manage the knowledge assets of the company, which form the basis of its knowledge-creating process. Recently, many companies have created the position of chief knowledge officer (CKO) to perform this function.[30] However, the role of these CKOs has so far been mostly limited to managing knowledge assets as a static resource to be exploited. Top management has to play a more active role in facilitating the dynamic process of building knowledge assets from knowledge.

Since knowledge is unbounded, top management has to redefine the organization on the basis of the knowledge it owns, rather than by using existing definitions such as technologies, products and markets. Top management and knowledge producers have to read the situation, in terms of what kind of knowledge assets are available to them. It is perhaps even more important to read the situation in terms of what kind of knowledge they are *lacking*, according to the knowledge vision that answers the question 'Where are we going?'

To do so, they can take an inventory of the knowledge assets and on that create a strategy to build, maintain and utilize the firm's knowledge assets effectively and efficiently. For example, after studying a hybrid power system that uses both a conventional engine and an electric motor, Toyota realized that it did not have the technology to make the main components of the hybrid system, such as the battery, motor, converter and inverter. Realizing that it lacked knowledge assets that could determine the future of the firm, the top management of Toyota took a major initiative to research, develop and produce the hybrid system internally.

It is also important to have knowledge producers who know where they can find the knowledge or personnel that will enable the firm to create and exploit its knowledge. It is often difficult for a large organization to know exactly what it knows. Top management has to foster and utilize knowledge producers who can keep track of the firm's knowledge assets, and utilize them when they are needed.

It should be noted that knowledge assets, especially routine knowledge assets, can hinder as well as foster knowledge creation. Organizations are subject to inertia and it is difficult for them to diverge from the course set by their previous experiences. Successful experience leads to excessive exploitation of the existing knowledge, and in turn hinders the exploration of new knowledge.[31] Therefore, current capabilities may both impel and constrain future learning and actions taken by a firm.[32] Core capabilities may turn into 'core rigidities'[33] or a 'competence trap',[34] which hinders innovation rather than promotes it. To avoid rigidities and traps, a firm can use an R&D project, which requires different knowledge from the existing knowledge assets, as an occasion for challenging current knowledge, and for creating new assets.

Building, Connecting and Energizing *Ba*

Ba can be built intentionally, or created spontaneously. Top management and knowledge producers can build *ba* by providing physical space such as meeting rooms, virtual space such as a computer network, or mental space such as common goals. Forming a task force is a typical example of the intentional building of *ba*. To build *ba*, leaders also have to choose the right mix of people to participate, and promote their interaction. It is also important for managers to 'find' and utilize spontaneously formed *ba*, which changes or disappears very quickly. Hence, leaders have to read the situation in terms of how members of the organization are interacting with each other and with outside environments in order to quickly capture the naturally emerging *ba*, as well as to form *ba* effectively.

Further, various *ba* are connected with each other to form a greater *ba*. For that, leaders have to facilitate the interactions among various *ba*, and among the participants, based on the knowledge vision. In many cases, the relationships among *ba* are not predetermined. Which *ba* should be connected in which way is often unclear. Therefore, leaders have to read the situation to connect various *ba* as the relationships among them unfold.

However, building, finding and connecting *ba* is not enough for a firm to manage the dynamic knowledge-creating process. *Ba* should be 'energized' to give energy and quality to the SECI process. For that, knowledge producers have to supply the necessary conditions, such as autonomy, creative chaos, redundancy, requisite variety, and love, care, trust and commitment.

Autonomy　Autonomy increases the chances of finding valuable information and motivating organization members to create new knowledge. Not only does self-organization increase the commitment of individuals, but it can also be a source of unexpected knowledge. By allowing the members of the organization to act autonomously, the organization may increase the chances of accessing and utilizing the knowledge held by its members.[35]

A knowledge-creating organization with autonomy can be depicted as an 'autopoietic system'.[36] Living organic systems are composed of various organs, which are made up of numerous cells. The relationship between system and organs, and between organ and cells, is neither dominant–subordinate nor whole–part. Each unit, like an autonomous cell, controls all of the changes occurring continuously within itself, and each unit determines its boundary through self-reproduction. Similarly, autonomous individuals and groups in knowledge-creating organizations set their task boundaries for themselves in pursuit of the ultimate goal expressed by the organization.

In the business organization, a powerful tool for creating autonomy is provided by the self-organizing team. An autonomous team can perform many functions, thereby amplifying and sublimating individual perspectives to higher levels. Researchers have found that the use of cross-functional teams that involve members from a broad cross-section of different organizational activities is very effective in the innovation process.[37] NEC has used autonomous teams to foster the expansion of its technology programme. Sharp uses its 'Urgent Project System' to develop strategically important products. The team leader is endowed by the president with responsibility for the project and the power to select his or her team members from any unit in Sharp.

Creative Chaos　Creative chaos stimulates the interaction between the organization and the external environment. Creative chaos is different from complete disorder; it is intentional chaos introduced to the organization by its leaders to evoke a sense of crisis among its members by proposing challenging goals or ambiguous visions. Creative chaos helps to focus members' attention and encourages them to transcend existing boundaries to define a problem and resolve it. Facing chaos, organization members experience a breakdown of routines, habits and cognitive frameworks. Periodic breakdowns or 'unlearning' provide important opportunities for them to reconsider their fundamental thinking and perspectives.[38] The continuous process of questioning and re-evaluating existing premises energizes *ba*, and hence fosters organizational knowledge creation. Some have called this phenomenon creating 'order out of noise' or 'order out of chaos'.[39] It is important for leaders to read the situation in order to introduce creative chaos into *ba* in the right place at the right time, and to lead the creation of order out of chaos so that the organization does not fall into complete disorder.

For example, when the development team of the Toyota Prius came up with a plan to improve fuel efficiency by 50%, which was ambitious enough, the top management rejected the plan and set a new goal to increase it by 100% instead. This threw the team into turmoil; it eventually discarded its original plan to use the direct injection engine, and developed the world's first commercially available hybrid car.

Redundancy 'Redundancy' refers to the intentional overlapping of information about business activities, management responsibilities and the company as a whole. Redundancy of information speeds up the knowledge-creating process in two ways. First, sharing redundant information promotes the sharing of tacit knowledge, because individuals can sense what others are trying to articulate. Redundant information enables individuals to transcend functional boundaries to offer advice or provide new information from different perspectives. Second, redundancy of information helps organizational members understand their role in the organization, which in turn functions to control their direction of thinking and action. Thus it provides the organization with a self-control mechanism for achieving a certain direction and consistency.

Redundancy of information is also necessary to realize the 'principle of redundancy of potential command' – that is, the principle whereby each part of an entire system carries the same degree of importance and has the potential to become its leader.[40] At Maekawa Seisakusho, different people take leadership in turn during the course of a project, from research and prototype building to implementation. The person whose abilities can best address the issues or problems at hand takes the leadership role to drive the project forward, guaranteeing 'the right man in the right place' in each phase of the project. Redundancy of information makes such a style of management possible, and allows team members to recognize the strengths of their colleagues. By the rotation of specialists in different positions and roles within the team, such as leader, support and so on, specialists gain additional knowledge in related fields as well as management skills and knowledge. In short, redundancy facilitates transcendence between leaders and subordinates, generalists and specialists, and creators and users of knowledge.

Redundancy of information, however, does increase the amount of information to be processed and can lead to information overload. It also increases the cost of knowledge creation, at least in the short run. Leaders have to read the situation to deal with the possible downside of redundancy by making it clear where information can be located and where knowledge is stored within the organization.

Requisite Variety Creation lies at the edge between order and chaos. Requisite variety helps a knowledge-creating organization to maintain the balance between order and chaos. An organization's internal diversity has to match the variety and complexity of the environment in order to deal with challenges posed by that environment.[41] To cope with many contingencies, an organization has to possess requisite variety, which should be at a minimum for organizational integration and a maximum for effective adaptation to environmental changes.

Requisite variety can be enhanced by combining information differently, flexibly and quickly, and by providing equal access to information throughout the organization. When an information differential exists within the organization, organization members cannot interact on equal terms, which hinders the search for different interpretations of new information. An organization's members should know where information is located, where knowledge is accumulated, and how information and knowledge can be accessed at the highest speed. Kao Corporation, Japan's leading manufacturer of household products, utilizes a computerized information network to give every employee equal access to corporate information as the basis for opinion exchanges amongst various organizational units with different viewpoints.

There are two ways to realize requisite variety. One is to develop a flat and flexible organizational structure in which the different units are interlinked with an information network, thereby giving organization members fast and equal access to the broadest variety of information. Another approach is to change organizational structure frequently or rotate personnel frequently, thereby enabling employees to acquire interdisciplinary knowledge to deal with the complexity of the environment.

Love, Care, Trust and Commitment Fostering love, care, trust and commitment among organizational members is important as it forms the foundation of knowledge creation.[42] For knowledge (especially tacit knowledge) to be shared and for the self-transcending process of knowledge creation to occur, there should be strong love, caring and trust among organization members. As information creates power, an individual might be motivated to monopolize it, hiding it even from his or her colleagues. However, as knowledge needs to be shared to be created and exploited, it is important for leaders to create an atmosphere in which organization members feel safe sharing their knowledge. It is also important for leaders to cultivate commitment among organization members to motivate the sharing and creation of knowledge, based on the knowledge vision.

To foster love, care, trust and commitment, knowledge producers need to be highly inspired and committed to their goal. They also need to be selfless and altruistic. They should not try to monopolize the knowledge created by the organization, or take credit for other members' achievements. Also, knowledge producers need to be positive thinkers. They should try to avoid having or expressing negative thoughts and feelings. Instead, they should have creative and positive thoughts, imagination, and the drive to act.

Promoting the SECI Process

The leadership should also promote the SECI process. Following the direction given by the knowledge vision, knowledge producers promote organizational knowledge creation by facilitating all four modes of knowledge conversion, although their most significant contribution is made in externalization. They synthesize the tacit knowledge of front-line employees, top management and outside constituents such as customers and suppliers, to make it explicit and incorporate it into new concepts, technologies, products or systems. To do so, knowledge producers should be able to reflect upon their actions. As Schon states, when one reflects while in action, one becomes independent of established theory and technique, and is able to construct a new theory of the unique case.[43]

Another important task for knowledge producers is to facilitate the knowledge spiral across the different conversion modes, and on different organizational levels. To facilitate the knowledge-creating process effectively, knowledge producers need to read the situation, in terms of where the spiral is heading and what kind of knowledge is available to be converted, both inside and outside the organization. With this reading, knowledge producers need to improvise to incorporate necessary changes in the knowledge-creating process. Improvisation is an important factor in dynamic knowledge creation, especially when dealing with tacit knowledge.[44] Knowledge producers should be able to improvise and facilitate improvisation by the participants in the knowledge-creating process.

Knowledge producers need to be able to create their own concepts and express them in their own words and thus should be able to use language effectively. Language here includes tropes (such as metaphor, metonymy, synecdoche), 'grammar' and 'context' for knowledge, and non-verbal visual language such as design. Each mode of knowledge conversion requires different kinds of language for knowledge to be created and shared effectively. For example, non-verbal language, such as body language, is essential in the socialization process, as tacit knowledge cannot be expressed in articulated language. In contrast, clear, articulated language is essential in the combination process, as knowledge has to be disseminated and understood by many people. In externalization, tropes such as metaphor, metonymy and synecdoche are effective in creating concepts out of vast amounts of tacit knowledge. Therefore, knowledge producers should carefully choose and design language according to the process of knowledge creation.

Conclusion

In this chapter we have discussed how organizations manage the dynamic process of knowledge creation, which is characterized by dynamic interactions among organizational members, and between organizational members and the environment. We have proposed a new model of the knowledge-creating process to understand the dynamic nature of knowledge creation and to manage such a process effectively. Three elements, the SECI process, *ba* and knowledge assets, have to interact with each other organically and dynamically. The knowledge assets of a firm are mobilized and shared in *ba,* where tacit knowledge held by individuals is converted and amplified by the spiral of knowledge through socialization, externalization, combination and internalization.

We have also discussed the role of leadership in facilitating the knowledge-creating process. Creating and understanding the knowledge vision of the company, understanding the knowledge assets of the company, facilitating and utilizing *ba* effectively, and managing the knowledge spiral are the important roles that managers have to play. Especially important is the role of knowledge producers, the middle managers who are at the centre of the dynamic knowledge-creating process.

All three elements of the knowledge-creating process should be integrated under clear leadership so that a firm can create knowledge continuously and dynamically. The knowledge-creating process should become a *discipline* for organization members, in terms of how they think and act in finding, defining and solving problems.

In this chapter we have focused primarily on the organizational knowledge-creating process that takes place within a company. We have described the knowledge-creating process as the dynamic interaction between organizational members, and between organizational members and the environment. However, the knowledge-creating process is not confined within the boundaries of a single company. The market, where the knowledge held by companies interacts with that held by customers, is also a place for knowledge creation. It is also possible for groups of companies to create knowledge. If we further raise the level of analysis, we arrive at a discussion of how so-called national systems of innovation can be built. For the immediate future, it will be important to examine how companies, governments and universities can work together to make knowledge creation possible.

Notes

1. A. Toffler, *Powershift: Knowledge, Wealth and Violence at the Edge of the 21st Century,* Bantam Books, New York, 1990.

2. R.M. Cyert, P.K. Kumar and J.R. Williams, 'Information, market imperfections and strategy', *Strategic Management Journal,* Winter Special Issue, 14: 47–58 (1993); P. Drucker, *Post-Capitalist Society,* Butterworth Heinemann, London, 1993; R.M. Grant, 'Prospering in dynamically competitive environments: organizational capability as knowledge integration', *Organization Science,* 7: 375–387 (1996); R. Henderson and I. Cockburn, 'Measuring competence: exploring firm effects in pharmaceutical research', *Strategic Management Journal,* 15(Winter Special Issue): 63–84 (1994); D. Leonard-Barton, 'Core capabilities and core rigidities: a paradox in managing new product development', *Strategic Management Journal,* 13(5): 363–380 (1992); D. Leonard-Barton, *Wellsprings of Knowledge,* Harvard Business School Press, Boston, MA, 1995; R.R. Nelson, 'Why do firms differ, and how does it matter?', *Strategic Management Journal,* 12(Winter Special Issue): 61–74 (1991); I. Nonaka, *Chishiki-Souzou no Keiei* (A Theory of Organizational Knowledge Creation), Nihon Keizai Shimbun-sha (in Japanese), 1990; I. Nonaka, 'The knowledge-creating company', *Harvard Business Review,* Nov.–Dec.: 96–104 (1991); I. Nonaka, 'A dynamic theory of organizational knowledge creation', *Organization Science,* 5(1): 14–37 (1994); I. Nonaka and H. Takeuchi, *The Knowledge-Creating Company,* Oxford University Press, New York, 1995; J.B. Quinn, *Intelligent Enterprise:*

A Knowledge and Service Based Paradigm for Industry, The Free Press, New York, 1992; K. Sveiby, *The New Organizational Wealth*, Berret-Koehler, San Francisco, 1997; S.G. Winter, 'Knowledge and competence as strategic assets', in D.J. Teece (ed.), *The Competitive Challenge: Strategies for Industrial Innovation and Renewal*, pp. 159–184, Ballinger, Cambridge, MA, 1987.

3. J.C. Spender and R.M. Grant, 'Knowledge and the firm: overview', *Strategic Management Journal*, 17(Winter Special Issue): 5–9 (1996).

4. R.M. Cyert and J.G. March, *A Behavioral Theory of the Firm*, Prentice-Hall, Englewood Cliffs, NJ, 1963; D. Levinthal and J. Myatt, 'Co-evolution of capabilities and industry: the evolution of mutual fund processing', *Strategic Management Journal*, 15(Winter Special Issue): 45–62 (1994).

5. J.B. Barney, 'Firm resources and sustained competitive advantage', *Journal of Management*, 17(1): 99–120 (1991); D. Lei, M.A. Hitt and R. Bettis, 'Dynamic core competences through meta-learning and strategic context', *Journal of Management*, 22(4): 549–569 (1996); Nelson (1991), op. cit.; D.J. Teece, G. Pisano and A. Shuen, *Firm Capabilities, Resources, and the Concept of Strategy: Four Paradigms of Strategic Management*, CCC Working Paper No. 90–8 (1990); M. Wilkins, *The History of Foreign Investment in the United States to 1914*, Harvard University Press, Cambridge, MA, 1989.

6. F.A. Hayek, 'The use of knowledge in society', *American Economic Review*, 35: 519–530 (1945).

7. A.N. Whitehead, as recorded by L. Price, *Dialogues of Alfred North Whitehead*, Little, Brown, Boston, MA, 1954.

8. Nonaka and Takeuchi, 1995, op. cit.

9. D.A. Schon, *The Reflective Practitioner*, Basic Books, New York, 1983.

10. M. Polanyi, *The Tacit Dimension*, Routledge and Kegan Paul, London, 1966.

11. L. Vygotsky, *Thought and Language*, Massachusetts Institute of Technology, Boston, MA, 1986.

12. I. Prigogine, *From Being to Becoming: Time and Complexity in the Physical Sciences*, W.H. Freeman, San Francisco, 1980.

13. Nonaka, 1990, 1991, 1994, op. cit.; Nonaka and Takeuchi, 1995, op. cit.

14. Adapted from I. Nonaka, P. Byosiere, C.C. Borucki and N. Konno, 'Organisational knowledge creation theory: a first comprehensive test', *International Business Review*, 3(4): 337–351 (1994).

15. J.L. Badaracco, Jr., *The Knowledge Link: How Firms Compete through Strategic Alliances*, Harvard Business School Press, Boston, MA, 1991; A.C. Inkpen, 'Creating knowledge through collaboration', *California Management Review*, 39(1): 123–140 (1996); Nonaka, 1990, 1991, 1994, op. cit.; Nonaka and Takeuchi, 1995 op. cit.; S. Wikstrom and R. Normann, *Knowledge and Value: A New Perspective on Corporate Transformation*, Routledge, London, 1994.

16. E. Jantsch, *The Self-organising Universe*, Pergamon Press, Oxford, 1980.

17. K. Nishida, *An Inquiry into the Good* (1921), trans. M. Abe and C. Ives, Yale University, New Haven, CT, 1990.

18. E.S. Casey, *The Fate of Place: A Philosophical History*, University of California Press, Berkeley, CA, 1997.

19. Nishida, 1921, op. cit.; K. Nishida, *Fundamental Problems of Philosophy: the World of Action and the Dialectical World*, Sophia University, Tokyo, 1970.

20. H. Shimizu, '*Ba*-principle: new logic for the real-time emergence of information', *Holonics*, 5(1): 67–79 (1995). However, the concept of place has also been talked about by philosophers such as Plato, Kant, Husserl and Whitehead.

21. I. Nonaka and N. Konno, 'The concept of *"ba"*: building a foundation for knowledge creation', *California Management Review*, 40(3): 1–15 (1998); I. Nonaka, N. Konno and R. Toyama, 'Leading knowledge creation: a new framework for dynamic knowledge management', 2nd Annual Knowledge Management Conference, Haas School of Business, University of California, Berkeley, 22–24 September 1998.

22. H.A. Simon, *Reason in Human Affairs*, Stanford University Press, Stanford, CA, 1983; R.M. Grant, 'Toward a knowledge-based theory of the firm', *Strategic Management Journal*, 17(Winter Special Issue): 109–122 (1996).

23. J. Lave and E. Wenger, *Situated Learning–Legitimate Peripheral Participation* Cambridge University Press, Cambridge, 1991; E. Wenger, *Communities of Practice: Learning, Meaning, and Identity*, Cambridge University Press, Cambridge, 1998.

24. R. Sanchez and J.T. Mahoney, 'Modularity, flexibility and knowledge management in product and organisation design', *Strategic Management Journal*, 17(10): 63–67 (1996).

25. L. Edivinsson and M.S. Malone, *Intellectual Capital*, Harper Business, New York, 1997; T. Stewart, *Intellectual Capital: The New Wealth of Organizations*, Doubleday, New York, 1997.

26. G. von Krogh, I. Nonaka and K. Ichijo, 'Develop knowledge activists!', *European Management Journal*, 15(5): 475–483 (1997).

27. Nonaka and Takeuchi, 1995, op. cit.; I. Nonaka, 'Toward middle-up-down management: accelerating information creation', *Sloan Management Review*, 29(3): 9–18 (1988).

28. Leonard-Barton, 1992, op. cit.

29. M. Polanyi, *Personal Knowledge*, University of Chicago Press, Chicago, 1958.

30. T.H. Davenport and L. Prusak, *Working Knowledge*, Harvard Business School Press, Boston, MA, 1998.

31. J. March, 'Exploration and exploitation in organizational learning', *Organization Science*, 2(1): 101–123 (1991); J. March, *The Pursuit of Organizational Intelligence* Blackwell Publishers, Malden, MA, 1999.

32. C.K. Prahalad and G. Hamel, 'The core competence of the corporation', *Harvard Business Review*, 68(3): 79–91 (1990).

33. Leonard-Barton, 1992, op. cit.

34. B. Levitt and J.G. March, 'Organisational learning', *Annual Review of Sociology*, 14: 319–340 (1988).

35. Grant, 'Prospering', 1996, op. cit.; 'Knowledge-based theory', 1996; K.H. Wruck and M.C. Jensen, 'Science, specific knowledge, and total quality management', *Journal of Accounting and Economics*, 18: 247–287 (1994).

36. G. von Krogh, *Organizational Epistemology*, St Martin's Press, New York, 1995; H.R. Maturana and E.J. Varela, *Autopoiesis and Cognition: The Realization of the Living*, Reidel, Dordrecht, 1980.

37. K.B. Clark and T. Fujimoto, *Product Development Performance: Strategy, Organization and Management in the World Auto Industry*, Harvard Business School Press, Boston, MA, 1991; W. Imai, I. Nonaka and H. Takeuchi, 'Managing the new product development process: how Japanese companies learn and unlearn', in K.B. Clark, R.H. Hayes and C. Lorenz (eds), *The Uneasy Alliance: Managing the Productivity–Technology Dilemma*, pp. 337–381, Harvard Business School Press, Boston, MA, 1985.

38. T. Winograd and F. Flores, *Understanding Computers and Cognition: A New Foundation for Design*, Addison-Wesley, Reading , MA, 1986.

39. H. von Foerster, 'Principles of self-organization in a socio-managerial context', in H. Ulrich and G.J.B. Probst (eds), *Self-Organization and Management of Social Systems*, pp. 2–24, Springer-Verlag, Berlin, 1984; T.J. Peters, *Thriving on Chaos*, Alfred A. Knopf, New York,

1987; I. Prigogine and I. Stengers, _Order Out of Chaos: Man's New Dialogue with Nature,_ Bantam Books, New York, 1984.

40. W. McCulloch, _Embodiments of Mind_, MIT Press, Cambridge, MA, 1965.

41. W.R. Ashby, _An Introduction to Cybernetics,_ Chapman & Hall, London, 1956.

42. G. von Krogh, 'Care in knowledge creation', _California Management Review,_ 40(3): 133–153 (1998); G. von Krogh, I. Nonaka and K. Ichijo, 'Enabling knowledge creation', in G. von Krogh, J. Roos and D. Kleine (eds), _Knowing in Firms. Managing and Measuring Knowledge_, 1999 SAGE, London.

43. Schon, 1983, op. cit.

44. K.E. Weick, 'The non-traditional quality of organizational learning', _Organizational Science,_ 2(1): 116–124 (1991).

3

Bridging Epistemologies: The Generative Dance between Organizational Knowledge and Organizational Knowing

S.D.N. Cook and J.S. Brown

It's funny what's happened to this word knowing. *... The actual* act *of apprehending, of making sense, of putting together, from what you have, the significance of where you are – this [now] oddly lacks any really reliable, commonly used verb in our language ... [one] meaning the* activity *of knowing. ... [Yet], every culture has not only its own set body of knowledge, but its own ways of [knowing]. Sir Geoffrey Vickers, 1976*

In recent years, knowledge has become a prominent theme in the organizational literature. However, in such discussions, as in informal contexts, knowledge is typically spoken of as though it were all of a piece, as though essentially it comes in only one kind. It is our contention that there are, in fact, a number of distinct forms of knowledge, and that their differences are relevant, both theoretically and practically, to an effective understanding of organizations.

There is now much discussion of organizational knowledge, knowledge-based organizations, knowledge-creating organizations, knowledge work, etc. There are numerous related themes such as organizational learning, the collective mind (Weick and Roberts, 1993) and the organizational brain. It has become common to talk of knowledge in the context of both individuals and groups, and even to consider knowledge in explicit and tacit senses (where, for example, explicit knowledge is treated as knowledge that can be spelled out or formalized and tacit knowledge as that associated with skills or 'know-how'). Accordingly, there are discussions about: how explicit knowledge acquired by individuals in an organization is associated with 'learning' at the level of the organization (March and Olsen, 1976; Argyris and Schon, 1978; Sims et al., 1986; Simon, 1991; Sitkin, 1992); how a group's mastering of explicit routines can be an aspect of organizational memory (Cohen and Bacdayan, 1994); how the tacit skills of an individual can and cannot be tapped for the benefit of the organization (Nonaka, 1994; Nonaka and Takeuchi, 1995; Spender, 1996); and how the activities of groups can constitute organizational learning (Weick, 1991; Weick and Westley, 1996). Meanwhile, such concepts are clearly vital to such concerns as the management of intellectual capital (Stewart, 1997), core competencies (Hamel and Prahalad, 1994), and innovation (Leonard-Barton, 1995).

Source: S.D.N. Cook and J.S. Brown (1999) '*Bridging epistemologies: the generative dance between organizational knowledge and organizational knowing*', *Organization Science*, 10 (4): 381–400. Edited version.

Increasingly, such work has pushed provocatively and insightfully at the boundaries of the theoretical frames used in understanding knowledge and organizations – as in Weick and Roberts's (1993) application of 'taking heed' and 'mindfulness' to operations of teams; in Cohen and Bacdayan's (1994) use of notions of procedural memory from psychology as a way of understanding organizational routines; in what Hutchins (1991: 2) sees as the 'pattern of communication' within the 'cognitive system' of a group; in Nonaka and Takeuchi's spiral of knowledge creation; and in Kogut and Zander's (1996) considerations of the interplay between individuals' social knowledge and the organizing principles of work in explaining what organizations know how to do.

Yet, even in this growing body of literature that explores epistemologically significant themes, there typically remains an expressed or implied tendency to treat knowledge as being essentially of one kind. That is, the epistemology assumed in the literature tends to privilege the individual over the group, and the explicit over the tacit (as if, for example, explicit and tacit knowledge were two variations of one kind of knowledge, not separate, distinct forms of knowledge). The former tendency is reflected in the insistence that organizational learning is really about individual learning since 'All learning takes place inside individual human heads' (Simon, 1991: 125). The latter, meanwhile, can be seen in Nonaka's argument that 'While tacit knowledge held by individuals may lie at the heart of the knowledge creating process, realizing the practical benefits of that knowledge centers on its externalization', where 'externalization' for Nonaka entails a process of 'converting' tacit knowledge into explicit knowledge (1994: 20). Cohen and Bacdayan, meanwhile (1994: 554) contend that organizational routines arise when 'individuals store components of a routine as a procedural memory'. And even Weick and Roberts (1993: 374) have made the epistemologically provocative move of describing 'collective mind' in terms of 'a distinct higher-order pattern of interrelated activities' grounded in and emerging from 'individual actions'. Meanwhile Hutchins (1991: 284) speaks of investigating the 'ways in which the cognitive properties of human groups may depend on the social organization of individual cognitive capabilities'.

As we will detail below, we believe that the tendency to treat all knowledge as being essentially the same severely limits the current work on epistemologically relevant organizational themes, both theoretically and operationally. Theoretically, these tendencies fail to honor aspects of the distinction between explicit and tacit, and individual and group knowledge that we see as germane to understanding the acquisition, maintenance and exercise of competencies by individuals and groups. Practically, it limits our ability to assess and support these competencies in their own right.

The first contention of this chapter is that each of the four categories of knowledge inherent in the explicit–tacit and individual–group distinctions is a distinct form of knowledge on equal standing with the other three (i.e none is subordinate to or made up out of any other). Also, this distinct character is reflected in the fact that each form of knowledge does work that the others cannot. We view these four forms of knowledge as constituting the appropriate focus of what we call *the epistemology*

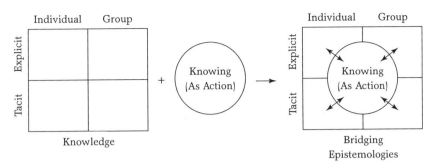

Figure 3.1 Knowledge and knowing

of possession, since these forms of 'what is known' are typically treated as something people *possess*.[1] To say, for example, 'Robert knows auto mechanics' points to Robert *possessing* knowledge of auto mechanics.

The second contention is that not all of what is known is captured by this understanding of knowledge. Put another way, there is more epistemic work being done in what we know how to do than can be accounted for solely in terms of the knowledge we possess.[2] So, in addition to talking about the four distinct forms of knowledge we *also* want to be able to speak about the epistemic work done by human action itself – that is, about what is *part of practice* as well as what is *possessed in the head*. To say, for example, 'Robert is fixing cars' points not only to knowledge he possesses but also to things he is doing. To give an account of what Robert knows, we claim, calls for an understanding of the epistemic work done, which needs to include both the knowledge he possesses and the actions he carries out.

Borrowing from the epistemological perspective of the American Pragmatist philosophers, we call what is possessed 'knowledge' and what is part of action 'knowing'. Individuals and groups clearly make use of knowledge, both explicit and tacit, in what they do; but not everything they know how to do, we argue, is explicable solely in terms of the knowledge they possess. We believe that understanding of the epistemological dimension of individual and group action requires us to speak about both knowledge *used in* action and knowing *as part of* action. Therefore, in addition to the traditional epistemology of possession, there needs to be, in our view, a parallel *epistemology of practice*, which takes ways of knowing as its focus. By this, we do not mean that practice needs to be brought under the umbrella of traditional epistemology (nor do we mean that all of human action needs to be accounted for epistemologically). Rather, we contend that there needs to be a radical expansion of what is considered epistemic in its own right, which includes knowledge and knowing.

Furthermore, we do not see knowledge and knowing as competing, but as complementary and mutually enabling (see Figure 3.1).[3] Indeed, as we will spell out in detail in what follows, understanding what is entailed in bridging the two epistemologies provides a more robust account of such matters as: how individuals and groups can draw on tacit and explicit knowledge simultaneously; how what individuals know tacitly can be made useful to groups; and how explicit instructions can be made more useful aids for the development of tacit skills. Also (and quite importantly) we see the interplay of knowledge and knowing as a potentially generative phenomenon. That is, for human groups, the source of *new* knowledge and knowing lies in the use of knowledge as a tool of knowing within situated interaction with the social and physical world. It is this that we call the *generative dance*. Understanding the generative dance (how to recognize, support and harness it) is essential, we believe, to understanding the types of learning, innovation and effectiveness that are prime concerns for all epistemologically oriented organizational theories.

In what follows, we explore the epistemologies of possession and practice and some implications of our perspective. We first sketch out our interpretation of the epistemology of possession, along with what we see as its strengths and limitations. Then we offer what in our view are some essential elements of an epistemology of practice – in particular, we define what we mean by: 1 the term *practice*; 2 the distinction between *knowledge* and *knowing*; 3 the Pragmatist philosopher John Dewey's concept of *productive inquiry*; 4 the notion of *interaction with the world*; and 5 the idea of *dynamic affordance*. Following this, we look at how seeing knowledge as a tool of knowing can help explain how individuals and groups draw on all four forms of knowledge and, importantly, how the interplay of knowledge and knowing can generate new knowledge and new ways of knowing. In the final section, we explore these ideas in the context of three cases, and consider some broader implications of them for a more robust understanding of the epistemological dimension of organized human activity.

The Epistemology of Possession

Each of the four categories that come from the explicit–tacit and individual–group distinctions identifies a unique and irreducible form of knowledge. We see each of the four as on equal footing with the other three, and hold that no one of them can be derived from or changed into one of the others. We believe that each needs to be understood *conceptually* as distinct, in no small part because *in practice* each does work that the others cannot. In arguing for this position, we first address the conventional inclination to treat knowledge either as if it were all of a piece or, if different forms are considered, to privilege explicit over tacit and individual over group knowledge.

Privileging the explicit and the individual is not unique to organizational studies. It reflects the dominant epistemology of Western culture for the last three centuries, at least. This view is often referred to as the Cartesian view, given its substantial grounding in the work of the seventeenth-century French philosopher René Descartes. For Cartesians past and present, the individual, indeed the individual analytic thinker, is taken as primary. All knowledge, accordingly, is believed to be best acquired through reason and the use of concepts and methods that are freed as much as possible from the fallibilities of our senses or the exigencies of given situations.

Descartes's famous 'Cogito ergo sum' (I think therefore I am) is both a beginning and a conclusion for the traditional epistemology. It is the conclusion that the thinking self is the one thing we cannot doubt – everything else, from the impressions of our senses to 'objective' claims about the world, is subject to one or another degree of uncertainty. It is through analytic reasoning, Cartesians maintain, that we can best minimize or 'control for' the clouding influences of our senses and subjective impressions, and thus acquire our most reliable knowledge about the world. It is a beginning in that the thinking (or reasoning or doubting) self becomes the one fundamental, irreducible starting point for any search for knowledge about the world, and the repository for that knowledge once acquired. All this should have a familiar ring to anyone who received a traditional introduction to 'the scientific method' and 'the scientific worldview'.

What follows from all this has become part of the conventional understanding of knowledge in our culture: the idea that knowledge, particularly anything that might pass as rigorous knowledge, is something that is held in the head of an individual and is acquired, modeled and expressed most accurately in the most objective and explicit terms possible. It is this Cartesian tradition, as well, that we see underlying such statements quoted above as 'All learning takes place inside individual human heads' (Simon, 1991) and 'realizing the practical benefits of [tacit] knowledge centers on its externalization' (Nonaka, 1994).

Our aim here, it should be noted, is not to reject the Cartesian epistemology wholesale. Rather, we wish to critique some of its elements that we believe have made difficult the development of a productive understanding of the forms of knowledge suggested by categories other than individual–explicit. We believe Cartesian epistemology needs to be broadened into an 'epistemology of possession' that can incorporate a conceptually sound and useful understanding of knowledge possessed tacitly and knowledge possessed by groups.

Explicit–tacit

The grip that the Cartesian tradition has had on the exploration of explicit and tacit knowledge has been particularly strong. When the idea of tacit knowledge is addressed, for example, it is most often treated as an informal, inchoate or obscure kind of knowledge, whose very nature calls for it to be made explicit in order to be truly understood or useful in practice. Indeed, the very term 'tacit' suggests to many people (quite understandably) the sense that any such knowledge must be 'hidden' from our understanding or 'inaccessible' for practical purposes. We believe that this predilection of the traditional epistemology has held back the development of an understanding of the explicit–tacit distinction that is called for and increasingly needed, given the growth of significant work on epistemological themes in the literatures concerned with organized human action. Indeed, we base our claim that the explicit–tacit distinction is one between two separate forms of knowledge on practical utility: we argue that the distinction needs to be *conceptually* clear because, in practice, each form of knowledge does work the other cannot. A sounder, more robust conceptual understanding of the distinction should help make it possible to recognize, support and harness the different forms of work that each, in fact, makes possible in practice.[4]

We base our understanding of the tacit–explicit distinction on the work of the scientist and philosopher Michael Polanyi (1983). Polanyi's distinction is exemplified very compellingly in the simple but rich example of riding a bicycle. Many people who say they can ride a bicycle will claim, when asked, that they do not know which way to turn the handlebars to prevent a fall to the left or right. However, since staying upright is part of knowing how to ride a bicycle, anyone who can ride must, by definition, know which way to turn the handlebars to avoid a fall. What they can't do is *say* which way to turn. So there's something known by everyone who can ride that most cannot say. What they can say is an example of what Polanyi called the explicit dimension of knowledge, while what is known by everyone who can keep upright on a bike is what he called the tacit dimension of knowledge.

Building on Polanyi, we argue that explicit and tacit are two distinct forms of knowledge (i.e. neither is a variant of the other); that each does work the other cannot; and that one form cannot be made out of or changed into the other. We explore these and other aspects of the distinction below, again beginning with the example of bicycle riding.

To be able to ride a bicycle, one needs to have the (tacit) knowledge of how to stay upright. This is knowledge one possesses; it is *not* the activity of riding itself but knowledge used in riding (you still possess the tacit knowledge even when you are not riding). Possessing this tacit knowledge makes it possible to keep upright, which is something that the explicit knowledge of which way to turn cannot do. We can't put a novice on a bicycle saying 'OK, take off – and if you start to fall like so, turn this way' and expect the person to be able to ride successfully. The novice would have the explicit knowledge but not the necessary tacit knowledge. Whatever epistemic work that explicit bit of knowledge can make possible, it cannot do *all* of the work that is necessary for someone to know how to ride. In order to acquire the tacit knowledge, a novice has to spend a certain amount of time on a bicycle. Indeed, it would even be possible for someone to be able to say in great technical detail what must be done to keep a bicycle upright, yet still be unable to ride one. No amount of explicit knowledge alone can enable someone to ride; it simply cannot enable all the necessary epistemic work.

At the same time, we argue that each form of knowledge can often be used as an *aid* in acquiring the other. If you know how to ride, for example, you might use your tacit knowledge to ride around in a way that helps you discover which way you turn when you begin to fall. Likewise, if a novice is told how to turn to avoid a fall, that explicit knowledge could be used while learning to ride as an aid in getting a feel for staying upright. However, neither tacit nor explicit knowledge can be used by itself to acquire the other: one must also, at the very least, get on a bicycle (an important point, to which we will return shortly).

We can now see that each form of knowledge does its own work. Explicit knowledge can be used as an aid to help acquire the tacit knowledge, but cannot by itself enable one to ride. The tacit knowledge is necessary in being able to ride, but it does not by itself enable a rider to say which way to turn.

Furthermore, it is important not to mistake using one form of knowledge as an aid in acquiring the other with one form being 'converted' into the other. Tacit knowledge cannot be turned into explicit, nor can explicit knowledge be turned into tacit. If you ride around using your tacit knowledge as an aid to discovering which way you turn, when you ultimately acquire the explicit knowledge you still possess the tacit knowledge, and you still use it in keeping upright. When we ride around with the aim of acquiring the explicit knowledge, we are not performing an operation on our tacit knowledge that turns it into explicit knowledge; we are using the tacit, within the activity of riding, to generate the explicit knowledge. The explicit knowledge was not lying inside the tacit knowledge in a dormant, inchoate or hidden form; it was generated in the context of riding with the aid of what we knew tacitly. Likewise, if you know explicitly which way to turn but cannot ride, there is no operation you can perform on that explicit knowledge that will turn it into the tacit knowledge necessary for riding. That tacit knowledge is acquired on its own: it is not made out of explicit knowledge. Prior to being generated, one form of knowledge does not lie hidden in the other.

Also, there is no guarantee that one form will always be a useful aid to acquiring the other. In fact, in some cases using one can be a hindrance to acquiring the other. In learning how to drive, for example, you may be told (explicitly) to accelerate when coming out of a turn, only to be told later that you are using this knowledge mechanically 'as a crutch' rather than 'getting a feel for it'. Similarly, in learning a skill, such as dancing or tennis, many people experience a period when explicit knowledge about how to move one's feet or hold one's shoulders can actually impair one's ability to acquire the tacit knowledge necessary to performing the skill in a fluid or masterful way. Even experts in a given skill can find their ability to use their tacit knowledge 'thrown off' when they are asked to describe explicitly what they are doing.

Individual–group

We have also inherited a cultural predilection for privileging the individual over the group. Whether stated emphatically or presented implicitly, a sense that whatever can be said about groups actually 'boils down' to things about individuals is taken almost as though it were self-evident, and particularly so when the concern at hand is an epistemological one (Cook, 1994). As the Cartesian view would have it, it is the *individual* thinker who is the primary (if not exclusive) wielder and repository of what is known. This predilection is reflected, for example, in Simon's insistence (noted above) that all learning takes place inside the heads of individuals. For many who are not as orthodox as Simon, such topics as 'organizational learning', 'organizational knowledge' or 'organizational routines' are still spoken of in ways that often leave it unclear as to whether groups are being treated on an equal footing with individuals or as a derivative of them. (This is often so, it should be noted, even in cases where it is not authors' intention either to address or to dodge the issue.)

In recent years, however, there has been a growing volume of research and publication that has begun to treat groups and organizations in their own right. This has been an implicit concern in our own work as well as that of a number of our colleagues at Xerox PARC and the Institute for Research on Learning. This trend is also strongly suggested in the literature treating such concepts as 'communities of practice' (Brown and Duguid, 1991; Wenger, 1997), 'core competencies' (Hamel and Prahalad, 1994), 'situated cognition', 'legitimate peripheral participation' (Lave and Wenger, 1991) and the 'spiral of organizational knowledge creation' (Nonaka and Takeuchi, 1995). Discussions of communities of practice look at how individuals establish themselves and function as a group by engaging in practices that are unique to or characteristic of that group. Within the growing body of work on core competencies one can see serious attention being given to how teams, as well as individuals, do 'real work' and how that work can be supported, enriched and directed. The concept of legitimate peripheral participation, originally used to explore apprenticeship learning, takes as its central concern the role of participation by seemingly peripheral individuals in the innovative and very *central* capacities of the group itself. In more and more instances, authors are addressing such epistemological issues at the level of the group, including recent direct explorations of such terms as 'organizational knowledge' and 'organizational epistemology' (Krogh and Roos, 1995). By taking the group as a primary unit of analysis, such approaches, implicitly at least, treat groups as something to be investigated in their own right with respect to epistemological concerns.

As with the explicit–tacit distinction, we propose that individuals and groups each do epistemic work that the other cannot. So, for example, while only individual physicians know how to diagnose nephritis using palpation (groups do not have hands), the knowledge of what constitutes acceptable and unacceptable practice in nephrology is possessed by nephrologists as a group. Likewise, while individual copier technicians have a sense of how a particular copier ought to sound when operating properly (groups do not have ears), it is a group of technicians that possess 'war stories' about what odd noises can mean. Indeed, an individual technician's account only becomes a 'war story' when it is held in common and can be used by the group in its discussions about machines (Orr, 1996). In both cases, part of what is known about a given domain is possessed by individuals, part by groups. Individual technicians and nephrologists possess various bits of knowledge in their respective fields, but the 'body of knowledge' of copier repair or nephrology is possessed by groups, not by individuals. Put another way, the body of knowledge of a group is 'held in common' by the group. We do not expect every individual in a group (discipline, profession, craft, etc.) to possess everything that is in the 'body of knowledge' of that group (in fact, this is likely to be impossible, unnecessary, and perhaps even undesirable). The body of knowledge is possessed by the group as a whole and is drawn on in its actions, just as knowledge possessed by an individual is drawn on in his or her actions. The work done by a group, as informed by the body of knowledge it possesses, is work that is epistemically distinct from work done by an individual in it, as informed by the knowledge he or she possesses.[5]

With respect to both distinctions, the lesson we wish to draw here is *not* that we ought now to reverse tradition and privilege the group and the tacit over the individual and the explicit. Indeed, our aim has been to argue for an expanded epistemology of possession that includes each of four types of knowledge and treats each as distinct from (not superior to) the other three, both conceptually and in the sense of each doing work that the others cannot.

Toward an Epistemology of Practice

We are now able to focus on an important aspect of what people know that is *not* captured by the four forms of knowledge considered above. In the bicycle example we argued that tacit and explicit knowledge alone are insufficient in acquiring the ability to ride; what has to be added is the actual act of riding (or trying to). This leads us now to make a specific claim: *the act of riding a bicycle does distinct epistemic work of its own*. Indeed, we hold that this type of epistemic work is an inextricable facet of human action itself, not something people possess. We mark this distinction by referring to it as 'knowing' rather than 'knowledge'. Furthermore, we believe that knowing does not belong to an epistemology of possession, but rather that it calls for an epistemology of practice. Following Vickers's (1976: 2) assertion that every human group 'has not only its own set *body* of knowledge, but its own *ways* of [knowing]', we now turn to outlining some of what we believe 'knowing' and an 'epistemology of practice' entail. In particular, we propose specific understandings of: 1 the term *practice*; 2 the distinction, drawn from the Pragmatists, between *knowledge* and *knowing*; 3 John Dewey's concept of *productive inquiry*; 4 the notion of *interaction with the world*; and 5 the idea of *dynamic affordance*.

Practice

Practice implies doing – intuitively, it refers to things we do as individuals and as groups. Conceptually, practice has received a growing amount of careful theoretical attention in recent years (see, for example, Bourdieu, 1977; Turner, 1994). In common usage, 'practice' can mean either to develop a competency through drill or rote actions as in 'to practice the piano' or to exercise a competency as in 'to practice medicine'. The former suggests drill in preparation for doing the 'real work', while the latter suggests the 'real work' itself. In our use of the term, we mean doing real work: the practice of engineers, managers, physicians, woodworkers, etc. (in which, meanwhile, drill and other rotelike activities can play an important part).

For our purposes, then, we intend the term 'practice' to refer to *the co-ordinated activities of individuals and groups in doing their 'real work' as it is informed by a particular organizational or group context.* In this sense, we wish to distinguish practice from both behavior and action. Doing of any sort we call 'behavior', while 'action' we see as behavior imbued with meaning. By 'practice', then, we refer to action informed by meaning drawn from a particular group context. In the simplest case, if Vance's knee jerks, that is behavior. When Vance raps his knee with a physician's hammer to check his reflexes, it is behavior that has meaning, and thus is what we call action. If his physician raps his knee as part of an exam, it is practice. This is because the meaning of her action comes from the organized contexts of her training and ongoing work in medicine (where it can draw on, contribute to, and be evaluated in the work of others in her field).

Knowledge and Knowing

Drawing a distinction between knowledge and knowing may seem at first pass an unduly subtle point. We believe it is at root quite a substantial one, both epistemologically and in its implications for understanding organized human activity. Above, we have expanded our understanding of knowledge to include the forms suggested by the explicit–tacit and individual–group distinctions. With respect to all four forms, however, we have maintained the sense of knowledge as something that is possessed. When we say 'Miriam has knowledge of physics', the knowledge is something that Miriam possesses (as concepts, rules, procedures, etc.). Furthermore, her knowledge (whether explicit or tacit) is abstract since it is something that is *about* but not *in* the tangible world. And it is static, in that possessing it does not require that it be always in use: when Miriam is playing tennis or sleeping she still has knowledge of physics. Finally, while knowledge itself is static, it is common to see it as necessary to action: 'Miriam can solve the problem because she has knowledge of physics' or 'Miriam cannot solve the problem until she acquires knowledge of the conservation of angular momentum.' That is, knowledge is commonly thought of as something we *use* in action but it is not understood to *be* action.

Accordingly, we use the term 'knowing' to refer to the epistemological dimension of action itself. By 'knowing' we do not mean something that is *used in* action or something *necessary to* action, but rather something that is a *part of* action (both individual and group action). 'Knowing' refers to the epistemic work that is done as part of action or practice, like that done in the actual riding of a bicycle or the actual making of a medical diagnosis. Knowing is dynamic, concrete, and relational.

If we talk about André reflecting 'knowing' in physics, our focus is on what he is actually doing; it is on the ways he deploys the knowledge he possesses in his interactions with the materials of a specific concrete task in physics (such as testing an experimental laser design).

In developing an understanding of the knowledge – knowing distinction, we have found it useful to draw on the work of the American philosophical school of Pragmatism, in particular the work of John Dewey, as an alternative to the dominant Cartesian perspective. Those interested in organizations have generally seen the work of the Pragmatists as limited essentially to educational settings. We believe that a new look at the Pragmatist perspective can yield very important and timely implications for organizations of all sorts. The resurgence of interest in American Pragmatism, which has centered on Dewey (see, for example, Rorty, 1982; Hickman, 1990), makes the re-examination of this perspective even more timely for organizational concerns.

A basic conviction of the Pragmatist perspective in both theory and practice is that our primary focus should *not* be (solely) on the likes of abstract concepts and principles (as has been common more broadly in philosophy and the social sciences) but on concrete action. Pragmatists have been centrally concerned with doing, particularly forms of doing that entail making or producing something (from technologies to ideas). Accordingly, when it comes to questions of what we know and how we know, the Pragmatist perspective takes a primary concern not with 'knowledge', which is seen as abstract and static, but with 'knowing', which is understood as part of concrete, dynamic human action. Following the Pragmatist perspective, for us 'knowing something' refers to an *aspect of* action, not to something assumed to underlie, enable, or be used in action.[6] By 'knowing' we mean that aspect of action or practice that does epistemic work.

'Knowing', Dewey maintained, 'is literally something which we do', not something that we possess. For Dewey, to talk about activity in terms of knowledge is to mistake an abstract, static concept for a concrete, dynamic activity. It is to make a kind of category error. To be accomplished in a profession, discipline, or craft, for example, is necessarily tied up with practicing it. This does not mean that its body of knowledge is useless to practice, only that it is not the same as the epistemic dimension of practice. An accomplished engineer may possess a great deal of sophisticated knowledge; but there are plenty of people who possess such knowledge yet do not excel as engineers (as is often observed in many fields). This means that if you want to understand the essentials of what accomplished engineers know, you need to look at what they do as well as at what they possess. It also means that our fundamental understanding of the relationship between a body of knowledge and activities of a practice must change: we must see knowledge as *a tool at the service of knowing* not as something that, once possessed, is all that is needed to enable action or practice. (Improved practice may not always be the product of acquiring more knowledge; at times it may be the result of developing innovative ways of using knowledge already possessed.)

This Pragmatist focus on action has broad implications for those areas where organizational and epistemological concerns intersect. And the value of these implications can be carried further, we believe, by drawing on the key Deweyan concept of 'productive inquiry'.

Productive Inquiry

One of the most important things that knowing can do in using knowledge as a tool is what Dewey called 'productive inquiry'. To engage in productive inquiry is to be actively pursuing a problem, puzzle, point of fascination, object of wonder, or the like; it is to seek an answer, solution or resolution. It is *inquiry* because what motivates us to action is in some sense a query: a problem, a question, a provocative insight, or a troublesome situation. It is *productive* because it aims to produce (to make) an answer, solution or resolution. Productive inquiry includes a broad range of actions from the problem solving of mathematics to computer programming to fixing a photocopier to finding the proper placement of the voice in singing. *Productive inquiry is that aspect of any activity where we are deliberately (though not always consciously) seeking what we need, in order to do what we want to do.*

Productive inquiry is not a haphazard, random search; it is informed or 'disciplined' by the use of theories, rules of thumb, concepts, and the like. These tools of productive inquiry are prime examples of what Dewey understands the term 'knowledge' to mean. Conversely, using knowledge in this way is an example of that particular form of knowing that Dewey called 'productive inquiry'. So, using knowledge in productive inquiry gives inquiry a systematic or disciplined character: just as knowledge is a tool of knowing, so must knowing respect the demands and constraints of knowledge. (To wield any tool skillfully, we must respect the constraints it places on our actions in using it, as the haphazard use of a hammer can all too painfully demonstrate.)

Significantly, Dewey also saw knowledge as one of the possible outcomes of productive inquiry: one end result of engaging in the (situated, dynamic) activity of productive inquiry is the production of (abstract, static) knowledge, which then can be used as a tool of further knowing, including knowing in the mode of productive inquiry.

Building on these key points from Dewey, we make a number of further arguments about the distinction between knowledge and knowing. Knowledge by itself cannot enable knowing. As a tool, knowledge disciplines knowing, but does not enable it any more than possession of a hammer enables its skillful use. Likewise, the principles of engineering alone cannot enable an accomplished engineer to engage in the productive inquiry of resolving a difficult design problem. However, it is precisely such things as the principles of engineering that an accomplished engineer uses *in practice* as tools in addressing a problem at hand, in interacting with it through the use of those tools, in seeking to resolve a design problem.

Furthermore knowing should not be confused with 'tacit knowledge'. As we have defined tacit knowledge, it is a tool or an aid to action, not part of action itself. Everyone who can ride a bike can be said to know tacitly which way to turn to avoid a fall, whether or not they are at that moment actually riding. Knowing requires present activity. Tacit knowledge does not. Knowing makes use of tacit knowledge as a tool for action – as when we ride around on a bike using our tacit knowledge to stay upright (acquiring the tacit knowledge of how to stay upright, meanwhile, is acquiring know-how useful to bike riding). Finally, tacit knowledge alone does not enable us to ride; there is more epistemic work that needs to be done. Being able to ride requires interaction between the (tacit) knowledge we possess and the present activity of being in motion on a bike. The activity of riding, itself, is a form of knowing; it does distinct epistemic work. *Knowing is that aspect of action (or practice) that does epistemic work* – including doing things we know how to do, and (through productive inquiry) producing what we need, in order to do something we want to do, which can include producing new knowledge. We will explore this notion further in the next two sections.

Interaction with the World

We act within the social and physical world, and since knowing is an aspect of action, it is about interaction with that world. When we act, we either give shape to the physical world or we affect the social world or both. Thus, 'knowing' does not focus on what we possess in our heads: it focuses on our interactions with the things of the social and physical world.

'Knowledge' is about possession; it is a term of predication. In all its forms we use it to indicate something an individual or group possesses, can possess, or needs to possess. 'Knowing' is about relation: it is about interaction between the knower(s) and the world.

To interact with the world effectively we need to honor it. One cannot make reliable objects through the haphazard use of clay or steel: it is possible to make the walls of a pot too thin or the span of a bridge too long: objects give way when design pushes them beyond the constraints of their materials. To make use of the power of materials, their inherent constraints must be honored. The master of a craft – whether potter or materials engineer – is constantly engrossed in a kind of conversation with the materials of his or her craft. The master puts out ideas by giving shape to the material, and 'hears back' from it as he or she discovers and explores what the material can and cannot make possible. Part of what it means to master any craft is to learn how to turn the constraints of its materials into opportunities for design.

Similarly, in the social world, one must honor the strengths, limitations, and character of individuals and groups to engender co-ordinated and directed action or practice – as all good managers, football coaches and orchestra conductors know, at least intuitively (as do the members of such groups).

Knowledge also helps us 'honor' the world in our interactions with it. As noted above, knowing as an aspect of action can make use of bits of knowledge (in any of its forms) as tools. In doing so, the knowledge about the social and physical world 'disciplines' our interaction with the world, just as the use of a pair of pliers gives particular form to how we interact with a bolt.

Within the relational and interactive character of knowing, the world shapes our actions by requiring that we honor it, just as we shape the world by interacting with it in a disciplined way. *Knowing is to interact with and honor the world using knowledge as a tool.* We will look more precisely at how this works in the next section.

Dynamic Affordance

We now wish to focus on some specific characteristics of 'interaction with the world' that are at the center of our understanding of 'knowing'. In doing so, we first borrow two general points from the work of the Spanish philosopher José Ortega y Gasset that frame 'interaction with the world' in a way that further develops an alternative to the Cartesian frame of the 'thinking self'. Then we explore the idea of 'affordance', as introduced in the work on perception by J.J. Gibson (1979) and as significantly developed in the design work of W.W. Gaver (1991, 1996). Finally we argue for our sense of what we call 'dynamic affordance'.

Interaction with the social and physical worlds is a central concern in the work of Ortega. Very much in keeping with the American Pragmatists, Ortega abandoned the frame of the abstracted, analytic thinking self and throughout his work approached questions of epistemology, action, etc. from the perspective of 'myself within this context'. For Ortega, what we can know and what we can do are not discovered through an abstract Cartesian thought experiment, but are products of ongoing concrete interaction between 'myself' (or 'ourselves') and the specifics of the social and physical 'context' or 'circumstances' we are in at any given time. 'I invent projects of being and of doing,' Ortega (1961a: 202) insisted, 'in light of circumstance'.

In keeping with this, Ortega (1961b) argues that in interacting with the world we encounter both 'facilities' and 'frustrations'. It is important to note that facilities and frustrations are *not* properties of the world, but properties that lie solely in our interaction with the world. The tensile strength of clay is a property of the world, but it becomes a facility or a frustration only when we are interacting with it (e.g. when we are making pots). Likewise, the bits of knowledge that members of a team may possess are a property of that social world. They can only become facilities or frustrations, however, when we are interacting with the group within the context of a specific piece of work (or when the members of the group interact with each other in such a context).

The phenomenon of certain properties arising solely in the context of interaction with the world can also be seen in connection with the idea of 'affordance'. There is a common meaning of 'affordance' that is a progenitor of the sense we have in mind, but it is one we need to go beyond, because it suggests a static (i.e. not 'interactive') character. This is the elemental sense of how a material, design or situation 'affords' doing something: metal affords making buckets; buckets afford carrying water; bucket brigades afford fire fighting.

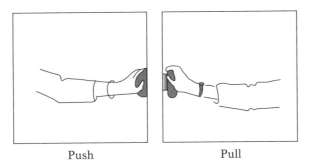

Push   Pull

Figure 3.2   Affordance

This sense of affordance is reflected in everyday objects in ways that can attract a great deal of conscious attention or none at all. This is particularly true of objects that are the product of human design. What they afford can give rise to shape and fluidity or incoherence and clumsiness in our activities. This can be seen, for example, even in the simple case of an ordinary book. The design of a book, as distinct from a newspaper or a scroll, affords such things as skimming or random access by using a thumb index or flipping from one part of the text to another and back again.

A doorknob, to take another example, affords opening and closing a door. The particular design of a doorknob can afford fluid or clumsy action. In Figure 3.2 we show the design of a doorknob that affords pushing or pulling the door from the appropriate side. On the side where the door needs to be pushed, the knob is a flattened hemisphere flush with the door; it is a knob that would, in fact, be difficult to pull. On the opposite side the same shape is raised from the surface of the door and one's fingers can fold easily around the edge so one's hand is almost invited to pull (particularly when paired with resistance from the door, if one should try pushing from that side). Although the design elements of common objects like books and doorknobs are often at the border of our attention, they nonetheless can constitute important resources in our interactions with them (Brown and Duguid, 1994).

How characteristics of the world give clues to our perceptions as to what we can and can't do with them is the sense of 'affordance' that is explored in depth in the work of Gibson (1979). Gaver has carried this notion further by arguing for an understanding of affordance that is not primarily about perception but about relationships between characteristics of the world and issues of inherent concern to people. For Gaver (1991, 1996), questions of affordance with respect to elevation in architecture, for example, emerge as issues of 'accessibility', which come from the relationship between elevation and the necessity of expending energy climbing to higher surfaces of support.

As we have indicated, there is a sense of affordance that lies beyond these inherently static senses, which deserves to be understood in its own right. We call this additional sense 'dynamic affordance' and mean by it forms of affordance that emerge as part of the (dynamic) interaction with the world. In talking about design elements of ordinary objects, for example, we said that they 'can give rise to shape and fluidity or incoherence and clumsiness in our activities'. We would note now that 'shape, fluidity, incoherence and clumsiness' are not properties of the objects (i.e. of the world). Rather, like Ortega's facilities and frustrations, they are properties of our interactions with those objects.[7] The emergence of these properties raises the question as to how we might deal with them: what use might we make of shape and fluidity, and how might we address incoherence and clumsiness are questions about what those properties of interaction afford. They are questions about dynamic affordance.

What we mean by 'dynamic affordance' has both an *intuitive* sense and a very particular *conceptual* sense. Both senses can be seen in the bicycle riding example. Intuitively, most of us understand that learning to ride requires 'getting a feel' for what it is like to stay in balance, and we recognize that we need to get on a bike to acquire that knowledge. So, the activity of riding around *dynamically affords* the acquisition of the needed knowledge.

Conceptually, we see 'dynamic affordance' as lying in the real and subtle interaction between the rider and the bike in motion. When bicycle wheels turn, they become gyroscopes – and like all gyroscopes their tendency is to remain in the plane of rotation: to get spinning bicycle wheels to tip to one side or the other requires that a force be applied to them that will overcome this gyroscopic tendency. A rider uses his or her body weight as that force: shifting one's weight pushes against the gyroscopic force of the moving wheels. This is what we do (or part of it) when we are riding or learning to ride. In the activity of riding, shifting our weight against the gyroscopic force of the wheels 'dynamically affords' learning to stay upright; it also 'dynamically affords' the enactment of that skill once acquired. These are things we can learn and do *only* when we are in dynamic interaction with bicycle wheels in motion. Without the dynamic affordance of that interaction there is no learning and no enactment of what is learned. Both are always inextricably tied to riding itself: without the activity of riding there is no gyroscopic force to be used or pushed against. This dynamic character is an essential element of our conceptual sense of 'dynamic affordance'.

Finally, because interaction between rider and bicycle dynamically affords *both* the acquisition of knowledge *and* the use of knowledge once acquired, we see it as doing epistemic work that the knowledge alone cannot. Indeed, we argue that dynamic affordance is intimately connected to the distinct epistemological form we have called 'knowing'. Dynamic interaction with the world opens the unique realm in which knowing takes place; the activity of addressing facilities and frustrations dynamically affords knowing.

We hold that dynamic affordance and knowing play an essential role in how knowledge – explicit and tacit, individual and group – is generated, transferred and used in organizations. We also hold that these activities acquire particular shape and meaning from their organizational contexts – that is, they are not only actions: they are also practices. Consequently, understanding how what is known functions in organizations requires understanding the interplay of the epistemology of

	Individual	Group
Explicit	Concepts	Stories
Tacit	Skills	Genres

Figure 3.3   Four forms of knowledge

possession and the epistemology of practice. It is to these matters that we now turn our attention.

Bridging Epistemologies

The four distinct forms of knowledge of the epistemology of possession as discussed above are displayed in Figure 3.3.

The cells of the figure array knowledge among the categories of individual – group and explicit – tacit. The upper left cell contains things an individual can know, learn and express explicitly. Examples of things that would fit this cell would include (but certainly not be limited to) concepts, rules and equations that typically are presented explicitly and are typically known and used by individuals. In the upper right are things that are also expressed explicitly yet typically are used, expressed or transferred in a group. This includes, for example, stories about how work is done or about famous successes or failures (Orr, 1990, 1996), as well as the use of metaphors or phrases that have useful meaning within a specific group. In the lower left are examples of tacit knowledge possessed by individuals, such as a skill in making use of concepts, rules, and equations or a 'feel' for the proper use of a tool or for keeping upright on a bike. Finally, in the lower right is tacit knowledge possessed by groups. Although everyone has daily experience with this form of knowledge, it is perhaps the most difficult of the four to define. A working definition of it, however, is crucial to understanding the relationships among the four forms of knowledge and to appreciating the distinction between knowledge and knowing. We wish to label this form of knowledge with an expanded definition of the term 'genre'.

Conventionally, 'genre' is most familiar as a literary term, where it refers to types of literature – for example 'novel' and 'biography' are two distinct literary genres. Such genres do more than constitute a tidy scheme of classification: they also provide frames for understanding arid interpreting what we read, without which a text could be utterly baffling or dangerously misleading. We read or 'take in' a text one way if we understand it to be a novel, quite another if we think it is a biography, Importantly, it is the meaning of the term 'novel' or 'biography' that constitutes the genre, not the actual text or the meaning the text acquires when it is understood to belong to a given genre. As literary historians would remind us, this meaning is constantly evolving and undergoing a kind of implicit negotiation among writers, readers and publishers as they read and discuss texts.

The power of genres to enable us to make sense of and use a text is so common in experience that we often are unconscious of it (Brown and Duguid, 1994). The characteristics of the genre 'newspaper' (folds, pulp paper, narrow columns of text, headlines, bylines, etc.) have meanings that we pay little, if any, conscious attention to; however, our ability to make sense of what newspapers say is highly dependent upon them. Without having been taught it or even reflecting on it consciously, most of us 'read' the importance of frontpage stories that appear above a newspaper's fold as greater than those that appear below it.

Genres are no less important to the organizational world than they are to the literary world (Orlikowski and Yates, 1994). A message from a co-worker can signal one thing if it arrives as a handwritten note, but quite another if it is a printed memo or a formal letter. The genre (note, memo or letter) provides a frame for interpreting a given text. Each of these forms of communication has a meaning understood and used by members of the organization. Indeed, employing genres is one way people in organizations communicate. As such, organizational genres acquire their very distinct (and quite effective) meanings not by deliberate design but (like that of 'novel' and 'biography') in the course of their being used (or misused) in the context of work practices.

The power of organizational genres is reflected, for example, in the case of the manager who reads email only as printed-out hard copy. After reading one such message, he phoned its author to tell him in no uncertain terms that such subjects 'should never be circulated in a memo'. The author replied that he had 'never written a memo like that', and that he had discussed the subject with people 'only through email'. In their organization, memos and email had in practice become two distinct genres; they had acquired two distinct meanings (with which the manager was perhaps not yet familiar). What was appropriate to communicate in one genre was inappropriate in the other. The boss misread the author's message (not necessarily his words) because he took what was intended as one genre (one form of communication) to be another.

We wish to generalize this sense of 'organizational genre' in defining what we mean by tacit group knowledge. For our purposes, 'organizational genre' applies not only to the distinctive and useful meanings a given group attaches to its various literary artifacts. It also applies to its various physical and social artifacts – that is, to different types of things (technologies or products, for example) and to different types of activities (such as ways of doing a task or types of meetings). These genres are not explicitly learned or known (although they can, for example, have explicit counterparts such as a label or a name). Their meanings emerge and undergo constant confirmation and/or modification through a kind of 'negotiation in practice' as they are used in the context of the group's ongoing 'real work'. What an organizational genre means at any one time is, in a sense, the accretion or product of the history of its use: it is meaning laid down in past use, and tapped into or 're-evoked' each time the members of the group use it in subsequent work. Accordingly, organizational genres have useful meaning solely in the context of a given group's practices – in this sense, they are possessed or 'held in common' by that group and are unique to it.

Two organizations, for example, could have ad hoc workgroup meetings, in each case called 'gatherings', that to an outsider could appear to be a single kind of semi-formal update. However, the meaning that 'gathering' has within each organization could be immensely different from its meaning in the other. In one, a 'gathering' could be understood by that organization's members to be where 'the real decisions' are made. In the other, it could be seen as a time to make subtle political moves. The events are alike. The names are the same. The genres are different. In each case, what 'gathering' means is known by the members of that organization; it is group knowledge. And that knowledge can be used effectively or ineffectively (as were 'email' and 'memo' in the above example) without any explicit discussion ever occurring. Accordingly, it is also tacit knowledge. For our purposes, then, this expanded sense of genre defines what we mean by group – tacit knowledge.

As group – tacit knowledge, genres do epistemically distinct work. This is reflected in a corporate executive's remarks on how a group of senior managers has made use of their organization's mission statement. 'The senior staff developed the statement', he reported, 'and the group has a sense of what it means, and we make use of that meaning in our discussions.' The group's 'sense' of what the mission statement means does not refer to its text but to the mission statement itself. Like 'novel' or 'memo' or 'gathering', it has become a genre within that group; it has acquired, in practice, tacit meaning that is known by the group. It can be used appropriately or inappropriately, effectively or ineffectively, but only in the context of group practice: as tacit – group knowledge (as an organizational genre), 'mission statement' does the epistemically distinct work of giving shape and direction to the group's discussions. This is under-scored by the executive's next remark. 'But when I think about the statement on my own,' he reflected, 'it can ... lead my thinking in directions I wouldn't go if I were working on the same issues along with members of the group.' How the genre func-tions within group practice is distinct from its role in the executive's thinking on his own. The group's 'sense' of what the mission statement means exemplifies what we have in mind by tacit knowledge possessed (or held in common) by a group.

Adding Knowing to Knowledge

Individuals and groups make use of knowledge in interaction with the things and activities of the social and physical world. Knowledge, as we have said, gives

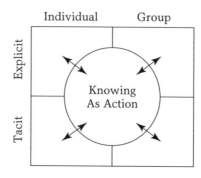

Figure 3.4   Adding knowing to knowledge

particular shape, meaning and discipline to our interactions with the world. At the same time, it has been our contention that not all of what we know in interacting with the world lies in our knowledge: some also lies in our actions themselves. Riding a bicycle requires that we use tacit knowledge in interaction with a bicycle in motion: some of what we know in being able to ride is in that interaction itself. For the manager mentioned above, being able to have effective communication with his colleagues required using the right genre ('email' rather than 'memo') in his interactions with messages (the action of interpreting them) and their authors (the action of conversing with them): some of what he knows in fostering success-ful communication in his organization is in those interactions themselves. In the example of the workgroup, a productive meeting is the product of the group using the genre 'the gathering' to help give the 'right' shape and meaning to the interac-tions that take place in their weekly sessions: some of what they know in con-ducting productive meetings is in their interactions with one another.

Each of these is an example of dynamic affordance – of what becomes possible when knowledge is used as a tool in the context of situated activity. Each is also an example of the importance of both knowledge and knowing in understanding the role played by what we know in organized human activity. It is by adding know-ing to knowledge that we can begin to account for the relationship between what we know and what we do. And it is also how we can begin to see how new knowl-edge and knowing are generated.

Figure 3.4 shows the four forms of knowledge from Figure 3.3, the focus of the epistemology of possession, with a circle superimposed that represents knowing, the focus of the epistemology of practice. The arrows suggest active use of knowl-edge in our interaction with the social and physical world. Within this interaction lies what we have called the generative dance.

Knowing does not sit statically on top of knowledge. Quite the contrary; since knowing is an aspect of our interaction with the world, its relationship with knowledge is dynamic. Each of the forms of knowledge is brought into play by knowing when knowledge is used as a tool in interaction with the world. Knowledge, meanwhile, gives shape and discipline to knowing.[8] It is this reciprocal interplay of knowledge and knowing that we call 'bridging epistemologies'.

It is by bridging epistemologies that it is possible to draw among the four forms of knowledge within the same activity. Individual and group knowledge are both used, for example, in activities that dynamically afford both the practice of a given skill by an individual and 'trying it out' by a group learning it – as when a choreographer teaches through demonstrations while a dance troupe follows. The group acquires tacit knowledge in practice as they develop a useful understanding, for example, of the moves employed in the piece through interacting with the demonstrations of the instructor (Cook, 1982; Lave and Wenger, 1991). It is within this interaction, moreover, that the troupe's new knowledge (genres) and new forms of knowing (performing the dance) are generated (a generative dance – literally).

What we are proposing here is more than a shift in language; it is a shift in focus from performing operations on existing knowledge to making something new. It is a shift in perspective that is meant to provoke different ways of assessing the role of what is known (both as knowledge and knowing) in an organization's ability to learn, to maintain quality, to develop competencies, to innovate, etc. Organizations not only create knowledge, they also – and usually primarily – create goods and services. In doing so, they need to be increasingly innovative. And this requires, we believe, attention not only to what they possess, but also to how they practice. This calls for a broadening of focus from one epistemology to two, including the generative potential of interplay between them.

In this sense, the generative dance entails productive inquiry in a substantial and robust sense: it is not only productive as a team is productive when it meets a preset quota; it is truly *generative*. By this we mean that it is a source of innovation, of productive change – as when a team invents new ways of working more effectively. In a very basic sense, for example, the activity that conversation affords is not limited to a merely additive back and forth exchange of information. When Emma says to Andrew 'I've been doing it this way', Andrew not only adds that knowledge to his own, but he also takes it into the context of his own experiences, skills, sensitivities, and the like (and vice versa when Andrew makes his reply). By placing Emma's knowledge into Andrew's contexts, the conversation can evoke novel associations, connections and hunches – it can generate new insights and new meaning. As everyone has experienced, a conversation's back-and-forth not only dynamically affords the exchange of knowledge, it can also afford the generation of new knowledge, since each remark can yield new meaning as it is resituated in the evolving context of the conversation. Through conversation, Emma and Andrew can negotiate a joint understanding of what 'doing it this way' means. This shared meaning, then, constitutes for them the genre 'Emma's way', which, in turn, can become an innovative and more effective means to read, understand, and carry out their work together. In this way, conversation affords more than an exchange in which the net sum of knowledge remains the same; it dynamically affords a *generative dance* within which the creation of new knowledge and new ways of using knowledge is possible.

Engaging in such conversation is a practice that does epistemic work; it is a form of knowing. Knowing entails the use of knowledge as a tool in the interaction with the world. This interaction, in turn, is a bridging, a linking, of knowledge and knowing. And bridging epistemologies makes possible the generative dance, which is the source of innovation. The generative dance, within the doing of work, constitutes the ability to generate new knowledge and new ways of using knowledge – which knowledge alone cannot do. And which the organizations of the future cannot afford to neglect.

Implications

We have found the perspective outlined above to have far-reaching implications for our work, in theory and in practice, and in assessing the work of others. Seeing each of the four forms of knowledge as unique, finding knowledge and knowing to be distinct, seeing how different epistemic work is done by different forms of knowledge and knowing, and understanding the notions of dynamic affordance and the generative dance – all this has not left our sense of how groups can and do work undisturbed. Below we briefly sketch out three cases that help make clearer some of the actionable and theoretically significant implications of this perspective.

The first case is drawn from Nonaka and Takeuchi's (1995) work on the 'knowledge-creating company'. Among their insightful explorations of 'knowledge creating' is a case of a company's development of a breadmaking machine. We build on their case, and argue that the perspective we have put forth here expands and makes more robust their notion of 'knowledge creation'. The second case deals with three Boston-area workshops that make world-class flutes. What the flutemakers know that enables them to make instruments of the highest quality, we argue, is found both in the knowledge they possess and in the ways they interact with the instruments and each other. The third case is a brief look at how a group of mechanical engineers in Xerox have created innovative *new* technologies in part through generative interactions with *old* mechanisms.

Machine Design

In their study of 'the knowledge-creating company' Nonaka and Takeuchi (1995) illustrate what they call the 'conversion' of tacit knowledge into explicit knowledge with the example of a company's development of a breadmaking machine. A good breadmaking machine must be able to knead dough properly. Yet, Nonaka and Takeuchi (1995: 63) note, this is something 'which is essentially tacit knowledge possessed by master bakers'. So one of the company's software developers became an apprentice to a prominent hotel's head baker. She was then able, according to Nonaka and Takeuchi's (1995: 104) interpretation, to 'transfer' the tacit knowledge she acquired in working with the master baker to the engineers who were designing the machine's kneading mechanism by 'converting' it into explicit knowledge 'by using the phrase "twisting stretch"'. The engineers used this knowledge in their work on the mechanism, and the software developer evaluated the results in a 'trial-and-error process [that] continued for several months' (1995: 104). Ultimately a good mechanism was produced. Nonaka and Takeuchi's argument, then, is that the tacit knowledge the software developer acquired by 'observing and imitating the head baker' was converted into explicit knowledge through the use of the phrase 'twisting stretch' (1995: 105), which, along with the engineers' technological knowledge, enabled the group to produce a prototype of the machine (1995: 106). In this way, they argue, the group was engaged in 'knowledge creation'.

We interpret this example somewhat differently. Yet, we believe an interpretation from the perspective of the generative dance serves to strengthen Nonaka and Takeuchi's central claims about 'knowledge creation'.

We see in the case the same distinct epistemological forms we saw in the bike-riding example, but now also at the organizational level. For us, the case is also an instance of bridging epistemologies, where the practices of the group (its ways of knowing) enabled it to draw simultaneously on different forms of knowledge possessed by different people. In this way, the individual tacit knowledge of the software developer and the explicit group knowledge of the engineers were both used by the team as a whole as tools within a productive inquiry (the trial-and-error process) that enabled them to design a successful kneading mechanism: various interactions by the group using specific tacit and explicit knowledge afforded the generation of both knowledge and new ways of knowing.

Following our interpretation, the example entails both 'bridging epistemologies' and the 'generative dance'. In making the machine, the design team drew on all four types of knowledge (by bridging epistemologies). There was the explicit technical knowledge each member of the team possessed. We imagine that there were also explicit group stories or metaphors, since such are all but universally found in groups. Individual tacit knowledge comes into play in both the master baker's skill and in what the apprenticed developer acquired. And there was group tacit knowledge, we claim, in the form of the useful meaning that 'twisting stretch' (as a genre) came to have for them (more on this in a moment).

In addition to the use of the different forms of knowledge, there was also knowing – that is, epistemic work that was part of the team's interaction with machine parts, bread dough and each other. This interaction (this way of knowing) entailed use of the team's various bits of knowledge as tools. The interaction also involved dynamic affordance within which (alone) the team was able to recognize and make use of the knowledge associated with the term 'twisting stretch' (just as being able to ride a bicycle requires the dynamic affordance of being on a bicycle in motion in order to make use of the knowledge associated with 'turn this way'). In particular, the term 'twisting stretch' referred to both the individual tacit knowledge of the developer and the tacit knowledge of the group. Using the term in the trial-and-error process provided a way of going back and forth between the two. In essence, the term functioned as a kind of 'boundary object' (Star and Griesemer, 1989) that straddled breadmaking and machine making. Through the successive iterations of mechanism design, the engineers negotiated with the developer the proper meaning and use of the term in application to the motion from breadmaking that they were aiming to capture in a machine operation. In this way, the meaning of the term 'twisting stretch' became a genre for the team as a whole (i.e. group tacit knowledge): it was the way they identified and understood the 'right' movement in both breadmaking and machine making. By bridging knowledge and knowing in actual interaction with the machine and each other (that is, by treating knowledge as a tool of knowing), the team was able to use the term 'twisting stretch' to draw on both individual and group tacit knowledge simultaneously in practice.

The generative dance can also be seen in the 'twisting stretch' example. 'Twisting stretch' as a genre (the shared meaning of the term), and the ability to use it in designing the prototype, were *new* things – a *new* bit of knowledge and a *new* way of knowing. They were not variant expressions of knowledge that already existed. They were created, we maintain, through the generative dance. That is, the design team used explicit and tacit knowledge as tools in interaction with machine parts and one another in an instance of productive inquiry that ultimately generated new knowledge and knowing. One of the team's aims was for the engineers to acquire a sense of the proper kneading motion. This entailed interaction between the engineers' machine making (a way of knowing) and the software developer's tacit knowledge (associated with her breadmaking). This resulted in the *generation* of the genre 'twisting stretch' (the group knowledge of what the term means). It was *not* tacit knowledge converted into explicit knowledge, it was *new* knowledge generated by the team. As a bit of knowledge, 'twisting stretch' became a meaningfully useful tool in two forms of knowing: the software developer's breadmaking and the engineers' machine making.

It is our focus on new knowledge and new knowing that leads us to prefer the concept of 'generating' to that of 'converting' (as used by Nonaka and Takeuchi, 1995). 'Conversion' tends to suggest an operation that is *applied to* knowledge rather than a concrete interaction with the world that generates knowledge. In converting feet to meters, an equation is applied to the measurement in feet and yields a measurement in meters, *without going back to the object at hand* to remeasure it. In our view, given one kind of knowledge, the only way to get the other is precisely *by going back to the object at hand* and *interacting* with it. For us, the 'trial-and-error process' Nonaka and Takeuchi identify is an example of just this sort of interaction with the world. What the design team did was not a conversion process applied to the software developer's tacit knowledge; it was an exercise in productive inquiry carried out by the group in interaction with bread dough, machine parts and each other. This interaction dynamically afforded the use of both explicit and tacit knowledge, and ultimately generated new knowledge and a new way of knowing.

Flutemakers

The case of the three flute companies that manufacture world-class instruments allows us to take these notions further. They are particularly illustrative of the notion of dynamic affordance and its role in the generative dance.

The Boston workshops produce flutes that are embraced by the flute world as instruments of the finest quality. And the flutes of each workshop have a distinctive character recognizable by knowledgeable flutists as the flute's 'feel' (generally, how the instrument feels when it is being played – not, incidentally, how it sounds). Both the high standard of quality and the unique character of each brand of flute are highly valued by the flute world.[9]

For most of their history, each workshop has had between 20 and 40 flutemakers (including those who are owners and managers) plus one or two office staff. The flutemakers work in teams, each flute being the product of a number of flutemakers, with each flutemaker working only on part of the instrument. (It is rare that a single person has the ability at any one time to make an entire flute, although some work on numerous aspects of flutemaking over the course of their careers.) A flutemaker, meanwhile, might work with a particular set of colleagues on one batch of flutes and with a different set on a later one. Over their history, the workshops have gone through generations of flutemakers (the oldest of the workshops dates from around 1900, the newest was established in 1977).

Because flutes are physical objects, the quality and character of each flute are inextricably tied to very fine degrees of dimension and tolerance in how their pieces work and fit together. Many of these dimensions and tolerances, however, are not known or used explicitly by the flutemakers. Rather, they are set by judgments of hand or eye. Typically, each flutemaker works on his or her part of the flute until it meets his or her standard of appearance and/or feel. Then it is handed on to the next flutemaker, who judges the work of the first by his or her own standards. If the work is not 'right', it goes back to the previous flutemaker to be reworked until both are satisfied. Some measurement tools are used, such as calipers and feeler gauges; but even when a part is measured, it is also checked out by feel or by eye, which are the final courts of appeal.

When an apprentice joins a workshop there are many things he or she must learn (apprenticeships have taken up to five years). Elements of what needs to be learned reflect all four forms of knowledge. There are concepts and rules about the types of parts, how they are connected, which tools are used for which functions, and so on. There are the skills needed to make flutes with the 'right feel'. These bits of explicit and tacit knowledge are learned and used by the individual apprentices just as they are used daily by master flutemakers.

At the group level, there are stories and metaphors used explicitly among flutemakers that help guide and co-ordinate their work. At one of the workshops flutemakers would argue that a piece of work or a new company policy ought to be 'the way the old man would want it', referring to the founder of the company (this continued long after 'the old man' had retired and died). There are also genres that constitute the shared meaning of the 'right way' to use certain equipment (feeler gauges, for example) or how to identify and understand what is wrong with a piece of work. When a part is handed back to a previous worker, for example, it can come with a comment such as 'this is a clunky one'. The flutemakers then hand the piece back and forth discussing its 'clunkiness'. This interaction with the piece and with each other dynamically affords a negotiation in practice as to what exactly 'clunky' means in reference to the piece at hand and concerning what work needs to be done to it. When the meaning associated with 'clunky' becomes commonly used by the flutemakers in recognizing, discussing and, working on subsequent problems, it functions as a genre in that workshop.

The examples above reflect different forms of knowledge that fit the four categories of the traditional epistemology. But having such knowledge is only part of what is needed to make world-class flutes. Knowing is required. Accordingly, it is typical for an apprentice to work on flutes starting on his or her first day in the shop: he or she engages in the practice of flutemaking, and begins to acquire not only knowledge but also ways of knowing. An apprentice may be told explicitly that 'these keys need to work more solidly'. But it is only through practice, through actual working jointly with other flutemakers on the piece, that he or she will 'get a feel' for what 'solidly' actually means in that shop ('solidly' could mean quite a different thing at one of the other workshops). When a master flutemaker says something such as 'this is what we call clunky' an apprentice can only know what that means by learning what it feels like – and a master flutemaker can only agree that an apprentice's work ultimately feels right by feeling the piece.

This is also true of accomplished flutemakers: part of what they know is in the daily handing of pieces back and forth and negotiating that a piece of work looks or feels right. Interaction with the instruments and other flutemakers dynamically affords the use, in practice, of the different forms of knowledge possessed by the flutemakers, individually and as a group. Another part of what the flutemakers know, another part of their epistemic work, is in their interactions themselves. The genre 'clunky' is a tool flutemakers use in their interactions with each other; it does the epistemic work of group tacit knowledge. Being able to recognize when 'clunky' gives way to that 'right feel' and being able to negotiate that with fellow flutemakers are also part of what flutemakers know, they are instances of epistemic work done as part of the practice of world-class flutemaking. And they are instances of knowing. The interaction with the instruments and among flutemakers also entails the generative dance; it is here that new knowledge and new ways of knowing are created. The back and forth between an apprentice and a master flutemaker, for example, dynamically affords two things at once: 1 the use, in practice, of existing tacit knowledge possessed by the master in judging the feel of the apprentice's work; and 2 the *generation* of new tacit knowledge and new ways of knowing for the apprentice. This is an instance of the generative dance.

An apprentice acquires new tacit knowledge in his or her interaction with the instrument and with a master flutemaker, and those interactions also dynamically afford the master using his or her tacit knowledge as a part of the practice of flutemaking. That is, the apprentice's *new* knowledge is *generated* in an interaction that has been given particular shape and form by the master's use of his or her *existing* knowledge. While on the surface this can appear to be a *transfer* of knowledge from the master to the apprentice, we see it as an interaction with the social and physical world (flutemakers and instrument parts) in which the master's knowledge is used and the apprentice's knowledge is *generated*.

The importance of tacit knowledge and its dissemination in organizations are also topics emphasized by Nonaka and Takeuchi (1995). For them this dissemination, including its role in the creation of new knowledge, occurs in a process they call 'socialization'. They hold that 'the sharing of tacit knowledge ... is a limited form of knowledge creation' because unless tacit knowledge 'becomes explicit, it cannot be easily leveraged by the organization as a whole'. They then contend that 'Organizational knowledge creation is a continuous and dynamic interaction between tacit and explicit knowledge' (1995: 70).

We propose three shifts that we believe build on and strengthen Nonaka and Takeuchi's general insight. First, as we have noted in detail above, we contend that it is not possible, under any circumstances, for tacit knowledge to become explicit (or vice versa). We do hold, however, that one can be a useful tool in the generation of the other through productive inquiry.

Second, since we hold that explicit and tacit knowledge are generated and disseminated each in its own right, whether either can 'be easily leveraged by the organization as a whole' depends, in our view, on the specific needs and resources that an organization has at hand in a given situation. The generation of explicit knowledge can, at times, be necessary to the dissemination of tacit knowledge (or even to making tacit knowledge more 'easily leveraged by the organization as a whole'). However, this is determined by its usefulness as a tool in productive inquiry in a given situation, not by general characteristics of explicit and tacit knowledge, as Nonaka and Takeuchi suggest. If explicit knowledge is needed, then it is explicit knowledge that needs to be generated and made sharable; if tacit knowledge is needed, then it must be generated and made sharable (as we see in the flute case). Or both (as is found in the case of the breadmaking machine).

Finally, for us, the production of new knowledge does not lie in 'a continuous interaction between tacit and explicit knowledge' but rather in our interaction with the world. Specifically, it lies in the use of knowledge (explicit and/or tacit) as tools of productive inquiry (of the sort we have called 'knowing') as part of our dynamic interaction with the things of the social and physical world.

Paper Handling

The significance of interaction with the *physical* world to dynamic affordance and the generation of knowledge and knowing found particular meaning for us in a recent research project in Xerox. In this research, it was discovered that, for a group of design teams, interacting with *old* artifacts is often a source of insights that are valuable in designing *new* technologies.

As part of a broader research project, what is known in Xerox about the design of 'paper paths' was examined.[10] These are the various electromechanical devices that move blank paper from a paper tray through a copier, printer, fax machine, etc. as it is 'marked' and then out of the machine as a printed page. These are surprisingly sophisticated devices, and there are often significant challenges in designing them as product cycles and technological innovations call for their evolution and change. This work is typically done by small teams composed mainly of mechanical engineers.

This expertise in paper path design is one of Xerox's traditional core competencies. Yet, through the course of the recent research, we came to recognize how some very valuable aspects of this competency are also embodied in the paper path mechanisms themselves. With time, engineers can forget, retire, move on, and the like – including, over enough time, entire cohorts or generations of engineers. By one way of thinking, then, some features of a given paper path's design and functioning, particularly subtle or sophisticated features, would no longer be available to Xerox. But the research revealed that when design teams sense that there is something in an old paper path that could be of use in designing new ones, they pull out the old one and begin to work with it. It is clear in this 'working with' old mechanisms that the teams are after tacit knowledge, not explicit knowledge (they have the technical drawings for that). In fact, they refer to being interested in how the mechanisms 'sound, feel, and work together' when in operation and when being assembled and disassembled.

This case complements Nonaka and Takeuchi's breadmaking machine example. In that example, what the engineers needed was *explicit* knowledge about the 'twisting stretch' movement so they could design a mechanism that would replicate it. While in the paper path example, the engineers needed *tacit* knowledge about the feel, sound and operation of older mechanisms, which they could use in designing new ones. Moreover, in the Xerox engineers' interactions with the older mechanisms, tacit knowledge was leveraged by the organization as a whole without requiring the use of explicit knowledge.

This research has led us to believe that we need radically to rethink what is needed to create and support 'core competencies'. Since part of Xerox's paper path competency is embodied in old artifacts, design teams need to have the kind of 'hands on' interaction with those artifacts that affords the recapture or (to follow our terminology) the regeneration of those particular bits of knowledge associated with that part of the competency. For the design team, this regeneration occurs as part of group practice: their dynamic interaction with the old paper path apparatus affords the acquisition by the team of (tacit) knowledge about significant aspects of how the mechanism looks, feels, and sounds when it is operating well. It can also afford the identification of significant dimensions, tolerances and functions (explicit knowledge) associated with the look, sound, and feel of proper operation.[11]

We also believe there is a need to rethink how competency is distributed – in particular, how it can be found both in what individuals and groups know and in their practices. Part of Xerox's competency in paper handling is embodied in existing artifacts, part in knowledge people possess. Part also lies in the ability of design teams to interact with old artifacts in ways that afford the regeneration, for the team, of the knowledge associated with those mechanisms. That is, the ability of these groups to do this is also part of Xerox's paper handling competency.

A design team's practices also include the generation of knowledge new to the group. This can be seen, for example, in the case of genres. In the context of their interaction with old mechanisms, a team will identify (through negotiation in practice) which aspects of how a mechanism sounds, feels and works are significant and which not. That is, bits of machine design and behavior will take on particular meaning (they will become genres), and those meanings will play a role in how the team frames, understands, or reads both their further interactions with the old mechanisms and their design work on the new one.

Finally, we would note that putting the knowledge associated with the older mechanisms in the context of new product design efforts results in more than adding old knowledge to new projects. It is a dynamic practice that can also afford the generation of new ideas and new ways of working – something that is not in the knowledge alone. Given this, we argue that understanding such things as the retrieval of 'intellectual capital' solely as a matter of tapping into a knowledge base (that is, as solely concerned with knowledge) leaves untapped (as well as unsupported, unrecognized, and underutilized) the generative power of the practices associated with recapturing old knowledge.

Conclusion

This chapter aims to broaden the existing understanding of what and how people know, as that relates to the epistemological dimension of organized human activity. We have offered the notions of distinct kinds of knowledge, productive inquiry, dynamic affordance, and the generative character of knowing to enrich such related themes as organization knowledge, knowledge creation, knowledge-based organizations, the management of intellectual capital, knowledge work, etc. Clearly, the perspective we have proposed both suggests and would benefit from further theoretical and empirical work. Among the numerous areas where further work could be done are the following.

How might issues of core competency be broadened if we were to ask not only what knowledge is entailed, but also what forms of knowing (how particular groups use the knowledge they have or acquire)? We see the core competencies of the flute workshops, for example, to include, along with the four forms of knowledge distributed among individuals and groups, ways of knowing reflected in the interactions flutemakers have with each other and the instruments. Such knowledge and knowing are essential to the organizations' world-class status, yet they are also unique to each workshop, and therefore cannot be transferred from one company to another. (In fact, when accomplished flutemakers have moved from one workshop to another, they have had to undergo 'retraining' in order to do work consistent with the new company's style and standards.) Thus, there is a need for a better understanding and better models of how this essentially nontransferable or 'situated' dimension of knowledge and knowing, as elements of an organization's core competency, can be 'generated in' (rather than 'transferred to') other groups or organizations.

There is a need for more case studies of knowledge-creating organizations, knowledge work, and knowledge management that focus not only on the body of knowledge that an organization acquires, stores and transfers. Equally important are the ways organizations can dynamically afford, within the situated practices of ordinary daily work, the productive inquiry essential to ongoing innovation.

There is also the very practical question of how training and educational programs can be redesigned. Such programs need to take as their aim both passing on knowledge to individuals *and* creating situations that help groups develop practices (ways of knowing) that make use of knowledge in new, innovative, and more productive ways.[12]

We hope that an expanded understanding of what and how people know can help provide an enriched, more robust way of assessing, supporting and honoring the epistemological dimension of all 'real work', which alone gives life and power to such concepts as core competency, knowledge creation, knowledge work and intellectual capital.

Acknowledgments

For their careful reading of and valuable comments on earlier drafts of this work the authors are indebted to Johan de Kleer, Daniel Denison, Paul Duguid, Larry Hickman, Kristian Kreiner, Charles F. Sabel, Edgar Schein, Sim Sitkin, Susan Stucky, Jeanne Vickers, Hendrik Wagenaar, Jay Zimmerman and Betty Zucker. They are also indebted to the anonymous reviewers of this chapter and, in particular, to Paul Adler for their exceptionally provocative and useful comments. Portions of the research that contributed to the writing of this chapter were supported by a grant from the National Science Foundation (#9320927).

Notes

1. The term 'epistemology' refers properly to the study of knowledge, including questions concerning what counts as knowledge and how bodies of knowledge can be systematically organized. More casually, it can also refer to knowledge and bodies of knowledge themselves (rather the way 'ecology' can refer both to the study of environmental systems and to those systems themselves). We make use of both senses of the term (depending on the context).

2. By 'epistemic work' we refer to the work people must do to acquire, confirm, deploy, or modify what needs to be known in order for them to do what they do.

3. We are indebted to Susan Stucky of the Institute for Research on Learning and to J.-C. Spender for the initial idea of this 2 × 2 table.

4. Discussion of explicit and tacit knowledge has a long history and has not by any means come to consensus. The terms used, how they are related, and the realities they point to vary considerably. Ryle (1949), for example, cast the discussion in terms of what it means to 'know *how*', and to 'know *that*'. For some (including us) the two types of knowledge are seen as quite distinct, while others may see them as two ends of a continuum.

5. The ontological status of groups has long been an unresolved issue. For our purposes, we take the view that not every action by a human collective can be meaningfully or usefully

reduced to an account of actions taken by the individuals in them (as the practices of coaches, orchestra conductors and organizational managers would suggest). To this extent, we believe collectives can be coherently and usefully considered in their own right with respect to actions they perform and with regard to the possession of any knowledge used in those actions.

6. Schon (1983), whose work also draws strongly on Dewey, makes a similar distinction in discussing what he sees as the need to shift from pure technical rationality to what he calls 'reflection-in-action' in professional practice.

7. This sense of significant properties arising in the interaction between the self (or group) and the world is also a central theme in the work of the twentieth-century Japanese philosopher Watsuji (1961).

8. Our language here (and at other points) suggests a resonance with structuration theory, especially with Giddens (see, for example, Giddens, 1979: especially Chapter 2; and Cohen, 1989: especially Chapter 1). Structuration theory's treatment of praxis as constitutive of social structure, while social structure informs praxis, parallels our characterization of knowledge as brought into play by knowing, while knowing is disciplined by knowledge. Some might reject any such parallel, given that our focus is essentially epistemological, while structuration theory (particularly Giddens himself) deliberately eschews epistemological concerns in favor of ontological ones. Others may see our treatment of the interaction of knowledge and knowing as an instance of structuration. For our part, we find the parallel a provocative one, both epistemologically and ontologically. Although a systematic consideration of this similarity is not within the scope of this chapter, we would make the following observations. We do not take the relationship between knowledge and knowing to be nothing more than a straightforward example of the more general relationship between structure and agency found in structuration theory (if for no other reason than that we believe neither structuration theory nor pragmatism makes the other epistemologically and/or ontologically redundant). At the same time, we believe that a fuller investigation of pragmatist epistemology and structuration ontology could find in the practice of productive inquiry a way to help the epistemological more fully rejoin the ontological within the purview of structuration theory.

9. A fuller presentation of this case focusing on organizational learning can be found in Cook and Yanow (1993). An extensive presentation and analysis of the case, focusing on tacit skills, judgment, and apprenticeship within the cultural context of groups can be found in Cook (1982).

10. This research was conducted as part of a project headed by Robert S. Bauer of Xerox Corporation and Estee Solomon Gray of Congruity. We are indebted to them for this example and for the project's influence on our thinking in general.

11. In addition to innovation, the use of older artifacts can also be seen in the case of training. Clark and Wheelwright (1992) have observed that Braun maintains a collection of their old products for use in training new product designers.

12. The theories and practices of 'progressive education' might offer some provocative points of reference in this regard.

References

Anderson, R. and W. Sharrock (1993) 'Can organizations afford knowledge?', Xerox Technical Report EPC-92–104.

Argyris, C. and D.A. Schon (1978) *Organizational Learning*, Addison-Wesley, Reading, MA.

Bourdieu, P. (1977) *Outline of a Theory of Practice*, Cambridge University Press, Cambridge.

Brown, J.S., A. Collins and P. Duguid (1989) 'Situated cognition and the culture of learning', *Educational Researcher*, 18(1): 32–41.

—— and P. Duguid (1991) 'Organizational learning and communities-of-practice: toward a unified view of working, learning, and innovation', *Organ. Sci.*, 2: 40–57.

—— and —— (1994) 'Borderline issues: social and material aspects of design', *Human-Computer Interaction*, 9(1): 3–36.

Clark, K.B. and S.C. Wheelwright (1992) *Managing New Project and Process Development*, Free Press, New York.

Cohen, I.J. (1989) *Structuration Theory: Anthony Giddens and the Constitution of Social Life*, St Martin's Press, New York.

Cohen, M.D. and P. Bacdayan (1994) 'Organizational routines are stored as procedural memory: evidence from a laboratory study'. *Organ. Sci.*, 5(4): 554–568.

Cook, S.D.N. (1982) 'Part of what a judgment is'. PhD dissertation, Massachusetts Institute of Technology (available from the author or from University Microfilms).

—— (1994) 'Autonomy, interdependence and moral governance: pluralism in a rocking boat', *Amer. Behavioral Sci.*, 38(1).

—— and D. Yanow (1993) 'Culture and organizational learning', *J. Management Inquiry*, 2(4): 373–90.

Gaver, W.W. (1991) 'Technology affordances', *Proceedings of CHI '91*. ACM Press, New Orleans: 79–84.

—— (1996) 'Affordances for interaction: the social is material for design', *Ecological Psych.*, 8(2): 111–129.

Gibson, J. (1979) *The Ecological Approach to Visual Perception*, Houghton Mifflin, New York.

Giddens, A. (1979) *Central Problems in Social Theory: Action, Structure and Contradiction in Social Analysis*, University of California Press, Berkeley and Los Angeles.

Hamel, G. and C.K. Prahalad (1994) *Competing for the Future*, Harvard Business School Press, Boston, MA.

Hickman, L. (1990) *John Dewey's Pragmatic Technology*, Indiana University Press, Bloomington, IN.

Hutchins, E. (1991) 'The social organization of distributed cognition', in L.B. Resnick, J.M. Levine and S.D. Teasley (eds) *Perspectives on Socially Shared Cognition*, American Psychological Association, Washington, DC.

Kogut, B. and U. Zander (1996) 'What firms do? – Coordination, identity, and learning', *Organ. Sci.*, 7(5): 502–519.

Krogh, G. von and J. Roos (1995) *Organizational Epistemology*, St. Martin's Press, New York.

Lave, J. and E. Wenger (1991) *Situated Learning: Legitimate Peripheral Participation*, Cambridge University Press, Cambridge.

Leonard-Barton, D. (1995) *Wellsprings of Knowledge: Building and Sustaining the Sources of Innovation*, Harvard Business School Press, Boston, MA.

March, J.G. and J.P. Olsen (1976) 'Organizational learning and the ambiguity of the past', *Ambiguity and Choice in Organizations*, Universitetsforlaget, Oslo, Norway.

Nonaka, I. (1994) 'A dynamic theory of organizational knowledge creation', *Organ. Sci.*, 5(1): 14–37.

—— and H. Takeuchi (1995) *The Knowledge-Creating Company*, Oxford University Press, New York.

Orlikowski, W.J. and J.Yates (1994) 'Genre repertoire: the structuring of communicative practices in organization', *Admin. Sci. Quart.*, 39: 541–574.

Orr, J.E. (1990) 'Sharing knowledge, celebrating identity: war stories and community memory in a service culture', in D.S. Middleton and D. Edwards (eds) *Collective Remembering: Memory in Society*, SAGE, London.

Orr, J.E. (1996) *Talking About Machines: An Ethnography of a Modern Job*, Cornell University Press, Ithaca, NY.

Ortega y Gasset, Jose (1961a) 'History as a system', in *History as a System*, W. W. Norton, New York. [Originally published in 1941.]

—— (1961b) 'Man the technician', in *History as a System*, W. W. Norton, New York. [Originally published in 1941.]

Polanyi, M. (1983) *The Tacit Dimension*, Peter Smith, Magnolia, MA. [Originally published in 1966.]

Rorty, R. (1982) *Consequences of Pragmatism*, University of Minnesota Press, Minneapolis, MN.

Ryle, G. (1949) *The Concept of Mind*, Hutchinson, London.

Schon, D.A. (1983) *The Reflective Practitioner: How Professionals Think in Action*, Basic Books, New York.

Simon, H.A. (1991) 'Bounded rationality and organizational learning', *Organ. Sci.*, 2(1): 125–134.

Sims, H.P., Jr, D.A. Gioia and associates (1986) *The Thinking Organization; Dynamics of Organizational Social Cognition*, Jossey-Bass, San Francisco, CA.

Sitkin, S.B. (1992) 'Learning through failure: the strategy of small losses', *Res. Organ. Behavior*, 14: 231–261.

Spender, J.-C. (1996) 'Competitive advantage from tacit knowledge? Unpacking the concept and its strategic implications', in B. Moingeon and A. Edmondson (eds) *Organisational Learning and Competitive Advantage*, SAGE, London.

Star, S.L, and J.R. Griesemer (1989) 'Institutional ecology, "translations" and boundary objects: amateurs and professionals in Berkeley's Museum of Vertebrate Zoology, 1907–39', *Soc. Stud. Sci.*, 19: 387–420.

Stewart, T.A. (1997) *Intellectual Capital: the New Wealth of Organizations*, Doubleday/Currency, New York.

Turner, S. (1994) *The Social Theory of Practices: Tradition, Tacit Knowledge, and Presuppositions*, University of Chicago Press. Chicago.

Vickers, G. (1976) 'Technology and culture', invited paper given at the Division for Study and Research in Education, Massachusetts Institute of Technology, Cambridge, MA.

Watsuji, T. (1961) *Climate and Culture*, Monbusho, Tokyo.

Weick, K.E. (1991) 'The nontraditional quality of organizational learning', *Organ. Sci.*, 2(1): 116–124.

—— and Roberts, K.H. (1993) 'Collective mind in organizations: heedful interrelating on flight decks', *Admin. Sci. Quart.*, 38: 357–381.

—— and F. Westley (1996) 'Organizational learning: affirming an oxymoron', *Handbook of Organization Studies*, SAGE, Thousand Oaks, CA.

Wenger, E. (1997) *Communities of Practice: Learning, Meaning and Identity*, Cambridge University Press, Cambridge.

What Is Organizational Knowledge?

Haridimos Tsoukas and Efi Vladimirou

This chapter explores the links between individual knowledge, organizational knowledge and human action undertaken in organized contexts. Those links have remained relatively unexplored in the relevant literature, a large part of which, captive within a narrowly Cartesian understanding of knowledge and cognition, has tended to privilege 'pure' knowledge and thinking at the expense of outlining the forms of social life that sustain particular types of knowledge (Tsoukas, 1996, 1997, 1998; Varela et al., 1991; Winograd and Flores, 1987).

Moreover, although most people intuitively identify knowledge with *individual* knowledge, it is not quite evident how knowledge becomes an individual possession and how it is related to individual action, nor is it clear in what sense knowledge merits the adjective *organizational*. Despite the insights gained by the research of leading experts on organizational knowledge, there are still crucial questions unresolved. For example, Nonaka and Takeuchi (1995, pp. 58–9) argue that:

> *Information is a flow of messages, while knowledge is created by that very flow of information, anchored in the beliefs and commitment of its holder. This understanding emphasizes that* knowledge is essentially related to human action. *(Emphasis in the original)*

Other researchers have similarly stressed the close connection between knowledge and action: whatever knowledge is, it is thought to make a difference to individuals' actions (Choo, 1998; Davenport and Prusak, 1998; Leonard and Sensiper, 1998; Suchman, 1987; Wigg, 1997). However, while this is a useful insight, it is not clear *how* knowledge is connected to action, nor, more fundamentally, what knowledge is. True, knowledge makes a difference, but how? How is knowledge brought to bear on what an individual does? What are the prerequisites for using knowledge effectively in action?

Davenport and Prusak (1998, p. 5) have provided the following definition of knowledge:

Source: H. Tsoukas and E. Vladimirou (2001) 'What is organizational knowledge?', *Journal of Management Studies*, 38(7): 973–93. Edited version.

> *Knowledge is a flux mix of framed experiences, values, contextual information, and expert insight that provides a framework for evaluating and incorporating new experiences and information. It originates and is applied in the minds of knowers. In organizations, it often becomes embedded not only in documents or repositories but also in organizational routines, processes, practices, and norms.*

While this definition correctly highlights the dynamic character of knowledge (i.e. knowledge is both an outcome – 'a framework' – and a process for 'incorporating new experiences and information'), it is not clear in what sense knowledge is different from information, nor how it is possible for values and contextual information to originate and apply in the minds of individuals alone. Moreover, Davenport and Prusak pack into knowledge too many things, such as 'values', 'experiences' and 'contexts', without specifying their relationships, thus risking making 'knowledge' an all-encompassing and, therefore, little-revealing, concept. Also, while it is acknowledged that knowledge becomes embedded in organizations, it is not mentioned in what form, nor how individuals draw on it.

For some researchers and practitioners (see Gates, 1999; Lehner, 1990; Terrett, 1998) organizational knowledge tends to be viewed as synonymous with information, especially digital information, in which case the interesting issue is thought to be how knowledge-as-information is best stored, retrieved, transmitted and shared (Brown and Duguid, 2000; Hendriks and Vriens, 1999). In contrast, for some researchers, such as Kay (1993), organizational knowledge becomes the essence of the firm. For example, as Kay (1993, p. 73) remarks, '[organizational knowledge] is distinctive to the firm, is more than the sum of the expertise of those who work in the firm, and is not available to other firms'. Here knowledge is thought to be profoundly collective, above and beyond discrete pieces of information individuals may possess; it is a pattern formed within and drawn upon a firm, over time. While few would take issue with this definition, it does not quite reveal what are the characteristic features of organizational knowledge, and does not even hint at the relationship between individual and organizational knowledge.

From the above admittedly cursory review, it follows that it is still not clear what knowledge is, nor what makes it organizational. Realizing that knowledge is indeed a tricky concept, some researchers have gone as far as to suggest (mostly in the context of academic conferences) that, perhaps, we do not need more formal definitions of knowledge, since they, very likely, end up complicating things further. We do not agree with this view. Our understanding of organizational knowledge (or any other topic of interest) will not advance if we resign ourselves to merely recycling commonsensical notions of knowledge for, if we were to do so, we would risk being prisoners of our own unchallenged assumptions, incapable of advancing our learning. On the contrary, what we need is ever more sophisticated theoretical explorations of our topic of interest, aiming at gaining a deeper insight into it. Those who think such an attempt is futile need to ponder the great extent to which Polanyi's notion of 'personal knowledge' has advanced our understanding of what knowledge is about and, accordingly, how much impoverished our understanding would have been without that notion. If theoretical confusion is in evidence the answer cannot be 'drop theory' but 'more and better theory'.

This chapter will argue that our difficulties in getting to grips with organizational knowledge stem from a double failure: to understand the generation and utilization of knowledge we need a theory of knowledge, *and* to understand *organizational* knowledge we need a theory of organization. Moreover, it needs to be pointed out that, although no self-respecting researchers have so far failed to acknowledge their debt to Polanyi for the distinction he drew between tacit and explicit knowledge, Polanyi's work, for the most part, has not been really engaged with. If it had been it would have been noticed that, since all knowledge has its tacit presuppositions, tacit knowledge is not something that can be converted into explicit knowledge, as Nonaka and Takeuchi (1995) have claimed (Cook and Brown, 1999; Tsoukas, 1996). Moreover, and perhaps more crucially, it would have been acknowledged that Polanyi (1962), more than anything else, insisted on the *personal* character of knowledge – hence the title of his magnum opus, *Personal Knowledge*. In his own words: '*All* knowing is personal knowing – participation through indwelling' (Polanyi, 1975, p. 44; emphasis in the original).

We will take on board Polanyi's profound insight concerning the personal character of knowledge and fuse it with Wittgenstein's claim that all knowledge is, in a fundamental way, collective, in order to show on the one hand how individuals appropriate knowledge and expand their knowledge repertoires, and, on the other hand, how knowledge, in organized contexts becomes organizational, with what implications for its management. We will ground our theoretical claims on a case study undertaken at a call centre in Panafon, the leading mobile telecommunications company in Greece.

The structure of the chapter is as follows. In the next section we describe what personal knowledge is and develop further the notion of organizational knowledge. In a nutshell, our claim is that knowledge is the individual capability to draw distinctions, within a domain of action, based on an appreciation of context or theory, or both. Similarly, organizational knowledge is the capability members of an organization have developed to draw distinctions in the process of carrying out their work, in particular concrete contexts, by enacting sets of generalizations whose application depends on historically evolved collective understandings. Following our theoretical exploration of organizational knowledge, we report the findings of a case study carried out at a call centre in Panafon, in Greece. In line with our argument that all organizations can be seen as collections of knowledge assets (Wenger, 1998, p. 46), we investigate how call operators at a call centre – a unit which, conventionally, would not be called knowledge-intensive – answer customer calls by drawing on and modifying organizational knowledge to suit their particular circumstances. Finally, we explore the implications of our argument by focusing on the links between knowledge and action on the one hand, and the management of organizational knowledge on the other.

On Personal and Organizational Knowledge

The distinction between data, information and knowledge has often been made in the literature (Boisot, 1995; Choo, 1998; Davenport and Prusak, 1998; Nonaka and Takeuchi, 1995). What differentiates knowledge from information, it has been argued, is that knowledge presupposes values and beliefs, and is closely connected with action. Similarly, Bell (1999, pp. lxi–lxiv) has provided a neat definition of these terms, which is particularly useful for our purpose here. For Bell *data* is an ordered sequence of given items or events (e.g. the name index of a book). *Information* is a context-based arrangement of items whereby relations between them are shown (e.g. the subject index of a book). And *knowledge* is the judgement of the significance of events and items, which comes from a particular context and/or theory (e.g. the construction of a thematic index by a reader of a book).

What underlies Bell's definition of knowledge is his view that data, information, and knowledge are three concepts that can be arranged on a single continuum, depending on the extent to which they reflect human involvement with, and processing of, the reality at hand. For example, the name index of a book is merely data, since it involves minimal effort on the part of an individual to make such an index – the names are there, it is just a matter of arranging them alphabetically. The subject index of a book, however, requires more processing on the part of the individual, since it depends on his/her judgement to construct the appropriate headings for such an index. Finally, when a reader relates the content of a book to his/her own interests, he/she may construct his/her own analytical index – in other words, the reader in this case has a far greater degree of involvement and exercises far greater judgement in organizing the material at hand. Put simply, data require minimal human judgement, whereas knowledge requires maximum judgement. Knowledge is the capacity to exercise judgement on the part of an individual, which is either based on an appreciation of context or is derived from theory, or both (Bell, 1999, p. lxiv).

Drawing on Dewey's (1934) conception of aesthetic experience, Bell (1999, p. lxiv) goes on to argue that 'judgement arises from the self-conscious use of the prefix *re*: the desire to *re*-order, to *re*-arrange, to *re*-design what one knows and thus create new angles of vision or new knowledge for scientific or aesthetic purposes'. The self-conscious desire to re-arrange what one knows implies that the individual wishes to see things differently, to disclose aspects of a phenomenon that were hitherto invisible, or simply to see more clearly than before. But this is not all: the individual will re-arrange his/her knowledge while being located somewhere – a certain standpoint or tradition. Thus the capacity to exercise judgement involves two things. First, the ability of an individual to draw distinctions (Reyes and Zarama, 1998; Vickers, 1983) and, second, the location of an individual within a collectively generated and sustained domain of action – a 'form of life' (Wittgenstein, 1958), a 'practice' (MacIntyre, 1985), a 'horizon of meaning' (Gadamer, 1989) or a 'consensual domain' (Maturana and Varela, 1988) – in which particular criteria of evaluation hold.

Why does the capacity to exercise judgement imply the capability of drawing distinctions? Because when we draw a distinction we split the world into 'this' and 'that', we bring into consciousness the constituent parts of the phenomenon we are interested in (Dewey, 1934, p. 310). Through language we name, and constantly bring forth and ascribe significance to, certain aspects of the world (including, of course, our own behaviour) (Schutz, 1970; Taylor, 1985; Winograd and Flores, 1987). When our language is crude and unsophisticated, so are our distinctions and the consequent judgements. The more refined our language, the finer our distinctions. Our attempt to understand and act on reality is simultaneously enabled and limited by the cultural tools we employ – with language being one of the most important (Vygotsky, 1978, pp. 23–30; Wertsch, 1998, p. 40). Just like someone with a rudimentary knowledge of English cannot easily tell the different kinds of accent of English speakers (that is, he/she cannot draw fine distinctions related to accent), so a person untrained into a particular activity has only a rule-based, undifferentiated outline of it in mind, rather than a set of refined distinctions (Dreyfus and Dreyfus, 1986). Polanyi (1962, p. 101) has perceptively captured this point in the following illustration:

> *Think of a medical student attending a course in the X-ray diagnosis of pulmonary diseases. He watches in a darkened room shadowy traces on a fluorescent screen placed against a patient's chest, and hears the radiologist commenting to his assistants, in technical language, on the significant features of these shadows. At first the student is completely puzzled. For he can see in the X-ray picture of a chest only the shadows of the heart and the ribs, with a few spidery blotches between them. The experts seem to be romancing about figments of their imagination; he can see nothing that they are talking about. Then as he goes on listening for a few weeks, looking carefully at ever new pictures of different cases, a tentative understanding will dawn on him; he will gradually forget about the ribs and begin to see the lungs. And eventually, if he perseveres intelligently, a rich panorama of significant details will be revealed to him: of physiological variations and pathological changes, of scars, of chronic infections and signs of acute disease. He has entered a new world. He still sees only a fraction of what the experts can see, but the pictures are definitely making sense now and so do most of the comments made on them.*

The medical student refines her ability to read an X-ray picture through her exposure to the relevant material (what Lakoff [1987, p. 297] calls 'the basic-level interactions with the environment') *and* the specialized language she is taught to apply to that material (Schon, 1983). How does this happen? Having a body, the medical student is capable of obtaining preconceptual experience, that is experience that is tied to gestalt perception, mental imagery and motor movement (Lakoff, 1987, pp. 267–8, 302–3). At the same time, being a language user, the medical student operates in the cognitive domain, namely a domain within which she recursively interacts with her own descriptions (i.e. thoughts). What initially appears only as a shadow of the heart and the ribs (i.e. a description), is further processed, through language and with the help of an instructor or with peers, until a much more refined picture emerges. As Mercer (1995, p. 13) remarks, 'practical, hands-on activity can gain new depths of meaning if it is *talked about'* (emphasis added). Relating her hitherto knowledge to the X-ray picture and talking about it with her instructor, the medical student is forced to revise and refine her understanding about the matter at hand (Hunter, 1991). In von Foerster's (1984, p. 48) second-order cybernetics language, cognitive processes are never-ending processes of computation. Cognition consists in computing descriptions of descriptions, namely in recursively operating on – modifying, transforming – representations. In doing so, cognizing subjects re-arrange and re-order what they know, thus creating new distinctions and, therefore, new knowledge (Bell, 1999, p. lxiv; Dewey, 1934).

Individuals draw distinctions within a collective domain of action, namely within a language-mediated domain of sustained interactions. For the medical student to be able to discern the medically significant pattern of an X-ray picture, she necessarily draws on medical knowledge, namely on a collectively produced and sustained body of knowledge (Hunter, 1991). Likewise, for an individual copier technician to be able to diagnose a faulty photocopier, he needs to draw on a specific body of expertise, which is produced and sustained by the company making photocopiers and by the community of technicians as a whole (Orr, 1996; cf. Wenger, 1998). Why is this so? The reason is that the key categories implicated in human action, for example, 'physiological variation', 'pathological change' (Polanyi, 1962, p. 101), 'faulty photocopier' (Orr, 1996) or 'clunky flute' (Cook and Brown, 1999, p. 396; Cook and Yanow, 1996), derive their meanings from the way they have been used within particular forms of life (the medical community or the community of photocopier technicians or the community of flutemakers). One learns how to recognize a pathology on the lungs or a 'clunky flute', only because one has been taught to use the category 'pathological lung' or 'clunky flute' within a domain of action (Toulmin, 1999).

In other words, knowing how to act within a domain of action is learning to make competent use of the categories and the distinctions constituting that domain (Wenger, 1998). As Spender (1989) has shown, upon entering a particular industry, managers learn a particular 'industry recipe', that is a set of distinctions tied to a particular field of experience. The distinctions pertain to a number of issues ranging from how markets are segmented to the kind of employees suited to an industry or to the technology used. To put it broadly, to engage in collective work is to engage in a discursive practice, namely in the normative use of a sign system which is directed at influencing aspects of the world and whose key categories and distinctions are defined through their use in discourse (Harré and Gillett, 1994, pp. 28–9; Taylor, 1993; Tsoukas, 1996, 1998).

On the basis of the preceding analysis, the definition of knowledge mentioned earlier may be re-formulated as follows: *knowledge is the individual ability to draw distinctions within a collective domain of action, based on an appreciation of context or theory, or both.* Notice that such a definition of knowledge preserves a significant role for human agency, since individuals are seen as being inherently capable of making (and refining) distinctions, while also taking into account collective understandings and standards of appropriateness, on which individuals necessarily draw in the process of making distinctions, in their work.

The individual capacity to exercise judgement is based on an appreciation of *context* in the ethnomethodological sense that a social being is (or, to be more precise, becomes) knowledgeable in accomplishing routine and taken-for-granted tasks within particular contexts (e.g. taking measurements, driving, holding a conversation, filling in a medical insurance form, etc.), as a result of having been through processes of socialization (Berger and Luckmann, 1966; Garfinkel, 1984; Schutz, 1970). We do not need a PhD in linguistics to carry out a conversation, nor do we need specialized training in economics or agricultural science to buy cheese at the grocers. We know how to deal with the practical things in life because we have picked up through interaction (with the world and with others) what is expected of us, or what works (Heritage, 1984; Wenger, 1998). 'We bring to situations of interaction', notes McCarthy (1994, p. 65), a 'tacit awareness of the normative expectations relevant to them and an intuitive appreciation of the consequences that might follow from breaking them'.

The individual capacity to exercise judgement is based on an appreciation of *theory* in the epistemic sense that, as Bell (1999, p. lxiii) has noted, 'theory allows one to take a finding and generalize from any one context to another context. From verified theory – Newton's laws of motion – we can accept the finding in a new context as knowledge'. Choosing a theory and applying it in a new context involves judgement, and the capacity to make such judgements is knowledge. The notion of 'theory' here is a broad one to include any framework, set of generalizing principles, or abstract instructions. Just as a judge brings a set of legal principles to bear on a particular situation, so a copier technician draws upon, among other things, a set of abstract instructions in order to repair a faulty photocopier. Whatever abstract principle enables an individual to generalize across contexts counts as theory and forms an additional basis for exercising judgement.

If the above is accepted then it becomes possible for us to see the sense in which knowledge becomes organizational. In a weak sense, knowledge is organizational simply by its being generated, developed and transmitted by individuals within organizations. That is obvious but unrevealing. In a strong sense, however, knowledge becomes organizational when, as well as drawing distinctions in the course of their work by taking into account the contextuality of their actions, *individuals draw and act upon a corpus of generalizations in the form of generic rules produced by the organization.*

Why is this the case? A distinguishing feature of organization is the generation of recurring behaviours by means of institutionalized roles that are explicitly defined. For an activity to be said to be organized it implies that *types* of behaviour in *types* of situations are connected to *types* of actors (Berger and Luckmann, 1966, p. 22; Scott, 1995). An organized activity provides actors with a given set of cognitive categories and a typology of action options (Scott, 1995; Weick, 1979). Such a typology consists of rules of action – typified responses to typified expectations (Berger and Luckmann, 1966, pp. 70–3). Rules are prescriptive statements guiding behaviour in organizations and take the form of propositional statements, namely 'If X, then Y, in circumstances Z'. As Twining and Miers (1991, p. 131) remark, 'a rule prescribes that in circumstances X, behaviour of type Y ought, or ought not to be, or may be indulged in by persons of class Z'.

On this view, therefore, *organizing implies generalizing*: the subsumption of heterogeneous particulars under generic categories. In that sense, formal organization necessarily involves abstraction. Since in an organization the behaviour of its members is formally guided by a set of propositional statements, it follows that an organization may be seen as a *theory* – a particular set of concepts (or cognitive categories) and the propositions expressing the relationship between concepts. Organization-as-theory enables organizational members to generalize across contexts. For example, the operators of the call centre we researched had been instructed to issue standardized responses to standardized queries: if this type of problem appears, then this type of solution is appropriate. From a strictly organizational point of view, the contextual specificity surrounding every particular call (a specificity that callers tend to expand upon in their calls) is removed through the application of generic organizational rules.

Rules, however, exist for the sake of achieving specific goals. The generalizations selected and enforced are selected from among numerous other possibilities. To have as a rule, for example, that 'no caller should wait for more than one minute before his/her call is answered' is not self-evident. It has been selected by the company, in order to increase its customer responsiveness, hoping that, ultimately, it will contribute to attracting more customers, thus leading to higher market share, and so on. In other words, a rule's factual predicate ('If X ...') is a generalization selected because it is thought to be causally relevant to a *justification* – some goal to be achieved or some evil to be avoided (Schauer, 1991, p. 27). A justification (or to be more precise, a set of logically ordered justifications) determines which generalization will constitute a rule's factual predicate. This is an important point for it highlights the fact that rules exist for the sake of some higher-order goals.

Moreover, rules do not apply themselves; members of a community-of-practice, situated in specific contexts, apply them (Gadamer, 1980; Tsoukas, 1996; Wittgenstein, 1958). Members of a community must share an interpretation as to what a rule means before they apply it. As Barnes (1995, p. 202) remarks, 'nothing in the rule itself fixes its application in a given case, ... there is no "fact of the matter" concerning the proper application of a rule, ... what a rule is actually taken to imply is a matter to be decided, when it is decided, by contingent social processes'. Since rules codify particular previous examples, an individual following a rule needs to learn to act in proper analogy with those examples. To follow a rule is, therefore, to extend an analogy. Barnes (1995, p. 55) has put it so felicitously that we cannot resist the temptation to quote him in full:

> To understand rule-following or norm-guided behavior in this way immediately highlights the normally open-ended character of norms, the fact that they cannot themselves fix and determine what actions are in true conformity with them, that there is no logical compulsion to follow them in a particular way. Every instance of a norm may be analogous to every other, but analogy is not identity: analogy exists between things that are similar yet different. And this means that, although it is always possible to assimilate the next instance to a norm by analogy with existing examples of the norm, it is equally always possible to resist such assimilation, to hold the analogy

insufficiently strong, to stress the differences between the instance and existing examples. If norms apply by analogy then it is up to us to decide where they apply, where the analogy is sufficiently strong and where not. (Emphasis added)

Notice that, on this essentially Wittgensteinian view, the proper application of a rule is not an individual accomplishment but is fundamentally predicated on collectively shared meanings. If formal organization is seen as a set of propositional statements, then those statements must be put into action by organizational members, who 'must be constituted as a *collective* able to sustain a shared sense of what rules imply and hence an agreement in their practice when they follow rules' (Barnes, 1995, p. 204; emphasis added). The justification (purpose) underlying a rule needs to be elaborated upon and its meaning agreed by the organizational collective. Organizational tasks are thus accomplished by individuals being able to secure a shared sense of what rules mean (or by agreeing upon, reinforcing and sustaining a set of justifications) in the course of their work. This suggests an organization as a densely connected network of communication through which shared understandings are achieved.

A collectivist understanding of organizational knowledge has been evident in Penrose's (1959) work on the theory of the firm. The key to understanding firms' growth, wrote Penrose, is to focus not on the given resources a firm possesses but on the *services* rendered by those resources. This means that, according to Penrose, firms have discretion over how they use their resources and, therefore, over the services derived from them. Such discretion stems from the fact that firms view, and thus utilize, their resources differently. On this view, organizational knowledge is the set of collective understandings embedded in a firm, which enable it to put its resources to particular uses. Penrose's view of organizational knowledge identifies the latter with cultural or collective knowledge (Blackler, 1995; cf. Collins, 1990) – *it is a distinctive way of thinking and acting in the world.*

There is an interesting parallel between the preceding Wittgensteinian view of rule following and Polanyi's conception of personal knowledge. Both philosophers showed that even the most abstract formalisms we use ultimately depend, for their effective deployment, on social definitions. Abstract systems cannot be self-sustained; they are necessarily grounded on collective definitions, hence they depend on human judgement (Toulmin, 1999). Polanyi extended this argument further. For him, human judgement is manifested not only at the level of collective significations that happen to have historically evolved; it is equally manifested at the individual level. All knowledge is personal knowledge.

Seeking to highlight the nature of science as a skilful practice, Polanyi described, time and again, the exact sciences as 'a set of formulae which have a bearing on experience' (Polanyi, 1962, p. 49). It is precisely the establishment of this 'bearing on experience' that renders all scientific knowing, ultimately, *personal* knowing. In so far as even the most abstract mathematical formalisms need to be empirically checked, that is predictions to be made, measurements to be taken, and predictions to be compared with measurements, there are bound to be discrepancies between theory and observations, no matter how minor, which will need to be assessed by personal judgement on the part of the scientist (Polanyi, 1975, p. 30). In his several illustrations, from map reading, through piano playing and bicycle riding, to scientific work, Polanyi consistently pointed out that all abstract systems, from the shortest set of instructions right to the most abstract and comprehensive set of formalisms, ultimately encounter experience – the real world with all its messiness, imperfection, and complexity – and that encounter is inevitably mediated through human judgement. In Polanyi's (1975, p. 31) words,

> *Even the most exact sciences must therefore rely on our personal confidence that we possess some degree of personal skill and personal judgement for establishing a valid correspondence with – or a real deviation from – the facts of experience.*

Acknowledging that all knowledge contains a personal element or, to put it differently, '[recognizing] personal participation as the universal principle of knowing' (Polanyi, 1975, p. 44), implies that knowing always is, to a greater or lesser extent, a skilful accomplishment, an art.

What is the structure of such a skill? What does it consist of? Either we refer to everyday or expert knowledge or, to use Bell's terminology, to knowledge based on an appreciation of context or theory, the structure of knowing-as-a-skill is identical. In order to know something, the individual acts to integrate a set of particulars of which he/she is subsidiarily aware. To make sense of our experience, we necessarily rely on some parts of it subsidiarily in order to attend to our main objective focally. We comprehend something as a whole (focally) by tacitly integrating certain particulars, which are known by the actor subsidiarily. Knowing has a *from–to* structure: the particulars bear on the focus *to* which I attend *from* them. Subsidiary awareness and focal awareness are mutually exclusive. Action is confused if the individual shifts his/her focal attention to the particulars, of which he/she had been previously aware in a subsidiary manner.

Thus, knowing consists of three elements: subsidiary particulars, a focal target, and, crucially, a person who links the two. Polanyi's (1975, p. 36) classic example is the blind man probing a cavity with his stick. The focus of his attention is at the far end of the stick, while attending subsidiarily to the feeling of holding the stick in his hand. The difference between a seeing man blindfolded and a blind man is that, for the former, probing feels like a series of jerks in his palm, whereas for the latter probing indicates the presence of certain obstacles of a certain hardness and shape. In the first case, the stick has not yet been assimilated (and, as a result, it receives focal awareness), while in the latter case the stick is being subsidiarily aware of and, as a result, it is used as a tool to a certain end.

On Polanyi's view, practical knowledge has two features. First, it is inevitably and irreducibly *personal*, since it involves personal participation in its generation. In his words, 'the relation of a subsidiary to a focus is formed by the *act of a person* who integrates one to another' (Polanyi, 1975, p. 38). And second, for knowledge to be effectively applied, it needs to be *instrumentalized* – to be used as a tool. On this point, Polanyi was very clear, echoing the Heideggerian line of thinking (Winograd and Flores, 1987). 'Hammers and probes', he wrote, 'can be replaced by intellectual tools' (Polanyi, 1962, p. 59). As we learn to use a tool, any tool, we gradually become unaware of how we use it to achieve results. Polanyi called this 'indwelling' – dwelling in the tool, making it feel as if it is an extension of our own body (Polanyi, 1962; 1975). We make sense of experience by assimilating the tool through which we make sense. The lapse into unawareness of the manner in which we use a tool is accompanied by an expansion of awareness of the experiences at hand, on the operational plane. We refine our ability to get things done by dwelling in the tools (both physical and intellectual) through which we get things done. The increasing instrumentalization of certain actions in the service of some purpose (or what we earlier called 'justification') enables the individual to expand his/her awareness of the situation he/she encounters and thus to refine his/her skills (Dreyfus and Dreyfus, 1986). The ongoing process of transforming experience into subsidiary awareness or, in Polanyi's (1962, p. 64) words, 'the pouring of ourselves into the subsidiary awareness of particulars', allows one to reach ever higher levels of skilful achievement (e.g. the improvement of the medical student's ability to read the X-ray picture).

To sum up, knowledge is the individual capability to draw distinctions, within a domain of action, based on an appreciation of context or theory, or both. Organizations are three things at once: concrete settings within which individual action takes place; sets of abstract rules in the form of propositional statements; and historical communities. Organizational knowledge is the capability members of an organization have developed to *draw distinctions* in the process of carrying out their work, in particular *concrete contexts,* by enacting sets of generalizations (*propositional statements*) whose application depends on historically evolved *collective understandings* and experiences. The more propositional statements and collective understandings become instrumentalized (in Polanyi's sense of the term); and the more new experiences are reflectively processed (both individually and collectively) and then gradually driven into subsidiary awareness, the more organizational members dwell in all of them, and the more able they become to concentrate on new experiences, on the operational plane.

Having developed the notion of organizational knowledge and shown its links with personal knowledge and human action, we will proceed below to empirically investigate these claims through a case study.

Organizational Knowledge in Action: A Case Study

Research Setting

A case study on organizational knowledge was undertaken at the Customer Care Department at Panafon, Greece's leading mobile phone operator. The company was formed in 1992, employs 900 people, and is controlled by the UK-based Vodafone group. With more than 2 million subscribers, Panafon holds a 38 percent share of the mobile phone market in Greece, one of the fastest growing markets in Europe (*Financial Times*, 28 December 2000). The company is listed on the Athens stock exchange and provides a wide range of standard and enhanced GSM services as well as services such as voice mail, short message services, personal numbering and data, fax transmission services, and internet-related services (Panafon, 1998).

The quality of customer care is, along with price, network coverage and range of services, a determining factor for customers to choose to subscribe to one of the three providers of mobile telecommunications services in Greece. Considering the great importance of customer care for Panafon's ability to maintain and attract customers, the empirical part of this study is focusing on organizational knowledge within the customer care department (CCD), although the latter is not what might be called a knowledge-intensive department. This, however, is immaterial for us, since, as was hopefully made clear in the preceding section, knowledge is de facto implicated in all types of organizational work (Wenger, 1998). Indeed, one of our claims in the preceding section has been that human action in organizations (all kinds of organizations) *necessarily* draws on organizational knowledge, namely on sets of generalizations underlain by collective understandings, activated in particular contexts. Of course, this is not to deny that there are, indeed, important differences between organizational forms concerning the dominant types of knowledge to be found in each one of them (Lam, 2000). But, such differences are not analytically relevant in the context of the present argument, just like differences between societies are not analytically relevant in the context of an inquiry that sets out to investigate the structuring and enactment of social relations (Garfinkel, 1984).

The CCD has been in operation since the commencement of Panafon's commercial operation, and it was the first customer care centre in Greece to operate 24 hours a day. Today the CCD has a total of 250 employees and consists of four call centres. The volume of calls to CCD has increased significantly in recent years, due to both the growth in the customer base and new services introductions. Currently, the department receives an average of 60,000 calls a day, although volumes fluctuate by month of the year, day of the week, time of the day and maturity of service. Operators, working in eight-hour shifts, are responsible for answering calls about specific Panafon services according to their experience and training on the corresponding services.

The aim of the CCD is to provide information support to Panafon subscribers, including directory inquiries, connection through directory assistance, secretarial messaging services, general information on the company's services (e.g. tariffs, network coverage), voice mail inquiries, as well as general information and assistance, including information about mobile phones, to both contract and pre-paid customers. Customer care is provided by customer care operators (hereafter referred to as operators), all of whom have been formally trained in Panafon's products and services and in the techniques of providing customer support. In addition, operators have received on the job training before taking on their duties.

Data Collection and Analysis

Data collection was conducted in two phases. In Phase I, we participated in a two-day induction programme, designed for new employees. Our aim was to familiarize ourselves with the company, and get an overall picture about its operation, products and services, departments, etc. In Phase II data about the CCD were collected using unstructured and semi-structured interviewing and document review. In addition, Phase II involved extensive on the job observation, and review of relevant work-related material.

Observation took the form of sitting with operators when they were on and off the phones as well as attending their coffee breaks, and taking notes on their work practices. Operators were encouraged to give explanations about what they were doing, and these descriptions were supplemented with questions probing particular issues, especially for explanations and clarifications both for the use of the available technology and work manuals, and for operators' initiatives and tacit understandings in dealing with customer calk. Materials reviewed included the work manuals provided by Panafon to employees and operators' personal notes. Detailed interviews in Phase II were taken from three operators, the fault coordinator, the shift supervisor, and supervisor of one of the four call centres, as well as three employees at engineering and one at operations & support departments who work in contact with customer care. Qualitative techniques were used to analyse the data collected, in line with the recommendations by Miles and Huberman (1984).

Knowledge Practices within Panafon's Customer Care Department

To answer most customer queries, operators draw upon electronically provided and printed information. Concerning electronically provided information, operators use computerized databases containing pertinent information for each of the services provided by CCD. For example, for general inquiries concerning contract customers, the computerized database contains, among other things, information about which services the customer has subscribed to and who is his/her service provider. This information enables operators to help customers identify whether, for example, a customer has indeed subscribed to a particular service the customer has inquired about (e.g. whether the customer has subscribed to having voice mail). The system can also help operators to activate the connection of pre-paid customers or even to activate call recognition for these customers if they wish.

The system is also used in the case of directory inquiries. Everyday operators are required to check their computer screens for new information that may have become available (concerning, for example, network coverage problems, tariff changes, etc.), which operators need to know about in order to answer customer queries accurately and efficiently. As for the printed material operators draw upon, it consists of company manuals containing information about a range of issues, such as details about all services provided by Panafon, countries in which roaming may be activated, information on different types of mobile phones, etc.

Drawing on both printed and electronically available information, operators are, in principle, in a position to handle customer queries. As an experienced operator put it:

> *Answers to 95 percent of the questions we are asked exist somewhere in the computer system, or in the manuals, or somewhere. Most likely the subscriber will be given the information he wants. The only question is how fast this will be done.*

Indeed, the question of speed is an important indicator of high-quality service since, if a particular customer is served quickly, he/she will very probably be a satisfied customer. Prompted to explain what she meant by 'somewhere', the above mentioned operator carried on exalting the significance of 'work experience' in that it provides operators with a repository of instances upon which they may regularly draw in their work.

Viewed this way, the information systems used by the operators include not only the organizationally provided technical means for accessing relevant information, but also the informal memory system (both individual and collective) which has gradually been built over time, consisting of the individual stocks of experience held by each operator, and by the stories shared in their community. As the operators often pointed out in their interviews with us, accessing that informal collective stock of knowledge is a valuable source of information for them. This is quite important because it highlights the significance of the web of social relations at work, since it is within those relations that such informal knowledge is preserved and drawn upon (Davenport and Prusak, 1998).

Indeed all operators interviewed emphatically mentioned how important it is for them to be able to draw upon the accumulated experience and knowledge of one another at work. We noticed that operators, while carrying out their tasks, often consulted one another about matters unknown to them. Communication about work-related issues occurs also during their breaks. It is noteworthy that such communication occurs naturally; it is part of the informal story telling that goes on among operators. Narrating work-related episodes to one another about, for example, awkward customers and uncommon questions tackled creates an environment in which the ties of community are reinforced, collective memory is enriched, and individual knowledge is enhanced. Researchers such as Orr (1996), Weick (1995), Brown and Duguid (1991) and Wenger (1998) have also mentioned the strong links between community ties, individual learning, and story telling.

Providing customer support is not as easy a job as it might first appear. Operators must be able to continuously provide efficient, courteous and helpful customer support services to subscribers – at least that is the official company policy. Moreover, customers are rarely 'sophisticated' mobile phone users, which often makes communication between operators and customers difficult: customers do not always express themselves in a clear and articulate manner, whereas sometimes they are not even sure what exactly they want. For example, we noticed that when asking for information, several customers tended to provide plenty of contextual details while describing their query. Often such contextual information was, strictly speaking, redundant and actually tended to blur, to some extent, the point of their query.

Customer queries thus contain some ambiguity. Such ambiguity requires that operators be adept in helping customers articulate their problems, probe them further in order to get customers to clarify what they want, and locate the appropriate information that will answer customers' queries. As well as doing all this, operators must be courteous towards customers and efficient in carrying out their tasks. Given that, as stated earlier, information about customers' calls normally exists 'somewhere' in the call centre, the primary task for the operator is to dispel the ambiguity surrounding customer calls and understand what the problem really is, and how, consequently, it ought to be solved. Even seemingly simple problems require diagnostic skills on the part of operators.

For example, a particular customer complained that he did not have the identification call service, whereby a caller's phone number appears on the receiver's mobile phone display, although he had paid for it. This could have been a technical problem (i.e. something wrong with his mobile phone), it could have been an error on the part of the company in having failed to activate that service, or it could have been the fact that certain callers did not wish that their phone numbers appear on other people's mobile phone displays. An inexperienced operator would probably have investigated all preceding possibilities. An experienced operator, however, would know that the first two possibilities were not very common and would, therefore, focus on the third. Indeed, through appropriate questioning, the particular operator observed first asked the customer about the extent to which the problem appeared and, when told that it tended to occur only in relation with a certain caller, the operator was immediately able to reach the conclusion that the caller, in all probability, did not wish for his/her number to be identified. The operator's ability to see through a customer's query, that is to make ever-finer distinctions, is an important skill, which is developed and constantly refined on the job.

Through experience and their participation in a 'community of practice' (Brown and Duguid, 1991; Wenger, 1998), operators develop a set of diagnostic skills which over time become instrumentalized, that is to say, tacit. This enables them to think quickly, 'on their feet', and serve customers speedily. Over time, operators learn to dwell in these skills, feel them as extensions of their own body and thus gradually become subsidiarily aware of them, which enables operators to focus on the task at hand.

For example, for operators to become effective in their job, they need to develop sophisticated perceptual skills in the context of mediated interaction (Thompson, 1995). Hearing only a voice deprives an operator of the multiple clues associated with face to face communication. The message a customer conveys to the operator is communicated not only through words but also through the tone of voice and other associated verbal clues. An operator realizes that she is dealing with an unhappy customer, a confused customer, or a puzzled customer not only by what they say to her but also by *how* they say it. High quality service means that the operator has instrumentalized her ability to discern such nuances in customer behaviour (i.e. to draw fine distinctions) and act accordingly.

An operator's perceptual skills, therefore, in understanding what is going on at the other end of the line is very important. It may be perhaps interesting to note that operators had refined their perceptual skills to the extent that they could tell straight away whether the caller at the other end was an electrical appliances retailer acting on behalf of a customer or whether it was the customer himself/herself. Recognizing nuances in callers' voices and acting accordingly (for example, to pacify an angry customer, to reassure a panic-stricken customer, or to instruct an utterly ignorant customer) was an important part of an effective operator's skill.

The tacitness of operators' knowledge was manifested when they were asked to describe how and why they tackled a particular problem in a particular way. To such questions, operators were at a loss for words; 'you feel it', 'you know so', 'I just knew it', were some of the most often repeated expressions they used (cf. Cook and Yanow, 1996). Such knowledge was difficult to verbalize, let alone codify. Although operators did make use of the information systems provided by the company, they did so in a manner whose distinguishing features were, on the one hand, the exercise of operators' judgement in diagnosing problems, while, on the other hand, the way in which operators' judgement was exercised had been crucially shaped by the overall company culture. Given that the latter placed heavy emphasis on high quality service, which was constantly reinforced through corporate announcements, induction programmes, training, and performance appraisal systems, the operators had internalized a set of values which helped them orient their actions accordingly.

Operators were drawing on a plethora of data and information (in Bell's sense of these terms), provided to them by the company in an electronic and printed form. Such data consisted of discrete items (e.g. addresses and phone numbers), while information consisted of generic propositional statements in the form of 'if this problem appears, then look at this or that' (Devlin, 1999). What was interesting to notice was the transformation of such information to knowledge by the operators themselves. To enact abstract 'if, then' statements, operators had to take into account the particular context of their conversation with a caller and quickly make a judgement as to what was required. To do so, the operators did not simply (and mindlessly) put the organizational rules into action, but they adapted those rules to the circumstances at hand.

As argued earlier, the encounter of a formalism with experience necessitates the exercise of human judgement, out of which new experience emerges, which is drawn upon on subsequent occasions. If Polanyi's claim that all knowledge is personal knowledge is accepted, it follows that, at least as far as organizational knowledge is concerned, there always is an improvisational element in putting knowledge into action. Indeed, this is the sense in which Bell differentiates knowledge from information: the former involves an active re-arrangement of the latter; it 'involves judgements, and judgements are derived from the knowledge of the "that it is so", or from a theory of the subject' (Bell, 1999, p. lxiv).

For example, through her experience, one operator knew that a particular type of mobile phone presented certain problems. The same operator also came to know that the set of instructions to customers to activate another type of card-based mobile phone were perceived as somewhat confusing by several customers. Having such knowledge, and faced with a particular problem, an operator might first ask what type of mobile phone a particular customer had been using and, depending on his/her answer, the operator would then proceed accordingly. Notice that such knowledge was not to be found in the official information system: it rather developed as a result of operators repeatedly facing (and learning from) particular types of problems to which they developed (i.e. they improvised) particular solutions.

As Orlikowski (1996) has persuasively shown, operators improvise in order to meet the demands of their tasks more effectively. Several operators observed were constructing their own personal information systems, which contained photocopies of the relevant corporate manuals plus personal notes. The latter consisted of notes they had taken during their training, and notes on which they had scribbled answers to customer queries they had faced in the past without, at the time, being able to locate the requisite information through the use of the formal information system. This is an important point that has not been given adequate coverage in the literature on knowledge management, although the phenomenon of 'improvisation' per se has received attention (Orlikowski, 1996; Weick, 1998): alongside formal organizational knowledge there exists informal knowledge that is generated in action. This type of knowledge (what Collins [1990] calls 'heuristic knowledge') is gained only through the improvisation employees undertake while carrying out their tasks. Heuristic knowledge resides both in individuals' minds and in stories shared in communities of practice. Such knowledge may be formally captured and, through its casting into propositional statements, may be turned into organizational knowledge. While this is feasible and desirable, the case still remains that, at any point in time, abstract generalizations are in themselves incomplete to capture the totality of organizational knowledge. In action, an improvisational element always follows it like shadow follows an object.

Discussion and Implications

From the preceding analysis it follows that what makes knowledge distinctly organizational is its codification in the form of propositional statements underlain by a set of collective understandings. Given, however, that individuals put organizational knowledge into action by acting inescapably within particular contexts, there is always room for individual judgement and for the emergence of novelty. It is the open-endedness of the world that gives rise to new experience and learning and gives knowledge its not-as-yet-formed character. As Gadamer (1989, p. 38) has perceptively noted, at issue is more than the correct application of general principles. Our knowledge of the latter is 'always supplemented by the individual case, even productively determined by it'. What Gadamer points out is that 'application is neither a subsequent nor merely an occasional part of the phenomenon of understanding, but codetermines it as a whole from the beginning' (p. 324). In other words, individuals are not given generalizations which must be first understood before being put into application afterwards. Rather, individuals understand generalizations only *through* connecting the latter to particular circumstances facing them; they comprehend the general by relating it to the particular they are confronted with. In so far as this process takes place, every act of interpretation is necessarily creative and, in that sense, heuristic knowledge is not accidental but a necessary outcome of the interpretative act.

A condition for organizational members to undertake action is to be placed within a conceptual matrix woven by the organization. Such a conceptual matrix contains generic categories (e.g. 'service quality', 'happy customer', 'efficient service') and their interrelations (e.g. 'high quality service makes customers happy'). By categorizing and naming the situation at hand, organizational members begin to search for appropriate responses. Commenting on Joas's (1996) *The Creativity of Action*, McGowan (1998, p. 294) aptly remarks: 'My judgement takes the raw data and raw feels of the present and names them. I decide to take this action because I deem this situation to be of this kind. The novelty of situations, the newness of the present, is tempered by this judgement'. Of course my judgement may be wrong. After all, it is only a guide to action, a tentative hypothesis, which may prove erroneous. The expected results may not occur; I need to reflect on this fact and revise my judgement. In other words, categorization and abstraction are conditions of possibility for human action (Lakoff, 1987). But categories *qua* categories may fail to match the particularities of the situation at hand. However, the abstract indeterminacy of categories is not a problem in practice, for it is situationally dealt with by the practical reasoning of competent language users. What gives organizational knowledge its dynamism is the dialectic between the general and the particular. Without the general no action is possible. And without the particular no action may be effective (McCarthy, 1994, p. 68).

If all organizational work necessarily involves drawing on knowledge, then the management of organizational knowledge must have been a time-old managerial activity. In a sense this is as true as the realization that marketing has been around since the dawn of the market economy. But, in another sense, this is not quite the case, if by management we mean the distinctly modern activity of purposeful coordination of socio-technical processes. For organizational knowledge to be managed, an unreflective practice needs to be turned into a reflective practice or, to put it differently, practical mastery needs to be supplemented by a quasi-theoretical understanding of what individuals are doing when they exercise that mastery.

An unreflective practice involves us acting, doing things, effortlessly observing the rules of our practice, but finding it difficult to state what they are. In that sense we are all unreflective practitioners: in so far as we carry out the tasks involved in our practice, we do so having instrumentalized, appropriated, the tools (i.e. abstract rules and collective understandings) through which we get things done. As Strawson (1992, p. 5) elegantly notes:

When the first Spanish or, strictly, Castilian grammar was presented to Queen Isabella of Castile, her response was to ask what use it was. [Her response was quite understandable since] the grammar was in a sense of no use at all to fluent speakers of Castilian. In a sense they knew it already. They spoke grammatically correct Castilian because grammatically correct Castilian simply was what they spoke. The grammar did not set the standards of correctness for the sentences they spoke; on the contrary, it was the sentences they spoke that set the standard of correctness for the grammar. However, though in a sense they knew the grammar of their language, there was another sense in which they did not know it.

What was that? If Queen Isabella had been asked to judge whether a particular sequence of Castilian words was grammatically correct, she would have to state the rules of the language in terms of which she would need to make her judgement. The speaking of Castilian sentences by the Queen and her subjects showed that they, indeed, observed such rules, but they could not easily state what they were, unless there was a grammar available.

The point of this example is that we may have (unreflectively) mastered a practice but this is not enough. If we need to teach efficiently new members to be effective members of the practice, or if we need to reflect on ways of improving our practice, or if we want to rid ourselves of likely confusions, then we need to elucidate our practice by articulating or making explicit its rules and principles. Knowledge management then is primarily the dynamic process of turning an unreflective practice into a reflective one by elucidating the rules guiding the activities of the practice, by helping give a particular shape to collective understandings, and by facilitating the emergence of heuristic knowledge.

Without any doubt the management of organizational knowledge today certainly implies the ever more sophisticated development of electronic corporate information systems, which enable a firm to abstract its activities and codify them in the form of generic rules (Gates, 1999). In this way, a firm provides its members with the requisite propositional statements for acting efficiently and consistently. Ideally, on this view, an organizational member should have all the information that he/she needs, instantly. To a considerable extent that was the case in the call centre under study, although the relative simplicity of operators' tasks does not make it look like an impressive achievement.

However, the above is only one aspect of organizational knowledge management. Another less appreciated aspect, one that has hopefully been made more evident in this chapter, is the significance of heuristic knowledge developed by employees while doing their job. This type of knowledge cannot be 'managed in the way formally available information can, because it crucially depends on employees' experiences and perceptual skills, their social relations, and their motivation. Managing this aspect of organizational knowledge means that a company must strive to sustain a spirit of community at work, to encourage employees to improvise and undertake initiatives of their own, as well as actively maintain a sense of corporate mission. To put it differently, and somewhat paradoxically, the management of the heuristic aspect of organizational knowledge implies more the sensitive management of social relations and less the management of corporate digital information (Tsoukas, 1998). In addition, the effective management of organizational knowledge requires that the relationship between propositional and heuristic knowledge be a two-way street: while propositional knowledge is fed into organizational members and is instrumentalized through application (thus becoming tacit), heuristic knowledge needs to be formalized (to the extent this is possible) and made organizationally available. Managing organizational knowledge does not narrowly imply efficiently managing hard bits of information but, more subtly, sustaining and strengthening social practices (Kreiner, 1999). In knowledge management digitalization cannot be a substitute for socialization.

References

Barnes, B. (1995) *The Elements of Social Theory.* London: UCL Press.

Bell, D. (1999) 'The axial age of technology foreword: 1999'. In *The Coming of the Post-Industrial Society.* New York: Basic Books, Special Anniversary Edition, ix–lxxxv.

Berger, P. and Luckmann, T. (1966) *The Social Construction of Reality.* London: Penguin.

Blackler, F. (1995) 'Knowledge, knowledge work and organizations: an overview and interpretation'. *Organization Studies,* 16, 6, 1021–46.

Boisot, M.H. (1995) *Information Space: A Framework for Learning in Organizations, Institutions and Culture.* London: Routledge.

Brown, J.S. and Duguid, P. (1991) 'Organizational learning and communities of practice: toward a unified view of working, learning and innovation'. *Organization Science,* 2, 1, 40–57.

Brown, J.S. and Duguid, P. (2000) *The Social Life of Information.* Boston, MA: Harvard Business School Press.

Choo, C.W. (1998) *The Knowing Organization: How Organizations Use Information to Construct Meaning, Create Knowledge, and Make Decisions.* New York: Oxford University Press.

Collins, M.H. (1990) *Artificial Experts: Social Knowledge and Intelligent Machines.* Cambridge, MA: MIT Press.

Cook, S.D. and Brown, J.S. (1999) 'Bridging epistemologies: the generative dance between organizational knowledge and organizational knowing'. *Organization Science,* 10, 381–400.

Cook, S.D. and Yanow, D. (1996) 'Culture and organizational learning'. In Cohen, M.D. and Sproull, L.S. (eds), *Organizational Learning.* Thousand Oaks, CA: SAGE, 430–59.

Davenport, T.H. and Prusak, L. (1998) *Working Knowledge.* Cambridge, MA: Harvard University Press.

Devlin, K. (1999) *Infosense: Turning Information into Knowledge.* New York: W.H. Freeman.

Dewey, J. (1934) *Art as Experience.* New York: Perigee Books.

Dreyfus, H.L. and Dreyfus, S.E. (1986) *Mind over Machine.* New York: Free Press.

Gadamer, H.-G. (1980) 'Practical philosophy as a model of the human sciences'. *Research in Phenomenology,* 9, 74–85.

Gadamer, H.G. (1989) *Truth and Method,* 2nd edition. London: Sheed & Ward.

Garfinkel, H. (1984) *Studies in Ethnomethodology.* Cambridge: Polity Press.

Gates, B. (1999) *Business @ the Speed of Thought.* London: Penguin Books.

Harré, R. and Gillett, G. (1994) *The Discursive Mind.* Thousand Oaks, CA: SAGE.

Hendriks, P.H.J. and Vriens, D.J. (1999) 'Knowledge-based systems and knowledge management: friends or foes?'. *Information & Management,* 35, 113–25.

Heritage, J. (1984) *Garfinkel and Ethnomethodology*. Cambridge: Polity Press.

Hunter, K.M. (1991) *Doctors' Stories*. Princeton, NJ: Princeton University Press.

Joas, H. (1996) *The Creativity of Action*. Cambridge: Polity Press.

Kay, J. (1993) *Foundations of Corporate Success*. New York: Oxford University Press.

Kreiner, K. (1999) 'Knowledge and mind'. *Advances in Management Cognition and Organizational Information Processing*, 6, 1–29.

Lakoff, G. (1987) *Women, Fire, and Dangerous Things*. Chicago, IL: The University of Chicago Press.

Lam, A. (2000) 'Tacit knowledge, organizational learning and societal institutions: an integrated framework'. *Organization Studies*, 21, 3, 487–514.

Lehner, F. (1990) 'Expert systems for organizational and managerial tasks'. *Information and Management*, 23, 1, 31–41.

Leonard, D. and Sensiper, S. (1998) 'The role of tacit knowledge in group innovation'. *California Management Review*, 40, 3, 112–32.

MacIntyre, A. (1985) *After Virtue*, 2nd edition. London: Duckworth.

Maturana, H. and Varela, F. (1988) *The Tree of Knowledge*. Boston, MA: New Science.

Mercer, N. (1995) *The Guided Construction of Knowledge*. Clevedon: Multilingual Matters.

McCarthy, T. (1994) 'Philosophy and critical theory'. In McCarthy, T. and Hoy, D.C. (eds), *Critical Theory*. Oxford Blackwell, 5–100.

McGowan, J. (1998) 'Toward a pragmatist theory of action'. *Sociological Theory*, 16, 292–7.

Miles, M.B. and Huberman, A.M. (1984) *Qualitative Data Analysis: A Sourcebook of New Methods*. Newbury Park, CA: SAGE Publications.

Nonaka, I. and Takeuchi, H. (1995) *The Knowledge-Creating Company: How Japanese Companies Create the Dynamics of Innovation*. New York: Oxford University Press.

Orlikowski, W.J. (1996) 'Improvising organizational transformation over time: a situated change perspective'. *Information Systems Research*, 7, 1, 63–92.

Orr, J.E. (1996) *Talking about Machines*. Stanford, CA: ILR Press/Cornell University Press.

Panafon, November (1998) Initial Public Offering.

Penrose, E. (1959) *The Theory of the Growth of the Firm*. New York: Wiley.

Polanyi, M. (1962) *Personal Knowledge*. Chicago, IL: University of Chicago Press.

Polanyi, M. (1975) 'Personal knowledge'. In Polanyi, M. and Prosch, H. (eds), *Meaning*. Chicago, IL: University of Chicago Press, 22–45.

Reyes, A. and Zarama, R. (1998) 'The process of embodying distinctions – a reconstruction of the process of learning'. *Cybernetics & Human Knowing*, 5, 19–33.

Schauer, F. (1991) *Playing by the Rules*. Oxford: Clarendon Press.

Schon, D. (1983) *The Reflective Practitioner*. New York: Basic Books.

Schutz, A. (1970) In Wagner, H. (ed.), *On Phenomenology and Social Relations*. Chicago, IL: The University of Chicago Press.

Scott, W.R. (1995) *Institutions and Organizations*. Thousand Oaks, CA: SAGE.

Spender, J.-C. (1989) *Industry Recipes*. Oxford: Blackwell.

Strawson, P.F. (1992) *Analysis and Metaphysics*. Oxford: Oxford University Press.

Suchman, L.A. (1987) *Plans and Situated Actions: The Problems of Human – Machine Communication*. Cambridge: Cambridge University Press.

Taylor, C. (1985) *Philosophy and the Human Sciences*, Vol. 2. Cambridge: Cambridge University Press.

Taylor, C. (1993) 'To follow a rule …'. In Calhoun, C., LiPuma, E. and Postone, M. (eds), *Bourdieu: Critical Perspectives*. Cambridge: Polity Press, 45–59.

Terrett, A. (1998) 'Knowledge management and the law firm'. *Journal of Knowledge Management*, 2, 1, 67–76.

Thompson, J.B. (1995) *The Media and Modernity.* Cambridge: Polity Press.

Toulmin, S. (1999) 'Knowledge as shared procedures'. In Engestrom, Y., Miettinen, R. and Punamaki, R.-L. (eds), *Perspectives on Activity Theory.* Cambridge: Cambridge University Press, 53–64.

Tsoukas, H. (1996) 'The firm as a distributed knowledge system: a constructionist approach'. *Strategic Management Journal*, 17, Winter Special Issue, 11–25.

Tsoukas, H. (1997) 'The tyranny of light: the temptations and the paradoxes of the information society'. *Futures*, 29, 9, 827–44.

Tsoukas, H. (1998) 'Forms of knowledge and forms of life in organized contexts'. In Chia, C.H.R. (ed.), *In the Realm of Organization.* London: Routledge, 43–66.

Twining, W. and Miers, D. (1991) *How to Do Things with Rules,* 3rd edition. London: Weidenfeld and Nicolson.

Varela, F.J., Thompson, E. and Rosch, E. (1991) *The Embodied Mind.* Cambridge, MA: MIT Press.

Vickers, G. (1983) *The Art of Judgement.* London: Harper & Row.

von Foerster, H. (1984) 'On constructing a reality'. In Watzlawick, P. (ed.), *The Invented Reality.* New York: W. W. Norton & Co., 41–61.

Vygotsky, L.S. (1978) *Mind in Society.* Cambridge, MA: Harvard University Press.

Weick, K.E. (1979) *The Social Psychology of Organizing,* 2nd edition. Reading, MA: Addison-Wesley.

Weick, K. (1995) *Sensemaking in Organizations.* Thousand Oaks, CA: SAGE.

Weick, K.E. (1998) 'Improvisation as a mindset of organizational analysis'. *Organization Science*, 9, 5, 543–55.

Wenger, E. (1998) *Communities of Practice.* Cambridge: Cambridge University Press.

Wertsch, J.V (1998) *Mind as Action.* New York: Oxford University Press.

Wigg, K.M. (1997) 'Integrating intellectual capital and knowledge management'. *Long Range Planning*, 30, 3, 399–405.

Winograd, T. and Flores, F. (1987) *Understanding Computers and Cognition.* Reading, MA: Addison-Wesley.

Wittgenstein, L. (1958) *Philosophical Investigations.* Oxford: Blackwell.

5

Do We Really Understand Tacit Knowledge?

Haridimos Tsoukas

Nisi credideritis, non intelligitis (Unless ye believe, ye shall not understand). (St Augustine [cited in Polanyi, 1962: 266])

Something that we know when no one asks us, but no longer know when we are supposed to give an account of it, is something that we need to remind ourselves of. (Wittgenstein, 1958: No. 89; emphasis in the original)

The act of knowing includes an appraisal; and this personal coefficient, which shapes all factual knowledge, bridges in doing so the disjunction between subjectivity and objectivity. (Polanyi, 1962: 17)

It is often argued that knowledge is fundamental to the functioning of late modern economies (Drucker, 1993; Stehr, 1994; Thurow, 2000). 'What's new here?', a critique might ask. 'Knowledge has always been implicated in the process of economic development, since anything we do, how we transform resources into products and services, crucially depends on the knowledge we have at our disposal for effecting such transformation. An ancient artisan, a medieval craftsman and his apprentices, and a modern manufacturing system all make use of knowledge: certain skills, techniques and procedures are employed for getting things done'.

What is, then, distinctly new in the contemporary so-called, 'knowledge economy'? Daniel Bell answered this question more than 30 years ago: theoretical (or codified) knowledge has acquired a central place in late modern societies in a way that was not the case before. Says Bell (1999: 20):

... Knowledge has of course been necessary in the functioning of any society. What is distinctive about the post-industrial society is the change in the character of knowledge itself. What has become decisive for the organization of decisions and the direction of change is the centrality of theoretical knowledge – the primacy of theory over empiricism and the codification of knowledge into abstract systems of symbols that, as in any axiomatic system, can be used to illustrate many different and varied areas of experience. (Emphasis in the original).

Source: H. Tsoukas (2003) '*Do We Really Understand Tacit Knowledge?*', in M. Easterby-Smith and M.A. Lyles (eds) *The Blackwell Handbook of Organizational Knowledge Management*, pp. 410–27. Oxford: Blackwell. Edited version.

Indeed, it is hard today to think of an industry that does not make systematic use of 'theoretical knowledge'. Products increasingly incorporate more and more specialized knowledge, supplied by R&D departments, universities and consulting firms; and production processes are also increasingly based on systematic research that aims to optimize their functioning (Drucker, 1993; Mansell and When, 1998; Stehr, 1994).

Taking a historical perspective of the development of modern market economies, as Bell does, one can clearly see the change in the character of knowledge over time. To simplify, modernity has come to mistrust intuition, preferring explicitly articulated assertions; it is uncomfortable with *ad hoc* practices, opting for systematic procedures; it substitutes detached objectivity for personal commitment (MacIntyre, 1985; Toulmin, 1990, 2001). Yet if one takes a closer look at how theoretical (or codified) knowledge is actually *used* in practice, one will see the extent to which theoretical knowledge itself, far from being as objective, self-sustaining and explicit as it is often taken to be, is actually grounded on personal judgements and tacit commitments. Even the most theoretical form of knowledge, such as pure mathematics, cannot be a completely formalised system, since it is based for its application and development on the *skills* of mathematicians and how such skills are used in practice. To put it differently, codified knowledge necessarily contains a 'personal coefficient' (Polanyi, 1962: 17). Knowledge-based economies may indeed be making great use of codified forms of knowledge, but that kind of knowledge is inescapably used in a *non-codifiable* and *non-theoretical* manner.

The significance of 'tacit knowledge' for the functioning of organizations has not escaped the attention of management theorists. Ever since Nonaka and Takeuchi (1995) have published their influential *The Knowledge-Creating Company*, it is nearly impossible to find a publication on organizational knowledge and knowledge management that does not make a reference to, or use the term 'tacit knowledge'. And quite rightly so: as common experience can verify, the knowledge people use in organizations is so practical and deeply familiar to them that when people are asked to describe how they do what they do, they often find it hard to express it in words (Ambrosini and Bowman, 2001; Cook and Yanow, 1996: 442; Eraut, 2000; Harper, 1987; Nonaka and Takeuchi, 1995; Tsoukas and Vladimirou, 2001: 987). Naturally, several questions arise: what is it about organizational knowledge that makes it so hard to describe? What is the significance of the tacit dimension of organizational knowledge? What are the implications of tacit knowledge for the learning and exercise of skills? If skilled knowing is tacit, how is it possible for new knowledge to emerge?

The purpose of this chapter is to explore the preceding questions. My argument will be that popular as the term 'tacit knowledge' may have become in management studies, it has, on the whole, been misunderstood. By and large, tacit knowledge has been conceived in opposition to explicit knowledge, whereas it is simply its other side. As a result of such a misunderstanding, the nature of organizational knowledge and its relation to individual skills and social contexts has been inadequately understood. In this chapter I will first explore the nature of tacit knowledge by drawing primarily on Polanyi (the inventor of the term), an author who is frequently referred to but little understood. Then I will explore how Polanyi's understanding of tacit knowledge has been interpreted by Nonaka and Takeuchi, the two authors who, more than anyone else, have helped popularize the concept of 'tacit knowledge' in management studies and whose interpretation has been adopted by most management authors (see for example, Ambrosini and Bowman, 2001; Baumard, 1999; Boisot, 1995; Davenport and Prusak, 1998; Devlin, 1999; Dixon, 2000; Leonard and Sensiper, 1998; Spender, 1996; von Krogh et al., 2000; for exceptions see, Brown and Duguid, 2000; Cook and Brown, 1999: 385, 394–5; Kreiner, 1999; Tsoukas, 1996: 14, 1997: 830–1; Wenger, 1998: 67). I will finally end this chapter by fleshing out the implications of tacit knowledge, properly understood, for an epistemology of organizational practice.

Polanyi for Beginners: A Guide

One of the most distinguishing features of Polanyi's work is his insistence on overcoming well established dichotomies such as theoretical vs. practical knowledge, sciences vs. the humanities or, to put it differently, his determination to show the common structure underlying all kinds of knowledge. Polanyi, a chemist turned philosopher, was categorical that all knowing involves *skilful action* and that the knower necessarily participates in all acts of understanding. For him the idea that there is such a thing as 'objective' knowledge, self-contained, detached, and independent of human action, was wrong and pernicious. '*All* knowing', he insists, 'is personal knowing – participation through indwelling' (Polanyi and Prosch, 1975: 44; italics in the original).

Take for example, the use of geographical maps. A map is a representation of a particular territory. As an explicit representation of something else, a map is, in logical terms, not different from that of a theoretical system, or a system of rules: they all aim at enabling purposeful human action, i.e. respectively, to get from A to B, to predict, and guide behaviour. We may be very familiar with a map per se but to *use* it we need to be able to relate it to the world outside the map. More specifically, to use a map we need to be able to do three things. First, we must identify our current position in the map ('you are here'). Second, we must find our itinerary on the map ('we want to go to the National Museum, which is there'). And third, to actually go to our destination, we must identify the itinerary by various landmarks in the landscape around us ('you get past the train station and then turn left'). In other words, a map, no matter how elaborate it is, cannot read itself; it requires the judgement of a skilled reader who will relate the map to the world through both cognitive and sensual means (Polanyi, 1962: 18–20; Polanyi and Prosch, 1975: 30).

The same personal judgement is involved whenever abstract representations encounter the world of experience. We are inclined to think, for example, that Newton's laws can predict the position of a planet circling round the sun, at some future point in time, provided its current position is known. Yet this is not quite the case: Newton's laws can never do that, only *we* can. The difference is crucial. The numbers entering the relevant formulae, from which we compute the future position of a planet, are readings on our instruments – they are not given, but need to be worked out. Similarly, we check the veracity of our predictions by comparing the results of our computations with the readings of the instruments – the predicted computations will rarely coincide with the readings observed and the significance of such a discrepancy needs to be worked out, again, by us (Polanyi, 1962: 19; Polanyi and Prosch, 1975: 30). Notice that, like in the case of map reading, the formulae of celestial mechanics cannot apply themselves; the personal judgement of a human agent is necessarily involved in applying abstract representations to the world.

The general point to be derived from the above examples is this: insofar as a formal representation has a bearing on experience, that is the extent to which a representation encounters the world, personal judgement is called upon to make an assessment of the inescapable gap between the representation and the world encountered. Given that the map is a representation of the territory, I need to be able to match my location in the territory with its representation on the map, if I am to be successful in reaching my destination. Personal judgement cannot be prescribed by rules but relies essentially on the use of our senses (Polanyi, 1962: 19, 1966: 20; Polanyi and Prosch, 1975: 30). To the extent this happens, the exercise of personal judgement is a skilful performance, involving both the mind and the body.

The crucial role of the body in the act of knowing has been persistently under-scored by Polanyi (cf. Gill, 2000: 44–50). As said earlier, the cognitive tools we use do not apply themselves; we apply them and, thus, we need to assess the extent to which our tools match aspects of the world. Insofar as our contact with the world necessarily involves our somatic equipment – 'the trained delicacy of eye, ear, and touch' (Polanyi and Prosch, 1975: 31) – we are engaged in the art of establishing a correspondence between the explicit formulations of our formal representations (be they maps, scientific laws or organizational rules) and the actual experience of our senses. As Polanyi (1969: 147) remarks, 'the way the body participates in the act of perception can be generalized further to include the bodily roots of all knowledge and thought ... Parts of our body serve as tools for observing objects outside and for manipulating them.'

If we accept that there is indeed a 'personal coefficient' (Polanyi, 1962: 17) in all acts of knowing, which is manifested in a skilful performance carried out by the knower, what is the structure of such a skill? What is it that enables a map-reader to make a competent use of the map to find his/her way around, a scientist to use the formulae of celestial mechanics to predict the next eclipse of the moon, and a physician to read an X-ray picture of a chest? For Polanyi the starting point towards answering this question is to acknowledge that 'the aim of a skilful performance is achieved by the observance of a set of rules which are not known as such to the person following them' (Polanyi, 1962: 49). A cyclist, for example, does not normally know the rule that keeps her balance, nor does a swimmer know what keeps him afloat. Interestingly, such ignorance is hardly detrimental to their effective carrying out of their respective tasks.

The cyclist keeps herself in balance by winding through a series of curvatures. One can formulate the rule explaining why she does not fall off the bicycle – 'for a given angle of unbalance the curvature of each winding is inversely proportional to the square of the speed at which the cyclist is proceeding' (Polanyi, 1962: 50) – but such a rule would hardly be helpful to the cyclist. Why? Partly because, as we will see below, no rule is helpful in guiding action unless it is assimilated and lapses into unconsciousness. And partly because there is a host of other particular elements to be taken into account, which are not included in this rule and, crucially, are not known by the cyclist. Skills retain an element of opacity and unspecificity; they cannot be fully accounted for in terms of their particulars, since their practitioners do not ordinarily know what those particulars are; even when they do know them, as for example in the case of topographic anatomy, they do not know how to integrate them (Polanyi, 1962: 88–90). It is one thing to learn a list of bones, arteries, nerves and viscara and quite another to know how precisely they are intertwined inside the body (1962: 89).

How then do individuals know how to exercise their skills? In a sense they do not. 'A mental effort', says Polanyi (1962: 62), 'has a heuristic effect: it tends to incorporate any available elements of the situation which are helpful for its purpose'. Any particular elements of the situation which may help the purpose of a mental effort are selected insofar as they contribute to the performance at hand, without the performer knowing them as they would appear in themselves. The particulars arc subsidiarily known insofar as they contribute to the action performed. As Polanyi (1962: 62) remarks:

> this is the usual process of unconscious trial and error by which we feel our way to success and may continue to improve on our success without specifiably knowing how we do it – for we never meet the causes of our success as identifiable things which can be described in terms of classes of which such things are members. This is how you invent a method of swimming without knowing that it consists in regulating your breath in a particular manner, or discover the principle of cycling without realizing that it consists in the adjustment of your momentary direction and velocity, so as to counteract continuously your momentary accidental unbalance. (Emphasis in the original)

There are two different kinds of awareness in exercising a skill. When I use a hammer to drive a nail (one of Polanyi's favourite examples – see Polanyi [1962: 55] and Polanyi and Prosch [1975: 33]), I am aware of both the nail and the hammer but in a different way. I watch the effects of my strokes on the nail, and try to hit it as effectively as I can. Driving the nail down is the main object of my attention and I am focally aware of it. At the same time, I'm also aware of the feelings in my palm of holding the hammer. But such awareness is subsidiary: the feelings of holding the hammer in my palm are not an object of my attention but an instrument of it. I watch hitting the nail by being aware of them. As Polanyi and Prosch (1975: 33) remark: 'I know the feelings in the palm of my hand *by relying on them for attending to the hammer hitting the nail*. I may say that I have a *subsidiary* awareness of the feelings in my hand which is merged into my *focal awareness* of my driving the nail' (italics in the original).

If the above is accepted, it means that we can be aware of certain things in a way that is quite different from focusing our attention on them. I have a subsidiary awareness of my holding the hammer in the act of focusing on hitting the nail. In being subsidiarily aware of holding a hammer I see it as having a meaning that is wiped out if I focus my attention on how I hold the hammer. Subsidiary awareness and focal awareness are mutually exclusive (Polanyi, 1962: 56). If we switch our focal attention to particulars of which we had only subsidiary awareness before, their meaning is lost and the corresponding action becomes clumsy. If a pianist shifts her attention from the piece she is playing to how she moves her fingers; if a speaker focuses his attention on the grammar he is using instead of the act of speaking; or if a carpenter shifts his attention from hitting the nail to holding the hammer, they will all be confused. We must rely (to be precise, we must learn to rely) subsidiarily on particulars for attending to something else, hence our knowledge of them remains *tacit* (Polanyi, 1966: 10; Winograd and Flores, 1987: 32). In the context of carrying out a specific task, we come to know a set of particulars without being able to identify them. In Polanyi's (1966: 4) memorable phrase, 'we can know more than we can tell'.

From the above it follows that tacit knowledge forms a triangle, at the three corners of which are the *subsidiary particulars*, the *focal target* and the *knower* who links the two. It should be clear from the above that the linking of the particulars to the focal target does not happen automatically but is a result of the *act* of the knower. It is in this sense that Polanyi talks about all knowledge being *personal* and all knowing being *action*. No knowledge is possible without the integration of the subsidiaries to the focal target by a person. However, unlike explicit inference, such integration is essentially tacit and irreversible. Its tacitness was earlier discussed; its irreversible character can be seen if juxtaposed to explicit (deductive) inference, whereby one can unproblematically traverse between the premises and the conclusions. Such traversing is not possible with tacit integration: once you have learned to play the piano you cannot go back to being ignorant of how to do it. While you can certainly focus your attention on how you move your fingers, thus making your performance clumsy to the point of paralysing it, you can always recover your ability by casting your mind forward to the music itself. With explicit inference, no such break-up and recovery are possible (Polanyi and Prosch, 1975: 39–42). When, for example, you examine a legal syllogism or a mathematical proof you proceed orderly from the premises, or a sequence of logical steps, to the conclusions. You lose nothing and you recover nothing – there is complete reversibility. You can go back to check the veracity of each constituent statement separately and how it logically links with its adjacent statements. Such reversibility is not, however, possible with tacit integration. Shifting attention to subsidiary particulars entails the loss of the skilful engagement with the activity at hand. By focusing on a subsidiary constituent of skilful action one changes the character of the activity one is involved with. There is no reversibility in this instance.

The structure of tacit knowing has three aspects: the functional, the phenomenal and the semantic. The functional aspect consists in the *from–to* relation of particulars (or subsidiaries) to the focal target. Tacit knowing is a from-to knowing: we know the particulars by relying on our awareness of them for attending to something else. Human awareness has a 'vectorial' character (Polanyi, 1969: 182): it moves from subsidiary particulars to the focal target (cf. Gill, 2000: 38–9). Or, in the words of

Polanyi and Prosch (1975: 37–8), 'subsidiaries exist as such by bearing on the focus *to* which we are attending *from* them' (italics in the original). The phenomenal aspect involves the transformation of subsidiary experience into a new sensory experience. The latter appears through – it is created out of – the tacit integration of subsidiary sense perceptions. Finally, the semantic aspect is the meaning of subsidiaries, which is the focal target on which they bear.

The above aspects of tacit knowing will become clearer with an example. Imagine a dentist exploring a tooth cavity with a probe. Her exploration is a from–to knowing (the functional aspect): she relies subsidiarily on her feeling of holding the probe in order to attend focally to the tip of the probe exploring the cavity. In doing so the sensation of the probe pressing on her fingers is lost and, instead, she feels the point of the probe as it touches the cavity. This is the phenomenal aspect whereby a new coherent sensory quality appears (i.e. her sense of the cavity) from the initial sense perceptions (i.e. the impact of the probe on the fingers). Finally, the probing has a semantic aspect: the dentist gets information by using the probe. That information is the meaning of her tactile experiences with the probe. As Polanyi (1966: 13) argues, the dentist becomes aware of the feelings in her hand in terms of their meaning located at the tip of the probe, to which she is attending.

We engage in tacit knowing through virtually anything we do: we are normally unaware of the movement of our eye muscles when we observe, of the rules of language when we speak, of our bodily functions as we move around. Indeed, to a large extent, our daily life consists of a huge number of small details of which we tend to be focally unaware. When, however, we engage in more complex tasks, requiring even a modicum of specialized knowledge, then we face the challenge of how to assimilate the new knowledge – to interiorize it, dwell in it – in order to get things done efficiently and effectively. Polanyi gives the example of a medical student attending a course in X-ray diagnosis of pulmonary diseases. The student is initially puzzled: 'he can see in the X-ray picture of a chest only the shadows of the heart and the ribs, with a few spidery blotches between them. The experts seem to be romancing about figments of their imagination; he can see nothing that they are talking about' (Polanyi, 1962: 101).

At the early stage of his training the student has not assimilated the relevant knowledge; unlike the dentist with the probe, he cannot yet use it as a tool to carry out a diagnosis. The student, at this stage, is a remove from the diagnostic task as such: he cannot think about it directly; he rather needs to think about the relevant radiological knowledge first. If he perseveres with his training, however, 'he will gradually forget about the ribs and begin to see the lungs. And eventually, if he perseveres intelligently, a rich panorama of significant details will be revealed to him: of physiological variations and pathological changes, of scars, of chronic infections and signs of acute disease. He has entered a new world' (Polanyi, 1962: 101).

We see here an excellent illustration of the structure of tacit knowledge. The student has now interiorized the new radiological knowledge; the latter has become tacit knowledge, of which he is subsidiarily aware while attending to the X-ray itself. Radiological knowledge exists now not as something unfamiliar which needs to be learned and assimilated before a diagnosis can take place, but as a set of particulars – subsidiaries – which exist as such by bearing on the X-ray (the focus) *to* which the student is attending *from* them. Insofar as this happens, a phenomenal transformation has taken place: the heart, the ribs and the spidery blotches gradually disappear and, instead, a new sensory experience appears – the X-ray is no longer a collection of fragmented radiological images of bodily organs, but a representation of a chest full of meaningful connections. Thus, as well as having functional and phenomenal aspects, tacit knowledge has a semantic aspect: the X-ray conveys information to an appropriately skilled observer. The meaning of the radiological knowledge, subsidiarily known and drawn upon by the student, is the diagnostic information he receives from the X-ray: it tells him what it is that he is observing by using that knowledge.

It should be clear from the above that for Polanyi, from a gnosiological point of view, there is no difference whatsoever between tangible things like probes, sticks or hammers on the one hand, and intangible constructions such as radiological, linguistic or cultural knowledge on the other – they are all *tools* enabling a skilled user to get things done. To use a tool properly we need to assimilate it and dwell in it. In Polanyi's (1969: 148) words, 'we may say that when we learn to use language, or a probe, or a tool, and thus make ourselves aware of these things as we are our body, we *interiorize* these things and *make ourselves dwell in them*' (italics in the original). The notion of *indwelling* is crucial for Polanyi and turns up several times in his writings. It is only when we dwell in the tools we use, make them extensions of our own body, that we amplify the powers of our body and shift outwards the points at which we make contact with the world outside (Polanyi, 1962: 59, 1969: 148; Polanyi and Prosch, 1975: 37). Otherwise our use of tools will be clumsy and will get in the way of getting things done.

For a tool to be unproblematically used it must not be the object of our focal awareness; it rather needs to become an instrument through which we act – of which we are subsidiarily aware – not an object of attention. To dwell in a tool implies that one *uncritically* accepts it, is unconsciously committed to it. Such uncritical commitment is a necessary presupposition for using the tool effectively and, as such, cannot be asserted. Presuppositions cannot be asserted, says Polanyi (1962: 60), 'for assertion[s] can be made only *within* a framework with which we have identified ourselves for the time being; as they are themselves our ultimate framework, they are essentially inarticulable' (italics in the original).

The interiorization of a tool – its instrumentalization in the service of a purpose – is beneficial to its user for it enables him/her to acquire new experiences and carry out more competently the task at hand (Dreyfus and Dreyfus, 2000). Compare, for example, one who learns driving a car to one who is an accomplished driver. The former may have learned how to change gear and to use the brake and the accelerator but cannot, yet, integrate those individual skills – he has not constructed a coherent perception of driving, the phenomenal transformation has not taken place yet. At the early stage, the driver is conscious of what he needs to do and feels the impact of the pedals on his foot and the gear stick on his palm; he has not learned to unconsciously correlate the performance of the car with the specific bodily actions he undertakes as a driver. The experienced driver, by contrast, is unconscious of the actions by which she drives – car instruments are tools whose use she has mastered, that is interiorized, and is therefore able to use them for the purpose of driving. By becoming unconscious of certain actions, the experienced driver expands the domain of experiences she can concentrate on as a driver (i.e. principally road conditions and other drivers' behaviour).

The more general point to be derived from the preceding examples is formulated by Polanyi (1962: 61) as follows: 'we may say ... that by the effort by which I concentrate on my chosen plane of operation I succeed in absorbing all the elements of the situation of which I might otherwise be aware in themselves, so that I become aware of them now in terms of the operational results achieved through their use'. This is important because we get things done, we achieve competence, by becoming unaware of how we do so. Of course one can take an interest in, and learn a great deal about, the gearbox and the acceleration mechanism but, to be able to drive, such knowledge needs to lapse into unconsciousness. 'This lapse into unconsciousness', remarks Polanyi (1962: 62), 'is accompanied by a newly acquired consciousness of the experiences in question, on the operational plane. It is misleading, therefore, to describe this as the mere result of repetition; it is a structural change achieved by a repeated mental effort aiming at the instrumentalization of certain things and actions in the service of some purpose'.

Notice that, for Polanyi, the shrinking of consciousness of certain things is, in the context of action, necessarily connected with the expansion of consciousness of other things. Particulars such as 'changing gear' and 'pressing the accelerator' are subsidiarily known, as the driver concentrates on the act of driving. Knowing something, then, is always a contextual issue and fundamentally connected to action (the 'operational plane'). My knowledge of gears is in the context of driving, and it is only in such a context that I am subsidiarily aware of that knowledge. If, however, I was a car mechanic, gears would constitute my focus of attention, rather than being an assimilated particular. Knowledge has, therefore, a *recursive* form: given a certain context, we blackbox – assimilate, interiorize, instrumentalize – certain things in order to concentrate – focus – on others. In another context, and at another level of analysis (cf. Bateson, 1979: 43), we can open up some of the previously blackboxed issues and focus our attention on them. In theory this is an endless process, although in practice there are institutional and practical limits to it. In this way we can, to some extent, 'vertically integrate' our knowledge, although, as said earlier, what pieces of knowledge we *use* depends, at any point in time, on context. If the driver happens to be a car mechanic as well as an engineer he will have acquired three different bodies of knowledge, each having a different degree of abstraction, which, taken together, give his knowledge depth and make him a sophisticated driver (cf. Harper, 1987: 33). How, however, he draws on each one of them – that is, what is focally and what is subsidiarily known – depends on the context-in-use. Moreover, each one of these bodies of knowledge stands on its own, and cannot be reduced to any of the others. The practical knowledge I have of my car cannot be replaced by the theoretical knowledge of an engineer; the practical knowledge I have of my own body cannot be replaced by the theoretical knowledge of a physician (cf. Polanyi, 1966: 20). In the social world, specialist, abstract, theoretical knowledge is necessarily refracted through the 'lifeworld' – the taken-for-granted assumptions by means of which human beings organize their experience, knowledge, and transactions with the world (cf. Bruner, 1990: 35).

The Appropriation of 'Tacit Knowledge' in Management Studies: The Great Misunderstanding

As was mentioned in the introductory section of this chapter, 'tacit knowledge' has become very popular in management studies since the middle 1990s, to a large extent, due to the publication of Nonaka and Takeuchi's (1995) *The Knowledge-Creating Company*. The cornerstone of Nonaka and Takeuchi's theory for organizational knowledge is the notion of 'knowledge conversion' – how tacit knowledge is 'converted' to explicit knowledge, and vice versa. As the authors argue, 'our dynamic model of knowledge creation is anchored to a critical assumption that human knowledge is created and expanded through social interaction between tacit knowledge and explicit knowledge. We shall call this interaction "knowledge conversion"' (Nonaka and Takeuchi, 1995: 61).

Nonaka and Takeuchi distinguish four modes of knowledge conversion: from tacit knowledge to tacit knowledge (socialization); from tacit knowledge to explicit knowledge (externalization); from explicit knowledge to explicit knowledge (combination); and from explicit knowledge to tacit knowledge (internalization). Tacit knowledge is converted to tacit knowledge through observation, imitation and practice, in those cases where an apprentice learns from a master. Tacit knowledge is converted to explicit knowledge when it is articulated and it takes the form of concepts, models, hypotheses, metaphors and analogies. Explicit knowledge is converted to explicit knowledge when different bodies of explicit knowledge are combined. And explicit knowledge is converted into tacit knowledge when it is first verbalized and then absorbed, internalized by the individuals involved.

The organizational knowledge-creation process proceeds in cycles (in a spiral-like fashion), with each cycle consisting of five phases: the sharing of tacit knowledge among the members of a team; the creation of concepts whereby a team articulates its commonly shared mental model; the justification of concepts in terms of the overall organizational purposes and objectives; the building of an archetype which is a tangible manifestation of the justified concept; and the cross-leveling of knowledge, whereby a new cycle of knowledge creation may be created elsewhere (or even outside of) the organization.

To illustrate their theory, Nonaka and Takeuchi describe the product development process of Matsushita's Home Bakery, the first fully automated bread-making machine for home use, which was introduced to the Japanese market in 1987. There were three cycles in the relevant knowledge-creation process, with each cycle starting in order to either remove the weaknesses of the previous one or improve upon its outcome. The first cycle ended with the assemblage of a prototype which, however, was not up to the design team's standards regarding the quality of bread it produced. This triggered the second cycle which started when Ikuko Tanaka, a software developer, took an apprenticeship with a master baker at the Osaka International Hotel. Her purpose was to learn how to knead bread dough properly in order to 'convert' later this know-how into particular design features of the bread-making machine under development. Following this, the third cycle came into operation whereby the commercialization team, consisting of people drawn from the manufacturing and marketing sections, further improved the prototype that came out of the second cycle, and made it a commercially viable product.

To obtain a better insight into what Nonaka and Takeuchi mean by 'tacit knowledge' and how it is related to 'explicit knowledge', it is worth zooming into their description of the second cycle of the knowledge-creation process, since this is the cycle most relevant to the acquisition and 'conversion' of tacit knowledge. In the section below I quote in full the authors' description of this cycle (references and figures have been omitted) (see Nonaka and Takeuchi, 1995: 103–6).

A Case Study: The Second Cycle of the Home Bakery Spiral

The second cycle began with a software developer, Ikuko Tanaka, sharing the tacit knowledge of a master baker in order to learn his kneading skill. A master baker learns the art of kneading, a critical step in bread making, following years of experience. However, such expertise is difficult to articulate in words. To capture this tacit knowledge, which usually takes a lot of imitation and practice to master, Tanaka proposed a creative solution. Why not train with the head baker at Osaka International Hotel, which had a reputation for making the best bread in Osaka, to study the kneading techniques? Tanaka learned her kneading skills through observation, imitation, and practice. She recalled:

> *At first, everything was a surprise. After repeated failures, I began to ask where the master and I differed. I don't think one can understand or learn this skill without actually doing it. His bread and mine [came out] quite different even though we used the same materials. I asked why our products were so different and tried to reflect the difference in our skill of kneading.*

Even at this stage, neither the head baker nor Tanaka was able to articulate knowledge in any systematic fashion. Because their tacit knowledge never became explicit, others within Matsushita were left puzzled. Consequently, engineers were also brought to the hotel and allowed to knead and bake bread to improve their understanding of the process. Sano, the division chief, noted, "If the craftsmen cannot explain their skills, then the engineers should become craftsmen."

Not being an engineer, Tanaka could not devise mechanical specifications. However, she was able to transfer her knowledge to the engineers by using the phrase "twisting stretch" to provide a rough image of kneading, and by suggesting the strength and speed of the propeller to be used in kneading. She would simply say, "Make the propeller move stronger", or "Move it faster". Then the engineers would adjust the machine specifications. Such a trial-and-error process continued for several months.

Her request for a 'twisting stretch' movement was interpreted by the engineers and resulted in the addition inside the case of special ribs that held back the dough when the propeller turned so that the dough could be stretched. After a year of trial and error and working closely with other engineers, the team came up with product specifications that successfully reproduced the head baker's stretching technique and the quality of bread Tanaka had learned to make at the hotel. The team then materialized this concept, putting it together into a manual, and embodied it in the product. ...

In the second cycle, the team had to resolve the problem of getting the machine to knead dough correctly. To solve the kneading problem, Ikuko Tanaka apprenticed herself with the head baker of the Osaka International Hotel. There she learned the skill through socialization, observing and imitating the head baker, rather than through reading memos or manuals. She then translated the kneading skill into explicit knowledge. The knowledge was externalized by creating the concept of "twisting stretch". In addition, she externalized this knowledge by expressing the movements required for the kneading propeller, using phrases like "more slowly" or "more strongly". For those who had never touched dough before, understanding the kneading skill was so difficult that engineers had to share experiences by spending hours at the baker to experience the touch of the dough. Tacit knowledge was externalized by lining special ribs inside the dough case. Combination took place when the 'twisting stretch'concept and the technological knowledge of the engineers came together to produce a prototype of Home Bakery. Once the prototype was justified against the concept of "Rich," the development moved into the third cycle. (Emphasis in original).

How Should We Understand Tacit Knowledge?

The preceding account of tacit knowledge has very little in common with that of Polanyi. Nonaka and Takeuchi assume that tacit knowledge is knowledge-not-yet-articulated: a set of rules incorporated in the activity an actor is involved in, which is a matter of time for him/her to first learn and then formulate. The authors seem to think that what Tanaka learned through her apprenticeship with the master baker can be ultimately crystallized in a set of propositional 'if–then' statements (Tsoukas, 1998: 44–8), or what Oakeshott (1991: 12–15) calls 'technical knowledge' and Ryle (1963: 28–32) 'knowing that'. In that sense, the tacit knowledge involved in kneading that Tanaka picked up through her apprenticeship – in Oakeshott's (1991: 2–15) terms, the 'practical knowledge' of kneading, and in Ryle's (1963: 28–32) terms, 'knowing how' to knead – the sort of knowledge that exists only *in use* and cannot be formulated in rules, is equivalent to the set of statements that articulate it, namely it is equivalent to technical knowledge.

Tacit knowledge is thought to have the structure of a syllogism and as such can be reversed and, therefore, even mechanized (Polanyi and Prosch, 1975: 40). What Tanaka was missing, the authors imply, were the premises of the syllogism, which she acquired through her sustained apprenticeship. Once they had been learned, it was a matter of time before she could put them together and arrive at the conclusion that 'twisting stretch' and 'the [right] movements required for the kneading propeller' (Nonaka and Takeuchi, 1995: 103–6) were what was required for designing the right bread-making machine.

However, although (Nonaka and Takeuchi, 1995: 103) acknowledge that Tanaka's apprenticeship was necessary because 'the art of kneading' could not be imparted in any other way (e.g. 'through reading memos and manuals', [1995: 105]), they view her apprenticeship as merely an alternative mechanism of transferring knowledge. In terms of content, knowledge acquired through apprenticeship is not thought to be qualitatively different from knowledge acquired through reading manuals, since in both cases the content of knowledge can be articulated and formulated in rules – only the manner of its appropriation differs. The mechanism of knowledge acquisition may be different, but the result is the same.

The 'conduit metaphor of communication' (Lakoff, 1995: 116; Reddy, 1979; Tsoukas, 1997) that underlies Nonaka and Takeuchi's perspective – the view of ideas as objects which can be extracted from people and transmitted to others over a conduit – reduces practical knowledge to technical knowledge (cf. Costelloe, 1998: 325–6). However, while clearly Tanaka learned a technique during her apprenticeship, she acquired much more than technical knowledge, without even realizing it: she learned to make bread in a way which cannot be formulated in propositions but only manifested in her work. To treat practical (or tacit) knowledge as having a precisely definable content, which is initially located in the head of the practitioner and then 'translated' (Nonaka and Takeuchi, 1995: 105) into explicit knowledge, is to reduce what is known to what is articulable, thus impoverishing the notion of practical knowledge. As Oakeshott (1991: 15) remarks:

> *a pianist acquires artistry as well as technique, a chess-player style and insight into the game as well as a knowledge of the moves, and a scientist acquires (among other things) the sort of judgement which tells him when his technique is leading him astray and the connoisseurship which enables him to distinguish the profitable from the unprofitable directions to explore.*

As should be clear from the preceding section, by viewing all knowing as essentially 'personal knowing' (Polanyi, 1962: 49), Polanyi highlights the skilled performance that all acts of knowing require: the actor does not know all the rules he/she follows in the activity he/she is involved in. Like Oakeshott (1991), Polanyi (1962: 50) notes that 'rules of art can be useful, but they do not determine the practice of an art; they are maxims, which can serve as a guide to an art only if they can be integrated into the practical knowledge of the art. They cannot replace that knowledge'. It is precisely because what needs to be known cannot be specified in detail that the relevant knowledge must be passed from master to apprentice. 'To learn by example', says Polanyi (1962: 53):

> is to submit to authority. You follow your master because you trust his manner of doing things even when you cannot analyse and account in detail for its effectiveness. By watching the master and emulating his efforts in the presence of his example, the apprentice unconsciously picks up the rules of the art, including those which are not explicitly known to the master himself. These hidden rules can be assimilated only by a person who surrenders himself to that extent uncritically to the imitation of another.

Like Polanyi's medical student discussed earlier, Tanaka was initially puzzled by what the master baker was doing – 'at first, everything was a surprise' (Nonaka and Takeuchi, 1995: 104), as she put it. Her 'repeated failures' (1995: 104) were due not to lack of knowledge as such, but due to not having interiorized – dwelled in – the relevant knowledge yet. When, through practice, she began to assimilate the knowledge involved in kneading bread – namely, when she became subsidiarily aware of how she was kneading – she could, subsequently, turn her focal awareness to the task at hand: *kneading* bread, as opposed to imitating the master. Knowledge now became a tool to be tacitly known and uncritically used in the service of an objective. 'Kneading bread' ceased to be an object of focal awareness and became an instrument for actually kneading bread – a subsidiarily known tool for getting things done (Winograd and Flores, 1987: 27–37). For Tanaka to 'convert' her kneading skill into explicit knowledge, she would need to focus her attention on her subsidiary knowledge, thereby becoming focally aware of it. In that event, however, she would no longer be engaged in the same activity, namely bread kneading, but in the activity of thinking about bread kneading, which is a different matter. The particulars of her skill are 'logically unspecifiable' (Polanyi, 1962: 56), in the sense that their specification would logically contradict and practically paralyse what is implied in the carrying out of the performance at hand.

Of course, one might acknowledge this and still insist, along with Ambrosini and Bowman (2001) and Eraut (2000), that Tanaka could, *ex post facto*, reflect on her kneading skill, in the context of discussing bread-kneading with her colleagues – the engineers – and articulate it into explicit knowledge. But this would be an erroneous claim to make for, in such an event, she would no longer be describing her kneading skill *in toto* but only its technical part: that which is possible to articulate in rules, principles, maxims – in short, in propositions. What she has to say about the 'ineffable' (Polanyi, 1962: 87–95) part of her skill, that which is tacitly known, she has said already in the bread she kneads and cannot put it in words (cf. Oakeshott, 1991: 14; Janik, 1992: 37). As Polanyi so perceptively argued, you cannot view subsidiary particulars as they allegedly are in themselves for they exist always in conjunction with the focus to which you attend from them, and that makes them unspecifiable. In his words:

> Subsidiary or instrumental knowledge, as I have defined it, is not known in itself but is known in terms of something focally known, to the quality of which it contributes;

and to this extent it is unspecifiable. Analysis may bring subsidiary knowledge into focus and formulate it as a maxim or as a feature in a physiognomy, but such speci-fication is in general not exhaustive. Although the expert diagnostician, taxonomist and cotton-classer can indicate their clues and formulate their maxims, they know many more things than they can tell, knowing them only in practice, as instrumental particulars, and not explicitly, as objects. The knowledge of such particulars is there-fore ineffable, and the pondering of a judgement in terms of such particulars is an ineffable process of thought. (Polanyi, 1962: 88)

If the above is accepted, it follows that Tanaka neither 'transferred' her tacit knowl-edge to the engineers, nor did she 'convert' her kneading skill into explicit knowl-edge, as Nonaka and Takeuchi (1995: 104–5) suggest. She could do neither of these things simply because, following Polanyi's and Oakeshott's definitions of tacit and practical knowledge respectively, skilful knowing contains an ineffable element; it is based on an act of personal insight that is essentially inarticulable.

Well, so far so good, but how are we to interpret Tanaka's concept of 'twisting stretch', which turned out to be so useful for the making of Matsushita's bread-making machine? Or, to put it more generally, does the ineffability of skilful know-ing imply that we can never talk about a practical activity at all? That the skills involved in, say, carpentry, teaching, ship navigation, or scientific activity will ulti-mately be mystical experiences outside the realm of reasoned discussion?

Not at all. What we do when we reflect on the practical activities we engage in, is to re-punctuate the distinctions underlying those activities, to draw the attention of those involved to certain hitherto unnoticed aspects of those activities – to see connections among items previously thought unconnected (cf. Weick, 1995: 87, 126). Through instructive forms of talk (e.g. 'look at this', 'have you thought about this in that way?', 'try this', 'imagine this', 'compare this to that') practitioners are moved to *re*-view the situation they are in, to relate to their circumstances in a dif-ferent way. From a Wittgensteinian perspective, Shotter and Katz (1996: 230) sum-marize succinctly this process as follows:

to gain an explicit understanding of our everyday, practical activities, we can make use of the very same methods we used in gaining that practical kind of understand-ing in the first place – that is, we can use the self-same methods for drawing our attention to how people draw each other's attention to things, as they themselves (we all?) in fact use!.

Notice what Shotter and Katz are saying: we learn to engage in practical activities through our participation in social practices, under the guidance of people who are more experienced than us (MacIntyre, 1985: 181–203; Taylor, 1993); people who, by drawing our attention to certain things, make us 'see connections' (Wittgenstein, 1958: No. 122), pretty much like the master baker was drawing Tanaka's attention to certain aspects of bread-kneading. Through her subsequent conversations with the engineers, Tanaka was able to form an explicit understanding of the activity she was involved in, by having her attention drawn to how the master baker was drawing her attention to kneading – hence the concept of 'twisting stretch'. It is in this sense that Wittgenstein talks of language as issuing reminders of things we *already* know: 'Something that we know when no one asks us, but no longer know when we are supposed to give an account of it, is something that we need to *remind* ourselves of' (Wittgenstein, 1958: No. 89; italics in the original).

In her apprenticeship, Tanaka came eventually to practice 'twisting stretch' but she did not know it. She needed to be 'reminded' of it. When we recursively punctuate our understanding, we see new connections and '[give] prominence to distinctions which our ordinary forms of language easily makes us overlook' (Wittgenstein, 1958: No. 132). Through the instructive (or directive) use of language we are led to notice certain aspects of our circumstances that, due to their simplicity and familiarity, remain hidden ('one is unable to notice something – because it is always before one's eyes' (Wittgenstein, 1958: No. 129)). This is, then, the sense in which although skilful knowing is ultimately ineffable, it nonetheless can be talked about: through reminding ourselves of it, we notice certain important features which had hitherto escaped our attention and can now be seen in a new context. Consequently, we are led to relate to our circumstances in new ways and thus see new ways forward.

Conclusion

Tacit knowledge has been greatly misunderstood in management studies – or so I have argued in this chapter. Nonaka and Takeuchi's interpretation of tacit knowledge as knowledge-not-yet-articulated – knowledge awaiting for its 'translation' or 'conversion' into explicit knowledge – an interpretation that has been widely adopted in management studies, is erroneous: it ignores the essential ineffability of tacit knowledge, thus reducing it to what can be articulated. Tacit and explicit knowledge are not the two ends of a continuum but the two sides of the same coin: even the most explicit kind of knowledge is underlain by tacit knowledge. Tacit knowledge consists of a set of particulars of which we are subsidiarily aware as we focus on something else. Tacit knowing is vectorial: we know the particulars by relying on our awareness of them for attending to something else. Since subsidiaries exist as such by bearing on the focus *to* which we are attending *from* them, they cannot be separated from the focus and examined independently, for if this is done, their meaning will be lost. While we can certainly focus on particulars, we cannot do so in the context of action in which we are subsidiarily aware of them. Moreover, by focusing on particulars after a particular action has been performed, we are *not* focusing on them as they bear on the original focus of action, for their meaning is necessarily derived from their connection to that focus. When we focus on particulars we do so in a new context of action which itself is underlain by a new set of subsidiary particulars. Thus the idea that somehow one can focus on a set of particulars and convert them into explicit knowledge is unsustainable.

The ineffability of tacit knowledge does not mean that we cannot discuss the skilled performances in which we are involved. We can – indeed, should – discuss them provided we stop insisting on 'converting' tacit knowledge and, instead, start recursively drawing our attention to how we draw each other's attention to things. Instructive forms of talk help us re-orientate ourselves to how we relate to others and the world around us, thus enabling us to talk and act differently. We can command a clearer view of our tasks at hand if we 'remind' ourselves of how we do things so that distinctions which we had previously not noticed, and features which had previously escaped our attention, may be brought forward. Contrary to what Ambrosini and Bowman (2001) suggest, we do not so much need to operationalize tacit knowledge (as explained earlier, we could not do this, even if we wanted) as to find new ways of talking, fresh forms of interacting, and novel ways of distinguishing and connecting. Tacit knowledge cannot be 'captured', 'translated' or 'converted' but only displayed, manifested, in what we do. New knowledge comes about not when the tacit becomes explicit, but when our skilled performance – our praxis – is punctuated in new ways through social interaction (Tsoukas, 2001).

References

Ambrosini, V. and Bowman, C. (2001) Tacit knowledge: Some suggestions for operationalization, *Journal of Management Studies*, 38: 811–29.

Bateson, G. (1979) *Mind and Nature: A Necessary Unit*. Toronto: Bantam Books.

Baumard, P. (1999) *Tacit Knowledge in Organizations*, translated by S. Wauchope. London: SAGE.

Bell, D. (1999) The axial age of technology foreword: 1999. In D. Bell (ed.), *The Coming of the Post-Industrial Society*. New York: Basic Books, Special Anniversary Edition, pp. ix–lxxxv.

Boisot, M.H. (1995) *Information Space: A Framework for Learning in Organizations, Institutions and Culture*. London: Routledge.

Brown, J.S. and Duguid, P. (2000) *The Social Life of Information*. Boston, MA: Harvard Business School Press.

Bruner, J. (1990) *Acts of Meaning*. Cambridge, MA: Harvard University Press.

Cook, S.D.N. and Brown, J.S. (1999) Bridging epistemologies: The generative dance between organizational knowledge and organizational knowing, *Organization Science*, 10: 381–400.

Cook, S.D.N. and Yanow, D. (1996) Culture and organizational learning. In M.D. Cohen and L.S. Sproull (eds), *Organizational Learning*. Thousand Oaks, CA: SAGE, pp. 430–59.

Costelloe, T. (1998) Oakeshott, Wittgenstein, and the practice of social science, *Journal for the Theory of Social Behaviour*, 28: 323–47.

Davenport, T.H. and L. Prusak (1998) *Working Knowledge*. Cambridge, MA: Harvard University Press.

Devlin, K. (1999) *Infosense*. New York: W.H. Freeman & Co.

Dixon, N.M. (2000) *Common Knowledge*. Boston, MA: Harvard Business School Press.

Dreyfus, L.H. and Dreyfus, S.E. (2000) *Mind Over Machine*. New York: Free Press.

Drucker, P. (1993) *Post-Capitalist Society*. Oxford: Butterworth/Heinemann.

Eraut, M. (2000) Non-formal learning and tacit knowledge in professional work, *British Journal of Educational Psychology*, 70: 113–36.

Gill, J.H. (2000) *The Tacit Mode*. Albany, NY: State University of New York Press.

Knowledge for Development (1998/99) World Development Report. Oxford: Oxford University Press.

Harper, D. (1987) *Working Knowledge*. Berkeley, CA: University of California Press.

Janik, A. (1992) Why is Wittgenstein important? In B. Goranzon and M. Florin (eds), *Skill and Education*. London: Springer-Verlag, pp. 33–40.

Kreiner, K. (1999) Knowledge and mind, *Advances in Management Cognition and Organizational Information Processing*, 6: 1–29.

Lakoff, G. (1995) Body, brain, and communication (interviewed by I.A. Boal). In J. Brook and I.A. Boal (eds), *Resisting the Virtual Life*. San Francisco, CA: City Lights, pp. 115–29.

Leonard, D. and S. Sensiper (1998) The role of tacit knowledge in group innovation, *California Management Review*, 40(3): 112–32.

Maclntyre, A. (1985) *After Virtue*, 2nd edition. London: Duckworth.

Mansell, R. and When, U. (1998) *Knowledge Societies*. New York: Oxford University Press.

Nonaka, I. and Takeuchi, H. (1995) *The Knowledge-Creating Company*. New York: Oxford University Press.

Oakeshott, M. (1991) *Rationalism in Politics and Other Essays*. Indianapolis, IN: Liberty Press.

Our Competitive Future: Building the Knowledge Driven Economy (1998) Presented to Parliament by the Secretary of State for Trade and Industry. London: The Stationery Office.

Polanyi, M. (1962) *Personal Knowledge*. Chicago, IL: University of Chicago Press.

Polanyi, M. (1966) *The Tacit Dimension*. London: Routledge & Kegan Paul.

Polanyi, M. (1969) *Knowing and Being*, ed. M. Grene. Chicago, IL: University of Chicago Press.

Polanyi, M. and Prosch, H. (1975) *Meaning*. Chicago, IL: University of Chicago Press.

Reddy, M.J. (1979) The Conduit Metaphor: A Case of Frame Conflict in our Language about Language. In A. Ortony (ed.), *Metaphor and Thought*. Cambridge: Cambridge University Press, pp. 284–324.

Ryle, G. (1963) *The Concept of Mind*. London: Penguin.

Shotter, J. and Katz, A.M. (1996) Articulating a practice from within the practice itself: Establishing formative dialogues by the use of a 'social poetics', *Concepts and Transformation*, 1: 213–37.

Spender, J.-C. (1996) Making knowledge the basis of a dynamic theory of the firm, *Strategic Management Journal*, 17(Special Winter Issue): 45–62.

Stehr, N. (1994) *Knowledge Societies*. London: SAGE.

Taylor, C. (1993) To follow a rule … . In C. Calhoun, E. LiPuma and M. Postone (eds), *Bourdieu: Critical Perspectives*. Cambridge: Polity Press, pp. 45–59.

Thurow, L. (2000) *Creating Wealth*. London: Nicholas Brealey Publishing Ltd.

Toulmin, S. (1990) *Cosmopolis*. Chicago, IL: University of Chicago Press.

Toulmin, S. (2001) *Return to Reason*. Cambridge, MA: Harvard University Press.

Tsoukas, H. (1996) The firm as a distributed knowledge system: A constructionist approach, *Strategic Management Journal*, 17(Winter Special Issue): 11–25.

Tsoukas, H. (1997) The tyranny of light: The temptations and the paradoxes of the information society, *Futures*, 29: 827–43.

Tsoukas, H. (1998) Forms of knowledge and forms of life in organized contexts. In R.C.H. Chia (ed.), *In the Realm of Organization*. London: Routledge, pp. 43–66.

Tsoukas, H. (2001) Where does new organizational knowledge come from? Keynote address at the International Conference *Managing Knowledge: Conversations and Critiques*, Leicester University, 10–11 April 2001.

Tsoukas, H. and Vladimirou, E. (2001) What is organizational knowledge?, *Journal of Management Studies*, 38(7): 973–93.

Von Krogh, G., Ichijo, K. and Nonaka, I. (2000) *Enabling Knowledge Creation*. New York: Oxford University Press.

Weick, K. (1995) *Sensemaking in Organizations*. Thousand Oaks, CA: SAGE.

Wenger, E. (1998) *Communities of Practice*. Cambridge: Cambridge University Press.

Winograd, T. and F. Flores (1987) *Understanding Computers and Cognition*. Reading, MA: Addison-Wesley.

Wittgenstein, L. (1958) *Philosophical Investigations*. Oxford: Blackwell.

An Overview: What's New and Important about Knowledge Management? Building New Bridges Between Managers and Academics

6

J.-C. Spender

The most obvious news is that knowledge management (KM) has become big business, growing explosively since Drucker drew attention to it in 1988 (Drucker, 1988). We now see KM conferences all over the world, a huge number of KM trade journals, and battalions of KM consultants. The majority of organizations, both private and public, have KM projects of various types and their spending is enormous, perhaps 40 per cent of their entire capital outlay. Along with these projects there are all manner of new KM job titles such as chief knowledge officer (CKO), knowledge engineers, knowledge authors and, of course, knowledge workers (Reich, 1992). There has been a parallel growth of academic discussion about knowledge, especially about organizational learning and the knowledge-based theory of organizations and alliances, for example, Choo and Bontis (2002), Cohen and Sproull (1996), Easterby-Smith and Lyles (2003) and Holsapple (2003).

As KM has risen in importance and managerial fashionability the hype and confusion has multiplied, leading some to argue that KM is a fad of little long-term significance, for example, Kalling (2003), Marren (2003) and Storey and Barnett (2000). Such critical notes are partly sour grapes in the sense that much of what passes for KM is conventional information systems design and analysis, or conventional job training or business process re-engineering (BPR) relabelled. However, there is mounting pressure from theorists and managers alike to understand the specific contributions that KM can make, especially when they reach beyond conventional managerial and consulting practice (Alvesson and Kärreman, 2001). The good news is that the outlines of KM as a coherent system of analysis and practice are beginning to gel; the confusion in the literature diminishes and its potential becomes clearer (Gray and Meister, 2003). The main argument of this chapter is that we can get a clearer sense of KM only by differentiating it from other fields such as information technology (IT), organization communications, institutional and cultural theory, or organizational development, which are already established. So I shall argue the theory or scheme of KM, and of knowledge-based organizations, must begin with an appreciation of the underlying differences between data and meaning and practice (Figure 6.1).

| Knowledge-as-data |
| Knowledge-as-meaning |
| Knowledge-as-practice |

Figure 6.1   Three types of knowledge

Since any substantial knowledge-based theory of the organization and its management must encompass all three types of knowledge, we must also appreciate why the relationships between these types are complex rather than simple. Eventually the difficulties of relating either data or meaning to practice give us fresh insight into what management generally, and KM in particular, is all about.

Where to Begin?

Explanations of KM often begin with writers asserting knowledge's rising importance as the source of competitive advantage (Beerli et al., 2003; Rumizen, 2002). Others begin by defining knowledge so as to contrast it with conventional organizational assets, arguing that knowledge assets cannot be managed in the same manner (Firestone and McElroy, 2003). Yet others begin by defining KM as a process that uses IT to manage the collection and distribution of organizational and environmental information (Bergeron, 2003). Economists tend to the first, treating knowledge as the crucial or strategic organizational asset (Boisot, 1998; Grant, 2003; Teece, 2003). Organization theorists incline to the second, seeing knowledge as the outcome of some crucial knowing and learning organizational processes (Brown and Duguid, 2001; Weick, 1995). Information technologists incline to the last, seeing collecting and moving useful data as crucial. Comparing these positions we see crucial differences in their underlying assumptions; organization theorists tending to assume employees hold the knowledge, perhaps as tacit skills, while IT or management information systems (MIS) theorists and economists normally treat knowledge as separable from the people who generate and use it in their decision-making.

It does not really matter where we start – provided we do not stop theorizing before reaching a position that encompasses all three types of knowledge. This moves towards a theory of KM that embraces, inter alia, (i) assets (knowledge) and (ii) processes (knowing), which are either (iii) objective, in the sense of being handled by information systems, or (iv) subjective, being handled by people – so we can imagine yet another two-by-two matrix, illustrated in Figure 6.2.

For the most part we work in ways that reflect our prior training and experience. Managers focus on knowledge as a precursor to control, their primary task, but probably add some concerns about the strategic relationship between what the

	assets	processes
Objective		
Subjective		

Figure 6.2 Overall scope of KM

business knows and the challenges that can be safely undertaken on that basis, so avoiding committing themselves to operate in unfamiliar territory. Data about products and markets, for instance, can support data-driven decisions, the type familiar to business school students. However, problems of meaning – connecting the dots and interpreting the data – lead to strategic discussion, insight, hunches and so forth. There is also the matter of practice, knowing how to do things, so thinking about what organizations can undertake safely means taking into account their external networks, employee skills and organizational procedures (routines) along with their equipment, designs, company records, patents and data on hard drives (Nelson and Winter, 1982).

The literature seems confusing because it is not obvious how to bring such varied ideas together; especially when it is clear most of the KM discourse and activity is about IT or MIS (Gray and Meister, 2003). Thus Bergeron (2003) and Groff and Jones (2003) define KM as the business of managing IT to improve employee performance and organizational competitiveness. Looking at these books and the KM trade press it is clear that most of the activity and investment is devoted to organizational data collection, selection, manipulation and delivery. Information scientists have developed a wide range of KM tools to support these tasks (Awad and Ghaziri, 2003; Liebowitz, 2001; Ruggles, 1998; Sharp, 2003; Tiwana, 2002). Some are simple, such as effective use of Microsoft products costing a few hundred dollars; others are complex and cost millions, such as those from Convera, SAP, ServiceWare (now called Knova) or Vivisimo. Readers focusing on the IT and MIS aspects of KM should pay close attention to trade journals such as *KM World* and *KM Review*, and to the KM trade conferences where the relative merits of these tools and the best practices for their implementation are discussed.

These comments may seem dismissive given many see IT and MIS as the core of KM and assume it is the development of IT that has led to today's interest in KM – and, no question, it is easy to miss the contemporary organization's prodigious appetite for information. For instance, the average hospital produces several terabytes of information every day. Businesses and organizations are increasingly integrated by information rather than by physical inspection of the goods being produced or moved and services supplied.

Garment companies collect point-of-sale data in their outlets and analyse it in close to real-time to generate orders on fabricating plants thousands of miles from the stores being monitored. No longer do managers look in stock rooms and order on the basis of what they find there; shelving and racking plans are remade daily and carefully sequenced inventory packs are shipped nightly. Likewise auto assembly companies have adopted integrated just-in-time methods, managing the flow of product from design to sale and no longer ordering components on the basis of minimum stock levels. Today's organizations do their utmost to reduce inventories, often held only in sealed containers as they move across the oceans, for less inventory means less working capital and a better return, and a leaner and more agile operation. In the public sector 'legacy' databases are pulled together to minimize abuse of services and maximize operating efficiency and system-wide surveillance. The MIS aspects of KM have contributed significantly in all these respects and may well be among the most significant of productivity and profit drivers (Gray and Meister, 2004).

The point here is less to diminish these achievements than to see how their background complexities reveal the core issues that differentiate KM from MIS and IT. KM adds little to our broader understanding of knowledge's place in the organization, or the management problems arising from knowledge's special characteristics and challenges, so long as we see it lying within the boundaries of IT. Then it would be no more than a sub-set of IT. For instance Awad and Ghaziri (2003: 305) review KM tools such as neural networks, data mining systems and knowledge portals. These are framed by the axioms and theories of information technology and, as such, cannot help us understand KM as different from IT. Here we are in danger of missing the most important aspects of KM. Thus the main 'what's new' is that KM is now becoming distinguishable from a variety of closely related areas of thought and analysis, such as IT, cognitive science, institutional theory, culture theory, organization design and corporate strategy. Nevertheless much of what people in businesses call knowledge management seems, at least at first sight, to be about collecting information from one set of people in the organization and delivering it to others. This is what IT has been doing since it was called electronic data processing (EDP) so there is nothing to be gained by calling this KM. Again, the main argument of this note is that we get a clearer sense of KM only by differentiating it from such specific areas of study. How is this to be done?

For example, MIS designers go beyond the interface between the IT system and the people whose behaviour is being affected whenever they consider the knowledge-driven system as a socio-technical whole. To do this they must use theories about how people generate and use information. IT generally assumes away the problems at this interface, focusing narrowly on technology and taking people's responses to the data delivered for granted. But we also appreciate value is added only when such systems are integrated into an organizational system composed of people, and thence into markets composed of suppliers and consumers. The critical issue is that managers know that people seldom respond to information in simple ways; that is on the basis of the data alone. More often the data is merely one of several inputs reflected in their behaviour – even when there is no problem with understanding the data offered. This kind of complexity drives us towards cognitive psychology or other kinds of thinking about human behaviour; beyond the logical operations basic to IT. We are suggesting that KM is better understood as related to this more complex analysis embracing both IT and people. IT professionals confronting these complexities need to bring in non-IT models of the workplace or socio-economic system into which their IT system is being projected. This draws us to analyse the initial crucial distinction between data and information.

Data Versus Information

A hard drive carries data. But looking directly at the data cannot tell us what it means. Meaning is what our minds add to the data – we connect the dots in a system of meaning, a frame for cognizing within which we are comfortable placing the data, and so turn it into information. The data can be a number – fine and precise, but for it to be information we need to know if the number refers to the temperature, your bank balance, or this week's casualties, etc. Textual data can describe variables, but we still have to know what these symbols mean. We sense an endless regression to find the ultimate source of meaning. This seems a simple enough point but it is so often glossed over that we tend to miss that communicating data – which IT systems do well – is utterly different from communicating the meaning of the data, which has to be known before the recipient can understand the data. Communicating meaning – as a framework for analysis – means setting up or changing the cognitive framework which enables us to make sense of the signals being received. Communicating 'information' gets these two tangled up.

This analysis raises a major conceptual question – if data can only be understood when a frame of meaning is in place, how is this initial frame put in place? Where does it come from? Are we born with a basic way of understanding what is going on around us, a sort of initial 'cognitive boot program'? Absorptive capacity is a popular term in our literature; it means the ability to acquire further knowledge (Cohen and Levinthal, 1990). But it is not clear how the process of acquiring meaning can begin. Acquiring data is no problem; we can start with a blank sheet, zero data. But acquiring meaning is a puzzle since we cannot convey meaning by transmitting data. As soon as we 'problematize' meaning, which means arguing that the relationship between data and meaning is neither self evident nor necessary, we must presume meaning is something we create in our own heads, a product of our imagination, rather than extracted from data through rigorous analysis. Are there constraints on our imagination; or can we imagine that things mean whatever we like?

The philosophy of language offers us some suggestions about the ways in which a word's meaning might be warranted – thing theories, idea theories and practice theories (Stainton, 2000). The first might be that a word corresponds to the thing perceived and indicated, or alternatively that it can be analysed in terms of its etymological 'roots'. Thus 'strategy' is derived from the Greek word *strategos* the ship's helmsman – or the commander of the phalanx of hoplites who defended the city-state. The second is that the word is completely arbitrary, without any necessary correspondence between it and the thing perceived. It has meaning merely because we are all agreed on the meaning to be attached to it – for instance, 'quark'. The third implies a relationship but not so much in the word itself as in the way the word is used and the social practices to which it refers – for instance 'courage', defined inevitably in terms of 'courageous' behaviour.

This kind of philosophizing can get complicated and confusing so we need to focus on the implication for managers – which is that meanings are acts of imagination constrained in some ways that seem puzzling but important. In the normal organization answers to the questions about warranting or justifying the meanings created fall into two categories, power and experiment. First, senior managers have power, and one aspect of this is that the meanings they choose become those for the rest of the organization. The mission statement is a manifesto of the meanings to be attached to particular words and practices. Senior managers often try to control organizations by determining the meaning systems adopted – searching for excellence, respecting customers' needs, being world class and so forth, and chief executive officers (CEOs) are sometimes changed as a way of changing the organization's meaning system. Second, these meanings guide the organization's actions and are thus exposed to a certain kind of pragmatic experiment, being tested against the world outside the organization. When the meanings are 'incorrect', things do not turn out as expected – pragmatists might say the ideas have little 'cash value'. Managers will say 'we know that does not work'.

In spite of the puzzles above, it seems meanings can be communicated. The whole point of the mission statement is to establish a shared pattern of meaning across the organization or in its markets – even though we are not quite clear how this works. At the same time meanings may be communicated through practice, for actions often speak louder than words – especially when those imagining new meanings and turning them into novel practices get rewarded or punished. Meanings can also be communicated through stories, so storytelling is rapidly becoming a KM specialty (Brown et al., 2005).

It is usual to define 'information' as data with meaning, that is lying within a framework that tells us what to make of it. Sixty kilometers per hour – too fast in a built-up area but possibly dangerously slow on the motorway, but as simple data we do not know what to make of it. Businesses need information to manage their affairs, not data, so it is CIO not CDO and MIS not EDP. Yet often in this curiously named Information Age we are awash with data, much of it clearly not information. We hope that we have complete information and that the surplus data, and the uncollected data, does not matter. When this is not the case we suffer increasing 'information anxiety' as we struggle to deal with what seems to be the rising uncertainty and complexity of contemporary life (Wurman, 1989).

The design of an information system begins with establishing the meaning system that enables its users to distinguish the useful data from the useless. Aspects of meaning become evident in the classification categories and data structures, as well as in the data collection facilities themselves, those interfaces between the 'information system' – which is actually only a data system – and the world of social activity and meaning outside. The meaning systems are also crucial to the human computer interface where the IT system's presentation of the data needs to be aligned to the users' meaning systems. Ideally the 'information system' translates the world to the decision makers in ways that seem completely transparent. Nintendo games, or their grown-up military battle simulations, seek to present the world in the static and dynamic detail necessary to ensure success.

The news with regards to meaning is that cognitive science has moved forward rapidly in the last few decades. We have an increasing appreciation for the way in which our imagination works. For instance, we understand our natural modes of thought are 'biased' when compared with the rational or logical decision-making presumed by utility theory. Prospect theory shows we humans are risk and loss averse, and suffer from reflection and framing effects which are clearly far from rational (Hogarth, 1980; Kahneman and Tversky, 1979). At another level we know more about the ways in which human cognitions are structured and how learning occurs (Anderson, 1983; Caine and Caine, 1991). This is a huge specialist field which we shall neither explain nor critique. Our point here is that our imagination is, inevitably, constrained by the neurophysiologic circumstances of the human brain.

At this point in the chapter the main thing is to see there is no necessary relationship between data and meaning, and that the information content of data is therefore always problematic. Managing data, which IT illustrates well, is quite different from managing meaning, which is what senior managers do by deploying their powers of leadership, or using culture management tools (Hislop, 2002). Meaning is also shaped as we observe the actions of others, through signalling, both attributing the actions' meanings to them and understanding the actions' meanings for us.

As soon as we separate data and meaning, which are melded together in the term 'information', we understand we are covering different ideas, especially about learning and management's roles. When knowledge is defined as data, learning implies more data. This might be called the 'accretion' model of learning. We learn as we sit at a desk and are given more facts, or as we read more books. Learning theorists know this is an impoverished theory in the sense it is so simplistic it tells us nothing of importance. When knowledge is meaning, then we see learning is either the acquisition of a framework of meaning, or a change to one we already have in place. The contrast is well expressed in Kuhn's famous thesis of scientific advancement (Kuhn, 1970). Normal science is the elaboration or accrual of 'facts' within a seeming stable framework. Revolutionary or radical progress occurs when there is a 'paradigm shift', a move to a new system of meaning. Similar notions are familiar from Henderson and Clark's (1990) analysis of the different types of innovation. Since meaning is made and implies an act of imagination, management's role in the creation of new meaning is both to invent and convey it and, perhaps, clarify the constraints on others' imagination by setting limits.

Missed in the discussion so far is the realization that we cannot collect data without a frame. Instrumentation is the implementation of a frame that has been invented, since there is no self-evident set of variables or metrics for measuring anything – whether the phenomena of interest be speed, intelligence or market share. As we turn this thought back onto itself we see that data is actually the prisoner of a meaning system that we treat as 'unproblematic' – to be accepted without question.

Thus data is a kind of information in that what we treat as data is hung in a specific system of meaning.

To complicate things further, we cannot really describe a meaning system without referring to the data it captures. We might illustrate the difference between, say, Inuit and English culture by comparing their notions of marital fidelity. However, to get a complete picture of each culture we would have to identify every element or axiom underpinning each and this turns out to be way beyond the possible when we are dealing with everyday life and social and personal meanings. The task is easier when we distinguish, as did Kuhn, the pre- and post-Copernican or pre- and post-Freudian world views. We get close to a complete explanation contrasting, say, the mathematics of Euclid and Riemann. Again, the point is that in practice both data and meaning are different, though both are aspects of information. When we call what we have 'data', we are stressing the specific observations and pushing the frame into the background and taking it for granted. When we call it 'meaning' we are foregrounding and problematizing the frame. Knowledge managers need to be conscious of the difference. As communications theory recognizes, it is easy to transfer data, implying the recipient has an appropriate meaning system with which to absorb the information being communicated – its meaning being beyond doubt. On the other hand it is quite different, and maybe more difficult, to communicate a new meaning system and so help the recipient see old data in new ways.

While it is easy to talk about meaning as an 'act of imagination', it is less easy to be clear about the circumstances under which this is either possible or necessary. This will become much more important as we proceed, but we can anticipate the argument by pointing out that such acts of imagination may be quintessentially human responses to the absence of meaning, our desire to make sense of something that seems puzzling. We suggest an alternative model of man. On the one hand we have the familiar man the decision-maker, driven by data, albeit with biases. On the other hand, we see man the meaning creator, confronting a universe full of stimuli and data that is not fully comprehensible. Thus one aspect of KM is about collecting and analysing data, while another is about managing our responses to uncertainty, the absence of information. It is the growing appreciation of the second that is the really big 'what's new' in KM theorizing and we only reach this by understanding the differences, as well as the interrelationships, between data and meaning. How these get handled leads us to see how KM differs from IT and disciplines such as rational decision analysis and organization theory.

From Imagination to Practice

Our general method is to seek defining differences, in this case mostly epistemological, that must then be overcome in order to create a theory of the phenomena. This contrasts sharply with those KM theorists who argue all types of knowledge shade into each; those who deny the differences we make central to our theory. The most obvious squabble of this type is between those who see tacit knowledge as quite distinct from explicit knowledge (Gourlay, 2004; Tsoukas and Vladimirou, 2001), and those who 'smoosh' them together saying all 'knowledge' is on a spectrum that has 'completely explicit' at one end and 'completely tacit' at the other.

Before getting into this we need to recognize that the KM literature has been hugely influenced by early work in decision-making and systems theory, in particular the work of Ackoff (1989). These writers downplay the epistemological differences I explore above being seen as matters of degree. In his 1989 paper, Ackoff proposed what has become the widely used DIKW model (data, information, knowledge, wisdom) model. It suggests some kind of ladder of increasing cognitive power, though few authors tell us how any of this works, using it more as a self-evident mantra. Ackoff's model is actually a five-step one, somewhat better thought out, embracing data, information, knowledge, understanding and wisdom. He argued data is without meaning – it just is. Knowledge is useful aggregations of information. Understanding is interpolative, enabling one to generate new knowledge from old, and understanding differs from knowledge as learning differs from memorizing. Finally, he considered that wisdom is about locating understanding into the context of the human condition. While there is much good stuff here, it does not really help us towards a theory of KM because the differences cannot be related. More importantly, we take a different line on the significance of practice.

One of the most important aspects of the new KM literature is that in addition to considering knowledge-as-data and knowledge-as-meaning, it also embraces the notion of knowledge-as-practice. Typically, this begins with references to Ryle's (1949) distinction between knowing what and knowing how or James's (1950) between knowledge about and knowledge of acquaintance or with illustrations from non-English languages – for instance, the distinction between *savoir* and *connaître*. The classic examples of knowledge-as-practice are taken from Polanyi – cycling and swimming. The point here is to show people can demonstrate their knowledge as practical competence, even though they might be unable to 'verbalize' or explain how they are doing what they are doing. Those who say all knowledge is more or less explicit say that with help and encouragement people can generally explain their practice. The relevant competence or 'tacit' knowledge is simply 'difficult to articulate' or codify and a temporary rather than a permanent knowledge condition (Boisot, 1998; Nonaka and Takeuchi, 1995).

Again, our method is to look for grounds for separation before beginning to work on bringing the dissimilar together. The essence of the distinction between data and meaning is that the data is exogenous, driven by stimuli from the world outside us, while meaning is endogenous, created within us. So there is a reflection of the difference between objectivity and subjectivity. If KM is to encompass practice as well as the objective and subjective 'knowledge', how can practice be distinguished?

At this point we can say three things. First, we should understand knowledge is a problematic concept – after several millennia of thought philosophers are still unable to agree on what, if anything, it is – and we should not raise our hopes of a thorough understanding of it too high. Indeed there is a paradox about what it means to theorize about knowledge. Is such theory meta-knowledge, or just more knowledge, and how would we tell the difference anyway? One way of proceeding is to put the whole discussion in philosophical terms. There is a huge literature here and not much of it is adapted to managers' concerns and tastes though the work of Tsoukas is a notable exception (Tsoukas and Mylonopoulos, 2004b; Tsoukas and Vladimirou, 2001).

Second, much of this discussion is simply the impact within managerial discourse and organizational theorizing of matters well known within philosophical and sociological circles, especially the various disputes about method (Lakatos and Feyerabend, 1999). We have two prevailing epistemologies or frameworks within which academic knowledge is hung: realism and idealism (Delanty, 1997). The first, which embraces various forms of positivism, starts out from the assumption that there is a 'knowable reality out there'. Science seeks to understand its fundamental nature through questioning experiment and exposing hypotheses to falsification. The second epistemology, idealism or interpretivism, argues that we can never have certain or immediate knowledge of what lies outside our minds – we have no hotline to God – so our thoughts and language relate only on the images, models and other cognitive constructions we create through acts of imagination.

While the realist position seems obvious and commonsensical to most of us, it turns out that for several hundred years – since Kant – we have had to grapple with the compelling arguments of the sceptics that we have no certain knowledge. We realize we have no 'frame-free' sense data, and that what we see must first be imagined. Kuhn's (1970) work is justly famous because it presented this argument in a very accessible way. If we are limited to the realist and idealist positions, as are most discussions about knowledge and its management, then we adopt an interesting and important assumption about practice. We are saying that cognition – what goes on in our heads, whether we think as individuals or as groups – always precedes action (Argyris, 1982). If there are other kinds of action they are beyond explanation and get dismissed as irrational, inexplicable or deviant. Thereby we arrive at one of the most fundamental assumptions within organizational and managerial theorizing – that managers can, or should, control organizations by shaping the decision-making thoughts of employees, associates, customers, competitors, etc. Within this framework practice can always be explained by reference to the thinking behind it, typically in terms of the goal-orientation of the actor. This leads to the third thing we can say at this stage – which is that if practice is always explainable in terms of the ideas that shape it, we have no need of a theory of knowledge-as-practice. We might want to have a category of deviant or mindless action to oppose that of mindful action (Weick and Roberts, 1993), but we are looking to help knowledge managers not psychologists or theorists of crowd hysteria.

So, in spite of the seeming commonsensicality of knowledge-as-practice it is not obvious how we can have an academically sustainable theory of practice without it collapsing into either the realist or idealist frameworks into which we have been trained. Again there is a huge philosophical and sociological literature seeking a theory of practice – simply because the idea of explaining all practice by reference to the goal-oriented thinking that precedes it is inappropriately narrow. Too much human activity seems to fall outside its scope in spite of the seminal work of sociological theorists such as Parsons (1968). But before we drown in the complexities of social theorists like Bourdieu (1977), Habermas (1984), de Certeau (1984), Rorty (1991) and Luhmann (1995) there are some things we can say about justifying a theory of prac-tice. The challenge is to show there is a meaningful or analytically significant notion of practice lying beyond the bounds of the reasoning-driven concepts of practice that we have, in fact, inherited from Parsons. This is crucial if we are to establish there are parts of KM that lie beyond the grasp of the disciplines grounded on notions of rational decision-making – which includes organization and manage-ment theory, among others.

One way of justifying a theory of practice, and thereby helping us understand knowledge-as-practice, is to problematize consciousness and thus the reasoning on which it stands. We can do this without it getting too complicated by referring to the debate between Vygotsky (1978) and Piaget (1972), two theorists of the develop-ment of human consciousness. These writers have had a huge impact on educational theorizing (Tharp and Gallimore, 1988). At the risk of gross over-simplification we can say both recognized that consciousness is problematic, that it is not a 'natural' and inevitable feature of being alive. Piaget's theory was that what we call conscious-ness unfolds during the child's first four or so years – at which point reasoning, memory, observation (especially the observation of self) – are in place. The process, he suggested, is basically genetically given. Vygotsky, starting with the same prob-lematic, argued that consciousness is socially shaped, typically through the inter-active practices between child and parent or other 'care-givers'. In the latter case there is the implication that practice precedes and shapes our consciousness.

It is no great leap from this educational psychology to appreciating that what we do does, in fact, have a significant impact on how we think about the world. Kant quipped 'to do is to be'. This is especially true of 'professionals', those whose work depends on a developed body of knowledge, typically controlled by others (Abbott, 1988). Medical doctors, for example, surely see the world quite differently than priests, pilots or engineers. This kind of argument might lead us to the need for a theory of practice that distinguishes between purposive practices such as those ori-ented towards organizational goals that require the application of professional skills and practices which are simply about us, in the sense of shaping, maintaining and protecting our consciousness – or what we might call our social identity.

Again, these are deep waters and there is a huge literature created by those who study these matters closely (Blackler et al., 2000; Chi et al., 1988; Dougherty, 1992; Gherardi, 2000; Nicolini et al., 2003; Scarbrough, 1996; Sternberg et al., 2000; Turner, 1994). Managers normally learn to be sensitive to the relationship between people's work and their attitudes. There is much classic sociology about how workers seek to resist the power structures in which they are embedded. Decorating one's cubicle, Dilbert's comments aside (www.dilbert.com), is one way in which we personalize our workplace and so attempt to 'possess' it psychologically. Roy's (1952) observation of 'gold bricking', working ahead of the piece-work requirement so that one has the flexibility to go for a smoke or chat to someone elsewhere in the plant, is such a classic. In more useful managerial terms, if we are able to develop this broader theory of organizational practice, we shall be in a position to distinguish three kinds of practice: goal-oriented, identity-oriented, and what remains as an unexplained residue, rather than the two suggested by rationalists like Argyris. This framework also recalls Bales's (1950) classic work on group activity, and his distinction between task orientation and group maintenance activities.

The challenge of developing a third epistemological position that stands outside both realism and idealism is considerable, but it is central to paying serious attention to knowledge-as-practice. The 'what's new' here is that it is precisely at this point that KM begins to be clearly separable from the disciplines around it and on which it draws. These are typically constrained by the realist–idealist dispute, the one seeking external causes and denying imagination, looking for a natural science of human behaviour, the other surrendering to it entirely and risking the anarchic relativism of the imagination unconstrained. Nor is this a simple pursuit of pure behaviourism as Skinner (1953) framed it – bypassing or ignoring consciousness. There are paradoxes here; for to speak of practice is to bring it into the domain of language, thought and reasoning. We might ask, if knowledge-as-practice is ultimately tacit, then what can one usefully say about it, beyond merely observing its application in practice?

In the section above we proposed at least one kind of practice that *ex definitio* lies outside consciousness and thus the possibility of being explained as purposive. Managers do well to distinguish between purposive, identity-related and inexplicable practices. Different kinds of knowledge and learning, and, thus, KM are implied.

There is a trick here, of course, since all philosophizing is a sort of mental trickery undertaken to reveal our initial assumptions. The focus is on the limits to the imagination as an aspect of consciousness; in this case evolutionary and contingent not on the genetic makeup, as Piaget argued, but rather as Vygotsky suggested, on the socializing process and context in which consciousness is acquired. Consciousness is being re-defined to comprise both reasoning and imagination, recalling Adam Smith's comment that what distinguishes the human race is our senses, our ability to reason and our imagination (Skinner, 2001).

Bringing the Different Kinds of KM Together

At the outset we suggested a theory of KM must begin with an understanding of the differences between data, meaning and practice and then second, offer some suggestions about how the three might be brought back together again in ways useful to managers. To appreciate the differences between data and meaning is, of course, to understand something of the irreconcilable differences between the realist and idealist epistemologies, between objectivity and subjectivity. In the previous section, we considered this distinction by differentiating practice from thought, arguing there were types of practice that could not be explained rationally, by reference to the goals sought. We do this by problematizing the assumption of consciousness and logical reasoning shared by the realist and idealist epistemologies. We show up the taken-for-granted mental practices behind consciousness, as well as the cognitive structures and data perception processes which flesh it out. Inasmuch as we imagine any practices lying below or beyond consciousness we merely suggest an epistemology of practice without being clear about how it would look, or even how we might talk about it. In the next section I shall touch on the radical constructivist literature to make some suggestions in this direction. Before doing so it might be helpful to indicate where this is leading, what the eventual theory of KM is going to look like.

Once we have concepts of data, meaning and practice in place we can consider the management of each. We know the bulk of KM is about managing data and that is what CKOs, CIOs and their colleagues – and the majority of KM industry players – are doing. This is not only about computers; there is a comprehensive system of professionalized practices and attitudes. We know the psychological, social and political contexts into which their systems are projected must be negotiated, raising difficult questions about the sources of the meanings used to (i) construct and collect the data and (ii) deliver it back to those using it. Meanings can be communicated, though clearly not in the same way as data, but they can also be controlled to some extent by signalling or punishments and rewards. Managing meaning shapes the organization, its decision-making premises and behaviours, and the data being generated and used.

The most familiar way of controlling practice is via managerial direction, an appeal to the employee's own initiative and decision-making, by indicating the activity's purpose, so subordinating the analysis of practice to that of rational analysis. But practices can be controlled directly, for instance, by process instructions by funding or not funding projects, supplying equipment and resources, etc. Practice takes us instantly into a world of constraints, finite spaces, technological limits, frictions and transactions costs where the Second Law of Thermodynamics applies – and away from the abstract frictionless world of thought. We eventually understand practice by discovering how interacting with the world constrains our imagination.

With the separations between data meaning and practice in place we can see that each suggests a quite different theory of learning – more data is not the same as establishing or changing meanings – and neither is the same as creating a new practice. The role of management towards each is different. Data is only unproblematic when part of the realist position. Reality is presumed to exist so observations of it are relatively straightforward. Managers can initiate the discovery of data, and its collection, transportation and delivery. Meaning is more fundamental to the

K-type	Learning mechanisms	Managerial roles
Data		
Meaning		
Practice		

Figure 6.3   A new scope for KM?

idealist or interpretive position. Managers and others create meaning through acts of imagination, and then communicate it. Practice belongs in a third epistemology, one in which there are external and internal constraints that can be associated with the psychological world, as in the discussion above of the growth of consciousness, or the physical world, as in our concern with the Second Law of Thermodynamics, or in the social world, such as the Law. Managers can shape practice by communicating their thoughts and by their decision-making, but also by manipulating the constraints over which they have power. Perhaps we can fill out a table like that in Figure 6.3.

Most importantly, because data, meaning and practice derive from essentially incommensurable epistemologies, we see few obvious relationships between them; a theoretical and practical matter that tells us the kinds of problem our KM theory must address.

From the Knowledge We Have to the Knowledge We Haven't

At this point we might recall earlier comments about the difference between managing the knowledge we have – clearly the central theme in the KM literature – and a quite different but complementary conception of KM as dealing with the absence of knowledge. The first focuses on theorizing how to manage the organization's knowledge assets or processes to ensure the best outcomes – collect and deliver data, manage meaning, discover and transfer best practice. We shall see that the second plunges us into practice, and is more about identifying the acts of imagination and creativity that managers perform when confronting uncertainty, circumstances under which they have inadequate data or need to create meaning. This is the realm of heuristics rather than rationality (Simon, 1960).

Simon (1960, 1981, 1987, 1991, 1999) bade us pay close attention to these heuristics, rules which cannot be justified theoretically but deal effectively with the uncertainty and knowledge absences. This additional uncertainty-coping dimension illustrates KM's most fundamental novelty, its new balance between logical reasoning and imagination. This firmly distinguishes KM from the organization

Type of knowledge	Consciousness		
	Reason-dominated		Imagination-dominated
	Static	Dynamic	Dynamic
Data	Rational decision-making	Discovery and communication	Awareness
Meaning	Paradigms communicated through language, narrative or observation		Creating new meanings, paradigm shifts
Practice	Enacting established logical rules	Goal-oriented learning, evolving new rules	Explorative practice and the production of consciousness

Figure 6.4   A broader range for a new KM

sciences, since they mostly stand on assumptions about causality and rational decision-making. We also pick up the challenge Simon (1958) presented us with his concept of 'bounded rationality'. This is crucial since, as he noted, absent bounded rationality, there is little need for managers and none for an administrative science. Overall, then, the new parts of KM may be more to do with the bounds and constraints to rationality than with new versions of decision-making under certainty.

When it comes to understanding data, imagination is written out of the analysis as soon as we accept the realist definition of data as about a 'reality out there' that pre-exists our imagination. We assume we do not imagine data, rather that we observe it. It is objective by definition; and when absent we find it by making further observations of reality. Meaning, on the other hand, is a consequence of our imagination. It is not 'out there' and when absent we must create it. As soon as we eschew transcendentalism or Divine Insight – a considerable assumption, of course – we can no longer find meaning or purpose in the world; only reflections of our own meaning-making (Polanyi, 1959). The imagination in action may be more than our own, others may create meaning with or for us. Many theorists, following Durkheim and including Kuhn, suggest meaning-making is a collective project (Jones, 1986; Sandelands and Stablein, 1987). Finally we see practice is always unique, created afresh and constrained by the unique time–space situation in which it takes place.

This leads us towards a broader notion of KM (see Figure 6.4). We are familiar with the reason-dominated left side of Figure 6.4. But a radical theory of KM opens up the right-hand creative side as well. If this works it can take us far beyond the causality and control aspects of reason-dominated kinds of KM to cover the management or shaping of our acts of imagination. These cannot be made subject to predictive causal laws, so the analysis must focus on the constraints, bounds and limits to the imagination.

That imagination leads to new meanings is easy to grasp, though the ways in which these get warranted remain problematic, as noted above. Our empirical tradition focuses on practice, on doing experiments, ultimately prioritizing practice as the final source of meaning, and this is central to the radical constructivist epistemology we shall touch on next. It also reflects Wittgenstein's (1972) maxim that use determines meaning. We must see practice as inherently creative, for even when it seems just the enactment of a generalized decision its circumstances are unique. This creativity actually places practice beyond the bounds of complete rational analysis for that necessarily abstracts from the particular. There is an unbridgeable gap between anticipation and experience in that our models are always simplifications of the world rather than complete pictures (Tsoukas and Mylonopoulos, 2004a). Practice, on the other hand, takes place in a real world constrained by all its experienced complexity. Thus the idea of controlling practice by controlling the actor's decision-making can never be entirely effective because as we act our thinking selects only a sub-set of the world we experience.

There is also the related matter of coherence, whether it be of thought or of action. Uncertainties arise from lack of coherence as well as from lack of data. Rational decision-making requires a coherent model of the world. We cannot know whether the world is actually coherent, though realists assume it is. Our models of the world are coherent only because we select the variables that we can bring into our models – so we must start out by creating the meaning system that dictates what we select. The meaning system is prior to any data we have of the world – while at the same time we know the world can surprise us even as we do not 'know' what has happened. A tsunami happens, even though some understand it as the consequence of an under-sea earthquake while others see it as punishment from the gods. The point is that coherence is something we impose on our experience of the world. It is not a feature of the world in the sense of our finding it in the world for we never have such complete knowledge of the world. Practice, on the other hand, seems coherent as we experience it in context. There is an integrity and wholeness about our experience that is central to its immediacy and rawness. It is only when we reflect on our experience that we discover its many facets and implications as we try to fit it into the multiple dimensions of our identity – the many 'hats' that we wear in the world.

These comments about the coherence of experience begin to show how radical constructivism, as a third epistemology, might help us handle the theory of KM implied in Figure 6.4. But we also reconnect with a question that permeates the KM literature – the nature of tacit knowledge. As noted above, some see tacit knowledge as under-articulated knowledge of the same basic type as well-articulated explicit knowledge, that is it is equally in the mind but difficult to put into language and so communicate to others. Others see tacit knowledge as in a different domain altogether and point to embodied knowledge or practical skills e.g. (Blackler, 1995; Harper, 1987; Kusterer, 1978).

However, following Gourlay (2004), we suggest that what is tacit about all our knowledge, and remains inexplicable because it is the result of our creativity, is not so much its embodied dimension but the process of selection which, as we have seen above, must precede all coherent explicit knowledge. The strength of Polanyi's example of bicycle-riding is that both novice and expert experience the same context of activity and receive the same stimuli. But they differ radically in what they pay attention to; the novice does not know how to pay attention correctly to balance and hand motion, so mis-selecting from the various stimuli he/she is receiving. The expert has learned, through imaginative experiment or instruction, how to attend selectively and so construct a coherent and workable model of the situation. Likewise, expert radiographers see the same X-ray films as their novice colleagues, but know better what to pay attention to. In short, tacit knowledge is evidence of the human imaginative act, whether that be physical or mental. It is the coherence we put into the world as we make it sensible, and it is necessarily prior to and for ever distinct from our knowledge of the world. Without the tacit knowledge that we alone create we can have no explicit knowledge; indeed we cannot be conscious of the world. It is our attitude towards the world, which Polanyi (1959, 1962) illustrates, how we pay attention, and is thus closely integrated into our sense of identity.

Since tacit knowledge is not data about the world it is not contingent on our rationality, rather it is the other way around – what we take to be rationality is a consequence or evidence of our tacit knowledge. But the connection between tacit knowledge and practice is suggestive, for one way of explaining how we develop tacit knowledge is through practice, most particularly explorative practice, practice that is not the enactment of an idea, even planned discovery. Studies of the actual processes of science, of the experience of scientific work, suggest a great deal of it is explorative in this sense and not, as the rhetoric suggests, logically planned (Latour and Woolgar, 1986).

Here we turn the whole analytic schema upside down and instead of starting our theorizing at the top left corner of Figure 6.4, with rational thought, we start at the bottom right with raw practice. In philosophical terms we replace initial assumptions about rational man, *homo economicus* or *homo sapiens* with those of *homo ludens* (Huizinga, 1955) or *homo faber* (Bergson, 1983) or man the *bricoleur* (Brown and Duguid, 1998; Harper, 1987) – man who explores the world as a matter of practice and experience rather than intellectually through models of the world. We prioritize exploratory practice over thought and reasoning, and become exposed to being surprised by the world rather than protecting ourselves as we restrict what we can learn to knowledge gained by selecting and anticipating our experiences, which is what happens when we simply test out hypotheses.

On Radical Constructivism

Having sketched a scheme of KM that covers both rational analysis and imaginative practice which, at the same time, covers three types of knowledge, we can make some tentative remarks about the managerial implications and begin to wrap up the discussion. It is still not quite clear how we pull the cells of Figure 6.4 together, so bridging the various epistemologies. My argument is that a rich notion of practice helps us do this. We must approach practice in at least two ways (i) by treating it as the enactment of a goal-oriented cognition, or (ii) by understanding the constraints to explorative practice. The first prioritizes thought over action, in the second these are reversed. There are echoes of March's (1991) discussion of exploitation and exploration here, though this may be little more than a re-articulation of Kuhn's (1970) distinction between normal science and paradigm shifts or architectural versus radical change (Henderson and Clark, 1990); it does not turn critically on our notions of practice. However, explorative practice is essentially unplanned, with activity preceding analysis, though it is probably problemistic in the sense of being driven by the need to address some problems (March and Simon, 1958).

The second kind of practice is direct exploration of the context or medium itself, as opposed to an intellectual analysis of the potentialities derived from abstracted or codified models of the context of practice. It should not be confused with 'messing about' or 'tinkering' in the hope of turning up something interesting. To take Polanyi's example of bicycle-riding, explorative practice is not about the novice becoming an expert in the sense suggested by the Dreyfus (Dreyfus and Dreyfus, 1986) ladder of skill acquisition. Explorative practice is the generation of paradigm shifts in the domain of practice, about creating imaginative extensions that may lead to radically different patterns of practice. They change the discipline. Reg Harris and Lance Armstrong, for instance, both created transforming competitive cycling practices, forever changing their sport. How they did this is almost incomprehensible (or tacit) to ordinary cyclists. Because we do not understand it we assume they are doing what we are doing, but better. This, of course, is not the case. They are doing something quite different which sometime has something, but generally not all that much, to do with the equipment being used. This kind of exploration-driven shift in knowledge-as-practice is suggested by 'transformational' leadership or by firms 'reinventing' themselves when their original markets and lines of business disappear.

To grasp such breakthroughs one must have experienced the limits and constraints of the practice oneself. Musicians provide us some good examples. Haydn is considered to have changed classical music forever by inventing the string quartet, just as Hendrix changed the scope of electric guitar work. Most people, being outsiders, uncomprehendingly observe the new practice and sense something is different, but do not know the boundaries that have been transcended. Nor are such transformations mere happenstance. On the contrary, they are the outcomes of considerable imaginations confronting the constraints of the medium, which can only occur after prodigious disciplined effort. Yes, Armstrong trained and Hendrix practised – but they worked and thought extremely hard about what they were doing. Likewise, both Newton and Einstein remarked the transformations they generated came about only because they were able to focus their imaginations and carry the disciplinary constraints in question in their 'mind's eye' for months at a time.

The essential puzzle behind an epistemology of practice is the relationship proposed between practice and thinking. Absent any links we are unable to say anything about practice; we are condemned to observing it without comment. If the links are too close and determining, we need not observe practice – it can be collapsed into thinking. The rational decision-making model presumes practice is framed by thinking, to the extent that the practice can be fully explained by the decision-making model and its objective function. This immediately sets up the conflict between the realist and idealist positions because each offers a different source of meaning. We introduce Vygotsky's ideas to suggest that there are questions which cannot be resolved in this way. The key to understanding KM as a discipline, therefore, is not merely to see the discontinuity between the realist and idealist positions – between data and meaning – but also to unhook practice from rational decision-making as framed within either. In this sense, at its most powerful, KM becomes a critique of rational decision-making, and begins to follow through on Simon's critique. If this is supportable it has ramifications across the entire spectrum of organizational analysis and managerial theorizing.

What are we to say about the relationship between thought and practice? We have suggested radical constructivism gives us some useful clues. Similar to most philosophical positions there is variety here and many disagreements too. But a summary of key points might go like this. Rorty (1991) introduced the notion of 'anti-representationalism'. Both realists and idealists are focused on creating representations to use in meaningful statements, the former referring to the real as a warrant for the representation, the latter to their conceptualizing. Anti-representationalists consider such efforts misdirected. Instead they argue language should capture our experience of practice, hence provide a guide to further practice rather than discover anything about the reality that provides the practice's context. Reality is not 'out there', rather the only reality is our experience. That, and the way it interacts with our ideas, are all we have to go on – an epistemological position that goes back to Vico who argued in 1725 that we can only see what we have already created (von Glasersfeld, 2002).

The core axiom of radical constructivism is that we waste our time trying to 'represent' the 'out there' reality for it is forever unknown to us. But at the same time we cannot deny its impact on us. But we cannot understand this by making representations of that reality. Rather we must focus on modelling our experience of that external reality and using those models to direct our practice since it takes place within, and is bound by, that unknowable context. In spite of this attempt to find middle ground, radical constructivism always seems to be falling into one or other of the realist and idealist camps it opposes (Rasch, 2000). In one instant it seems like a re-articulation of idealism, in the next, of realism – an unfortunate overhang from our previous philosophizing, that seems constantly to snap us back to seeking representations and 'mental maps' of reality. There is a sense in which radical constructivism takes the Popperian use of 'temporary truths' to another level as it continues to waver between the realist and idealist positions (Rasch, 2000). Either position becomes increasingly temporary.

What does this mean in practice, so to speak? Pickering's analysis of the ways in which scientific explanations are developed is helpful for non-philosophers (Pickering, 1995). One way of summarizing this is to remind ourselves constantly that our language is rooted in our experience and has nothing to say about the way reality might or might not be. This sounds like idealism all over again, raising questions about how we avoid the slippery slope into anarchic relativism where things seem true simply because we say them. But this is where practice takes hold for it is contextualized or situated practice (Lave and Wenger, 1992; Scribner, 1984). The fundamental assumption under radical constructivism is that when we use our imaginings to guide our actions we run up against the world and may find things do not turn out as expected. We experience the world falsifying our practice, some-what along the lines of Popper's (1968) understanding of experimental evidence as falsifying our ideas. But in Popper's argument it is the representations of reality (hypotheses) that are being falsified. In radical constructivism it is our practices that are being falsified. To confuse the two is to slip back into realism. Our thinking presents us only with our experience, not with representations of the real or psychological context of our actions (von Glasersfeld, 2002).

The critical point is that radical constructivism survives the sceptical critique of the realist and idealist positions and allows the process of interacting with the world to constrain our imagination. Social constructionists presume the final constraint on the imagination is the given-ness of the social process itself (Gergen, 1994). In addition to its acceptance of the social and psychological constraints, radical constructivism allows the physical (non-perceptual) limits over our actions to impress themselves onto our experience without, at the same time, insisting we build representations of the physical world. We can know surely our attempts to make pigs fly will come to naught without having the aerodynamics or a Holy Book to explain it. Again, the crucial point is that in a radical constructivist epistemology some forms of explo-rative practice precede thought in ways that complement the Vygotskian arguments presented earlier, and it is this that helps us drive the crucial wedge between thought and practice.

These epistemological comments may not seem all that productive, but they matter hugely when it comes to grasping the differences between data, meaning and practice, and between rational decision-making and using our imaginations – and it is these differences that comprise the core of our theory of KM. We have seen above that data and meaning are different and essentially incommensurate aspects of 'information'. But as we bring a richer notion of practice into the discus-sion the emphasis shifts from trying to pull together coherent cognitive models of the world in which we want to act – impossible when saddled with incommensu-rable epistemologies – to trying to create a coherent practice that can be conducted in its unrepresented and only experienced context.

It seems curious we are so trained to look for coherence in our intellectualizing and world views when we are perfectly comfortable without the same sense of coherence in the ways in which we act in the world. We refer to the many different 'hats' we wear as we present different faces to the world according to our assess-ment of the situation. We accept that we have multiple personalities or identities, and a complex inventory of behaviours corresponding to each one. Identity and behaviour are mirrors of each other, for it is the practice that shapes the thinking as much as the other way around, as Vygotsky showed us. This makes us aware that the most profound practice of all is our ongoing struggle to develop and sustain these multiple identities. Each of our identities reflects choices about, and our attitudes towards, our social and psychological context, each is the locus for the power experienced or exercised in this context, and each is consequently the locus of emotion as we act out our identity (Nussbaum, 2001).

Conclusion

The core argument of this chapter is that my theory of KM opens up new ways of understanding organizations and their management. The justification for the epistemological discussions above is the need to illustrate how it does this by confronting rather than suppressing the distinctions between data, meaning and practice. The theory also confronts the distinction between the mental acts of rational decision-making and imagination. Much of what is different and new is that these differences are driving the theory, for without them there is no theory. The underlying agenda, of course, is to critique the rational decision-making model on which so much of our analysis is grounded and which suppresses the discussion of uncertainty, creativity, constraints, power and emotion. As we progress from the top-left corner of Figure 6.4 to its bottom-right corner we move in a direction that takes us from abstractions about management towards their on-going sense of practice.

Driving us in this direction is the fact that our classroom conceit that the appropriate information is available for us to think through to the optimal decision is almost never validated. Our first awareness that we must leave the Eden-like top-left comfort zone comes when we realize we cannot make sense of the data. We have a meaning problem and cast about for alternative meanings. Not finding any, perhaps, we look for 'expert practitioners', people who can deal with our problem without knowing how to explain what they are doing. All this, of course, is about our shrinking from using or considering imagination and creativity. We fear the loss of control when we hand over to 'creative types'. So the other side of KM is precisely about managers' imaginative and creative practices as they respond to uncertainties and their lack of knowledge. Creativity is in play all the time in organizational life and the suggestion that everyone is always being rational and following rules is patently ridiculous. The essential poverty of managerial and organizational theorizing is that it has refused to leave its comfort zone at the top-left of Figure 6.4.

Conversely, there are many practitioner-oriented writers anxious to tell us how to 'release the hidden energy of our employees in the pursuit of sustainable competitive advantage'. They tell us little, of course, except that there is a huge market for some ideas about how to escape the bounds of rationality in an indirectly controllable manner. In this chapter I argue creativity itself cannot be part of a theory of knowledge management until we can either explain it with a causal (rational) model – a contradiction in terms – or, and this is the important novelty, showing something about how our imaginations are constrained by choices of context and boundaries.

When Simon (1958) advanced his theory of bounded rationality he was ambiguous on its causes, but he was also thinking as a psychologist. On the one hand, he pointed out both our limited computational abilities and our limited information gathering capabilities. In this note we supplement rather than ignore the idea of psychological constraints on the imagination. The popularization of the inherently Vygotskian work of Lave and Scribner as 'communities of practice' shows the widespread acceptance of social constructionism (Cole and Scribner, 1974; Rogoff and Lave, 1984; Scribner, 1984; Tobach et al., 1997). The imagination is clearly constrained in the context of shared practice, indeed the essence of the idea of a community of practice is agreement on context, not on concepts or purpose (Amin and Cohendet, 2004; Knorr-Cetina, 1999). But nothing in the theorizing about social constraints is able to escape the realist's criticisms of idealist epistemologies and their attachment to the modernist project of finding causal mechanisms for all phenomena. The importance of the radical constructivist approach is that it is able to bring in constraints arising from the non-social world that are not subject to these charges of relativism; but this may seem too esoteric a point. What is key is to see, paradoxically, that there is seldom any explicit theory of practice in the burgeoning 'community of practice' literature (Wenger et al., 2002).

It is important to point out that other authors have been working along similar lines though without explicitly adopting the same epistemological position, but they provide interesting insights into the ideas explored in this note. Carlile (2003, 2004), for example, sets up an important three-way discussion based on realist, idealist, and pragmatist positions. Thiétart (2001) does something similar, exploring organizational science's methodologies and differentiating its positivist, interpretive and constructionist paradigms. But neither of these authors develops the analysis of knowledge-as-practice suggested here.

It is also important to point to one part of the KM literature we seem to have ignored completely; that about the ownership of organizational knowledge (Nonaka and Teece, 2001; Teece, 2000). One of the penalties for using the term knowledge is that it is so expansive – indeed it can embrace everything known, imagined, or sought after. The ownership discussion is not, of course, about knowledge management at all, as conceived in this note. It is an exploration of the limits of the institutional practices prevalent in capitalist society. It is about how data, meaning, and practices can be brought under the existing property-rights laws which underpin our version of democratic capitalism. We know that as technologies change the boundaries between what can or cannot be so captured change too. Should genomic knowledge be privatized? Can places in space, off the Earth's surface be made private? Can there be legally binding agrements that give firms ownership of all of the fruits of their employees' imaginings? The confusion arises because we think ownership resolves the problems of management whereas, of course, it only initiates them.

The practical implications of this kind of rich theorizing about KM are legion. First, the new way of thinking lets managers distinguish between decision-making under conditions adequately close to certainty, when they have high confidence

	Managing what we have	**Responding to what we lack**
Data	Rational decision-making	Data collection and systematic discovery
Meaning	Communicating meaning	Creating meaning and heuristics
Practice	Executing decisions	Explorative practice

Figure 6.5 Overall KM schema

that causal models can be applied, and that they know the meaning of the data available, and the 'wicked' situations when such confidence is absent (Churchman, 1967). Working managers readily understand the retreat from high confidence in data to puzzling about meaning, and about the need to communicate the new meanings on which they settle. This is KM and often the core of their strategizing. The circumstances may require they retreat even further, forced into categorizing the on-going 'buzzing booming confusion' they are experiencing and evolving organizational routines and managerial heuristics – this is KM too. Pressed even further by their knowledge shortages, they must make recourse to their sense of identity by projecting themselves into the situation, making the selections which seem to others to indicate their possessing tacit managerial skills. This is KM too, and if we can make this new kind of KM work, it may well help narrow the widening gap between organizational theorists and practising managers, giving them deeper insight into their essentially creative work.

By way of summary, we can simplify Figure 6.4 by stressing the distinction between managing the knowledge we have, and managing the consequences of not having appropriate knowledge (Figure 6.5). The left-hand column of Figure 6.5 stresses thought and rational approaches. The right-hand column stresses creative practice as the visceral and natural response to uncertainty and thus source of all human knowledge. In the latter case, after evolving successful practice we may codify it into heuristics. Thus we attach meaning to our practice and develop language to enable us to collect and analyze what we call data. When we start with data and rational decision-making in mind, we start at the top left of the matrix. When that fails, because we lack sufficient data we collect additional data, or create it through systematic scientific practice. On other occasions we see we lack the ability to make sense of the data and we look for new patterns of meaning. Sometimes these are available as alternative views. On other occasions we have to create anew. In this way, under the press of uncertainty, we move away from the top left and down towards the bottom right. Eventually we have neither data nor meaning and we confront the context of our being and activity directly. This chapter has assumed that to be human is to be able to respond to such total uncertainty with explorative practice – even though we may have learned, in our hyper-rationalist culture, that we must only talk of this as 'play' (Huizinga, 1955).

References

Abbott, A. (1988) *The System of Professions: An Essay on the Division of Expert Labor*. Chicago, IL: University of Chicago Press.

Ackoff, R.L. (1989) 'From data to wisdom', *Journal of Applied Systems Analysis*, 16: 3–9.

Alvesson, M. and Kärreman, D. (2001) 'Odd couple: making sense of the curious concept of knowledge management', *Journal of Management Studies*, 38(7): 995.

Amin, A. and Cohendet, P. (2004) *Architectures of Knowledge: Firms, Capabilities, and Communities*. Oxford: Oxford University Press.

Anderson, J.R. (1983) *The Architecture of Cognition*. Cambridge, MA: Harvard University Press.

Argyris, C. (1982) *Reasoning, Learning and Action: Individual and Organizational*. San Francisco, CA: Jossey-Bass Publishers.

Awad, E.M. and Ghaziri, H.M. (2003) *Knowledge Management*. Upper Saddle River, NJ: Prentice-Hall.

Bales, R.F. (1950) *Interaction Process Analysis*. Cambridge, MA: Addison-Wesley.

Beerli, A.J., Falk, S. and Diemers, D. (eds) (2003) *Knowledge Management and Networked Environments: Leveraging Intellectual Capital in Virtual Business Communities*. New York: AMACOM.

Bergeron, B. (2003) *Essentials of Knowledge Management*. Hoboken, NJ: John Wiley & Sons.

Bergson, H. (1983) *Creative Evolution*. New York: Rowman & Littlefield.

Blackler, F. (1995) 'Knowledge, knowledge work and organizations: an overview and interpretations', *Organization Studies*, 16(6): 1021–46.

Blackler, F., Crump, N. and McDonald, S. (2000) 'Organizing processes in complex activity networks', *Organization*, 7(2): 277.

Boisot, M. (1998) *Knowledge Assets: Securing Competitive Advantage in the Information Economy*. Oxford: Oxford University Press.

Bourdieu, P. (1977) *Outline of a Theory of Practice*. Cambridge: Cambridge University Press.

Brown, J.S., Denning, S., Groh, K. and Prusak, L. (2005) *Storytelling in Organizations: Why Storytelling is Transforming 21st Century Organizations and Management*. Burlington, MA: Elsevier Butterworth-Heinemann.

Brown, J.S. and Duguid, P. (1998) 'Organizing knowledge', *California Management Review*, 40(3): 90–111.

Brown, J.S. and Duguid, P. (2001) 'Knowledge and organization: a social-practice perspective', *Organization Science*, 12(2): 198–213.

Caine, R.N. and Caine, G. (1991) *Making Connections: Teaching and the Human Brain*. Alexandria, VA: ASCD.

Carlile, P.R. (2003) 'A pragmatic view of knowledge and boundaries: boundary objects in new product development', *Organization Science*, 13(4): 442–55.

Carlile, P.R. (2004) 'Transferring, translating, and transforming: an integrative framework for managing knowledge across boundaries', *Organization Science*, 15(5): 555–68.

Chi, M., Glaser, R. and Farr, M.J. (eds) (1988) *The Nature of Expertise*. Hillsdale, NJ: Lawrence Erlbaum Associates.

Choo, C.W. and Bontis, N. (eds) (2002) *The Strategic Management of Intellectual Capital and Organizational Knowledge*. New York: Oxford University Press.

Churchman, C.W. (1967) 'Wicked problems', *Management Science*, 4(14): 141.

Cohen, M.D. and Sproull, L.S. (eds) (1996) *Organizational Learning*. Thousand Oaks, CA: SAGE Publications.

Cohen, W.M. and Levinthal, D.A. (1990) 'Absorptive capacity: a new perspective on learning and innovation', *Administrative Science Quarterly*, 35: 128–52.

Cole, M. and Scribner, S. (1974) *Culture and Thought: A Psychological Introduction*. New York: John Wiley & Sons.

de Certeau, M. (1984) *The Practice of Everyday Life*. Berkeley, CA: University of California Press.

Delanty, G. (1997) *Social Science: Beyond Constructivism and Realism*. Minneapolis, MN: University of Minnesota Press.

Dougherty, D. (1992) 'A practice-centered model of organizational renewal through product innovation', *Strategic Management Journal*, 13 (Special Issue Summer): 77–92.

Dreyfus, H.L. and Dreyfus, S.E. (1986) *Mind over Machine: The Power of Human Intuition and Expertise in the Era of the Computer*. New York: Free Press.

Drucker, P.F. (1988) 'The coming of the new organization', *Harvard Business Review*, 66(1): 45–53.

Easterby-Smith, M. and Lyles, M.A. (eds) (2003) *The Blackwell Handbook of Organizational Learning and Knowledge Management*. Malden, MA: Blackwell.

Firestone, J.M. and McElroy, M.W. (2003) *Key Issues in the New Knowledge Management*. Burlington, MA: Butterworth-Heinemann.

Gergen, K.J. (1994) *Toward Transformation in Social Knowledge*, 2nd edn. London: SAGE Publications.

Gherardi, S. (2000) 'Practice-based theorizing on learning and knowing in organizations', *Organization*, 7(2): 211.

Gourlay, S. (2004) 'Knowing as semiosis: steps towards a reconceptualisation of "tacit knowledge"', in H. Tsoukas and N. Mylonopoulos (eds), *Organizations as Knowledge Systems*. Basingstoke: Palgrave Macmillan. pp. 86–105.

Grant, R.M. (2003) 'The knowledge-based view of the firm', in D.O. Faulkner and A. Campbell (eds), *The Oxford Handbook of Strategy*, Vol. 1. Oxford: Oxford University Press. pp. 197–221.

Gray, P.H. and Meister, D.B. (2003) 'Introduction: fragmentation and integration in knowledge management research', *Information, Technology and People*, 16(3): 259–65.

Gray, P.H. and Meister, D.B. (2004) 'Knowledge sourcing effectiveness', *Management Science*, 50(6): 821–34.

Groff, T.R. and Jones, T.P. (2003) *Introduction to Knowledge Management: KM in Business*. Burlington, MA: Butterworth-Heinemann.

Habermas, J. (1984) *Theory of Communicative Action*, trans. T. McCarthy. Boston, MA: Beacon Press.

Harper, D.A. (1987) *Working Knowledge: Skill and Community in a Small Shop*. Chicago, IL: University of Chicago Press.

Henderson, R.M. and Clark, K.B. (1990) 'Architectural innovation: the reconfiguration of existing product technologies', *Administrative Science Quarterly*, 35(1): 9.

Hislop, D. (2002) 'Mission impossible? Communicating and sharing knowledge via information technology', *Journal of Information Technology*, 17(3): 165.

Hogarth, R.M. (1980) *Judgement and Choice: The Psychology of Decision*. New York: John Wiley & Sons.

Holsapple, C.W. (ed.) (2003) *Handbook on Knowledge Management*. Berlin: Springer-Verlag.

Huizinga, J. (1955) *Homo Ludens: A Study of the Play-Element in Culture*, trans. R.F.C. Hull. Boston, MA: Beacon Press.

James, W. (1950) *The Principles of Psychology*, Vols. I & II. New York: Dover Publications.

Jones, R.A. (1986) *Emile Durkheim: An Introduction to Four Major Works*. Newbury Park, CA: SAGE.

Kahneman, D. and Tversky, A. (1979) 'Prospect theory: an analysis of decisions under risk', *Econometrica*, 47: 262–91.

Kalling, T. (2003) 'Knowledge management and the occasional links with performance', *Journal of Knowledge Management*, 7(3): 67–81.

Knorr-Cetina, K. (1999) *Epistemic Cultures: How the Sciences Make Knowledge*. Cambridge, MA: Harvard University Press.

Kuhn, T.S. (1970) *The Structure of Scientific Revolutions*, 2nd edn. Chicago, IL: University of Chicago Press.

Kusterer, K.C. (1978) *Know-How on the Job: The Important Working Knowledge of the 'Unskilled' Workers*. Boulder, CO: Westview Press.

Lakatos, I. and Feyerabend, P. (1999). *For and Against Method*. Chicago, IL: University of Chicago Press.

Latour, B. and Woolgar, S. (1986) *Laboratory Life: The Construction of Scientific Facts*. Princeton, NJ: Princeton University Press.

Lave, J. and Wenger, E. (1992) *Situated Learning: Legitimate Peripheral Participation*. New York: Cambridge University Press.

Liebowitz, J. (2001) *Knowledge Management: Learning from Knowledge Engineering*. Boca Raton, FL: CRC Press.

Luhmann, N. (1995) *Social Systems*, trans. J. Bednarz and D. Baecker. Stanford, CA: Stanford University Press.

March, J.G. (1991) 'Exploration and exploitation in organizational learning', *Organization Science*, 2: 71–87.

March, J.G. and Simon, H.A. (1958) *Organizations*. New York: John Wiley.

Marren, P. (2003) 'Where did all the knowledge go?', *Journal of Business Strategy*, 24(3): 5.

Nelson, R.R. and Winter, S.G. (1982) *An Evolutionary Theory of Economic Change*. Cambridge, MA: Belknap Press.

Nicolini, D., Gherardi, S. and Yanow, D. (eds) (2003) *Knowing in Organizations: A Practice-Based Approach*. Armonk, NY: M.E. Sharpe.

Nonaka, I. and Takeuchi, H. (1995) *The Knowledge-Creating Company: How Japanese Companies Create the Dynamics of Innovation*. New York: Oxford University Press.

Nonaka, I. and Teece, D.J. (eds) (2001) *Managing Industrial Knowledge: Creation, Transfer and Utilization*. London: SAGE.

Nussbaum, M.C. (2001) *Upheavals of Thought: The Intelligence of Emotions*. Cambridge: Cambridge University Press.

Parsons, T. (1968) *The Structure of Social Action: A Study in Social Theory with Special Reference to a Group of Recent European Writers*. New York: The Free Press.

Piaget, J. (1972) *Psychology and Epistemology: Towards a Theory of Knowledge*. London: Allen Lane.

Pickering, A. (1995) *The Mangle of Practice: Time, Agency, and Science*. Chicago, IL: University of Chicago Press.

Polanyi, M. (1959) *The Study of Man*. Chicago, IL: The University of Chicago Press.

Polanyi, M. (1962) *Personal Knowledge: Towards a Post-Critical Philosophy*. Chicago, IL: University of Chicago Press.

Popper, K. (1968) *The Logic of Scientific Discovery*. London: Hutchinson.

Rasch, W. (2000) *Niklas Luhmann's Modernity: The Paradoxes of Differentiation*. Stanford, CA: Stanford University Press.

Reich, R.B. (1992) *The Work of Nations: Preparing Ourselves for 21st Century Capitalism*. New York: Vintage Books.

Rogoff, B. and Lave, J. (eds) (1984) *Everyday Cognition: Its Development in Social Context*. Cambridge, MA: Harvard University Press.

Rorty, R. (1991) *Objectivity, Relativism, and Truth: Philosophical Papers, Vol. 1*. Cambridge: Cambridge University Press.

Roy, D. (1952) 'Quota restriction and gold-bricking in a machine shop', *American Journal of Sociology*, 67: 427–42.

Ruggles, R. (1998) 'The state of the notion: knowledge management in practice', *California Management Review*, 40(3): 80.

Rumizen, M.C. (2002) *The Complete Idiot's Guide to Knowledge Management*. Indianapolis, IN: Alpha Books.

Ryle, G. (1949) *The Concept of Mind*. London: Hutchinson.

Sandelands, L.E. and Stablein, R.E. (1987) 'The concept of organization mind', in S. Bacharach and N. DiTomaso (eds), *Research in the Sociology of Organizations*, Vol. 5. Greenwich, CT: JAI Press Inc. pp. 135–61.

Scarbrough, H. (ed.) (1996) *The Management of Expertise*. Basingstoke: Macmillan Press.

Scribner, S. (1984) 'Studying working intelligence', in B. Rogoff and J. Lave (eds) *Everyday Cognition: Its Development in Social Context*. Cambridge, MA: Harvard University Press. pp. 9–40.

Sharp, D. (2003) 'Knowledge management today: challenges and opportunities', *Information Systems Management*, 20(2): 32.

Simon, H.A. (1958) *Administrative Behavior: A Study of Decision-Making Processes in Administrative Organization*, 2nd edn. New York: Macmillan.

Simon, H.A. (1960) *The New Science of Management Decision*. New York: Harper & Row.

Simon, H.A. (1981) *The Sciences of the Artificial*, 2nd edn. Cambridge, MA: MIT Press.

Simon, H.A. (1987) 'Making management decisions: the role of intuition and emotion', *Academy of Management Executive*, 1: 57–64.

Simon, H.A. (1991) 'Bounded rationality and organizational learning', *Organization Science*, 2(1): 125–34.

Simon, H.A. (1999) 'The many shapes of knowledge', *Revue d'Economie Industrielle*, 88(2e): 23–39.

Skinner, A. (2001) 'Adam Smith, the philosopher and the porter', in P.L. Porta, R. Scazzieri and A. Skinner (eds), *Knowledge, Social Institutions and the Division of Labour*. Cheltenham: Edward Elgar. pp. 35–51.

Skinner, B.F. (1953) *Science and Human Behavior*. New York: Macmillan Free Press.

Stainton, R.J. (ed.) (2000) *Perspectives in the Philosophy of Language: A Concise Anthology*. Peterborough, Ont: Broadview Press.

Sternberg, R.J., Forsythe, G.B., Hedlund, J., Horvath, J.A., Wagner, R.K., Williams, W.H., Snook, S.A., and Grigorenko, E. (2000) *Practical Intelligence in Everyday Life*. Cambridge: Cambridge University Press.

Storey, J. and Barnett, E. (2000) 'Knowledge management initiatives: learning from failure', *Journal of Knowledge Management*, 4(2): 145.

Teece, D.J. (2000) *Managing Intellectual Capital: Organizational, Strategic, and Policy Dimensions*. Oxford: Oxford University Press.

Teece, D.J. (2003) 'Knowledge and competence as strategic assets', in C.W. Holsapple (ed.), *Handbook on Knowledge Management*, Vol. 1. Berlin: Springer-Verlag. pp. 129–52.

Tharp, R.G. and Gallimore, R. (1988) *Rousing Minds to Life: Teaching, Learning, and Schooling in Social Context*. Cambridge: Cambridge University Press.

Thiétart, R.-A. (ed.) (2001) *Doing Management Research: A Comprehensive Guide*. London: SAGE Publications.

Tiwana, A. (2002) *The Knowledge Management Toolkit: Orchestrating IT, Strategy, and Knowledge Platforms*, 2nd edn. Upper Saddle River, NJ: Prentice-Hall.

Tobach, E., Falmagne, R.J., Parlee, M.B., Martin, L.M.W. and Kapelman, A.S. (eds) (1997) *Mind and Social Practice: Selected Writings of Sylvia Scribner*. Cambridge: Cambridge University Press.

Tsoukas, H. and Mylonopoulos, N. (2004a) 'Introduction: what does it mean to view organizations as knowledge systems', in H. Tsoukas and N. Mylonopoulos (eds), *Organizations as Knowledge Systems*. Basingstoke: Palgrave Macmillan. pp. 1–26.

Tsoukas, H. and Mylonopoulos, N. (eds) (2004b) *Organizations as Knowledge Systems: Knowledge, Learning and Dynamic Capabilities*. Basingstoke: Palgrave Macmillan.

Tsoukas, H. and Vladimirou, E. (2001) 'What is organizational knowledge?', *Journal of Management Studies*, 38(7): 973.

Turner, S. (1994) *The Social Theory of Practices: Tradition, Tacit Knowledge, and Presuppositions*. Chicago, IL: University of Chicago Press.

von Glasersfeld, E. (2002) *Radical Constructivism*. London: Routledge/Falmer.

Vygotsky, L.S. (1978) *Mind in Society: The Development of Higher Psychological Processes*. Cambridge, MA: Harvard University Press.

Weick, K.E. (1995) *Sensemaking in Organizations*. Thousand Oaks, CA: SAGE Publications.

Weick, K.E. and Roberts, K.H. (1993) 'Collective mind in organizations: heedful interrelating on flight decks', *Administrative Science Quarterly*, 38: 357–81.

Wenger, E., McDermott, R., and Snyder, W.M. (2002) *Cultivating Communities of Practice: A Guide to Managing Knowledge*. Boston, MA: Harvard Business School Press.

Wittgenstein, L. (1972) *On Certainty*, trans. G.E.M. Anscombe and G.H. von Wright. New York: Harper & Row.

Wurman, R.S. (1989) *Information Anxiety: What To Do When Information Doesn't Tell You What You Need to Know*. New York: Bantam Books.

PART II: KNOWING IN PRACTICE

7 Deep Smarts

Dorothy Leonard and Walter Swap

Your best employees' deepest knowledge can't be transferred onto a series of PowerPoint slides or downloaded into a data repository. It has to be passed on in person – slowly, patiently and systematically.

When a person sizes up a complex situation and comes to a rapid decision that proves to be not just good but brilliant, you think, 'That was smart.' After you've watched him do this a few times, you realize you're in the presence of something special. It's not raw brainpower, though that helps. It's not emotional intelligence, either, though that, too, is often involved. It's deep smarts, the stuff that produces that mysterious quality, good judgment. Those who have deep smarts can see the whole picture and yet zoom in on a specific problem others haven't been able to diagnose. Almost intuitively, they can make the right decision, at the right level, with the right people. The manager who understands when and how to move into a new international market, the executive who knows just what kind of talk to give when her organization is in crisis, the technician who can track a product failure back to an interaction between independently produced elements – these are people whose knowledge would be hard to purchase on the open market. Their insight is based more on know-how than on facts; it comprises a system view as well as expertise in individual areas. Deep smarts are not philosophical – they're not 'wisdom' in that sense – but they're as close to wisdom as business gets.

Throughout your organization, there are people with deep smarts. Their judgment and knowledge – both explicit and tacit – are stored in their heads and hands. Their knowledge is essential. The organization cannot progress without it. You will be a more effective manager if you understand what deep smarts are, how they are cultivated, and how they can be transferred from one person to another.

Very few organizations manage this asset well, perhaps because it's difficult to pin down and measure. Such neglect is risky. Individuals develop practical, often organization-specific expertise over the course of many years but can walk out the door in only a minute, taking their smarts with them. As the baby-boom-retirement tsunami approaches, lots of valuable employees and leaders will do precisely that. By 2006, for example, half of NASA's workforce will be eligible for retirement. It's not easy to harvest future retirees' knowledge, since much of it depends on context.

Source: D. Leonard and W. Swap (2004) 'Deep smarts', *Harvard Business Review*, September Issue: 88–97. Edited version.

Those with deep smarts know your business, your customers and your product lines, both overall and in depth. And much of their insight is neither documented nor even articulated. You may not know you have lost it until you feel the cold breezes of ignorance blowing through the cracks in your product or service architecture.

Smaller-scale losses occur when employees with deep smarts are transferred to new locations, functions, or roles. A marketing director we know was promoted to a general management position, which encompassed new functions and required new skills. Her predecessor was scheduled to be on a plane to take a new position in Thailand within two days of the promotion, so she needed to learn about engineering, manufacturing, finance and sales – fast. She couldn't possibly pick up the necessary skills in such a short time, but her superiors didn't even consider the costs of forcing her to muddle through on her own. Much of her predecessor's knowledge was lost.

When veterans leave, it is painful to lose strategic capabilities partly because growing them in the first place is extraordinarily challenging. Deep smarts are experience based. They can't be produced overnight or imported readily, as many companies pursuing a new strategy have discovered to their dismay. But with the right techniques, this sort of knowledge can be taught – if a company is willing to invest. Brad Anderson, the CEO of Best Buy, recently decided that the future success of his company depended on building an internal capability to innovate continuously. His employees were bright, hardworking and terrific at delivering on set goals, but innovation had never been part of their job. Exhortation alone would not change the DNA of the organization. Anderson needed to have some deep smarts about the innovation process transferred into the company. He hired the consulting firm Strategos to coach a cohort of employees through a six-month innovation journey. He hoped participants would gain enough experience to start embedding innovative practices throughout the organization.

Best Buy's deliberate decision to build company-wide expertise is unusual. In most organizations, deep smarts develop more by chance than by intent – and often in spite of management practices rather than because of them. Leaders toss people willy-nilly into new situations, incurring the costs of trial-and-error learning instead of those associated with more carefully planned transitions. But it is neither effective nor efficient to cultivate experience-based know-how in such an ad hoc fashion or to rely on a company's existing processes for transferring knowledge. Most organizational practices are not grounded in a fundamental understanding of how people learn. Furthermore, most companies' training and development programs are designed to transfer explicit technical or managerial knowledge – but not deep smarts.

We learned to appreciate the importance of deep smarts when we studied how novices acquire complex managerial skills. Over two years, we conducted research at 35 start-up companies in the United States and Asia, looking most closely at how experienced coaches helped novice entrepreneurs. We also examined a number of mature organizations, including Jet Propulsion Laboratory in Pasadena, California and Best Buy, in which managers were struggling with how to cultivate business wisdom. We interviewed more than 200 people (including each of the novice entrepreneurs and their coaches) twice, a year apart; sat in on dozens of meetings; shadowed one experienced leader as he made rounds to various protégés in India; and reviewed scores of videotapes made by people undergoing the intensive knowledge transfer effort at Best Buy. In the following pages, we draw on this field research to illustrate how organizations can develop and sustain profound institutional knowledge among their employees.

How Did He *Do* That?

Let's look in particular at two examples of deep smarts – one technical and the other managerial.

In the 1980s, two companies were competing for a multibillion-dollar, decades-long government contract for tactical missiles. Neither had a performance advantage. The stalemate was broken by a scientist in one of the companies who was not a member of the project team. His reputation as a technical wizard (based on more than 20 years of experience developing missiles) was such that when he called a meeting of the primary project participants, they all came. For several hours, he enthralled them with a detailed proposal for design changes that he had worked out over a single week of dedicated effort. Without notes, he walked them through the redesign of an entire weapon. To put the extensive software, wiring and hardware changes he suggested into production, as many as 400 people would have to work full-time for up to a year and a half – but the expert's audience saw immediately that the modifications would create tremendous competitive advantage. His proposal precipitated a frenzy of activity, and his company won the contract. More than 20 years later, it is still reaping the harvest sown by this man with deep smarts.

Deep smarts are most easily recognized when, as in the previous example, they are based on technical knowledge. Managerial deep smarts are harder to identify, but we know that people who have them are compelling leaders. Take the case of a CEO who, in an unusual reversal of roles, had to talk his board of directors out of allowing the company to miss its earnings commitment. In early 1997, Intuit had just sold off its bill-paying operations. The board met to consider a new strategic direction. Because revenues were down, the sentiment around the boardroom table was that the company would have to miss its earnings commitments not only for that quarter but for the foreseeable future. Board members were further resigned to a drop in stock price when the earnings were announced.

CEO Bill Campbell argued passionately against this fatalistic viewpoint. Wall Street analysts, he said, had already discounted the slower growth and the resulting decline in the top line. Lower revenues would not hurt the stock price. But deliberately deciding midway through the quarter to miss earnings was contrary to good management practices. Perhaps even more important, Campbell pointed out, if the stock dropped, employee options would be worthless – and some critical individuals might well leave the company. Such defections could hurt Intuit even more than the financial blow per se. It was pure baloney that they could not make the bottom line! He knew how to cut costs – and where to start.

The board members were persuaded by Campbell, and the next few months proved him right. Managers cut expenses and hit their quarterly financial targets, and the stock stayed steady. The course set out in the board meeting was successful for Intuit, and Campbell's promise to employees that the stock would double within a year was fulfilled. What smarts did Campbell have that allowed him to make the right decision – and to sway his board? He knew, of course, the details of his company's operations well enough to pinpoint areas for potential cost cutting. But he also understood the big picture, the financial environment within which he operated; he knew how resilient Intuit could be and how to release the company's untapped energies. He could foresee both Wall Street's reactions and those of his employees. And finally, he understood group dynamics and the personalities of his board members well enough to offer persuasive arguments.

Both the missile expert and Bill Campbell demonstrated an ability to do systems thinking *and* to dive into the details. The former, who redesigned a whole weapon by himself, knew a lot about each piece of software and hardware – but also about how they had to interact and which parts might need to be suboptimized in order to make the whole system perform better. Campbell could pull operational details about his company out of his head, but he also was emotionally intelligent about his organization as a collection of people and understood the larger financial milieu in which Intuit functioned.

The Science behind Deep Smarts

Experience is the obvious reason that such deeply knowledgeable individuals make swift, smart decisions. We would all rather fly with a pilot who has taken off, flown, and (especially) landed in all kinds of extreme weather than with one who has always enjoyed smooth conditions. Similarly, if we're about to go under anesthesia, we don't want to hear the surgeon exclaim, 'Wow – never seen one of *these* before!' And when launching a new product, we would prefer a boss who understands design, marketing and manufacturing over one who sees the world through only one lens. But what is it about experience that speakers separates from experts?

Think about something you are really, really good at – chess or cooking or interviewing job candidates. Chances are, if you are not just competent, but truly expert, it took 10 years or more to develop that expertise – in which time you've come across countless different situations. With so many of them under your belt, you have likely found some common ground and discovered a few rules of thumb that usually work: 'Control the center of the board' in chess, for instance, or 'Err on the side of letting people go early rather than late' in management. However, as an expert, you have the perspective to go beyond generalizations and respond to unusual situations. You know when facile rules don't apply, because you've seen so many exceptions. When confronted with a setback or a surprise, you can modify your course of action by combining elements from your menu of familiar options. In short, you can exploit an extensive *experience repertoire*.

Experts who encounter a wide variety of situations over many years accumulate a storehouse of knowledge and, with it, the ability to reason swiftly and without a lot of conscious effort. Those with keen managerial or technical intuition can rapidly determine whether current cases fit any patterns that have emerged in the past; they're also adept at coherently (though not always consciously) assembling disparate elements into a whole that makes sense. They can identify both trends and anomalies that would escape the notice of less-experienced individuals. When you ask your financial wizard how she decided so quickly that there was something wrong with the numbers on a page, she may not be able to tell you exactly how she homed in on the odd figure. In fact, when asked to explain a decision, experts often cannot re-create all the pathways their brains checked out and so cannot give a carefully reasoned answer. They chalk up to gut *feel* what is really a form of gut *knowledge*.

Of course, the experts aren't always right. Their confidence can lead to myopia or arrogance, blinding them to truly novel solutions or causing them to reject contributions from others. They can underestimate the extent to which knowledge is actually a set of beliefs and assumptions. When a physician confidently prescribes an acid suppressant for a woman who is in fact having a heart attack, not indigestion, he may be fitting her symptoms into a schema built on research about men. No chest pains–ergo, no heart attack. Only as research reveals that women's heart attack symptoms differ from men's, and as medicine builds enough knowledge to characterize these differences, will the physician be prepared to recognize the danger of his snap judgment.

Making Sure the Catcher Is Ready Before You Pitch

Many times in our lives, we need either to transfer our knowledge to someone else (a child, a junior colleague, a peer) or to access bits of wisdom accumulated in someone else's cranium. But before we can even begin to plan such a transfer, we must understand how our brains process incoming information.

What we already have in our heads determines how we assimilate new experiences. Without receptors – hooks on which to hang new information – we may not even perceive and process the information. It's like being sent boxes of documents but having no idea how they could or should be organized. Scientists who study specialized functions of the brain note that specific areas link our perceptions to long-term memory. For someone to capture complex, experience-based knowledge, his brain has to contain some frameworks, domain knowledge or prior experiences to which current inputs can connect. Otherwise, the messages and information sent remain relatively meaningless suggestions. To a person who is unfamiliar with finance, the following advice is merely a string of words: 'If you borrow money to buy back a lot of stock, you increase return on equity, but not in a way that those hawks at Moody's would approve of.' Take a non-business example: 'What three-dimensional avatar would you like to be in the next MUD you enter?' To many people, that question is almost unintelligible – but not to an online gamer who has represented herself in cyberspace as a three-dimensional object (an avatar) while playing in a multiuser domain (MUD). Even when the terms are explained, however, a non-gamer will not know what criteria to use in selecting an avatar. Someone who has not played such games lacks the receptors to process the query intelligently.

This cognitive limitation exists at an organizational level as well. When GE Healthcare sets up or transfers operations from one location to another, for instance, it appoints an experienced manager and team to be the 'pitcher' and a team in the receiving plant to be the 'catcher'. These two teams work together, often over a period of years, first at the pitcher's location and then at the catcher's. To ensure a smooth transition, the pitcher team needs to be sensitive to the catcher team's level of experience and familiarity with GE Healthcare procedures. When a veteran operations manager arrived at a growing GE Healthcare plant in China, the local team was getting ready to move raw materials from the manufacturing facility into a warehouse. The operations manager could see numerous potential problems with the chosen site, but he knew that simply vetoing it would have transferred little knowledge. So he helped the team develop a list of critical-to-quality (CTQ) factors against which to evaluate potential sites. (Although this analytic process is standard operating procedure at GE, the Chinese plant hadn't adopted it yet.) The list included such factors as proximity to the manufacturing plant, easy access for large trucks, road conditions between facilities and basic amenities for employees. List in hand, the catchers visited the selected site and could see that it met few of their criteria. They then understood the reasons for using the CTQ model for even apparently simple choices; they had a framework and some basic experience on which to build future decisions.

In many situations requiring the transfer of deep smarts, new people are thrown in to sink or swim. Sometimes they make it. They're often quick studies and have other adaptive skills. If they come into the job with few preconceptions about what does and doesn't work, they may suggest smart changes. So a deliberate decision *not* to transfer knowledge to the newcomer can have advantages. But usually, the sink-or-swim strategy is inefficient and – more important – ineffective. It is far better to deliberately create receptors by providing frameworks and tools or other types of mental structures to which experience can be tied.

Transfer Techniques

Receptors, of course, are not enough. The most valuable part of deep smarts is the tacit know-how (and often, know-who) that a person has built up over years of experience. This knowledge cannot be easily documented and handed over in a filing

PASSIVE RECEPTION						ACTIVE LEARNING	
Directives, presentations, lectures	Rules of thumb	Stories with a moral	Socratic questioning	Guided practice	Guided observation	Guided problem solving	Guided experimentation

Figure 7.1   Moving toward deep smarts

cabinet or on a CD. Managers are sophisticated; they recognize that documentation and software are inadequate to capture deep knowledge. Why, then, do they persist in relying on a thick deck of PowerPoint slides, a Web site of best practices, a repository of project reports, online training, or even in-person lectures for the transfer? Even the smartest people have difficulty gaining insight from such materials, because so much of the knowledge they need is tied to specific contexts and has tacit dimensions.

The central paradox in transferring deep smarts is that constantly reinventing the wheel is inefficient, but people learn only by doing. So what's the best way to get them up to speed? In our research, we identified a number of techniques used by what we call knowledge coaches – experts who were motivated to share some of their deep smarts with protégés. While some played the traditional mentor role of helping their protégés navigate organizations or providing personal advice, the coaches primarily served as teachers transmitting experience-based expertise.

As Figure 7.1 suggests, approaches vary considerably – and predictably – in how effectively they address the deep-smarts paradox. Most of these modes are well understood. A number of books have been written about storytelling, for example, as a potent way to convey nuanced information. And Socratic questioning is pretty common. Queries such as 'How do you know?' and 'What would happen if …?' stimulate reflection and active learning. However, the learning-by-doing methods are not as familiar to many readers. They require active engagement from both the teacher and the student, they take time, and they usually happen one-on-one.

Recall that deep smarts are based on an extensive experience repertoire. While it's true that merely describing experiences to people (or telling them what to do or giving them rules) may create some mental receptors upon which to hang experience, the tacit dimensions of an expert's deep smarts have to be *re-created* to take hold. That is, the novice needs to discover the expert's know-how through practice, observation, problem solving and experimentation – all under the direction of a knowledge coach. In the process, the smarts of both the expert and the novice are deepened.

Guided Practice

The old adage is right: Practice *does* make perfect – or at least better. But mindless repetition can hone the wrong skills. Better is mindful, reflective practice, in which

Guided experience – learning by doing, with feedback from a knowledge coach, creates deep understanding. It is especially valuable when:

Situations	Examples
The skills to be learned involve interpersonal relations, so there is no set of absolute steps but rather an array of possible responses to the actions and emotions of others.	➤ working with a board of directors ➤ negotiating a merger or acquisition ➤ handling a talented prima donna
There are many tacit dimensions to the skills, so even an expert may not be able to make them all explicit.	➤ closing a sale ➤ dissipating tension in a meeting ➤ creating a new perfume or best-selling wine
The knowledge is context specific, so it's appropriate to be adaptive rather than apply formulas.	➤ managing in a foreign culture ➤ manufacturing with proprietary, plant-specific equipment ➤ handling sexual harassment cases
The situation is new, so there is great uncertainty.	➤ launching a new service product in a new market ➤ using a new mode of manufacturing

Rules create a mental scaffold on which to hang experience. They help people make sense of their experience but do not serve as a substitute for it. People with deep smarts will know exceptions to the rules in their domain and will feel comfortable augmenting them. But guidelines can be appropriate and helpful as a starting point, especially when:

Situations	Examples
The skills to be learned are largely cognitive, generate little emotion, and are relatively independent of individual differences.	➤ accounting practices ➤ statistical analysis of market segments
There are explicit, communicable ideas and models.	➤ strategic analysis using Michael Porter's 'five forces' model ➤ financial analysis of a business plan
The processes are unvarying and relatively independent of context.	➤ Six Sigma applications ➤ the running of democratic meetings
The domain is well understood and explored, and there is little uncertainty about what works.	➤ high-volume assembly line manufacturing ➤ product positioning on shelves

Figure 7.2　Guided experience versus other types of learning

Sometimes an expert is the key actor in a managerial setting. Sometimes a novice is. Give them both a managerial task, and they'll approach it in characteristically different ways. And the experts aren't always right – they run risks, too.

Tasks	Novice	Expert	Expert's Limitations
Making decisions	Needs to review all facts and choose deliberately among alternatives	Makes decisions swiftly, efficiently, without reviewing basic facts	→ Overconfidence; expert may ignore relevant data
Considering context	Relies on rules of thumb that minimize context	Takes context into account when solving problems	→ Difficulty transferring expert knowledge, because it is highly contextualized
Extrapolating information	Lacks receptors and thus has limited basis for extrapolation	Can extrapolate from a novel situation to find a solution	→ May base solution on inappropriate pattern
Exercising discrimination	Uses rules of thumb to obscure fine distinctions	Can make fine distinctions	→ May not communicate well to a novice who lacks receptors to understand distinctions
Being aware of knowledge gaps	Doesn't know what he doesn't know	Knows when rules don't apply	→ May assume expertise where none exists
Recognizing patterns	Has limited experience from which to draw patterns	Has large inventory of patterns drawn from experience	→ May be no better than novice when no patterns exist
Using tacit knowledge	Relies largely on explicit knowledge	Uses extensive tacit knowledge to drive decision making	→ May have a hard time articulating and thus transferring tacit knowledge

Figure 7.3 Characteristics and limitations of deep smarts

outcomes are assessed and the method adjusted appropriately. But best of all is practice under the tutelage of someone who can guide the reflection and provide performance feedback. This is where an experienced coach comes in.

At SAIC, a consulting firm in San Diego that works primarily with the US government, consultants learn their trade from a seasoned pro first by watching the expert help a client pick up a particular knowledge management process, next by leading a client session and receiving feedback from the coach, and then by teaching another consultant how to work with a client. This 'see one, lead one, teach one' approach is one of SAIC's most useful knowledge transfer tools.

Guided Observation

Another powerful technique, guided observation, can be used for two very different purposes: to re-create deep smarts and to challenge ossified assumptions that may be based on outdated experience.

If your goal is to re-create deep smarts, you can have a 'catcher' shadow an experienced, skilled colleague and arrange for the two to meet afterward to discuss what the catcher observed. A top consultant was once asked where and how he learned his skills in closing deals with clients. He explained that when he joined the company, an elder statesman in the firm asked him to sit in on client meetings. 'You don't have to say a word', the older consultant told him, 'Just listen and learn'. The junior consultant rightly took that invitation as more than a suggestion and sat at the back of the room. After the meetings, he and the older consultant discussed what had occurred. 'I learned more from those debriefs', he said, 'than in four years at my prior company and two years of business school.'

The combination of shadowing and feedback sessions works because, as we have said, deep smarts are based largely on pattern recognition and are highly contextual. Because there are so many tacit dimensions to this sort of insight, the individual possessing it will not always realize what she knows until a particular challenge calls her knowledge forth. This makes it difficult for her to give her protégé absolute, detailed directives to follow in general. She might not be able to tell a novice what the response should be to a particular situation, but she can show him.

What if the issue is not so much teaching new skills but convincing individuals to unlearn what they take for granted? We can't deepen our smarts without challenging our beliefs about our clients, our organizations, our services. Field trips – playing anthropologist for a few days to observe behaviors at other sites or companies – can help. Exposed to foreign ways of thinking and behaving, people not only extend their experience repertoire but are often shocked into questioning their own complacent understanding of the world.

When consultants from Strategos guided teams from Best Buy through the intricate steps of identifying, exploring, and prototyping new business opportunities, they first challenged the team members' assumptions about the company's uses of technology to attract typical Best Buy customers – young males who purchase powerful, feature-rich electronics. The consultants then sent team members on the road. Best Buy's Toby Nord took a trip with some colleagues to American Girl Place in Chicago that proved invaluable, though initially unsettling. American Girl specializes in a line of dolls representing historical eras. More of a destination than a retail outlet, the store features doll-centric activities: You can get a new hairdo for your doll, for example, or have tea and scones at the American Girl Cafe, where dolls sit at the table. Nord and his male colleagues were pushed out of their comfort zone. But Nord realized that the dolls at American Girl Place were a kind of platform for intergenerational socializing among grandmothers, mothers and daughters. The store was entertaining, and its business focused tightly on a community built for a given demographic: women and girls.

The Best Buy team combined observations from this trip to Chicago and others to Mexico City, the Amish countryside in Indiana, and Seoul, South Korea, and began to see behavior patterns. All these visits stimulated thinking about social, communal behavior focused on a platform, product or technology. The team began to generate ideas for products and services that would offer an experience or a social happening. Inspired by the groups of teens they saw in Seoul gathering to play video games, the Best Buy folks came up with a youth-centered entertainment concept: a 'PCBang', where teenagers and people in their early 20s (a demographic group younger than Best Buy's typical consumers) will be able to play computer games together and socialize.

Guided Problem Solving

Guided problem solving serves different purposes and requires more active engagement from the protégé than does guided observation. A knowledge coach may or may not already know the answer to a problem. But either way, if he works on it with his protégé, the novice can learn how to approach the problem. That is, the knowledge coach transfers know-how more than know-what. During their residencies, newly minted physicians convert their book smarts into deeper, experience-based smarts as they work beside veteran doctors over a period of years.

Apprenticeships in business are less formalized – but they do occur in companies where managers are alert to the need for re-creating tacit knowledge. In an engineering company, a highly experienced design engineer was asked to train a younger colleague in the kind of systems thinking for which the older man was renowned. One of the senior engineer's most valued skills was the ability to bring multiple perspectives to any design – not just engineering knowledge about every component (software and hardware) in the complex systems the company manufactured, but also an understanding of how the systems were to be produced. He was famous for detecting and avoiding potential assembly problems and performance shortfalls. To transfer his understanding of the overall product architecture and his respect for manufacturing constraints, he had his protégé go down to the assembly line and work on problems with a test engineer for several months. The senior engineer joined many of these problem-solving sessions, adding information that the test technician lacked, such as historic customer biases and preferences. While the protégé gained specific knowledge about component parts, the more important know-how transferred was the ability to look at the whole system, see how the interfaces worked and understand how different functional priorities led to specific design flaws. The protégé also got to know and respect the knowledge of people working on the assembly line. This experience enhanced his organizational know-who, altered his belief systems, and contributed to his technical expertise.

Guided problem solving combines many of the best features of the transfer techniques mentioned previously: focusing attention, sharpening process skills, giving feedback, providing an opportunity to mimic an expert, engaging the learner actively in developing her own deep smarts, and building an experience repertoire.

Guided Experimentation

In the first few years of their lives, children learn at a fantastic rate, partly because they are constantly experimenting. (Of course, that's what makes parents of toddlers so nervous.) Too often in organizations, we assume that experimentation is both a risky and an expensive way of learning. It doesn't have to be. The best entrepreneurial coaches in our study of 35 start-ups encouraged their charges to set up deliberate but modest experiments. This was the case with ActivePhoto, a company based on a software system that instantly downloads and catalogs digital photographs for use in a business process. In search of its best market, ActivePhoto initially considered three promising customer bases: public emergency services; insurance claims processing; and online auctioning. The tiny seven-person firm would ultimately have to choose one or two markets, but in its first few months of life it experimented with all three. Pilot studies, along with discussions with knowledge coaches, allowed the ActivePhoto people to evaluate the results of each experiment and quickly eliminate the first market.

Most retail companies use pilot markets to test new products – rolling them out in one area of the country before going national. When Whirlpool was considering custom-built appliances, the company was advised to find out whether customers were interested and whether customization would generate more market share or more profit. In a fairly simple and inexpensive experiment, Whirlpool selected two retail outlets in each of two cities (Dallas and Philadelphia) in which to set up tests for custom appliances. To draw crowds, the stores funded local advertising campaigns ('Come build your own Whirlpool refrigerator down at XYZ Appliances'). Computer kiosks in the stores allowed customers to choose from a variety of appliance features, and workers in the back busily assembled what people ordered. What did Whirlpool learn? As expected, customizing helped in the share game, at least for these four outlets. But the experiment also produced an unanticipated outcome: Customers ordered more features – approximately $70 more per refrigerator.

Coaches can offer good advice about where and how much to experiment – and more important, they can improve a team's attitude toward adding to deep smarts through experimentation. The Toyota Production System is admired for its efficient manufacturing and has attracted imitators worldwide. But researchers who have investigated the deep smarts underlying TPS have discovered that the explicit techniques so widely copied (kanban cards, andon cords, just-in-time inventory delivery) do not account for the true advantage that Toyota has. The real secret to Toyota's success is the mind-set of its employees: to constantly hypothesize about possible improvements and test those hypotheses in experiments. (See 'Decoding the DNA of the Toyota Production System,' by Steven Spear and H. Kent Bowen, in the September–October 1999 issue of Harvard Business Review.) This sort of mind-set is possible in any industry, including service. At any given time, Bank of America's innovation and development teams are conducting more than two dozen experiments in operating branches, such as 'virtual tellers', video monitors displaying financial and investment news, computer stations where customers can upload images of their canceled checks, and kiosks staffed by associates ready to open accounts or process loan applications.

But Does It Cost Too Much?

In our world of fast brain food, one might think that guided experience is passé at best – or at least too costly. We have heard an executive from a well-run *Fortune* 100 company say, 'The days of apprenticeship are over. We don't have enough people to mentor newcomers'. Many who share this view will nonetheless willingly spend millions of dollars and years of effort on data repositories and formal training. We certainly do not wish to suggest that all such investments are wasteful. But we're convinced that guided experience is the only way to cultivate deep smarts and that managers need to be realistic about how much tacit, context-specific knowledge can be created or transferred through other means.

Fortunately, guided experience can deliver two benefits simultaneously and thus is not as costly as it might seem: first, a lasting asset in the form of transferred know-how, and second, delivery of a new business process, product idea or capability. The learning happens on the job, so the business situations are real and relevant to today's problems. SAIC's training of US Army personnel in the 'peer assist' technique, for example, not only transfers process knowledge but does so in the context of a real problem – how to improve the performance of contract officers. Similarly, Strategos consultants were not only training Whirlpool and Best Buy employees to develop innovation processes; they were also showing these clients how to identify new business opportunities.

Guided experience increases value exponentially – it promotes dual-purpose learning and builds on all that we know about how people accumulate and retain knowledge. How can companies afford *not* to invest in it?

8

Organizational and Occupational Commitment: Knowledge Workers in Large Corporations

May Yeuk-Mui Tam, Marek Korczynski and Stephen J. Frenkel

The belief that advanced western economies are becoming knowledge economies has become conventional wisdom in the organizational studies and management literature (Blackler et al., 1993; Drucker, 1993). It has been claimed that expertise and specialized knowledge are increasingly important to corporate performance and are replacing capital as the basis of social status and power (Bell, 1973). Management increasingly turn to new expertise for efficient problem-solving and provision of customized services. New occupations like financial and management consultants, information technology analysts, project engineers and computer technologists have emerged in response to demands of modern corporations. Incumbents of these new occupations have been referred to as knowledge workers (Reed, 1996; Scarbrough, 1996). They are expanding occupational groups and are increasingly being considered as key expert groups in advanced western economies.

In the recent discussion of expertise and knowledge workers, three interrelated areas of theoretical and empirical work can be discerned (Abbott, 1991; Bacharach et al., 1991; von Glinow, 1988). The first area concerns the cognitive basis and the nature of knowledge workers' expertise and knowledge. The second area focuses on the strategies knowledge workers use to establish and guard exclusionary claims to their expertise and to maximize economic and symbolic rewards. The third area is about the management–employee relationships in which these workers are involved. One of the important issues in the third area is the commitment of knowledge workers to the organization vis-à-vis their occupations (Alvesson, 2000; Kanter, 1993; Zuboff, 1988). It has been argued that organizations compete with work teams or occupational groupings for the commitment of knowledge workers (Causer and Jones, 1996; Raelin, 1985). Organizational commitment has long been a concern in the studies of organizational behaviours and job satisfaction. There is also a vast amount of research on the impacts of organizational commitment on work effort and job satisfaction (Angle and Lawson, 1994; Becker et al., 1996; Kalleberg and Marsden, 1995; Mathieu and Zajac, 1990; Meyer and Allen, 1997; Mowday et al., 1982; Wallace, 1993, 1995a, 1995b). Generally, researchers agree that while organizational commitment reduces turnover rates and absenteeism, it does not have definitive positive impacts on work effort and job satisfaction.

Source: M.Y.-M. Tam, M. Korczynski and S. Frenkel (2002) 'Organizational and occupational commitment: knowledge workers in large corporations', *Journal of Management Studies*, 39(6): 775–801. Edited version.

The alleged rivalry between occupations and organizations as the bases of employee loyalty has been extensively researched in the case of traditional professions like lawyers, nurses, doctors and engineers. Likewise, the relationship between commitment and work effort has also been investigated for conventional professionals. However, we know little about the commitment and work attitudes of knowledge workers, particularly those who are employed in large corporations. The management of knowledge workers' commitment has become a key management concern as intellectual and human capital become increasingly important to the corporation's functioning and services provision. The spread of communication technologies and extensive ties between corporations have enhanced the access and flow of information and knowledge. Clients have become more knowledgeable. They, therefore, demand for more customized services and products. The use of new communication and informational technologies within the corporation creates new technological and management problems. Management, therefore, need to rely on new experts and specialists for efficient problem-solving and the provision of tailored services. The loyalty of knowledge workers and ways to minimize their exit are critical management problems (Alvesson, 2000).

One of the major factors that affects the commitment, work effort and job satisfaction of knowledge workers is the way they are organized and relate to management. In the extant work, Reed (1996) presented a theoretical and historical analysis of knowledge workers as the third type of experts in advanced western economies. He argued that knowledge workers, as a new expert group, adopt a marketization power strategy to build up and maintain their expertise status. Unlike traditional professionals, knowledge workers do not rely on conventional occupational or organizational credential systems to establish and gain economic and political advantages for their expertise. Instead, they make use of the esoteric and intangible nature of their knowledge to create market niches for themselves. In terms of their labour market positions, these workers are located in external rather than internal labour markets (Berg, 1981). Reed (1996, p. 586) suggested that this pushes knowledge workers towards an organic or network organizational form which is characterized by decentralized flexibility and autonomy.

In a similar vein, recent discussions about changes in employment relations systems claim that management increasingly adopt a market model to organize the employment relationships of salaried experts (Cappelli, 1999; Scarbrough, 1996). Management adopt new practices and measures that bring market pressures into the firm to manage employment relations and work motivation. The psychological contract that used to bond employees and corporation together is in decline. Employment relations are made highly contingent. As a result, employees orient themselves towards the external labour market.

Whether as a power strategy pursued by knowledge workers themselves or as practices adopted by management, the market model and its implications for knowledge workers' work attitudes have not been adequately assessed, especially for employees in large corporations. This chapter seeks to fill this gap by first, examining critically Reed's model; second, proposing an alternative; and third, drawing on findings from a group of knowledge workers ($n = 134$) employed in two large corporations in Australia. These employees were in two types of knowledge work occupations: computer information systems developers and money market dealers. They held expertise knowledge in specific fields in infor- mation technology and finance. Unlike traditional professionals who usually belong to professional associations, only 15 per cent of these knowledge workers claimed to be members of professional associations and only 2 per cent said they were union members.

In the following sections, we shall first examine Reed's model and supplement the discussion with the market model proposed by researchers on employment relations. We shall then draw from these two analogous models postulates about the commitment, work effort and job satisfaction of knowledge workers. A critical assessment of Reed's model suggests that the relationship between management and knowledge workers in large corporations can be of a dualistic nature. We shall explicate this dualistic model and the postulates about commitment, work effort and job satisfaction that can be derived from it. Our findings will then be exam- ined. The ensuing discussion of our findings will focus on four major aspects of work organization: work skills and knowledge; co-workers relations; the reward system; and control relations. Other studies have noted that these four aspects are crucial elements in work organizations. They have strong impacts on employee commitment, work effort and job satisfaction (Clark, 1996; Gallie et al., 1998; Gunz and Gunz, 1994; Pitt et al., 1995). In the conclusion, we shall discuss the managerial implications of the findings.

The Market Model of Knowledge Work Organization and Its Implications

In his discussion of expert power in advanced capitalist economies, Reed (1996) distinguished three main groups of experts: traditional or liberal professions (example, lawyers); organizational professions (managers, administrators); and knowledge workers (information technology analysts). For each of these groups, Reed high- lighted its knowledge base, power strategy and organizational form. He argued that the knowledge base of knowledge workers is esoteric, non-substitutable, global and analytical. These workers are less concerned with formal occupational and organi- zational credentialism, compared to traditional professionals. Reed (1996, p. 585) claimed that '[knowledge workers] specialize in complex task domains which are inherently resistant to incursions by the carriers of bureaucratic rationalization and control'. They then aggressively market their refined and portable knowledge and skills. This process implies that they are not tied to one particular organization. Reed called this strategy marketization and argued that knowledge workers use this strategy to build and maintain their exclusionary claims to their knowledge and skills domains. He also called knowledge workers entrepreneurial professions, a term which implies self-employment and a high degree of work autonomy. In terms of labour market positions, the marketization strategy implies that knowledge workers are in external rather than internal labour markets. The marketization strategy results in an organic or network organizational form with the features of decentralized flexibility and autonomy.

Both theories and previous research note that employment relations have significant effects on the work commitment and attitudes of employees (Morrow, 1993). As noted earlier, current changes in employment systems are said to be moving towards a market model. Non-standard forms of employment like short-term hires, fixed-term contract, part-time employment and sub-contracting replace regular, full-time and permanent employment (Carré et al., 2000). Management increasingly introduce practices that bring market pressures into the corporation. Examples of these practices are: performance-related instead of seniority-related pay; outside benchmarking; explicit training contracts that require employees to stay for some minimum periods after receiving their training; and a flatter organizational structure that provides limited senior positions for promotion. Workers are expected to be self-reliant for their own career development and employability, both inside and outside the corporation. Employee development and their interests are not the main concerns of the corporation. Neither management nor employees expect a long-term employment relationship. Knowledge workers' primary interest is the marketability of their own skills and knowledge in the external labour market, instead of the well-being of the corporation. Their values and goals diverge from those of their employing organization. Their loyalty to the organization depends on the extent to which their job expectations are met by the corporation, and on the options available to them in the external labour market. Thus, similar to the marketization strategy Reed proposed, the market model of employment relations system implies that knowledge workers are oriented, in principle, towards the external labour market.

From the marketization strategy or the market model, we can derive the following propositions about the commitment and work attitudes of knowledge workers: first, as occupations rather than the corporation comprise the base of their expertise status and economic advantage, knowledge workers will be more committed to their occupations than to the organization. Second, the orientation of knowledge workers towards external labour markets implies that occupational and organizational commitment are unrelated to each other, and if they are related at all, the association will be tenuous. For the same reason, we can postulate that organizational commitment will have insignificant effects on workers' work effort and job satisfaction whereas occupational commitment will have positive effects. The market model also implies that pay is significant to knowledge workers. Pay matters because it carries both economic and symbolic meanings. It represents the going market price of knowledge workers' expertise in the external labour market. It indicates how much knowledge workers are worth in the eyes of management. Pay is a badge of status with implications for self-esteem and exercise of influence. We can, therefore, postulate that satisfaction with pay is positively related to work effort and job satisfaction.

The Importance of Contextual Knowledge and Management Strategy: An Alternative to the Market Model

Reed's analysis has two major weaknesses. First, his analysis posits that organizational forms can simply be derived from the knowledge base and power strategy of an expert group. This view also posits knowledge workers as autonomous actors. The crucial element of management strategy is mistakenly neglected. The reason for this omission is Reed's assumption that knowledge workers tend to be self employed, or they work in small specialist firms outside of large corporations. If this assumption holds, then management strategy would not matter much in shaping the power strategy of knowledge workers. However, the literature on knowledge work occupations shows that many knowledge workers are employed in large corporations, particularly in the occupations with which we are concerned (Fincham et al., 1994; Gibbons et al., 1994). For these knowledge workers, in contrast to contractors or entrepreneurs, management strategy is important for understanding knowledge workers' commitment and work attitudes.

The second weakness of Reed's model is his characterization of the base of knowledge work. Reed (1996, p. 585) wrote: '[knowledge workers] rely on a sophisticated combination of theoretical knowledge, analytical tools and tacit or judgmental skills that are very difficult, but not impossible, to standardize, replicate and incorporate within formalized organizational routines.' However, while esoteric, abstract and theoretical knowledge is a key feature of knowledge work, contextual knowledge is equally important. As Koestler (1970), Gibbons et al. (1994) and Frenkel et al. (1999) argued, one of the key features of knowledge work is the synthesis of theoretical and contextual knowledge. The latter refers to knowledge of non-generalizable company policies or procedures and task-objects. Such knowledge may be formalized or tacit, and may range from lower-order forms such as company policies and individual clients' needs to higher-order forms, such as industry trends.

Gibbons et al. (1994) reviewed the latest development of knowledge creation in advanced industrial economies. They noted that in a wide range of areas of knowledge work, there have been significant moves towards what they refer to as 'Mode 2' knowledge production. This mode involves the creation of knowledge in the context of application. General, theoretical knowledge needs to be combined with non-generalizable contextual knowledge through an iterative process of diagnosis, inferencing and application to resolve complex problems. The synthesis of theoretical and contextual knowledge is particularly important for the provision of sophisticated and tailored services and advices to customers. Theoretical and contextual knowledge are, therefore, equally important. Knowledge workers employed in large corporations depend on the corporation for resources including contextual knowledge to create new knowledge. Their status as employees and the importance of contextual knowledge mean they cannot autonomously pursue the marketization strategy suggested by Reed. They are constrained to a certain extent by their dependence on the organization. Therefore, both management strategy and workers' power strategy need to be considered when the organizational form of these knowledge workers is examined.

Recently, there has also been discussion on the way organizations limit the work autonomy of knowledge workers. Alvesson (2000, p. 1109) noted that since knowledge work occupations are less uniform than conventional professional occupations, there are spaces for an organizational-specific knowledge base. This implies that organizational contexts are critical to the creation of knowledge and the expertise status of knowledge workers. Alvesson's argument, therefore, highlights knowledge workers' dependence on organization. Hill et al. (2000) studied a sample of British companies to examine the organization of research and development (R&D). They found most firms had centralized instead of decentralized their R&D. Their study also implies that there are organizational limits to knowledge workers' autonomy.

To understand the organizational form of knowledge workers employed in a large corporation, an alternative model is needed.[1] This model needs to recognize the dual dependent relationship between knowledge workers and the organization. On the one hand, for the purpose of channelling the motivation and effort of employees to serve the interest of the corporation, management will seek to exploit knowledge workers' need to rely on the organization for resources (for example, advanced computer softwares and hardwares which are available at a high cost) to accomplish their worktasks. On the other hand, management depend on knowledge workers for their esoteric and advanced knowledge and their ability to synthesize theoretical and contextual knowledge. Management, therefore, need to meet these employees' aspirations and expectations. As for knowledge workers, they need to depend on the organization as the locale to develop contextual knowledge and to create new knowledge. However, their ability to apply theoretical knowledge in other contexts, that is, in other organizations, means that to a certain extent, they are also able to pursue a limited form of marketization. This enables them to reap market-level rewards for their expertise.

One of the organizational forms that can result from this dual dependent relationship between the knowledge workers and the corporation is the creation of an enclave within the corporation. In this organizational form, management cede a high degree of autonomy to knowledge workers in their work process. This is partly due to the difficulty in applying process-related control to the complex work undertaken by knowledge workers, and partly to management's desire for workers to build and share relevant contextual knowledge. An enclave organizational form will also satisfy knowledge workers' desire for work autonomy. Structurally, this form is like an independent section made up of specialist teams within the corporation (Riain, 2000). Within the enclave, co-worker relationships among knowledge workers will be characterized by a high degree of interdependence. This arises from the need to supplement each other's expertise when individual knowledge workers apply their theoretical knowledge to analyse complex work problems. Interdependence between co-workers is especially salient in project work which brings together the specialties of different knowledge workers. However, the enclave organizational form does not mean that management delegate to knowledge workers absolute discretion. The form also rests upon a performance-based reward system through which market pressures and management control are realized. Under this reward system, knowledge workers' pay is made highly contingent upon their work outcomes, that is, their performance.

The dualistic model and its enclave organizational form can lead to the following postulates about knowledge workers' commitment, work effort and job satisfaction. First, as knowledge workers' expertise status is based on both their occupationally-specific theoretical knowledge of their occupation and contextual knowledge (embedded in the organization), they will be similarly committed to their occupations and the organization. The dual dependent relationship between them and the organization means that the two types of commitment will be positively related. However, the association may be weak as knowledge workers will try to reduce their dependence on the organization in order to pursue more completely a marketization strategy and maximum work autonomy. Third, the relationships between organizational commitment on the one hand, and work effort and job satisfaction on the other hand, will depend on the extent to which management can meet knowledge workers' job expectations. The dualistic model suggests that knowledge workers will value pay and influence over work-related decisions. Pay will be emphasized as it indicates *both* the market value of knowledge workers' esoteric expertise in the external labour market and their worthiness within the corporation. Influence over work-related decisions will augment the autonomy of knowledge workers and thereby minimize their dependence on the organization. Fourth, the more knowledge workers are committed to their occupation which is closely tied to their expertise status, the higher will be their levels of work effort and job satisfaction. Fifth, since pay is an indicator of knowledge workers' status both inside and outside the organization, pay satisfaction will positively affect work effort and job satisfaction. Table 8.1 summarizes the postulates about commitment, work effort and job satisfaction that are derived from both the market and the dualistic model.

The Empirical Cases: Background and Research Methods

Our empirical cases come from a larger research project which was conducted between the end of 1994 and 1996 in specific work sections of several corporations in Australia, Japan and the USA.[2] This chapter focuses on three work sections located in two companies, one in the financial services and the other one in the telecommunications sector in Australia. These sections will be called IT, MM and TELHI. Sites IT and MM were sections in a multinational company (hereafter referred to as Company A) which was among the top ten US companies in the financial services industry, according to the Fortune 1996 industrial ranking. The Australian arm was one of the leading companies in the local financial services sector. Site IT aimed to enhance the competitiveness and flexibility of the company

Table 8.1 Postulates on employee commitment and work attitudes from the market model and the dualistic model

	Postulates from the market model and marketization strategy	Postulates from the dualistic model
The relative levels of organizational commitment and occupational commitment	Occupational commitment higher than organizational commitment	Occupational commitment same as organizational commitment
The correlation between organizational and occupational commitment	Negative or absent	Positive
The effect of organizational commitment on work effort and job satisfaction	Absent	Depends on whether the corporation can meet workers' job expectations regarding pay and influence over work- related decisions
The effect of occupational commitment on work effort and job satisfaction	Positive	Positive
The effect of pay satisfaction on work effort and job satisfaction	Positive	Positive

through constructing a business information technology system. Employees in Site MM offered advice and undertook transactions in money markets for corporate and institutional fund managers. Site TELHI was located in a company (hereafter referred to as Company B) whose corporate ranking was in the top 5 per cent in Australia, according to the 1996 Dun and Bradstreet league table. This company is among the largest providers of telecommunication services in Australia, employing 4352 employees when our research was undertaken. The system developers in Site TELHI were involved in building a communication infrastructure for a large client. Work in these three sites had a number of common features, hence the sites will be discussed collectively.

Research Methods

Data were collected in two ways: on-site field research and an employee survey. During the fieldwork stage, researchers conducted interviews with management personnel and individual employees, undertook observations at the workplace and examined company documents. The interviews were semi-structured in nature and questions were open-ended. Interviewees were asked to relate specific incidents from the recent past when they made general comments. In total, over 30 interviews with management and supervisors were conducted, over 60 individual workers were interviewed, and more than 20 team meetings were observed. A broad range of company documents were also examined. These documents included minutes of meetings, organizational charts, recruitment guides, management strategy documents, policy papers and annual reports of the company. A total of over 130 documents were examined. Data collected through interviews, observations and documents for each site were sifted systematically according to coded categories which were listed as a template. These categories covered main areas of work organization and comprised a number of sub-categories. The coded data were then analysed by a field researcher. The analysis document was then reviewed by another field researcher who made comments where appropriate concerning ambiguities of meanings and differences in understanding. Appendix 8.1 gives a sample of the template used to code and analyse the field research data.

The survey comprised self-administered questionnaires which included questions on occupational and organizational commitment, skills and knowledge require-ments of the job, work effort and satisfaction as well as basic demographic data.[3] A total of 134 employees responded to the survey, giving an average response rate of 83 per cent across all three sites. Table 8.2 gives some basic demographic and work experience information about the survey respondents in these three sites taken together.

A majority of the respondents were university degree holders, and nearly one quarter held a post-graduate degree. More than half of the respondents were married and a majority were male. Many of them were in their late 20s or early 30s and the average age was 32 for the sample as a whole. A majority of the repondents (76 per cent) had been in their occupation (including their current job) for more than three years, whereas less than 5 per cent were novices who had spent six months or less in the occupation. The distribution in terms of company tenure was slightly skewed towards longer-serving employees. While 11 per cent of the respon-dents had worked in their company for six months or less, 36 per cent had been employed for more than three years. The average occupation tenure was about eight years, whereas the average company tenure was about three years.

The Expertise of Knowledge Workers: The Importance of Context

We noted earlier that contextual knowledge is as important as general and theoretical knowledge in understanding knowledge work. Customers of our knowledge workers were either external organizations or departments internal to the company. The nature of work was complex and involved much problem-solving and considerable

Table 8.2 Distribution of the survey respondents by gender, education level, marital status, age, occupational and company tenure

Gender	
Men	78%
Women	22%
Education level	
University degree-holder[1]	81%
Non-degree holder[2]	19%
Marital status	
Married[3]	58%
Single	42%
Age	
Less than 25	21%
26–30	26%
31–35	26%
36–40	17%
41 or above	10%
Average	32 years old
Length of time spent on similar occupation	
Less than one year	6%
1–2 years	4%
2–3 years	10%
3 years or more	80%
Average duration	98 months
Company tenure	
Less than one year	22%
1–2 years	25%
2–3 years	15%
3 years or more	38%
Average duration	39 months
Total number of respondents	134

[1]This includes both undergraduate and post-graduate degree. Only 8 per cent of the pooled sample held a post-graduate degree.
[2]This category combines advanced certificate/vocational qualification and secondary school or below qualification.
[3]This refers to both de facto and legal partnership.

customization of services. Employees often had to draw on theoretical and generalizable knowledge and a relatively high level of analytical skills. These skills and knowledge were then applied to diagnose and resolve specific work problems or to give customers appropriate and specialized advices. Money market dealers drew heavily on theories in finance, marketing and advanced mathematics to structure complex derivative deals for their fund managers' clients. These theories also helped them understand market developments and present complex arguments to clients. System developers used electronic engineering theory. They pointed out in interviews that common theoretical knowledge facilitated communications among themselves. It also enabled them to have a holistic understanding of the system.

The work of both developers and dealers involved considerable uncertainty. This arose from developments in their occupational fields and in the market. For the system developers, one of the main sources of uncertainty was rapid technological progress in the tools they used for design and implementation. Dealers faced uncertain market developments and needed to interpret market movements and elicit their clients' changing objectives and concerns. They also needed to influence customers' perceptions and tailored the products to meet clients' requirements. Contextual knowledge was, therefore, important in service provision and task accomplishments. The following quotes from employee interviews illustrate how developers and dealers applied both theoretical and contextual knowledge as well as analytical skills to provide customized services and identify problems in a creative manner:

> [Customers' requests] are more complex, where clients want something particular, for example, want to keep ahead of some benchmarks they are evaluated by. So they might ask for a package that will give them what they want.

> There is a fascination of technologists with technology itself – what's the latest whizbang, Windows 95 needs ... we keep looking for the next one to solve problems.

> Quite a few things can knock out a network which allows you to brainstorm what might be wrong, so you must be creative.

> On this project, we have to be both specialists and generalists.

The use of considerable analytical skills, theoretical knowledge and a relatively high level of creativity were reflected in the employee survey. Respondents at the three sites were asked to rank the importance of analytical skills against four other types of skills. Out of the five types of skills, analytical skills was nominated by the greatest proportion of respondents (64 per cent) as the first or second most important skills, while the smallest proportion (5 per cent) rated it as the least important type of skills.[4] Respondents were also asked to choose five out of seven types of knowledge and then rank their importance in their work. Knowledge specific to their occupation had the greatest proportion (66 per cent) of respondents ranking it as the first or second most important, and the smallest proportion (3 per cent) who did not nominate it as one of the five most important types of knowledge. Knowing where to go within the corporation to get things done was ranked as the second most important type of knowledge; 48 per cent of the survey respondents nominated this type of knowledge as the first or second most important and only 4 per cent of respondents did not include this in their ranking exercise. The needs of individual customers were deemed as the third most important type of knowledge: 45 per cent of the respondents regarded this as the first or second most important and 16 per cent did not include it in their ranking list. These findings indicate clearly the importance of both theoretical and contextual knowledge in the work of our knowledge workers.[5] Responses to the survey questions used to calibrate creativity level also indicated that a majority of the respondents (83 per cent) reported that they frequently had to try new ways to solve work problems; 85 per cent said they often had to deal with non-routine or unique problems, or to have to come up with new ideas and ways of accomplishing worktasks.

Taking the fieldwork and survey data together, it is clear that the work of our knowledge workers involved both theoretical and contextual knowledge. They needed to apply their specialized and theoretical knowledge to analyse and diagnose context-specific problems. They were engaged in what Gibbons et al. (1994) called 'Mode 2' production of knowledge mentioned earlier. Our cases highlighted various contexts that knowledge workers had to be well-acquainted with before they could apply their theoretical knowledge. These contexts ranged from the different institutions to which dealers' clients belonged, the developmental trend of technologies that were related to developers' fields and the corporate environment.

Enclave-like Work Teams: Team-work, Peer Learning and Self-discipline

The nature of work skills and knowledge to a great extent shaped the co-workers relations among developers and dealers. Specialization in complex task domains means that knowledge workers need to work in groups to complement each other's expertise and knowledge. Employees with different expertise are mixed and matched by management to form temporary project teams for problem-solving. In our cases, dealers and developers worked in teams. Dealers were organized according to 'desks' – long tables on which sat banks of computer screens and where workers sat so close to each other that telephone conversations could be easily overheard. System developers also worked alongside one another. They frequently moved from one project to another and worked with teams comprising specialists in different technical domains of information system building. A high degree of inter-dependence prevailed in both the dealers' and developers' teams as team members specialized in different tasks and products and had varying levels of experience. In both cases, the products and services required the combined expertise of various specialists.

Besides collaborative work relationships, peer learning prevailed in the work teams and was considered significant by the employees themselves. The survey data clearly indicated that these knowledge workers relied more on workplace peers than on other sources to keep themselves abreast of the latest development in their expertise fields. Respondents were asked to choose five out of 10 sources of learning and then ranked their importance. Immediate colleagues in the work team were nominated as the first most important source of learning. It had the greatest proportion (63 per cent) of respondents reporting it to be the first or second most important source and the smallest proportion (5 per cent) who did not nominate it in their ranking lists. In contrast to immediate colleagues, only 14 per cent of knowledge workers considered immediate supervisors or team leaders as the first or second most important source of learning; and a majority of the knowledge workers (65 per cent) did not include the item in their ranking list.[6] This result echoed with the relatively small proportion (52 per cent) of respondents who agreed that their surpervisors helped them develop their skills. Training courses were also ranked as a relatively unimportant source of learning: only 17 per cent of the respondents nominated it as the first or second important source of learning and 37 per cent did not include it in their ranking list.

Our field research indicated three reasons for the importance of peer learning. First, there was the need to supplement one's expertise with that of the more experienced colleagues or expertise of another type. Second, highly collaborative working relationships and specialization facilitated learning from peers. Third, there was generally a lack of proper documentation of the work process. This was partly due to the rapidly changing working environment, which made any documentation obsolete and irrelevant very quickly; and partly to the fact that 'learning by doing' and on-the-job experience were more important sources of acquiring knowledge, compared to formal sources like manuals and training sessions. For the same reasons, employees did not evaluate the training courses set up by management favourably. The following remarks made by employees in interviews illustrate the importance of peer learning vis-à-vis formal training courses:

Learning from (others') experience is important. I chose this project partly because there were more talented people to learn from.

I talk to a lot of people. [I have] only been on one or two courses. I learn hands-on, make my own mistakes, also learn from peers with experience.

Little of the information was documented and hence there was a greater dependence on learning from team members.

Courses are no good, therefore people get best value from learning at their own pace, learning by doing and on the job training. I think courses generally are a waste of money.

Since the team is working at the leading edge of systems developments, formal courses are dated by nature.

Besides being the bases of skills and knowledge formation, co-workers also acted as agents of control, resulting in self-discipline and peer censure where norms were transgressed. In all three sites, although there were formally designated immediate supervisors or project leaders, the notion of formal line supervision was fluid, ambiguous and was even considered irrelevant. Issues and differences of opinion were resolved through discussion, and consensus was arrived at collectively, rather than through a formal subordinate–superordinate authority hierarchy. The primary agent of control was the peer group rather than formal supervisors. The following interview comments bear these points out:

> *Responsibilities are often shared. Most decisions are made by consensus, no one has clear authority.*

> *We don't really have a project leader. [The project leader's role] is pretty administrative, a communicator. He reports on what is being done. Although in the business design stage he was more hands on, in design and construction, he's more hands off.*

> *I don't believe in [project] management. The project manager has no tools to evaluate the tasks. In our case you cannot break the tasks into components, so you can't know how long it will take. Schedules cannot be valid in this type of project.*

> *I think they rely on culture to give feedback. Culture is strong, if people fit in with culture they will succeed, they will get feedback from the peer group. This seems to be pretty good. [Manager] rarely says to an individual that was good or not good. He tends to look at the team.*

Our employee survey asked respondents about the effectiveness of teams and relationships between team members. The results indicated that generally, favourable relationships prevailed among team members: 77 per cent of respondents considered their work teams effective in helping everyone do their jobs well, 66 per cent regarded their team effective in developing new team members, 80 per cent felt that they were part of their work team, 72 per cent said they looked forward to working with their team members every day, although only 22 per cent socialized a lot with their team members outside work.[7] Employees commented on relationships between team members in the following ways:

> *There were different views within the team, but nothing unusual, from the team's point of view, we could come to a consensus. Because of discussion, most of the time we were working as a tight team. In the midst of an uncertain environment, it made us closer.*

> *If you have a problem you can sort it out with [the manager]. Or more generally we debate and sort it out in our meeting.*

Favourable co-worker relationships were reflected in the survey findings. When survey respondents were asked how satisfied they were with co-worker relations, 80 per cent of survey respondents reported satisfaction and only 7 per cent reported dissatisfaction.[8]

Our field research and survey results indicate that generally, work teams of developers and dealers were imbued with the collegial ethos. These teams were egalitarian, autonomous and self-disciplining in the way they functioned. Together with the esoteric and complementary nature of employees' skills and knowledge, these teams were like independent enclaves in the corporation. Discussion in the next section shows that the strategy management used in the rewards system further augmented the enclave-like nature of these work teams.

Reward System: The Market Orientation of Management

In managing and motivating work effort, management of developers and dealers adopted an orientation which is similar to the market model. The lack of formal human resources (HR) management policies for these employees, the absence of internal career ladders and performance-related pay were the main features of this orientation. The HR department of the corporation was involved minimally in conventional HR functions like recruitment, training, rewards management, and performance appraisal of developers and dealers. The onus of employee development was on the dealers and developers themselves. They had to seek their own learning opportunities, instead of relying on management's initiatives. Other HR functions were performed, sometimes reluctantly, by team leaders or line supervisors as suggested by the following interview remarks:

Fifteen per cent of my time is dedicated to the HR aspect ... I feed up to management. They [senior management] had decided that we need a dedicated HR person in information technology, but the company refused to fund a person in HR ... I am not really interested in the HR area.

Individuals [employees] must manage [their] manager to ensure [skills and knowledge] development happens.

Management in Company A encouraged work effort by the use of performance-based pay. Bonuses made up a substantial proportion of the total pay of employees at Sites IT and MM. On average, bonuses contributed 15 per cent of the salary of Site IT's employees. At Site MM, the share of bonus in employees' salary was much higher, averaging at 45 per cent with considerable variations between individual employees. Bonus payments were set unilaterally by team leaders in consultation with supervisors. Employees had almost no influence or participation in the bonus-setting process. An employee at Site IT reported that: 'there is no appeal against the bonus decisions. I got zero per cent last year and went to see a guy [in management] who said there was no real tribunal, and that the human resource department would side with team leaders.'

The external labour market for developers was tight. This, together with the lack of internal promotion chances could lead to turnover problems. This was duly recognized by management and employees, as indicated by corporate discussion documents and interview remarks:

The loss of staff and key skill sets from [Company B] to competitor companies is [another] threat. This places [Company B] in a vulnerable position in terms of resourcing and expertise ... A title, a recognized place in the organization and a career path are often more important. A career structure will assist in the retainment of staff.

People are not sitting out on street corners. It's a seller's market.

As soon as I hit the wall here, I will look for something else here or elsewhere.

However, internal career ladders that offered promotion opportunities within the corporation were absent at all three sites. The need to provide employees with internal career paths was dismissed by senior management as dysfunctional in Site IT and Site MM. The management of performance incentive was primarily dealt with by offering employees a generous pay package which management claimed to be well above the going market rate. Thus, management considered bonus payments as sufficient incentive which therefore did not require supplementation by structured promotion opportunities. This is indicated by the following quotes from interviews with managers:

The reason for paying bonuses high relative to salary is that it reduces overhead and means that costs vary with performance of the company.

There is no structured career path. We look for individuals who like to be challenged, and well remunerated.

I don't know what a career means in technology in 1996. Some people still want to be a project manager. I don't agree with that as an automatic aim. It takes the creating initiative away from the individual.

Control Relations: Job Autonomy and Employee Participation

With respect to control relations, developers and dealers individually and jointly as teams enjoyed substantial autonomy and discretion at the task level. The complexity and fluidity of the work in the three sites meant that management could not predefine a routine that specified the way work should be accomplished or problems be resolved. Substantial task discretion, therefore, was given to the employees. This is clearly indicated by the responses to the survey question which asked respondents the amount of influence they had on a number of issues at work. A great majority

(93 per cent) of respondents reported substantial influence in deciding how to do their job and organize their work. Two-thirds said they had considerable involvement in setting their work schedules. The degree of task-level autonomy given to workers was highlighted when one of the employees at Site IT left the company. It was only after his departure that the rest of the team found that he had left a considerable 'black hole' in the work he had been doing, without informing the rest of the team. An employee at Site MM commented on the task autonomy that employees enjoyed in the following way: 'here there is a lot of discretion, lot of self-managing, own responsibility. You need to weigh pros and cons of time spent with different customers. As long as you can convince your peers. If you don't do well on something, they will tell you'.

The amount of influence which dealers and developers had over issues beyond the task level was, however, minimal. Their participation in higher level decision-making was very limited. There were three unions at the corporate level of Company B within which Site TELHI was located. They were concerned with corporate-level issues and their presence at the workplace was minimal. In Company A, there were no collective voice mechanisms apart from occasional employee opinion surveys. Findings from the employee survey show that less than half of the survey respondents (42 per cent) reported that they had considerable influence over the decision to replace equipment with new ones or to set team goals, and a majority (75 per cent) reported little or no influence at all on promotion and hiring decisions. The following comments employees made in interviews converge with these survey findings:

Many people feel out of the loop, unsure what is happening, rumours proliferate in this kind of environment; issues are blown out of proportion.

One issue is lack of communication from management down, people would move jobs but you don't know, there is a bit of an air of secrecy around here.

People in management think there is participation in [business] strategy level, but there isn't. Reality is different, unless you are [seniors] who go off and have meetings all the time. You've got no idea what they are discussing – only find out when it's a done deal. [I have] suggested ideas but not taken up, [we were] not encouraged to develop strategy paper.

Management in Site IT once attempted to encourage participation by creating a debating forum through company-wide common access to a software package. Initially there was a high degree of involvement. However, when the employees noticed that the discussion in the forum did not have much impact on concrete decisions, participation dwindled. An employee explained the loss of interest in the following way: '[it] was a horizontal tool, top [management] did not look at it. I think people don't use it much any more ... when it was found that high level decision-makers were not using it ... people decided it was not useful'. The lack of communication was starkly revealed in a presentation at Site IT which aimed at discussing a work process improvement model. The commitment of workers to the model was necessary for its implementation and success. However, only four out of 200 technologists knew about it. Lack of communication bred mistrust of senior management. Only 39 per cent of the survey respondents agreed that senior management could be trusted to do what they said; and only 47 per cent agreed that they were sincere in dealing with employee problems.

From the above findings about work skills and knowledge, co-worker relations, the rewards system and control relations, it is clear that the work teams of developers and dealers functioned as distinct groups to provide strategic services to internal and external clients. Management conceded to them task autonomy and some decision-making influence and rewarded them with relatively generous pay. This was in exchange for their intangible and scarce expertise and appropriate performance. However, in the absence of institutional participatory mechanisms and internal career progression, these employees remained 'enclaved' – working for, but not being strongly integrated into the corporation. This led to a sense of isolation, communication gaps and mistrust between employees and senior management. The ways these problems affected organizational vis-à-vis occupational commitment, work effort and job satisfaction are examined in the next section.

Job Expectations of Knowledge Workers

In the earlier discussion of the dualistic model, we noted that the extent to which management meet the job expectations of employees affects employee commitment, work effort and job satisfaction. To gauge job expectations, respondents to the employee survey were asked to choose and then rank out of 14 job aspects the five that are most important to them in their working lives.[9] The results showed that among all 14 aspects, pay was regarded as the first or second most important job aspect by the greatest proportion (60 per cent) of respondents and had the smallest proportion (12 per cent) not nominating it in their ranking lists. The intrinsic nature of work in terms of its variety, challenge and learning opportunities was ranked as the second most important job aspect. More than half of the respondents (55 per cent) nominated it as their first or second most important job aspect. The intrinsic nature of work was followed by promotion prospects (22 per cent ranked this as first or second most important), co-worker relations (16 per cent) and amount of influence over decisions that affect one's job (13 per cent).

Testing of Postulates: Organizational and Occupational Commitment, Work Effort and Job Satisfaction

Mowday et al. (1982, p. 27) defined organizational commitment as 'the relative strength of an individual's identification with and involvement in a particular organization'.

Their measures have been widely adopted by other studies and were used in our employee survey. Occupational commitment can be defined as identification and involvement in a particular occupation. We adopted the measures used by McCloskey and McCain (1987). Job satisfaction refers to a pleasurable or positive emotional state resulting from the appraisal of one's job or job experiences (Locke, 1976, p. 1300). Our measure of job satisfaction was adapted from Quinn and Shepard (1974). Since it was impossible to obtain standardized job performance data across the three sites, we relied on self-reports that measured the willingness of employees to expend work effort beyond the required level. Bailey (1993) called this discretionary effort and suggested that it is the crucial link between organizational characteristics and levels of individual job performance.[10] Detailed wordings of the survey questions used to gauge these four types of work attitudes, their descriptive statistics and alpha coefficients (which measure their internal consistency) are given in Appendix 8.2. Reliability analysis indicated that they were all internally consistent. Factor analysis was conducted on each set and it was noted that only one factor underlay each one of them. In the following discussion, responses to questions used to gauge the level of occupational and organizational commitment are examined first. This is followed by two sets of statistical analyses.

Table 8.3 gives the response distributions to questions about occupational and organizational commitment. Except for the statements about being proud of the occupation and organization which had the same proportions of respondents expressing agreement, the results in Table 8.3 indicate that respondents were more committed to their occupation than to the organization. For example, while 91 per cent of the respondents planned to be active in their occupation, a smaller proportion (59 per cent) said they would turn down a job at comparable pay and prospects in another company to stay with the current company. Two scales were calculated from each of these two sets of questions. The average for the occupational commitment scale is 4.24 (1 = lowest to 5 = highest), while that for the organizational commitment scale is 3.87. This indicates that our knowledge workers were more committed to their occupation than to the corporation.

Two factors indicating occupational and organizational commitment were derived from the above two sets of questions. The two factors were positively and significantly correlated to each other $(r = + 0.28, p = 0.001)$. The correlation is weaker than those noted in previous studies of employee commitment.[11] The third set of analyses assesses the independent effects of organizational and occupational commitment on work effort and job satisfaction. We noted in our earlier discussion that the market model highlights the importance of pay, and according to our employee survey findings, pay was considered the most important job aspect. Other studies have noted that satisfaction with pay contributes to overall job satisfaction (Clark, 1996; Gallie et al., 1998). We also take into account the effects of gender, marital status, age and educational level. Previous studies have noted that these socio-demographic factors have independent effects on work effort and job satisfaction. We used ordinary least squares regression in the analysis. The results are given in Table 8.4.

Table 8.4 shows that the effect of occupational commitment on discretionary work effort was significant and positive. The higher the level of occupational commitment,

Table 8.3 Percentage distribution of responses to questions that measure occupational and organizational commitment

	Strongly agreed or agreed (%)	Neither agreed nor disagreed (%)	Disagreed or strongly disagreed (%)	Total ($n = 134$)
Occupational commitment				
I plan to continue to be active in the occupation I am in now	91	2	7	100
I am proud to work in this occupation	86	11	3	100
Pursuing a career in this occupation is important to me	78	13	9	100
Organizational commitment				
I am willing to work harder than I have to in order to help this company succeed	73	18	9	100
I am proud to tell others that I work for this company	86	13	1	100
I feel much loyalty to this company[1]	61	21	18	100
I would turn down a job at comparable pay and prospects in another company to stay with this company	59	19	22	100

[1]The original question was negatively worded. For the sake of presentation, it is positively worded here.

Table 8.4 Ordinary least squares regression results for discretionary work effort and overall job satisfaction

Independent variable	Discretionary work effort B (s.e.)	Overall job satisfaction B (s.e.)
Occupational commitment	0.18 (0.08)***	0.270 (0.09)***
Organizational commitment	0.008 (0.08)	0.266 (0.08)***
Satisfaction with pay	−0.11 (0.09)	0.356 (0.08)***
Age	−0.008 (0.01)	−0.02 (0.01)
Education level (1 = degree-holder; 0 = non-degree holder)	0.05 (0.18)	−0.03 (0.18)
Marital status(1 = married; 0 = otherwise)	0.03 (0.16)	−0.19 (0.18)
Gender (1 = male; 0 = female)	−0.05 (0.18)	−0.03 (0.18)
Constant	0.92 (0.64)	−0.25 (0.69)
R^2	0.084	0.36

B = unstandardized regression coefficient; s.e. = standard error, $*p < 0.1$; $**p < 0.05$; $***p < 0.001$.

the greater the amount of discretionary effort expended. We noted earlier that the intrinsic nature of the work of our knowledge workers was characterized by challenges and uncertainties which, in turn, required considerable creativity and initiatives. Alvesson (2000, p. 1104) suggested that these features enhanced occupational commitment and work motivation. On the contrary, organizational commitment did not have significant effect. Despite the fact that pay was linked to performance, satisfaction with pay did not have a significant effect. This may be due to pay being a hygiene rather than a motivating factor (Herzberg et al., 1959) and is partly explained by the unsystematic and highly subjective application of performance appraisal to knowledge work, especially at Site IT. Our survey shows that among those survey respondents whose performance had been appraised ($n = 105$), only 56 per cent agreed that the appraisal was based on facts rather than management opinion, and 51 per cent agreed that the criteria were made clear to them well ahead of time. The level of satisfaction among the appraisees was, therefore, not particularly high: only 46 per cent were satisfied with the way their job performance was appraised.

We next examine the results for job satisfaction. Table 8.4 shows that organizational and occupational commitment as well as pay satisfaction each independently contributed to overall job satisfaction. The higher the levels of occupational and organizational commitment and pay satisfaction, the higher the level of satisfaction with the job as a whole. A comparison of the coefficients suggested that pay satisfaction had the strongest effect, followed by occupational and organizational commitment. As our knowledge workers attached great importance to pay, it is, therefore, not surprising that pay satisfaction was positively related to overall job satisfaction and its effect was greater than those of occupational and organizational commitment. To sum up, the regression analyses show that it is occupational commitment and pay satisfaction which contributed to our knowledge workers' job satisfaction and work effort. Organizational commitment was either insignificant or has a weaker effect. None of the demographic factors were significant in the work effort and job satisfaction regression analyses.

Table 8.5 summarizes the above four sets of findings and their associated postulates which we derived from the market and dualistic model in the earlier discussion.

The results from field research and the employee survey show that the dualistic model receives more empirical support than the market model. Our knowledge workers were, to a certain extent, committed to the corporation, though they were more attached to their occupation. Loyalty to the occupation and the corporation were related. However, the lack of institutional channels for knowledge workers to participate in the corporation's decision-making process led to unmet job expectations. This is reflected in the weak correlation between organizational and occupational commitment and in the insignificant effect of organizational commitment and pay satisfaction on work effort. Our research indicates that the work attitudes of knowledge workers are an interplay between the functioning of their enclave-like work team and management's market orientation that is reflected in the reward system. The interplay between these two factors created communication gaps and integration problems. The absence of organizational career paths and institutional participatory mechanisms meant that management did not meet two important job expectations of employees, namely, promotion prospects and influence over work-related decisions. Thus, only 38 per cent of the respondents were satisfied with their promotion opportunities and 25 per cent expressed dissatisfaction (the remaining 37 per cent were neither satisfied nor dissatisfied). The level of satisfaction with

Table 8.5 A summary of the postulates from the market model and dualistic model and the empirical findings

	The empirical findings	Result for the postulate of the market model	Result for the postulate of the dualistic model
The relative levels of organizational commitment and occupational commitment	Occupational commitment higher than organizational commitment	Supported	Not supported
The correlation between organizational commitment and occupational commitment	Positive but weak	Not supported	Supported
The effect of organizational commitment on work efffort and job satisfaction	Insignificant for work effort, positive for job satisfaction	Postulate about work effort supported; postulate about job satisfaction not supported	Supported
The effect of occupational commitment on work effort and job satisfaction	Positive and significant for both work effort and job satisfaction	Supported	Supported
The effect of pay satisfaction on work effort and job satisfaction	Insignificant for work effort, positive for job satisfaction	Postulate about work effort not supported; postulate about job satisfaction supported	Postulate about work effort not supported; postulate about job satisfaction supported

work influence was not particularly high as only 49 per cent of the respondents expressed satisfaction, and only 32 per cent were neither satisfied nor dissatisfied.

Conclusion

This chapter reported a study of knowledge workers employed as money market dealers and computer system developers in large corporations. In response to Reed (1996) who claimed that knowledge workers tend to pursue a marketization strategy to protect their expertise and gain economic advantages, we noted that this way of understanding knowledge workers overlooks 1 the importance of contextual knowledge in the creation of knowledge and 2 the possible constraints knowledge workers face as employees in large corporations. Taking account of these points, we suggested a dualistic model which stresses the interdependence between knowledge workers and the corporation and the ways corporations can both enable and limit knowledge workers' autonomy.

The market model and the dualistic model were then applied to 134 knowledge workers employed in two large corporations, part of which were located in Australia. The empirical findings lend more support to the dualistic model than to the market model. The knowledge workers in our cases differed from the type Reed discussed: on the one hand, they sought specialization and knowledge advancement through their enclave-like work teams; on the other hand, they looked to the corporation for promotion chances. They also desired more participation in the decision-making process of senior management. Promotion to higher-ranking positions along internal career ladders offered both recognition of their expertise and greater institutionalized and formal influence over relatively higher-level decisions in the corporation. Formal power in decision-making would enable knowledge workers to mobilize corporate resources to protect and advance their interests. Management in our cases, however, relied primarily on extrinsic rewards and job autonomy as the major levers to manage work motivation. Our analyses indicated that these levers were not successful in enhancing work effort. This suggests that more systematic, jointly determined appraisal systems which include employee participation will be crucial for effective performance-based reward systems.

Our study suggests that the reliance on the external labour market and centralized decision-making seemed to be counter productive in the management of knowledge workers. A managerialist conclusion would suggest that management should introduce career ladders and forms of participation for the knowledge workers. However, whether these actions are effective is questionable. If career ladders are developed to allow knowledge workers access to other sections of the corporation, then, quid pro quo, similarly the knowledge work enclave careers may be opened up to other job-holders of the corporation. If participation opportunities are given to knowledge workers in the decision-making process of senior management and above, a logical quid pro quo is that the enclave-like work team would be open to senior management's and corporate influence. These are important implications to management practitioners.

The dualistic model developed in this paper was applied to two occupational types of knowledge workers. Very few of them were members of professional associations. The general applicability of the model awaits future and comparative research on: 1 other types of knowledge workers like computer engineers, financial analysts, information technology analysts who are similarly employed in large corporations; and 2 knowledge workers who are organized into professional associations.

Notes

The authors would like to thank Leigh Donoghue for his valuable contributions to the field-work data collection and analysis. We would also like to thank Andersen Consulting and the Australian Research Council for funding the research on which this chapter is based.

1 The issue of employee loyalty to the organization was addressed by Lincoln and Kalleberg (1990). From their comparative study of work organizations in Japan and the USA, they developed a corporatist model to understand the commitment and work attitudes of workers. The model was subsequently used to study new organizational forms of traditional and new professionals (Wallace, 1995a, 1995b). However, the corporatist model stresses the assimilation of the worker into the organization. It does not feature the possible dynamic and dualistic relationship between workers and the organization as in the case of knowledge workers.

2 The primary purpose of the project was to examine the way customer services were delivered and complex work tasks were undertaken and organized in advanced service sectors. For details of the research, see Frenkel et al. (1999).

3 To ensure a relatively high response rate, the survey was conducted through on-site administration. Where on-site administration was hampered by practical constraints, respondents were supplied with a self-addressed envelope to return the completed questionnaire by mail.

4 The other four types of skills are computer skills, interpersonal skills, self-management skills and adaptive skills.

5 Other types of knowledge included in the question are: company's formal policies, systems and procedures; market and other trends in the industry; competitors' products and services; post-secondary school education.

6 Other sources of learning included in the question are: employees from other departments/sections with whom the employee currently was in contact; experience gained from job rotation; team leader or supervisor; computer systems; work-related associates outside the company; written manuals and reference guides; publications and research in the employee's area of expertise; customers with whom you are, or have been, in contact.

7 It is likely that socialization outside work was limited by long working hours and by family responsibilities; 58 per cent of the respondents were married and 40 per cent of these respondents had one dependant child.

8 Favourable relationships between team members were negatively affected when the annual bonus payments were decided. Employees reported in interviews in-fighting and conflicts around the time when management decided on the bonus payments of individual knowledge workers.

9 The 14 job aspects are: promotion prospects, pay, capability and efficiency of management, the flexibility of working hours, the nature of work (variety, challenge, opportunities to learn), workload, training provision, people whom I work with, influence over decisions that affect one's job, work technology, the way one's job performance is measured, the amount of leisure time, relations with customers, job security.

10 Self-reports of work effort or job performance have been criticized on the grounds that people cannot evaluate their performance accurately and there is likely to be social desirability effect and hence inflation in the responses given by the employees. These criticisms are open issues rather than definitive verdicts. Heneman (1974, p. 638) pointed out that studies have shown opposite results regarding whether there is convergent and discriminant validity for self- and superior ratings. Heneman noted in his comparison of self- and superior ratings of performance that self-ratings tended to be less lenient and more variable than superior ratings. He recommended that self-ratings were likely to be more appropriate for research purposes than for organizational evaluations.

11 Wallace (1993) conducted a meta-analysis of 25 studies which examined occupational and organizational commitment and found that the true correlation coefficient was + 0.45. Morrow (1993, pp. 83–4) noted in her review of studies that the correlation coefficients generally ranged from + 0.31 to + 0.52. Thus, in our case, the relation is not particularly strong, compared to these analogous previous studies.

Appendix 8.1

A Sample of the Template Used to Code and Analyse Field Research Data

1   Context of work organization
- Macro
  - Product market or industry
  - Organizational strategy
  - Organization structure
  - Organization culture

- Mezzo
  - Work organization history
  - Structure, key roles and functions, etc.
  - Trajectory and process of change
  - Workforce demographics

2   Pattern of work organization
- Work relations
  - Act of work: creativity, forms of knowledge, skills
  - Vertical relations
  - Lateral relations
  - Customer–worker relations
  - Role of information technology
  - Spatial arrangements and physical work environment

- Employment relations
  - Selection criteria and process
  - Employment contract and actuality
  - Training and development
  - Performance management
  - Remuneration and recognition
  - Career opportunities and aspirations
  - Industrial relations

3   Outcomes of work organization
- Employee interests
- Management interests
- Customer interests

Appendix 8.2

Definitions of variables, descriptive statistics and results of reliability tests are given in Table 8.A1.

Table 8.A1 Definitions of variables, descriptive statistics and results of reliability tests

Variable	Definition (mean, standard deviation)	Cronbach's alpha coefficient
Discretionary work effort	In doing your work, how often do you do each of the following (1 = never to 5 = very often) • go beyond the scope of your duties when necessary (4.01, 0.83) • put in extra effort (4.30, 0.69) • do more than the acceptable level (4.21, 0.77)	0.84
Job satisfaction	• All in all, how satisfied are you with your job? [1 = very dissatisfied to 5 = very satisfied] (3.8, 0.83) • If you were free to go into any type of job you wanted, what would your choice be? 1 = I want the job I have now 2 = I want to retire and not work at all 3 = I prefer some other job to the job I have now [the above three pre-coded choices were recoded] • If a good friend of yours told you he or she was interested in working in a job like yours for your employer, what would you tell him or her? 1 = I would strongly recommend it 2 = I would have doubts recommending it 3 = I would advise the friend against it [the above three pre-coded choices were recoded]	0.67
Occupational commitment	Thinking about your occupation, how much do you agree or disagree with each of the following? (1 = strongly disagree to 5 = strongly agree) • I plan to continue to be active in the occupation I am in now (4.35, 0.90) • I am proud to work in this occupation (4.31, 0.79) • Pursuing a career in this occupation is important to me (4.08, 1.00)	0.82
Organizational commitment	Thinking about this company, how much do you agree or disagree with each of the following? (1 = strongly disagree to 5 = strongly agree) • I am willing to work harder than I have to in order to help this company succeed (3.89, 0.98) • I am proud to tell others that I work for this company (4.25, 0.71) • I feel very little loyalty to this company [reverse coded] (3.69, 1.18) • I would turn down a job at comparable pay and prospects in another company to stay with this company (3.66, 1.28)	0.63

References

Abbott, A. (1991) 'The future of professions: occupation and expertise in the age of organization'. In Tolbert, P.S. and Barley, S.R. (eds), *Research in the Sociology of Organizations*, 8. Greenwich, CT: JAI Press, 17–42.

Alvesson, M. (2000) 'Social identity and the problem of loyalty in knowledge-intensive companies'. *Journal of Management Studies*, 37, 8, 1101–23.

Angle, H.L. and Lawson, H.B. (1994) 'Organizational commitment and employees' performance ratings: both type of commitment and type of performance count'. *Psychological Reports*, 75, 1539–51.

Bacharach, S. et al. (1991) 'Negotiating the "see-saw" of managerial strategy: a resurrection of the study of professionals in organizational theory'. In Tolbert, P.S. and Barley, S.R. (eds), *Research in the Sociology of Organizations*, 8. Greenwich, CT: JAI Press, 217–38.

Bailey, T. (1993) *Discretionary Effort and the Organization of Work, Employee Participation and Work Reform since Hawthorne*. Discussion Paper, Teacher College, University of Columbia, New York.

Becker, T. et al. (1996) 'Foci and bases of employee commitment: implications for job performance'. *Academy of Management Journal*, 39, 469–82.

Bell, D. (1973) *The Coming of Post-industrial Society*. New York: Basic Books.

Berg, I. (1981) *Sociological Perspectives on Labor Markets*. New York: Academic Press.

Blackler, F. et al. (1993) 'Editorial introduction: knowledge workers and contemporary organizations'. *Journal of Management Studies*, 30, 6, 851–62.

Cappelli, P. (1999) *The New Deal at Work*. Boston, MA: Harvard Business School Press.

Carré, F. et al. (eds) (2000) *Non-standard Work: the Nature and Challenges of Changing Employment Arrangements*. Industrial Relations Research Association Series. Champaign, IL: Industrial Relations Research Association.

Causer, G. and Jones, C. (1996) 'Management and control of technical labour'. *Work, Employment and Society*, 10, 105–23.

Clark, A. (1996) 'Job satisfaction in Britain'. *British Journal of Industrial Relations*, 34, 2, 189–217.

Drucker, P. (1993) *Post-capitalist Society*. New York: Harper.

Fincham, R. et al. (1994) *Expertise and Innovations*. Oxford: Clarendon Press.

Frenkel, S. et al. (1999) *On the Frontline: Work Organization in the Information Economy*. New York: Cornell University Press.

Gallie, D. et al. (1998) *Restructuring the Employment Relationship*. Oxford: Clarendon Press.

Gibbons, M. et al. (1994) *The New Production of Knowledge*. London: SAGE.

Gunz, H.P. and Gunz, S. (1994) 'Professional/organizational commitment and job satisfaction for employed lawyers'. *Human Relations*, 47, 801–28.

Heneman, H.G. II (1974) 'Comparisons of self- and superior ratings of managerial performance'. *Journal of Applied Psychology*, 59, 5, 638–42.

Herzberg, F., Mausner, B. and Snyderman, B. (1959) *The Motivation to Work*. New York: Wiley.

Hill, S., Martin, R. and Harris, M. (2000) 'Decentralisation, integration and the post-bureaucratic organization: the case of R&D'. *Journal of Management Studies*, 37, 4, 563–85.

Kalleberg, A.L. and Marsden, P.V. (1995) 'Organizational commitment and job performance in the U.S. labor force'. In Simpson, I.H. and Simpson, R.L. (eds), *Research in Sociology of Work*, 5, Greenwich, CT: JAI Press, 235–57.

Kanter, R.M. (1993) *Men and Women of the Corporation* (2nd edition). New York: Basic Books.

Koestler, A. (1970) *The Act of Creation*. London: Picador.

Lincoln, J.R. and Kalleberg, A.L. (1990) *Culture, Control and Commitment*. Cambridge: Cambridge University Press.

Locke, E.A. (1976) 'The nature and causes of job satisfaction'. In Dunnette, M.D. (ed.), *Handbook of Industrial and Organizational Psychology*. Chicago, IL: Rand McNally, 1297–349.

McCloskey, J.C. and McCain, B.E. (1987) 'Satisfaction, commitment and professionalism of newly employed nurses'. *Image: Journal of Nursing Scholarship*, 19, 20–4.

Mathieu, J.E. and Zajac, D. (1990) 'A review and meta-analysis of the antecendents, correlates and consequences of organizational commitment'. *Psychological Bulletin*, 108, 171–94.

Meyer, J.P. and Allen, N.J. (1997) *Commitment in the Workplace*. Thousand Oaks, CA: SAGE.

Mintzberg, H. (1993) *Structure in Fives*. Upper Saddle River, NJ: Prentice-Hall, Inc.

Morrow, P.C. (1993) *The Theory and Measurement of Work Commitment*. Greenwich, CT: JAI Press.

Mowday, R.T., Steers, R.M. and Porter, L. (1982) *Employee-Organization Linkages: the Psychology of Commitment, Absenteeism and Turnover*. New York: Academic Press.

Pitt, L.F., Foreman, S.K. and Bromfield, D. (1995) 'Organizational commitment and service delivery: evidence from an industrial setting in the UK'. *The International Journal of Human Resource Management*, 6, 1, 369–89.

Quinn, R.P. and Shepard, L.J. (1974) *The 1972–73 Quality of Employment Survey*. Ann Arbor, MI: Institute for Social Research, University of Michigan.

Raelin, J.A. (1985) *The Clash of Cultures: Managers and Professionals*. Boston, MA: Harvard Business School Press.

Reed, M.I. (1996) 'Expert power and control in late modernity: an empirical review and theoretical synthesis'. *Organization Studies*, 17, 4, 573–97.

Riain, S.O. (2000) 'Net-working for a living: Irish software developers in the global work-place'. In Burawoy, M. et al. (eds), *Global Ethnography: Forces, Connections, and Imaginations in a Postmodern World*. Berkeley, CA: University of California Press, 175–202.

Scarbrough, H. (1996) 'Understanding and managing expertise'. In Scarbrough, H. (ed.), *The Management of Expertise*. London: St. Martin's Press, 23–47.

von Glinow, M.A. (1988) *The New Professionals*. Cambridge, MA: Ballinger.

Wallace, J.E. (1993) 'Professional and organizational commitment: compatible or incompatible'. *Journal of Vocational Behaviour*, 42, 333–49.

Wallace, J.E. (1995a) 'Organizational and professional commitment in professional and non-professional organizations'. *Administrative Science Quarterly*, 40, 228–55.

Wallace, J.E. (1995b) 'Corporatist control and organizational commitment among professionals: the case of lawyers working in law firms'. *Social Forces*, 73, 3, 811–39.

Zuboff, S. (1988) *In the Age of the Smart Machine*. London: Heinemann.

Human Resource Policies for Knowledge Work

9

John Storey

Knowledge of some kind has always constituted some element in work of all kinds: hunter-gatherers, early farmers, builders of temples, canals and railways all required knowledge as well as materials and muscles. So, why the recent focus on the knowledge component? Moreover, in so far as the knowledge component of work has become increasingly significant, what are the human resource management implications?

It is the latter question that forms the agenda for this chapter. But it is necessary to address the former question first. The thesis argued by a range of writers, many from the domains of economics, strategic management and sociology of work, is that many if not all economic enterprises are now operating in a new competitive landscape. Knowledge-based industries such as biotechnology have come to represent the new age in place of the capital-based industries such as steel, which represented the industrial age. Moreover, changes in technology, transport and (de)regulation have opened up economic competition onto a global scale. As a result, players have to abide by new rules. On the demand side, consumer markets are more volatile, product life cycles are shorter than before and product segmentation and market segmentation require variety rather than standardization of products. The mass production and economies of scale paradigm is under threat. In its place, variety, novelty, agility and responsiveness are critical.

Under such conditions, the new orthodoxy has it that knowledge-based resources have become paramount in the quest for competitiveness comparative to (though not of course entirely displacing) other resources such as capital or natural resources. Capabilities and competences (underpinned by knowledge) are regarded as the most important strategic assets (Prahalad and Hamel, 1990; Stalk et al., 1992). Within this same strategic management framework, the creation and sharing of knowledge are thus regarded as major contributors to organizational advantage (Nahapiet and Ghoshal, 1998).

Two interrelated questions arise from this diagnosis of the changing game of competitive advantage. What are the implications, first, for the role of people within organizations? and second, for managing these human resources (HR)? One perceived implication might be, for example, its explanation of the so-called 'war for talent';

the critical priority for organizations being to hire the most talented individuals at virtually any price. This could be classified as the individualistic response. An alternative view is that such an individualized conception is both morally distasteful and possibly factually incorrect. It is argued, for example, that even exceptionally talented individuals require the support of many other people, appropriate systems and procedures. Indeed, complex products (e.g. films, aeronautical engines, etc.) require collaborative and aligned inputs from many sources and thus much of the knowledge resource is embedded in the underlying systems and processes – including the adaptability of those systems and processes.

The existing literature tends to adopt variously one of these stances or the other (the 'star' individualist or the systems perspective) and sometimes both, without proper recognition that they could require different HR approaches. Much recent literature addresses the theme of 'managing knowledge workers' (Amar, 2002; Horibe, 1999). The agenda, from this perspective, is one of training, empowering, rewarding knowledge and encouraging people to learn. The objective is to ensure these individuals and teams are 'willing' to share their knowledge *with* the group and to use the shared knowledge *of* the group. Hence, providing the conditions and the incentives for this becomes the managerial mission. A somewhat different proposition is that knowledge is embedded in the processes and systems of the organization. The implication one could derive from this would seem to be that a less individualistic approach is required and that those involved in people management should set high on their agenda aspects such as recruiting people who have the 'correct' orientations and attitudes; who are willing to conform to these systems; and who are willing to contribute to jointly-produced operations. Horibe (1999) follows other writers in distinguishing between 'human capital' (brainpower) and 'structural capital' (in part database systems but also the wider infrastructure that supports and allows optimal use of human capital). The HR aspects relating to both, however, amount to largely the same agenda – namely encouraging learning and use of the available knowledge.

Work and enterprise design tend to derive from the economic and the business models that are predominant at any one time. During the mass production, industrial era, F.W. Taylor (1911) designed-out the legacy work patterns of the previous craft era. The 'principles of scientific management' formed the engineered prospectus for a new labour process better fitted to the new product market context and the new industrial organization context that was being created. The break-up of whole work tasks into fragmented elements (the division of labour) was one key principle (Gilbreth, 1914). The insistence on managers holding all the decision-making power was a second. It should be recalled that the central tenet of 'knowledge management' at this time was to *prevent* workers using their knowledge. Henry Ford continued the mission with the logic of the moving assembly line. The fundamental idea was to squeeze out discretion, creativity and variation. Conformity was required in order to meet the goal of industrial standardization. Contrary to the emphasis in recent years on learning as a critical factor in knowledge age work, the main principle in Taylor's scientific management was to drive-out inherited skills and craft learning; all that was required was to conform to industrial routines.

The varied and multiple changes that have characterized economic competition during the past 20 to 30 years have called into question this industrial formula and made it look increasingly vulnerable. The industrial behemoths, such as General Motors, General Electric and Chrysler, found to their surprise that their size, routines and command of vast material resources did not offer a sustainable entry barrier to new upstart competitors. The command and control approach seemed unable to meet the new challenge of competitors who were producing products better suited to changing consumer demands. A seismic shift was occurring: the ossified, centralized knowledge, owned or controlled by the entrepreneur or by the small group of agents retained by owners of stocks and shares, proved a poor match for the vibrant, more dispersed knowledge exercised by the new producers.

Thus, within this context – one where more knowledge is required, where frequent changes of knowledge are required and where more multiple sources of knowledge are required – HR management policies come into play.

This chapter examines the implications for the way people are managed under current circumstances in which 'knowledge' is identified as a major concern. Such circumstances arise, for example, when knowledge is perceived as being the key to delivering competitive advantage. This chapter is organized in three main sections. First, a brief review of the nature of knowledge work and its apparent implications for HR. Second, the nature and evolution of HR. Third, a conceptual framework is presented and a detailed analysis carried out of the knowledge organization and its HR linkages.

The Nature of Knowledge Work and Implications for HR

An underlying key theme in much research is the idea that knowledge intensive firms (KIFs) represent and presage the firms and work of the future. Notably, Drucker (1993) observed that knowledge was becoming the critical resource in the new economy.

This same idea is to be found stated explicitly in the CIPD report by Swart et al. (2001). Echoing the work of Starbuck (1992) on knowledge intensive firms, they (2001: vii–viii) state: 'the knowledge intensive sector ... reflects likely changes in the UK economy in the future'. These firms, it is contended, 'challenge widely held beliefs about how organizations should be structured and managed; they are said to be developing a model for people management which is different ...', 'a new model of people management is emerging in knowledge intensive firms' (Angela Baron (2001), CIPD).

Swart et al. themselves suggest that there are three critical elements to this new management: developing individual knowledge; sharing this across the organization; and sharing and developing knowledge across clients, partners and suppliers (i.e. across the supply chain).

Such ideas are now relatively commonplace (though the problematic nature of the idea of KIF has been noted) (Alvesson and Karreman, 2001). The interrelationship between human resource management (HRM) and knowledge work is two-way. That is, work situations where knowledge is intensive, or in some other way especially critical, can be expected to present special challenges to the practice of HR. It cannot be assumed that conventional HR priorities, policies and practices are necessarily equally appropriate to such situations. Indeed, there could be said to be a prima facie assumption that sets of different and distinctive practices will be required. In so far as this is the case, the crucial question therefore becomes: in what ways will HR have to change in order to fit the special circumstances of knowledge work? By the same token, the reverse relationship should also be considered: what insights into the optimal organization and management of knowledge work can be identified by drawing on insights from HR?

It needs to be noted at the outset that when the term HRM is used in this chapter, it does not solely refer to the officially designated HR specialist function. The usage here also embraces the management of human resources by any person within and across organizations, including, for example, line managers.

The kinds of issues and questions which arise when the relationships between HR and knowledge work are juxtaposed are many. A couple of the overarching ones we have already alluded to, but in addition to the 'big' question about the possible overall reconfiguration of the HR approach, there are many other interesting and important questions that nest within it. For example, if there is such a concept as 'knowledge work' which has, it is widely claimed, assumed special critical importance in recent years as a source of competitive advantage and sustainability, then does that mean there are, by implication, new types of workers, 'knowledge workers', who undertake this work? Posing this question raises others; for example, is knowledge work concentrated in specialist hands, and if so is the agenda therefore one which concerns the special treatment of an elite or special cadre (such as an expanded or redrawn mode of 'professional worker')? Or is knowledge-at-work now so widely dispersed and infiltrated into work in general that the issue is how to manage virtually all work with this new priority in mind? Wherever and however – widely or tightly drawn – knowledge work is located and distributed, the central question in relation to the people-and-relationships management point of view is what set of policies seem most pertinent for this kind of work. This central question will form the heart of this chapter and in order to assess it in a rounded manner the chapter will also examine the other questions posed above.

The Human Resource Management Contribution

So what can HRM contribute to the new challenge of management? In order to answer this question we first have to ask what HRM is. Human resource management can itself be seen to be part of the same evolutionary economic forces as outlined above. There has been immense debate within the specialism about the extent to which it differs from traditional personnel management. The broad answer is, that in many respects, HRM shares many – though not all – of the techniques and methodologies of personnel management. Both disciplines are concerned with the fundamental processes of recruitment and selection, training and development, pay and rewards, and so on. To this extent HRM and personnel management can virtually be regarded as the same. But in another respect they could be said to be different. The differences may at times be subtle but in terms of the present topic of managing knowledge they could be said to be nonetheless hugely significant.

The key differences relate first to beliefs and assumptions underlying the two approaches, second to their strategic intent, third the relationship between line managers and the people-management specialists, and fourth the key levers used by both approaches (Storey, 1992: 35). In brief, while some people management specialists still call themselves personnel managers and their departments personnel departments there was a discernible transition period from the late 1980s onwards during which the ways in which 'labour' was managed began to shift in significant ways. Notably, the shifts in approach were often driven not by the personnel specialists themselves but by general managers and line managers who took it upon themselves to manage people in ways different from the then prevailing norms. Ironically, people practising 'personnel' as specialists were sometimes the most resistant to change and often warned against the changes. The shift or transition can be briefly shown in Table 9.1.

Table 9.1 gives a summary of 10 features that form part of a wider more elaborated analysis but which are sufficient to convey the flavour of the shift to HRM. In essence, it is a transition from industrial-age procedures and labour-management inspired negotiated 'temporary truces'/agreements, to a post-industrial-age doctrine that recognizes 'labour' as a potential source of competitive advantage – a resource rather than a nuisance and a cost. Thus, while HRM can be used to facilitate 'knowledge management' it is simultaneously itself part of the phenomenon that it is being used to manage. Hence, this is highly relevant to our focus on managing knowledge; the shift can be seen as a part of the wider transformation to a new competitive landscape of the nature and breadth sketched above. In other words, HRM can be viewed as a management theory and technology which emerged as part of the knowledge economy.

It should be noted, however, that not all companies and organizations have shifted in this manner. Even today we have segmented labour markets and diverse employment strategies. At one extreme end there is the highly casualized employment system with low pay, no training and no employment security: the 'gang-masters' employing immigrant labour virtually on a day-to-day basis reminiscent of casualized dock work at the end of the 19th century. Also at this end of the spectrum, low-pay, low-skilled and low-knowledge work persists – and may even have grown – in some parts of the catering, cleaning, hotel and related trades where contract workers are allowed minimal discretion and minimal reward. Such work and such work systems are not normally considered to be part of the 'new economy' or the 'knowledge economy' and they are usually simply ignored. In another sense, they

Table 9.1 Shift from personnel/IR to HRM

Dimension	Personnel & IR	HRM
Beliefs and assumptions		
Contract	Careful negotiation of written contract	Aim to go beyond contract
Rules	Importance of clear rules	Aim to instil 'can-do' outlook
	Appeal to custom and practice	Appeal to business need
Strategy		
Key relationship	Labour-management	Customer
Initiatives	Piecemeal	Integrated
Relationship to business strategy	Marginal to	Central to
Line management		
Management role	Transactional	Transformational leadership
Key managers	Personnel/IR specialists	General/business/line managers
Key levers		
Selection	A marginal second-order task	Integrated key task
Job categories and grades	Many	Few
Nature of interventions	New personnel procedures	Wide-ranging cultural, structural and personnel strategies

could perhaps be seen as the hidden, subterranean foundation of the visible knowledge economy offering support services upon which the more fortunate depend.

However, the HRM strategies described and analysed in this chapter are those which are designed to address the needs of the 'knowledge work' end of the spectrum. At this end, work is more knowledge-intensive, and human capital is the vital ingredient for organizational survival and success. Human capital can be considered to comprise reputation, drive, skills and knowledge. In this chapter therefore we will treat knowledge as a sub-set of human capital resources.

Human Resource Policies for Knowledge Work: A Conceptual Framework

As pointed out in Table 9.1 earlier, a distinctive feature of the HRM approach is that it seeks to manage work in an integrated way. That is, an organization that simply initiates a whole series of interventions, such as a recruitment system, a payment

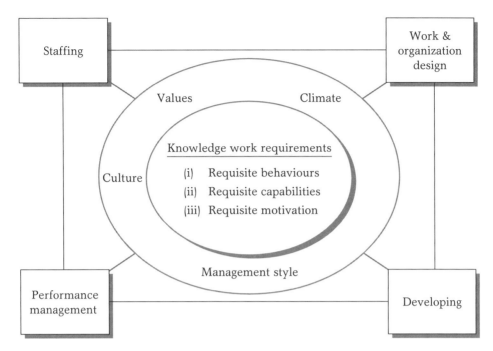

Figure 9.1 Link between HRM and knowledge work

system, an appraisal system and so on, in a series of isolated and disconnected steps and which manages these as separate sub-systems, should not really be considered as practising HRM as properly understood. Thus, integrated, compatible sub-systems are one key element to be recalled from the discussion above. A second, is that the integrated HR system should also be aligned to the mission and strategy of the organization. With these two points in mind we can now turn to Figure 9.1, which shows a conceptual framework linking HRM with knowledge work requirements. The figure illustrates the set of knowledge work 'requirements' and how these are secured through a constellation of HR sub-systems.

Knowledge Work Requirements

Knowledge work requirements are based around a set of behaviours, capabilities and motivations.

Requisite Behaviours   People working in knowledge-intensive environments can be expected to, and will be required to, behave differently from workers in traditional industrial settings. To a considerable extent, management are in fact wanting and requiring the converse of the behaviours instilled and learned under Taylorism. Instead of compliance, with instructions from the top and repeat routine behaviours, there is a need for creative solutions and self-starting behaviour. Workers in these environments will usually be expected to come with a body of knowledge (both formal knowledge and experiential). Thus educational qualifications supplemented by relevant experience is normally expected. Equally important, if not even more so, is evidence of ability to learn anew. Such workers need to behave in ways that allow the organization to access new knowledge, to adapt knowledge, to share it and to apply it in new innovative ways.

Requisite Capabilities Capabilities are related to behaviours but they are worth highlighting as a necessary element underpinning behaviours. The kinds of capabilities usually required for knowledge work situations relate to the capacity for new learning and the capacity to make sense of large amounts of complex information and data. Additionally, a competence in interpreting changes in the marketplace and in other forces in the external environment will be important at least for some of the knowledge workers in the organization.

Beyond the individual level, there is a need for capabilities located within organizational routines. This implies the importance of complementary capabilities distributed across the organization (Tsoukas, 1996).

A further capability worthy of note, in the new competitive landscape we have been sketching, is the need for emerging businesses, such as design, engineering services, software design and so on, to actively shape customer expectations and not merely respond to expressed demand (Lei et al., 1999).

Requisite Motivation Capability per se is not of course sufficient. People in knowledge work environments need to be motivated enough to seek out opportunities and to design their work and their priorities for themselves – often with little or no instruction.

Values, Culture and Climate

Values, culture and organizational climate are organization-level attributes. They can be absolutely crucial because few if any organizations will be able to sustain competitive edge simply by relying on a few talented and motivated individuals. Even these individuals will find it hard to make any significant impact without the complementary support of myriad other organizational members. Thus, if the organization is to work together as a team then it must have and must live a set of relevant values.

A distinction has to be made between actual, lived values and culture, and aspired-to values and culture. Most of the writing about cultures for knowledge intensive organizations addresses mainly the latter – they are prescriptive but they often imply they are also descriptive. However, numerous reports about prevailing cultures in knowledge-intensive firms reveal patterns of behaviour and cultures that are dramatically contrary to many of the prescriptions. For example, reports from a series of industrial tribunal cases involving international banks, computer companies and other work situations, in which high performance and high commissions are expected, point to aggressive rather than 'sharing' work cultures. For instance, a senior female manager at the UK headquarters of Oracle Computer company won an award of £98,000 in December 2004 for discrimination and unfair dismissal arising from what the tribunal chairman found to be a 'male oriented culture'. Her boss was reported to have said that his team members had to be 'young, virile, with plenty of debts, holidays and flash cars' (*Evening Standard*, 23 December 2004; *Daily Telegraph*, 23 December 2004). In May 2004 another high-ranking female investment banker received £1million for wrongful dismissal from Deutsche Bank in the City of London after exposing a culture of sexism. In America in May 2004 Merrill Lynch settled a 10-year battle with 1000 of its female brokers who claimed it had a culture of bias against women. *The Times* (26 June 2004) reported:

> *Female executives described a male-dominated work environment where women fail to reach the highest positions and are forced to tolerate sexist language or be excluded. An executive who brought a sex discrimination claim against the bank in 2001 said: 'It is a very tough culture. It is an aggressive, cold and results-oriented organisation'.*

Merrill Lynch won a sex discrimination case against one of its senior executives in December 2004. The tribunal found that her 'shabby treatment' was not based on grounds of sex.

In the management and academic literature much has been written about the importance of 'corporate culture' (Casey, 1996; Claver et al., 1998; Deal and Kennedy, 1991). In the main, the emphasis is upon a collective orientation directed towards excellence, customer-focus and the desire to perform beyond the norm. This performance driven prescription however does not envisage the version indicated in the cases reported above.

Knowledge is an essential element in securing innovation. In a recent study (using a research design of paired comparisons), which contrasted organizations that were more innovative with those which were less innovative – within the same sector, it was found that senior managers' orientations and perceptions were critical (Storey and Salaman, 2005). Organizational cultures and value systems were shown to be important in shaping the way in which and the extent to which organizations were able to utilize knowledge and deliver innovation with regard to products/services and processes. Top managers were setting the tone for the whole organization in ways which impacted on the orientation and delivery of innovation and on outcomes.

Managers' attitudes to innovation were found to be more important than other variables, such as whether an organization had an R&D unit, whether it had an innovation policy, or whether creativity courses had been run or not. The important point was that senior managers had their *own theories* of innovation. Some

Table 9.2 Managers' implicit theories of innovation

Core elements of managers' implicit theory of innovation	Poor innovating organizations	Well innovating organizations
Underlying attitude towards innovation	Dangerous, potentially improper, irresponsible, childish, conservative	Positive, celebratory, encouraging, radical
Consensus/differentiated definitions	Differentiated	Consensual
Recognition of role of balance, 'ambidexterity'	Conviction that one set of values should dominate	Search for balance, recognition that any 'solution' will fail
Innovating innovation	Traditional view and approach	Open, radical approach
Debate and discussion	Discouraged, not necessary	Encouraged, seen as central
Priority of organization or innovation	Organization, stability	Innovation, change

Source: Storey and Salaman (2005: 150)

managers were in reality rather suspicious of innovation, they viewed it as potentially dangerous and distracting. As a consequence of harbouring these attitudes they tended to set up procedures such as stage-gate review regimes, which could be used to screen out large numbers of innovative proposals. Perhaps more important than structures and procedures, they tended to set the tone with respect to the 'meaning' that innovation would convey in their organizations. This pattern of attitudes and behaviours tended to correlate with poor innovation performance. Conversely, in high performing innovative organizations, top managers' orientations and theories of innovation tended to be more positive and open with respect to innovation itself and to the associated changes which usually accompanied it. The main contrasts between organizations that innovated poorly and those that innovated well are shown in Table 9.2. It shows how managers' implicit theories of innovation were patterned across poor and effective innovating organizations.

The point about 'knowledge' here is rather a subtle one. What we were eliciting and capturing was 'management knowledge' in a rather literal sense. That is, we were researching managers' knowledge about management and about their business. Thus, 'knowledge of' and 'knowledge about' were influencing innovative performance in an important way. It was not only their knowledge of technologies, of customers, of strategic partners and so on – that is the normal building blocks of a successful innovation – but also their knowledge of innovation itself. These senior managers had ideas about, experiences of and theories of innovation – they 'knew' about its potential for good and for bad and they 'knew' about the processes and conditions which enabled or restricted it. This concept of 'knowledge' in the wider sense – as a set of experiences, as a set of understandings with moral, political and cognitive dimensions, and as a set of beliefs – has profound implications for innovation in organizations and for knowledge work more generally.

Management Style

Management style might be considered as a sub-set of culture. The way managers behave and the way they *enact* and *mediate* the policies shown in the outer parts of Figure 9.1 can be absolutely critical to the way the behaviours at the core of the figure have an impact. Studies have shown that even where companies have clear, uniform policies, the way these are *enacted* differs considerably and, moreover, that these differences matter (Purcell et al., 2003). For example, front line managers can be crucial in making the difference between poorly performing and highly performing organizations (Hutchinson and Purcell, 2003). Front line managers are defined as managers who have first line responsibility for work groups. An example from a hospital environment would be a ward sister. Research reveals that first line leadership has a very considerable effect on the attitudes and behaviours of employees. The implication is that these managers in turn require skilful management. Managers can be vital in making policies meaningful or, conversely, virtually meaningless. The emphasis on and the considerable rebuilding of the first line management (FLM) role itself formed part of the HRM model (Storey, 1992). In his study of organizations leading in HRM, Storey found that invariably part of the formula was a move away from the old style traditional supervisor roles and the purposeful creation of a new mode of first line managers. Across the cases examined it was revealed that 'few if any of the existing supervisory stock were thought to be suitable candidates' (Storey, 1992: 238). Whole tiers of supervision had been removed – charge hands and superintendents for example. The idea was to introduce a new breed of 'mini-managers' more highly qualified, with responsibilities for budgets, scheduling, quality assurance and team motivation:

> *First line managers were, as the case studies demonstrated, usually at the front line of moves towards human resource management. They were expected to embrace and embody the new management styles; they were the key channels in the open two-way communications; they were to be monitored for involving employees and for developing them. (Storey, 1992: 240)*

In a more recent study, the continued importance of this role is reinforced (Hutchinson and Purcell, 2003). In a multi-sector study which included organizations such as Clerical Medical, Nationwide, PWC and Selfridges there was a strong correlation between the role of the FLM and employee attitudinal and behavioural outcomes such as commitment, motivation, job satisfaction and the exercise of discretionary behaviour (2003: 15–16). It was further emphasized that the way these FLMs were themselves managed was an important determinant of their behaviour.

Staffing

Staffing, shown in the top left corner of Figure 9.1 refers to the set of HR policies and practices related to HR planning, recruitment and selection. Its relevance to the knowledge work debate stems from the increased importance of human capital in knowledge work organizations. While work in general in a knowledge economy may require increased applications of knowledge, nonetheless, it is argued that knowledge intensity is unequally distributed. Thus as argued by Lepak and Snell (2003: 127): 'whereas all people may contribute knowledge, innovation, creativity and the like, not all employees are equal in their knowledge-based contributions.' It would be 'misleading to suggest that all employees are likely to be knowledge workers. Rather, knowledge workers are likely to make up a proportion of the workforce' (2003: 130).

Lepak and Snell (2003) suggest shifting the unit of analysis from the job, to what people know and how they use that knowing. Also, they propose a reconceptualization of the firm as a portfolio of multiple types of human capital. They present a conceptual map of how firms make use of human capital (Lepak and Snell, 1999; also Chapter 13 in this volume). The important point they suggest is to shift from a basic conception of a job to be managed (therefore triggering an HR task of producing a 'job description') to a new perspective of leveraging the knowledge of people. Firms, they contend, will be constituted by portfolios of individuals with varying degrees of four types of knowledge: generic, industry, occupational and firm-specific. Part of the HR staffing task is to exploit these different profiles to the optimum degree. Issues of mobility arise (especially when knowledge of the non-specific types is involved). Human capital theory suggests that firms are more likely to invest in it when it is not transferable (Becker, 1964). So employees are generally expected to invest in their own transferable/generic skills.

The staffing perspective also relates to the way different HR practices are deployed for different categories of workers. They may have different recruitment routes, different job grades, different training opportunities and different psychological contracts (as well as explicit contracts). The staffing components of the architecture perspective are based on managing the overall balance between different inputs, for example, ensuring a sufficient number of customer service staff in a retail store appropriate to the level and type of service provision implied in the business model. This business requirement for different mixes of human capital underpins the staffing sub-techniques of HR planning, recruitment and selection.

Another staffing model is to acquire not just individuals but also whole teams or even whole companies through take-over. For example, the holiday and leisure company Center Parcs declared in December 2004 that its reason for acquiring a spa company in Cheltenham was in order to 'undertake R&D' in the spa sector.

Workers do not remain passive in this context. One tendency is for employees to position themselves more as free-agents prepared to sell their capabilities to the highest bidder. While the rumoured use of agents for these employees may be exaggerated, there are some signs that knowledge workers are able to 'reverse-use' headhunters as part of their external market positioning. That is, talented individuals are sometimes able to place themselves on the books of certain headhunters in case push and pull factors align at some point in the future.

Knowledge workers may respond better to recruitment strategies that emphasize the opportunity to do new things, to be innovative, to have considerable autonomy and to continue to learn and develop. The recruiting firm's image can also be critical. They may be recruiting not for a specific job but rather for a certain kind of person who could adapt to a range of opportunities and create opportunities. Stock options may play a more significant role for these creative workers. Recruitment sources for such workers may be professional associations, conferences, consultancy assignments. Conversely, ambitious recruits may also seek to be rapidly promoted or seek to leave. This can be an expensive process. Also, competitive rivalries between such personalities may also be damaging to the firm. Thus, future strategy might be to balance an outright war for talent with more judicious and measured approaches which consider trade-offs and which consider the costs, benefits and risks of different tactics for short-term gain.

In terms of the selection process, there is a need for a conception of what constitutes 'effective performance' for knowledge work. Some attempts have been made to specify the components. For example, Campbell (1999) and Pulakos (2000) suggest that a key element is 'the ability to adapt to new conditions' and that the indicators of this competence are: problems-solving, stress management, learning new tasks, demonstrating interpersonal adaptability and crisis management. Further suggested criteria for knowledge work jobs have included: capacity to build and apply knowledge, share knowledge and maintain knowledge. Examples of predictor constructs for these have been:

1 Building and applying knowledge: reasoning ability, critical thinking, fluency of ideas.
2 Sharing knowledge: active listening, cooperativeness, communication skills.
3 Maintaining knowledge: reading comprehension, willingness to learn.

In terms of selection methods, paper tests, computer simulation and job simulation have been proposed. It has been reported that conventional IQ tests did not differentiate 'stars' from 'solid workers' at Bell Labs (Pulakos et al., 2003). Further, when considering which selection methods are appropriate for hiring knowledge workers it is important to bear in mind candidate perception. Workers with scarce talents may be unwilling to jump through hoops, and so elaborate procedures may serve to deter the most desirable candidates.

Work and Organization Design

This set of HR interventions operates at three main levels: individual job design, unit level design and overall organizational design.

A first observation about work organization 'structures' in relation to knowledge and innovation is that because of the dynamic nature of environments and the need to adapt, existing structures and forms should not be fixed for too long (Mohrman, 2003). This principle was uppermost in the minds of chief executives in the most innovative firms studied by Storey and Salaman (2005). For example, the chairman of Nortel (Europe) told the authors that it was his policy to ensure that the fixed structures were periodically disturbed – indeed he referred to his policy to ensure that they were 'smashed' from time to time in order to avoid complacency and too many settled routines.

A second initial observation concerns the way in which people tend to think about knowledge management. It has been pointed out that the:

> Traditional approaches for knowledge management rest on a pipeline metaphor: knowledge is something that can be transmitted across locations much like piped water. From this perspective the volume and flow of knowledge can be managed directly, much as one can measure the flow of water in a pipeline. [An alternative view] is a river metaphor: knowing is a process that shifts and changes over time. The volume and flow of knowing can be supported by management structures and technologies only indirectly. (Fiol, 2003: 67)

By implication, 'structures' should not be too rigid. The designer of organizational forms needs to be sensitive to the dynamic elements of knowledge work. Three levels need to be borne in mind when designing the structure and form of knowledge work: the task level, the organization level and the inter-organizational level. We look briefly in turn at each of these.

Work Design and Job Design   We noted earlier the principles of scientific management (Taylor and Gilbreth). When organizational goal and means were meant to be in the hands of management, then a hierarchical organizational structure was assumed; the job design that accompanied this was of limited discretion. The initial idea was to divide labour, routine it and strip it of discretion as far as was possible. The industrial engineering studies of the early 19th century used photography to capture the minutest hand and body movements so that extraneous wasted effort could be eliminated. When subsequently the job-design movement developed ameliorative initiatives such as job enlargement (horizontal job expansion) and job enrichment (vertical job expansion) the aim was to overcome job dissatisfaction and reduce labour turnover rather than to infuse first line workers with knowledge-based jobs. From the 1950s onwards the socio-technical systems approach (Trist and Bamforth, 1951) also attempted to limit and to an extent reverse the fragmentation of jobs. Proponents advocated wider job roles and team-based working with some team autonomy. But the assumption was that these work reforms would operate within the managerially-designated overall framework. The extent to which these work design principles 'anticipated' the work design debate of the knowledge economy is a rather moot point (Mohrman, 2003).

Four factors have been identified as promoting knowledge production among successful medical research groups: strong leadership; strategies of related diversification; strongly linked theory and practice and network connectedness (Harvey et al., 2002).

Organizational Structures   Conventional structures under the industrial age were 'functional structures' – that is groupings based on specialized knowledge (finance and accounting, purchasing, engineering and so on). They were designed to maximize efficiency; they are perhaps less adept at permitting flexible responses, being receptive to change or allowing cross-functional learning.

Divisional structures organized on the basis of product or service types can overcome this cross-functional limitation but possibly at the price of building-in inflexibility around new product categories because of their designated mandates and domains of operation and their set targets.

To overcome these top-down structural limitations, flattened structures have been recommended for knowledge-age circumstances. These devolve knowledge, power and decision making to individuals and groups closer to the customer interface. Network forms represent one type of devolved, flatter structure.

In theory, flatter organizations draw on the core competences of each member. This should increase access to the most valuable knowledge ... should ensure flexibility ... with more permeable boundaries ... (Fiol, 2003: 80). But while practitioners and researchers have endorsed the flatter and condemned the hierarchical, Fiol wonders whether the pendulum may swing back the other way. Interactions – that is relationships – matter most, not the structure per se. 'Overspecified' structures according to Weick et al. (1999) can reduce the reliability needed in organizations where high reliability and safety are paramount (for example, nuclear power plants); the same principle may apply in relation to knowledge work.

Inter-organizational Networks   It is sometimes argued that the most valuable aspect of organizing for knowledge work is the self-organizing element. Indeed, in some analyses, knowledge work and conventional bureaucratic structural forms are seen as essentially antithetical. Hence the idea of informal and self-organizing 'communities of practice' has been enthusiastically received (Brown and Duguid, 1991; Wenger, 1998; Wenger and Snyder, 2000).

Communities of practice and informal social networks tend to be romanticized in the KM literature but such networks 'often compete with and are fragmented by such aspects of organisations as formal structure, work processes, geographic dispersion, human resource practices, leadership style and culture' (Cross et al., 2002: 25).

Summary of Work Design Issues   Knowledge work characteristics are seen to carry implications for work design and organizational design. A summary of many of the elements is shown in Table 9.3.

'Strategic competences' refers to the characteristic of knowledge age work where competence is intrinsic to the strategy. Mohrman gives the example of an equipment making firm that wants to shift its strategy from providing just equipment to providing 'hours of service'. To deliver on this strategic intent would require a whole host of adjustments in work. A far more collaborative approach would be needed with inputs from finance experts, sales and marketing, technologists and so on. 'Saturated interdependency' refers to the shift from linear work

Table 9.3 Characteristics of knowledge age work and the implications for work design

Characteristics	Implications			
	Dynamic work structures	**Cross boundary collaboration**	**System focus and integration**	**Work includes learning**
Strategic competences	Yes	Yes	Yes	Yes
Saturated interdependency		Yes	Yes	Yes
Process orientation		Yes	Yes	Yes
Geographical linkages		Yes	Yes	
Improvement and encoding	Yes	Yes		Yes
Generating and leveraging knowledge	Yes	Yes	Yes	Yes

Source: Adapted from (Mohrman, 2003: 98)

flows to work activities where it seems virtually everything depends on everything else almost simultaneously. 'Process orientation' denotes the shift from functional organizational design to a process focus. It should highlight activities that are not adding value for the customer. 'Geographical linkages' refer to the international dispersal and interrelationships in knowledge age work. Design teams and service delivery teams may be working virtually 24 hours a day on a series of projects. Coordinating such activity becomes a key capability. 'Improvement and encoding' relate to the expected continual improvement in work and the idea that process breakthroughs in one part of the organization can be encoded and shared with other parts. Finally, 'generating and leveraging knowledge' are also important features of knowledge age work. This characteristic refers to the local experimentation and active sense-making that is expected, in place of mere passive receipt of knowledge.

The six characteristics of knowledge work indicate the work design features that are required for organizations competing on knowledge. The implied work design features emphasize flexibility, collaboration and learning.

Developing for knowledge work

'Development' includes all aspects of training, learning, personal development and career management. What type of knowledge should be developed? Most specialists in the field recommend that special attention is paid to tacit as well as explicit knowledge. Examples of critical tacit knowledge include knowledge about customers, competitors and the organization's own business processes (Tobin, 1998). To this we can add knowledge about new opportunities, threats and supply-chain potential. To leverage this knowledge there will frequently be a need to transfer it to relevant business units and staff. This transfer can itself be a form of development for those involved.

The range of development methods include: senior management seminars, joint workshops, secondments and collaborative working on special problem-solving task forces. Technical experts may welcome attendance at leading edge conferences where a sense of exploring new frontiers is a reward. Some of this learning and development will be group as well as individual based. Indeed, for some categories of learning and development (new strategic positioning) it may be absolutely vital that the learning events are joint. With planning and careful thought, it is possible for teams to be engaged in learning while they are attending to what is largely perceived as business as usual. The joint working may also enhance 'social capital' as the teams develop their working relationships and common understandings (Nahapiet and Ghoshal, 1998).

The methods discussed so far are fairly conventional devices. A development experience that may be especially pertinent to those working with new knowledge is the opportunity to engage in constructive controversy. This means exposure to the open discussion of opposing views. Such a dialogical approach allows learning by confronting issues and views (Beer and Eisenstadt, 2004; Perlow, 2003). For example, innovation may be viewed as a sense-making process using discursive practices. Through these devices new configurations of meaning are constructed (Kleiner, 2003; Steyaert, 1996).

Beyond learning through constructive controversy, a related development opportunity, especially relevant to knowledge workers, is the learning through action process (Cook and Brown, 1999). The role for HR from this perspective would be to lend support for the creative ways in which knowledge-intensive work groups operate.

Performance Management

Performance management includes the whole cycle of agreeing goals and objectives, which may vary in their degree of specificity, providing feedback, offering coaching and advice and motivating staff to perform at a high level. The reward system must be sufficient also to assist in the staffing goal discussed above – to attract and retain the necessary human capital.

Knowledge-based organizations may require different forms of performance and reward management in contrast with traditional organizations which were 'not designed with an eye on knowledge management' (Lawler, 2003: 274). Traditional organizations often rewarded employees for the size of their job (measured for example by the number of direct reports a manager had and/or their length of service). However, knowledge-based organizations require new priorities and new incentives. Knowledge workers may have few direct reports and the length of their job tenure may be considered of less importance than was the case in traditional work settings when remuneration was indeed often largely based on tenure. Conversely, they are likely to give high value to personal growth and to personal development opportunities at work because they realize that this is how they will grow their human capital.

With regard to the reward aspect of performance management, there are three main ways of rewarding employees: paying the rate for the job; paying for competences; and paying for performance. The first of these three is conventionally the most used. It allows market-based comparisons using job evaluation techniques. But, from a knowledge work perspective, it has certain drawbacks. Job-based payment systems do not, for example, reward learning from lateral moves. Unless the organization needs more managers, this vertically-biased system may not lead to optimal behaviour especially if the organization structure (see above) is flat.

Hence, for knowledge work there may be a shift to the second type – paying what the person is worth rather than what the job is worth. It has been suggested by one leading expert in compensation that it is possible to set a market rate by using survey data for competency-based salaries (Gerhart, 2000). Such person-based pay or competency-based pay seem to fit well with the concept of human capital. For example, it rewards continuing skill development. But, on the other hand it can be difficult to administer. Moreover, there is little research evidence as yet on the impact of such systems on actual behaviour.

Paying for performance, the third type of reward system, was commonplace during the industrial era especially for routine production jobs. While performance pay may sound in tune with the achievement orientation of knowledge-age work it can be difficult to implement in the context of the intangible nature of knowledge work and in situations where there is extensive interdependency. Moreover, knowledge work (such as R&D) usually needs to be measured over a longer timescale than was the case with production work.

Beyond these three types of reward systems there are also systems which reward teams or reward employees in accord with organization-wide performance. The idea of team-based pay appeals, in principle, to many managers. However, it is often difficult to manage in practice. One possibility is simply to add a new criterion to the individual competency/behaviour profile of individuals. This, paradoxically, can lead to a new form of competition between individuals – based on who is being the more cooperative (Lawler, 2003).

Alternatively, it is possible to use team success, rather than team oriented behaviour. The team success device may best be used for exceptional (unscheduled) performance achievements.

Finally, organizational level awards may be managed through profit sharing schemes or through stock options. It has been found that these only have a limited impact when only a few shares are divided by the majority, and such schemes prove counterproductive if only the managerial elite benefit.

Conclusion

In working through the conceptual framework in this chapter it was inevitable that the focus was placed sequentially on a series of different elements. But of course, in reality, the crucial point is that, for knowledge to be leveraged, all of these elements need to operate in a mutually supportive way. For example, recruiting highly qualified staff but failing to locate them within a complementary context of supportive capabilities could be pointless. Organizational competitive advantage must derive from a conjoined series of complementary knowledge sub-systems. A company with knowledge and capabilities to design certain components of 3G mobile phones, for example, would need to have its knowledge and capabilities complemented with numerous other companies if it was to be able to utilize its knowledge. An infrastructure would be required. Human resource management in this cross boundary context would require expertise in alliances and in joint venture working.

Furthermore, an implication deriving from much of the discussion in this chapter is that HR itself may need to change if it is to meet the new challenges in managing knowledge work. For example, while industrial-age work prompted and impelled a personnel management specialism which emphasized welfare, discipline, rules and conformity, the new distinctive agenda for HR under a knowledge economy may require rather different underpinning priorities. The key requirements (as in Figure 9.1) may shift towards: attracting, rewarding and developing human capital; recognizing the importance of social capital; and building network management skills.

One final point in relation to this shifting agenda needs to be made. A great deal of the literature on managing knowledge work implies that overall, it marks a shift to a more benign and empowered regime. But, things may not be quite so straightforward or leading in such a uniform direction. Indeed, Hodgson (2002) refers to the signs pointing towards the 'disciplining of the professional'. The 'new' HR systems may thus possibly be interpreted not as the dawn of a new enlightenment, but as a temporary transition phase while management figures out ways to come to terms with new labour market conditions for certain types of worker.

References

Alvesson, M. and Karreman, D. (2001) 'Odd couple: making sense of the curious concept of knowledge management', *Journal of Management Studies*, 38(7): 995–1018.

Amar, A.D. (2002) *Managing Knowledge Workers: Unleashing Innovation and Productivity*. London: Quorum Books.

Baron, A. (2001) 'Preface', in J. Swart, N. Kinnie and J. Purcell, *People and Performance in Knowledge-Intensive Firms*. London: CIPD.

Becker, G. (1964) *Human Capital Theory*. Chicago, IL: University of Chicago Press.

Beer, M. and Eisenstadt, M. (2004) 'How to have honest conversations about your business strategy', *Harvard Business Review*, February (2): pp. 82–90.

Brown, J.S. and Duguid, P. (1991) 'Organizational learning and communities of practice: Towards a unified theory of working, learning and innovation', *Organization Science*, 2(1): 40–57.

Campbell, J.P. (1999) 'The definition and measurement of performance in the new age', in D. Ilgen and E.D. Pulakos (eds), *The Changing Nature of Performance: Implications for Staffing, Motivation and Development*. San Francisco, Jossey-Bass.

Casey, C. (1996) 'Corporate transformations: Designer culture, designer employees and "post-occupational" solidarity', *Organization*, 3(3): 317–39.

Claver, F., Llopis, J., Garcia, D. and Molina, H. (1998) 'Organizational culture for innovation and new technological behaviour', *The Journal of High Technology Management Research*, 9(1): 55–68.

Cook, S.D.N. and Brown, J.S. (1999) 'Bridging epistemologies: The generative dance between organizational knowledge and organizational knowing', *Organization Science*, 10(4): 381–400.

Cross, R., Borgatti, S. and Parker, A. (2002) 'Making invisible work visible: using social network analysis to support strategic collaboration', *California Management Review*, 44(2): 25–46.

Deal, T.E. and Kennedy, A.A. (1991) *Corporate Cultures*. Reading, MA: Addison-Wesley.

Drucker, P. (1993) *Post-Capitalist Society*. New York: HarperCollins.

Fiol, C.M. (2003) 'Organizing for knowledge-based competitiveness', in S.E. Jackson, M.A. Hitt and A.S. Denisi (eds), *Managing Knowledge for Sustained Competitive Advantage: Designing for Effective Human Resource Management*. San Francisco, CA: Wiley.

Gerhart, B. (2000) 'Compensation strategy and organizational performance', in S. Rynes and B. Gerhart (eds), *Compensation in Organizations: Current Research and Practice*. San Francisco, CA: Jossey-Bass.

Gilbreth, F.B. (1914) *Primer on Scientific Management*. New York: Van Nostrand Reinhold.

Harvey, J., Pettigrew, A. and Ferlie, E. (2002) 'The determinants of research group performance: Towards Mode 2', *Journal of Management Studies*, 39(6): 748–74.

Hodgson, D. (2002) 'Disciplining the professional: the case of project management', *Journal of Management Studies*, 39(6): 803–21.

Horibe, F. (1999) *Managing Knowledge Workers*. New York: John Wiley.

Hutchinson, S. and Purcell, J. (2003) *Bringing Policies to Life: The Vital Role of Front Line Managers in People Management*. London: CIPD.

Kleiner, A. (2003) 'Are you in with the in crowd?', *Harvard Business Review*, July: 86–92.

Lawler, E.E. (2003) 'Reward systems in knowledge-based organisations', in S.E. Jackson (ed.), *Managing Knowledge for Sustained Competitive Advantage*. San Francisco, CA: Jossey-Bass.

Lei, D., Slocum, J.W. and Pitts, R. (1999) 'Designing organizations for competitive advantage: the power of learning and unlearning', *Organizational Dynamics*, Winter: 24–38.

Lepak, D.A. and Snell, S.A. (2003) *Managing the Human Resource Architecture for Knowledge-based Competition*. San Francisco, CA: Jossey-Bass.

Lepak, D.P. and Snell, S.A. (1999) 'The human resource architecture: towards a theory of human capital allocation and development', *Academy of Management Review*, 24(1): 31–48.

Mohrman, S.A. (2003) 'Designing work for knowledge based competition', in S.E. Jackson, M.A. Hitt and A.S. Denisi (eds), *Managing Knowledge for Sustained Competitive Advantage*. San Francisco, CA: Wiley.

Nahapiet, J. and Ghoshal, S. (1998) 'Social capital, intellectual capital and the organizational advantage', *Academy of Management Review*, 23(2): 242–66.

Perlow, L. (2003) 'Is silence killing your company?', *Harvard Business Review*, May (5): 52–9.

Prahalad, C.K. and Hamel, G. (1990) 'The core competence of the corporation', *Harvard Business* Review, 68: 79–88.

Pulakos, E.D. (2000) 'Adaptability in the workplace: development of a taxonomy of adaptive performance', *Journal of Applied Psychology*, 84(1): 87–106.

Pulakos, E.D., Dorsey, D.W. and Borman, W.C. (2003) 'Hiring for knowledge-based competition', in S.E. Jackson (ed.), *Managing Knowledge for Sustained Competitive Advantage*. San Francisco, CA: Jossey-Bass.

Purcell, J., Kinnie, N. and Hutchinson, S. (2003) 'Inside the black box', *People Management*, May (15): 30–7.

Stalk, G., Evans, P. and Shulman, L.E. (1992) 'Competing on capabilities: the new rules of corporate strategy', *Harvard Business Review*, March–April: 57–69.

Starbuck, W. (1992) 'Learning by knowledge-intensive firms', *Journal of Management Studies*, 29(6): 713–40.

Steyaert, C. (1996) 'Conversational construction of new meaning configurations in organizational innovation: a generative approach', *European Journal of Work and Organizational Psychology*, 5(1): 67–89.

Storey, J. (1992) *Developments in the Management of Human Resources*. Oxford: Blackwell.

Storey, J. and Salaman, G. (2005) *Managers of Innovation: Insights into Making Innovation Happen*. Oxford: Blackwell.

Swart, J., Kinnie, N. and Purcell, J. (2001) *People and Performance in Knowledge-Intensive Firms: A Comparison of Six Research & Technology Organizations*. London: CIPD.

Taylor, F.W. (1911) *Principles of Scientific Management*: New York, Harper.

Tobin, D.R. (1998) *The Knowledge Enabled Organization: Moving from Training to Learning to Meet Business Goals*. New York: AMACOM.

Trist, E.L. and Bamforth, K. (1951) 'Some social and psychological consequences of the long-wall method of coal getting', *Human Relations*, 1: 3–38.

Tsoukas, H. (1996) 'The firm as a distributed knowledge system: a constructionist approach', *Strategic Management Journal*, Winter Special Issue (17): 11–25.

Weick, K., Sutcliffe, K.M. and Obsteld, D. (1999) 'Organizing for high reliability: processes of collective mindfulness', in R. Sutton and B.M. Staw (eds), *Research in Organizational Behavior*. Greenwich, CT: JAI.

Wenger, E. (1998) *Communities of Practice*. Cambridge: Cambridge University Press.

Wenger, E. and Snyder, W. (2000) 'Communities of practice: the organizational frontier', *Harvard Business Review*, January–February: 139–45.

Knowledge Management Initiatives: Learning from Failure

10

John Storey and Elizabeth Barnett

The scene is played out on a daily basis – Conference centres and hotels throughout the world entertain management gatherings with the usual paraphernalia of designer mineral water and glacier mints in imitation cut-glass containers. Our case-study begins in just such a setting one day in May 1998. The senior team of 'International Resources', a large, European-headquartered company, are gathered to participate in a strategy debate which includes the commencement of the firm's knowledge management initiative. There is a high-level executive sponsor, syndicate groups are mobilized to analyse the meaning of the concept, its implications for the company and the type of action plans required. The project gets off to a promising start and a project team is set-up to drive the initiative forward. But, 12 months later, despite a great deal of effort and commitment, it becomes clear that the initiative has failed.

In this chapter we seek to examine in some detail this example of a failed knowledge management initiative, to analyse what went wrong and to identify the key learning points. Large numbers of organizations are taking great interest in the idea of knowledge management and many are launching knowledge management initiatives and programmes. A significant proportion of such initiatives will fail. Charles Lucier, the first chief knowledge officer of Booz-Allen & Hamilton suggests that 84 per cent of all KM programmes will fail to have any real impact. Moreover, he notes that 'a disturbingly high proportion of programs initiated with great fanfare are cut back within two or three years' (Lucier and Torsiliera, 1997, p. 15). But so far, insufficient attention has been paid to why these initiatives fail and the learning points have not been adequately explored.

This chapter is organized in three sections: the first reviews the key elements of knowledge management initiatives and summarizes the literature which, to date, has speculated on the sources of failure for initiatives of this kind; the second section describes and analyses the failed attempt at a KM initiative in a significant European-based company; the third section revisits the main themes in the literature in the light of the analysis of the case study.

Source: J. Storey and E. Barnett (2000) 'Knowledge management initiatives: learning from failure', *Journal of Knowledge Management*, 4(2): 145–56. Edited version.

Knowledge Management and Knowledge Management Initiatives

Mainstream writing on knowledge management is overwhelmingly optimistic. The claims made on its behalf make the underlying proposition about the value of knowledge management almost irresistibly attractive. For example, 'KM is becoming a core competence that companies must develop in order to succeed in tomorrow's dynamic global economy' (Skyrme and Amidon, 1998). Another proponent observes 'Here's an uncontroversial thought if ever you've heard one: a firm's competitive advantage depends more than anything on its knowledge. Or to be slightly more specific, on what it knows, how it uses what it knows and how fast it can know something new' (Prusak, 1997, p. ix). While Nonaka (1994, p. 14) contends 'The ever increasing importance of knowledge in contemporary society calls for a shift in our thinking'. And Thomas Stewart (1991, 1997) argues 'Knowledge has become the most important factor in economic life. It is the chief ingredient of what we buy and sell, the raw material with which we work. Intellectual capital – not natural resources, machinery or even financial capital – has become the one indispensable asset of corporations.' And, at national level, government promotes the idea of the 'knowledge economy' (DTI, 1998).

The argument underlying these claims is that knowledge now represents the key competitive sustained resource (Quinn, 1992; Reich, 1992; Drucker, 1993) 'There is little doubt that we have entered the knowledge economy where what organizations know is becoming more important than the traditional sources of economic power' (KPMG, 1998). Most of the literature to date has focused on the nature of knowledge, types of knowledge and the theoretical bases of knowledge management. For example, one key strand associates KM with organizational learning (Polanyi, 1962, 1966; Spender, 1996a, 1996b; Cheng and Van de Ven, 1996). A second associates it with the resource-based view of strategic management (Penrose, 1959; Nelson and Winter, 1982). Within this strand, it is argued that the primary contribution of firms, as institutions, is the creation and integration of knowledge (Grant, 1996; Tsoukas, 1996). The 'greatest challenge for the manager of intellectual capital is to create an organization that can share the knowledge. When skills belong to the company as a whole, they create competitive advantages that others cannot match' (Stewart, 1997).

There are wider explanations for the amount of attention being paid to knowledge management. For example, growing interest in the resource-based view of the firm means strategy academics and others are paying more attention to problems of internal, cross-boundary knowledge sharing. Issues of horizontal as well as vertical co-ordination and organizational integration are therefore increasingly coming to the fore (Argyres, 1996). It has been argued that high-technology industries in particular have created new technologies with new technological inter-dependencies between business units (Doz et al., 1987). From the new strategy perspective, one can 'conceive of the firm as a portfolio of core competencies and disciplines'; this view then suggests that 'interfirm competition as opposed to inter-product competition, is essentially concerned with the acquisition of skills. In this view, global competitiveness is largely a function of the firm's pace, efficiency and extent of knowledge accumulation' (Hamel, 1991, p. 83).

Beyond the hype there is the serious business of finding useful ways in which to act on these insights. Knowledge may be important but in what sense can it really be 'managed'? There are two key issues here; first, what kind of interventions are managers being invited to make in order to effect and implement a knowledge perspective on business strategy and second, what kind of difficulties might be anticipated in this endeavour? Concerning the first, 'knowledge management' has come to be used to cover initiatives ranging from 'organizational learning' attempts to 'database management tools' (Ruggles, 1998, p. 80). A great deal of the literature on knowledge management is in fact concerned with its meaning and scope – (see, for example, Edvinsson and Sullivan, 1996; Stewart, 1997) and there is little need to rehearse these points here.

But it is the second issue, that is, the question of the problems and the barriers that we wish to focus our attention on in this chapter. Despite the generally optimistic nature of most KM literature there are a few examples to be found of attempts to probe this second issue. For example, an Ernst & Young survey of 431 US and European organizations conducted in 1997 found that the biggest reported difficulties were 'changing people's behaviour', and the existence of an inappropriate 'organizational culture' (Ruggles, 1998). Likewise, in his classic *Fortune* magazine article, 'Brainpower', Thomas Stewart (1991) argued that getting results from investing in knowledge requires 'a corporate culture that allows it to flow freely, which means breaking down hierarchies and getting rid of rules that stifle new ideas'.

Another common complaint is that the practice of knowledge management tends to be too IT/IS focused and too often IT/IS-led (Scarbrough and Swan, 1999; Scarbrough et al., 1999; Swan, 1999). It has even been suggested that KM in this regard could be seen as less developed than the literature on the learning organization. As attention on the former has increased, the attention to the latter has decreased. 'Far from being a development of the learning organization with its emphasis on people management, KM is a divergence with its own unique discourse and focus, specifically emphasizing IT and tools driven approaches' (Swan, 1999, p. 4). Such concerns are amplified when it is recalled that the contention has been made that there is in fact no direct link between investment in IT and subsequent business performance (Mulhotra, 1998).

The main allegation however is simply that, 'while the implications [of KM] for information systems development and practice have received close attention, the implications for personnel management development and practice have not' (Scarbrough et al., 1999, p. 25). The neglect of people management issues has also been noted by Ruggles. It has also been pointed out that 'By far the majority of articles have appeared in the IS/IT literatures with, for example, nearly 70 per cent of articles in 1998 appearing in these literatures' (Scarborough et al., 1999, p. 21). So far, knowledge management has been mainly sponsored by IS/IT specialists. It has been argued that few cases 'actually describe, in anything other than the broadest terms, the people management and organizational processes involved in KM initiatives' (Swan, 1999, p. 5). Our own reading of the literature concords with this assessment.

The different meanings of, approaches to, and possibilities for KM lead, therefore, to potential micro-political battles over the ownership of KM initiatives. There is plenty of scope for turf wars given the problems of getting to grips with such an elusive phenomenon as 'knowledge'. As Frank Blackler has observed, it is messy and hard to manage. How different specialists attempt to manage it to a large extent reflects how people understand and define it. 'Knowledge is multifaceted and complex, being both situated and abstract, implicit and explicit, distributed and individual, physical and mental, developing and static, verbal and encoded' (Blackler, 1995). These characteristics make not only the actual management of knowledge difficult but even achieving consensus around the meaning of the intent is inherently problematical. This is certainly an issue which we will surface in the case which follows. Moreover, intranets can themselves actually *exacerbate* turf wars' (Cohen, 1998) and IT/IS 'solutions' can in fact strengthen the barriers which already exist as well as creating firewalls by reducing informal contact.

So, broadly, two main points can be seen to arise in the literature to date: one, that KM initiatives so far have been IS/IT dominated and that they therefore neglect the complexities of organizational processes – and, further, that this is suboptimal for the organization; second, that the detailed processes which relate to people are also largely undescribed. The problems associated with the IT-driven approaches are several. Critically, they tend to be supply driven – focused on making existing knowledge more widely available. This assumes that people will be willing to share their knowledge and also assumes that people will use the information which is made available on intranets and the like. The emphasis so far has tended to be on knowledge as a commodity; making experts' knowledge more explicit and accessible via computer applications. Herein are seen the seeds of a further problem – such knowledge tends to be 'explicit knowledge' whereas the often more valuable 'tacit knowledge' (Grant, 1996) is neglected. Tacit knowledge is much more personal and is likely to be context specific. This latter form of knowledge is hard to make available through computer systems. Further learning occurs while applying and acting upon knowledge – as argued by Schon (1983) with regard to the idea of the 'reflective practitioner'. The realization of the tacit knowledge potential 'requires the close involvement and co-operation of the knowing subject' (Lam, 1998).

Attempts to codify tacit knowledge may only produce knowledge which is: useless (too difficult to explain); trivial; redundant (if subject to change); irrelevant to a wider audience; politically naïve; or inaccurate (Swan, 1999, p. 7). Some commentators have therefore stressed the inherent limits of intranets which merely capture the trivial and the codifiable.

To these complaints and reservations about the supply-driven IT/IS approach can be added the point that, in any case, most managers already suffer from information overload. In such circumstances, KM systems which concentrate on the capture, codification and archiving of knowledge need to take greater note of the issue concerning the demand for knowledge and the associated question of knowledge use.

This neglect of the users' perspective may not be accidental. Part of the rationale of KM is to reduce organizational vulnerability by transferring knowledge from individuals. The intent is to ensure that the intellectual property becomes owned by the organization. But this in turn may be what leads to a simplistic view of 'knowledge capture'. An entirely alternative approach would be to deal with the problem of potential knowledge loss by seeking to retain staff and by taking steps to win their commitment. In any case, the supply-driven and demand-driven approaches are perhaps not so far apart: 'getting people to share their knowledge requires not only new processes but also a new covenant between employer and employees' (Hibbard and Carillo, 1998).

Yet knowledge sharing across heterogeneous groups may be more difficult, yet ultimately more rewarding (Gibbons et al., 1994). Dialogue can lead to conflict and disagreement rather than necessarily to agreement. Issues of power and exclusion may therefore come to the fore. Moreover, the introduction of information technology can be used on the one hand to reinforce expert power or on the other hand to challenge it. Neither is pre-given by the technology itself. In addition, the literature warns that 'technology alone won't make a person with expertise share it with others. Technology alone won't get an employee who is uninterested in seeking knowledge to hop onto a keyboard and start searching or browsing. The mere presence of technology won't create a learning organization, a meritocracy or a knowledge-creating company' (Davenport and Prusak, 1998).

Even if these technological problems are surmounted, there will remain other managerial issues – not least of which is the question of the management of 'knowledge workers'. Henry Mintzberg has suggested that they respond to inspiration not supervision. He draws lessons from the way a symphony orchestra operates. 'Leadership at the individual level' he notes, is 'highly circumscribed. Empowerment is a silly notion here. Musicians hardly need to be empowered by conductors. Inspired maybe – infused with feeling and energy – but not empowered' (Mintzberg, 1998, p. 145). One of the ways in which such enthusing might be encouraged is through the encouragement of 'learning communities' and 'communities of commitment' (Koffman and Senge, 1993) but there are many aspects of organizational life which militate sharply against such ideals. These points too need to be borne in mind if the knowledge management roll-out is not to lead to failure.

Moreover, it has been noted that 'getting employees to share what they know is no longer a technology challenge – it's a corporate culture challenge' (Hibbard and Carillo, 1998, p. 49). 'Knowledge management is a business practice more than a technology' reports the research director of Delphi Consulting Group in Boston. 'In our research, users clearly identify cultural issues as the largest obstacles to implementing knowledge management' (1998, p. 49).

In this review of the literature we have identified a host of potential problems. The danger of IT/IS dominance clearly looms large in previous analyses. So too the need to have a clear business rationale for pursuing a KM initiative. And third, the needs of the 'users' have to be taken seriously into account. All of these we accept as valid points. However, as our case which follows will show, these nostrums only begin to scratch the surface of the managerial dilemmas which emerge when, even in the relatively propitious setting of a knowledge-rich business which is underpinned by technology and operational experience, a new knowledge management programme is launched for the first time in earnest.

The International Resources Case

We now return to the conference centre scene which opened this chapter. You will recall that the senior managers are gathered together to debate the launch of a new learning organization/knowledge management initiative. Those assembled, by and large, know each other – they work, or have worked, this corporate stage together for many years. They know the history, the political agendas, the gossip. Many aspects of the occasion are a reworking of previous performances: the enigmatic, possibly disapproving, reticent members again enacting their familiar role, and those usually relied on to offer commentary on each and every topic once more providing the entertaining thrust and parry of debate. A number of people look forward, with real concern, to achieving constructive consensus and commitment on fundamental issues facing the company; the price of the commodity which is the foundation of their business, always volatile, is beginning one of its nosedives at the same time that the under-performance of certain key projects are adding real business risks. The market and the analysts are less than enthusiastic.

The impacts of low prices, management of performance and risk, and environmental issues are all high on the agenda for this meeting. Lower on the agenda, but with some executive sponsorship, is a subject which is something of a surprise to some of those present – 'Knowledge management and the learning organization'. Papers on learning and knowledge management have been circulated prior to the meeting, although what proportion of the audience has bothered to read them remains very much open to question.

A short presentation is given, outlining the linkages in the view that strategy is about business purpose combined with developing insights, insight is about creativity and learning, and learning is key to competitiveness. Some definitions of learning and knowledge are highlighted and the benefits of working with this perspective in mind are summarized. Specific examples of processes, culture and behaviours within the company that could represent opportunities for learning, knowledge and insight development are proposed. The need for 'learning to learn' is especially noted. The discussion following the presentation is preliminary and exploratory – the topic is new to many and clearly of dubious validity to some who are in attendance. However, the presence of a key executive sponsor becomes clear and this very much helps to keep the proposal live. Syndicate groups are appointed to debate and report in depth on the main agenda topics and the learning/knowledge team duly retires to the sunlit terrace armed with flipchart and coloured pens.

The discussion is driven, as generally happens in syndicates, by a couple of enthusiasts, and the results reflect this. The plenary report-back talks about culture, removing the fear of failure, looking outside the box, and the importance of adaptation to change and uncertainty. The benefits of the new knowledge management initiative are described in terms specific to the company. They include the potential contribution to be made to the organization's declared commitment to teamwork-through-innovation; clarity of purpose; and the recruitment and retention of quality staff. Sharing of the mass of often tacit knowledge represented by the collective technical and operational experience of the company's world-wide staff is seen as key to cost-effectiveness, competitiveness and the management of business risks.

Setting up a project team is recommended, and an action list presented which has, at the top, sponsorship and active participation ('walking the talk') by executive management. Managers of the business units are identified as the key – knowledge sharing and helping the business across organizational boundaries have to be explicit objectives in their performance contracts, otherwise their people's time will just not be available for these activities. Cross-organizational and functional peer groups ('communities of practice') need to be identified and activated, the intranet needs to be used as a tool, processes to recognize innovation need to be considered and clear communication to all stakeholders is critical.

During the discussion, a core of participants who either have experience of knowledge management in other companies, or who buy into the need for it here, becomes apparent. Crucially, equally apparent are the early signs of resistance from business unit managers who see the expenditure of time and effort on this initiative as directly conflicting with their immediate business targets. Concerns are also expressed over managing or controlling the quality of shared knowledge, its proprietary sensitivity and the breadth of the potential audience within the company.

Nevertheless, the actions agreed at the conclusion of the meeting include, albeit with rumbling undercurrents of scepticism, the establishment of a learning organization/knowledge management project team.

Implementation – Phase 1

Thus was the initiative started. The project team was appointed by the usual smoke from the Vatican chimney process, and made up of nine members: the sponsoring executive, the technology and HR managers, the IT manager, three senior management enthusiasts and two overseas business unit managers who were to participate by virtual means. Notably absent were representatives of non-management employees but it was felt that others could be brought into the process 'as appropriate'.

Five of these team members attended the first 'brainstorming' meeting in June. Awareness was identified as the immediate priority – that is, ensuring that everyone in the organization would know what was going on, what projects were being worked on by whom, where specific technical experience lay, what priority issues were preoccupying the executives, and greater awareness about what the board and shareholders were saying. In addition, it was agreed by the team that there needed to be a clearer understanding of the company's strategy, the extent of progress being made in pursuing it, and individuals' responsibilities in relation to it.

Mechanisms for disseminating awareness and promoting feedback and ideas were drafted, including a more frequent use of 'town hall meetings', routine reporting cascade (both downwards and upwards) and a much-expanded use of the intranet (although opinion varied on the current level of use of the relatively new intranet, and the IT manager was unable to provide any relevant supporting data). A key recommendation was that the chief executive should have his own home page, ideally interactive, through which he could 'chat' with the organization and behind which would be a cascading series of pages from management, business units and functions that would provide the basis for the awareness campaign.

Interestingly, there was a considerable divergence of views as to whether only staff above a certain job grade should be included in this awareness and whether long-term contractors (of whom there were a significant number) should be excluded. The decision was eventually reached that privilege and discrimination had no place in the new knowledge-based learning organization. Further issues arose of how to involve the overseas offices (from an intranet hardware perspective rather than, perhaps more crucially, a cross-cultural one), who would pay for the time involved in the learning process, and what form of public recognition could be introduced for instances of innovation, knowledge sharing and so on (it was felt that the company had a poor record of celebrating success).

The principle of cross-discipline peer groups ('communities of practice') was endorsed and a potential structure of common business themes with similar challenges and expertise requirements was put together. The concept was developed that each should have its own 'champion'. Technology champions were already in place, each with their own intranet page. Peer reviews and post-project analysis were identified as needs that should be formalized.

It was agreed that a proposal would be made to the executive committee, which in due course was presented (by the executive members only of the project team). The proposal was fully endorsed by this committee. The endorsement included (to the evident surprise of many) a commitment to significant 'cultural change' to a more open culture. Further, it was accepted that the example for this had to be set from the top in terms of dialogue and a demonstrably no blame environment. The inevitable question of measuring the impact of the project was raised.

The decision was made that this would be a home-grown initiative – external facilitation and guidance would not be sought, nor was it considered a priority to seek advice from other companies in the industry and elsewhere who already had gained experience of such programmes of change. The reason for this insularity was that the organization was still sensitive in the aftermath of a very protracted 'business reengineering' exercise which had been conducted by external consultants. The decision to pursue this new project exclusively internally was in this context understandable but, in retrospect, turned out to be misguided. The concept of a pilot project never really arose; specific components (for example peer groups) would be started on a trial basis, but the underlying assumption, never fully examined, was that the project as a whole would be rolled-out to the entire organization. The structural scale that this required and the fact that so little time was spent considering possible organizational barriers to an initiative originating from a small group of enthusiasts also proved to be costly.

In the meantime, initial feedback from the absent project team members was generally positive. Emphasis was placed on the cultural and behavioural change imperatives if knowledge sharing was to occur and emphasis was also placed on the role of training and coaching. The appointment of a part-time 'chief knowledge officer' was recommended. It was also suggested (presciently as things turned out) that a dedicated IT resource might well be required. Failure to secure this eventually proved fatal.

Around this time, a note was issued to all staff introducing the new project. Its objectives were explained and emphasis was given to the high level commitment to the initiative by the company's top team. Little formal feedback from this communication was received, but corridor conversations were reassuring in so far as they seemed to reveal considerable grassroots enthusiasm. There was a sense of positive anticipation combined with a requirement for clarification of exactly what was involved. Some members of the project team held town hall meetings with their own staff and thus some level of feedback was achieved.

The next meeting of the project team was in mid-July; the structure and philosophy of the chief executive's home page, along with the underlying information cascade, was drafted. The idea that the project itself should have a home page to keep staff informed of what was going on was agreed, and actions on knowledge champions, communities of practice, and peer reviews were divided up among the group. The need to map the current information-sharing processes and evaluate their effectiveness was expressed. The IT manager was, unfortunately, ill and unable to attend this meeting. Nevertheless in his absence he was commissioned to report on the capacity of the intranet and associated issues – including the international dimensions and upgrade cost options.

For the subsequent meeting at the end of the month, a 12-page report from the IT department was submitted. This described all the constraints that the department was working under but it committed IT to developing the intranet as a vehicle for the knowledge management initiative – albeit at alarmingly high potential costs. This was, in retrospect, the first clear warning sign not only of IT barriers but of the perceived value of the project to various parties as a tool to pursue political agendas. These problems were however not realized at this stage. In part the problems were hidden because requests from the project team were responded to in highly technical terms and in a guarded way which failed to reveal the extent of the potential issues.

The IT manager reported that the basic company intranet would be available globally by September, but with certain constraints on data transmission volumes. A report on expansion plans and costs over the next year and beyond was promised (but no issues were identified that could not be solved by money).

In the meantime a complete draft of the project team's home page had been prepared for comment, introducing the background to the learning and knowledge management project. It also expanded on the 'jigsaw puzzle' image of the four integrated dimensions of content, process, culture and infrastructure as outlined by Bock (1998). The structure of these and other additional pages had already been designed and some draft content had been prepared. More content was being written, pilot communities of practice had been identified and the responsibilities for developing them were allocated. The project was rolling.

The related issues of quantifying the business case and measuring potential results were also initially addressed at this point. This was seen to be necessary especially since it was seeming likely that special funding for IT support would have to be sought. Moreover, the business environment continued to deteriorate as prices fell. Examples of cost savings that were identified included the savings in staff time achievable by knowledge sharing and the case was also made that there would be a lowering of investment risk, particularly with respect to technology as a result of the wider availability of knowledge. In addition, it was suggested that there would be increased quality of evaluation and a reduction of uncertainty leading to better investment decisions.

Implementation – Phase 2

The team meeting in mid-August was essentially both the high point of the project and the stage at which the weaknesses began to be more clearly visible. A great deal of progress had been made on drafting material for the intranet, involving more people and obtaining executive approvals. Targets were set for the launch of the knowledge management/learning organization home page (scheduled for early September) and the chief executive's home page with its underlying awareness structure (scheduled for October). The delicate issue of defining sensitive corporate information that could not be included had been addressed and resolved (with a clear agreement to be entirely open with the organization in terms of what knowledge could not be shared). The peer review and other processes were being developed. An article for the company magazine was planned.

The IT manager was not present at the meeting, but the team requested commitment from his department that the systems were in place to fully support the inauguration of the intranet pages world-wide on the agreed schedule. In addition, assurance was also sought that sufficient dedicated resources were available to build and maintain these systems (a 'Webmaster' etc.). However, there was a growing realization and consequent unease that the project had developed essentially on the assumption that IT systems would be the foundation for communication, knowledge sharing and feedback and that these systems would be simple, adequate and available. However, there were now clear signs that these assumptions were not valid.

The project team learnt, for the first time, that responsibilities for Website and intranet development within the company were, inexplicably, divided between IT and media affairs – two departments with very different agendas, priorities and views on how to best build and manage these processes. The sceptics in the team suspected that the KM and LO project had been viewed by the IT function as a means to achieve a dominant position in strategy, methodology and budget. This sceptical view was reinforced when it emerged that external IT consultants were being contracted by the IT function to recommend the best way forward for both the intranet and IT systems in general. It became difficult even for the KM project team to have confidence that the project's scope and targets could actually be achieved when other priorities and agendas were potentially competing.

Confidence among the project team members was further undermined by a communication from the IT manager. This came in response to a request for hardware and resources commitment, improved co-ordination, and a clear plan for developing an intranet system free from the instabilities that were admitted in the existing one. The project team was surprised to hear that, in the IT view, insisting on 'appropriate hardware' was a change of project priorities and would result in other approved projects being put on hold. This included the delivery of the intranet to overseas locations, the issues associated with which were the responsibility of those business units. The team also was advised that the purpose of the IT-initiated consultancy study was to define an outsourcing strategy, and that moreover the results would not be available until late September. The appointment of an intranet project manager would take several weeks.

The next revelation was that the IT plan for intranet development was to rebuild it as a part of the document management system (DMS) in which significant, and high profile, investment had been made, but which, after a considerable length of time, was yet to be functional and useable to business benefit. This plan would represent a complete change from the platform of the existing system and it raised fundamental questions concerning interfaces. The intranet group in the media affairs department were committed to continue with the existing platform, arguing that it offered simplicity, flexibility, speed, user-friendliness and cost-effective commercial maintenance. They further argued that moving to DMS would significantly change the way in which the KM/LO sites would work. It was apparent to the project team that these were significant conflicts of views and that they provided the backdrop to some, if not all, of the seemingly inexplicable but elusive issues that had arisen in the project to date. But the team, other than the IT manager, did not have the expertise to understand, still less resolve, the fundamental technical issues underpinning this controversy, and the only sources of expertise were the very people who were locked in this territorial conflict.

Implementation – Phase 3

Time dragged by – the basic material was ready to go on the intranet, staff were curious as to what the status of the project was, and the project team were frustrated but apparently impotent, finally becoming aware of the consequences of the focus on IT as the vehicle for a programme whose ambition overwhelmed the capacity of a system already weakened by political agendas.

No developments were forthcoming from the IT department and the tensions were exacerbated by the broadcast (via an imprudent error in the instantaneous and irrevocable act of e-mail addressee selection) to a wider audience than intended of a note expressing the exasperation of one member of the team and the suspicion that the commitment of the IT manager to the principles of the KM/LO initiative was very much open to question.

The last meeting of the project team took place in mid-September. Progress was reported on all areas except for IT. Although the need for a knowledge-sharing culture was highlighted by the problems already encountered in persuading potential communities of practice around the world that their practice was indeed common, this initiative was well underway. So too were the other components of the project but the launch of the project as a whole was clearly in jeopardy (the target date for the project home page launch having already passed). IT reported that a decision needed to be taken urgently on intranet standards, but that the prototype home pages would be assembled on the DMS system – the next meeting would be convened when the prototype pages were ready for demonstration. That was the last meeting of the project team.

More Pressing Matters

During October, the deterioration in the industry market conditions paralleled that in the prospect of a decision on IT systems. The company became, not surprisingly, more consumed with survival than learning.

In mid-November there was the announcement of a new project, this time to achieve major organizational restructuring in response to the unsustainable market conditions. This was to be managed by a small executive and senior management group with the assistance of external 'specialists in organizational development and breakthrough thinking'. Late in the month a sweeping outsourcing and staff reduction programme was announced, and the knowledge management initiative was lost in the subsequent turbulence.

Discussion

As the International Resources case demonstrates, knowledge management initiatives are prone to fail even when they are reasonably well resourced and there appears to be ample commitment from top management. In this section of the chapter we seek to diagnose the causes of the failure of this initiative and to set this diagnosis in the context of the wider literature on KM – especially that portion of the literature which tries to set out generalizable propositions about failure.

A number of problems that the case study surfaces can be identified quite readily.

First, top management was 'committed' only up to a point. As long as KM appeared simply to be an add-on to the existing organization and seemed to promise greater efficiency through the freer flow of information, the support was very evident. However, the commitment did not extend to a concerted willingness to overturn deeply ingrained cultural practices of the organization. Crucially, when business conditions began to deteriorate the safe response was perceived to be a reversal to traditional top-down methods. The principles of a learning organization were not instinctively realized as valuable or even reliable during a period of crisis. This incident was in this sense highly revealing: it points to the KM/LO initiative as a 'nice to have' rather than a mission-critical activity. Arguably, this is a widely held belief in the majority of the companies which even get around to launching initiatives of this kind – let alone those which merely toy with the concept. To put this point another way, it would seem that there was a greater need to ground the KM initiative in the firm's strategy – as Zack (1999) has recommended.

Second, as in so many other cases which we have witnessed, the initiative was undermined by divisions and differences in perspective between diverse functional 'camps'. In particular, the IT/IS department had its own 'take' on what the programme meant. In line with experience from other cases, this particular group perceived the programme as fitting within a broader vision which they already had for the future IT infrastructure. Initiatives of this nature rarely arrive on virgin territory. Here there was already underway a well-developed plan for intranet development founded on a new document management system. Aspirations and reputations were at stake and not surprisingly the IT specialists sought to safeguard the integrity of their pre-existing plans and investment. In this context, arguably the project team did not spend enough time listening to and understanding the perceptions and intentions of this crucial group. Meanwhile, another group, in this case, the media affairs department, was also an influential party which had its own agenda concerning corporate communications. The KM project team failed to appreciate the complexity of these micro-political processes, nor did it appear to have the authority to address them. To this extent, the team driving this KM initiative, despite its relative sophistication in many other respects, was open to the accusation of naïvety.

Third, and of a more subsidiary nature, more of these issues and tensions would have been surfaced in a less costly and in a more controlled way if a pilot for the KM initiative had been tried in one part of the company rather than planning for a total company-wide launch. Similarly, insufficient attempt was made to benefit from the learning and experience of other companies who had pursued similar initiatives. Likewise, no external advice or facilitation was sought. As explained early in the case, there were particular reasons why this rather obvious point was neglected at the time. But in hindsight the lesson can be learned that this temporary state of affairs was costly in its eventual consequences.

So, to what extent do the lessons in the literature align with the problems faced in this specific case? To put the point another way, how much more prepared would the project team have been if they had read the KM literature more carefully before they acted? As we pointed out at the beginning of this chapter, the vast bulk of the KM literature is overwhelmingly optimistic and even campaigning in nature and tone (Stewart, 1997; Huseman and Goodman, 1998). As such most of it pays little regard to the problems and barriers. That small section of the literature which is alert to the difficulties (for example, Lucier and Torsiliera, 1997; Ruggles, 1998; Scarbrough et al., 1999; Scarbrough and Swan, 1999) reports four main problems:

1 an insufficiently specific business objective. Instead companies launching knowledge management initiatives tend towards more general aspirations such as 'share best practice';
2 incomplete programme architecture that fails to build on the linked dynamics of organizational change and learning;
3 an insufficient focus on one or two strategic business priorities;
4 top management sponsorship without active ongoing involvement.

These sorts of issues certainly find resonance in our case. What is rather less usual about the case presented here when compared with most other studies, is the level of fine-grained detail that we have been able to provide. This detail is necessary in order to fully appreciate the meaning and reality of these rather abstract concepts. We suggest in this chapter, that any change agent contemplating involvement in a new KM initiative can learn a great deal from the detail of the dynamics described in our case. The warnings are present and there are concrete lessons to be learned. Here we highlight six:

1 Listen very carefully to the expectations, agendas and wants of all parties involved. They may appear to be using the same language and to be supporting the programme but in fact their understandings and plans may be very different.
2 Check continuously that top management support is continuing and is delivered in a practical and public way.
3 Be alert to the potential differences between a paradigm based on knowledge management which is IT-led and infused with priorities relating to knowledge capture, archiving and mining, and one based on the learning organization concept which may be inspired by wider developmental values. If handled with extra-ordinary skill the two approaches may reinforce each other but this cannot be expected simply to occur by happenchance.
4 It will be found useful to ensure that the purpose and reason for expending effort on knowledge sharing is clarified and understood by everyone involved. It needs to be seen to be useful to those who are, in effect, being asked to behave differently.
5 The interrelationship between knowledge sharing, knowledge creation and organizational change needs to be understood and realized. Reversal to traditional ways of operating based on low trust and direct command are too easily adopted when problems arise – as our case demonstrates.
6 If knowledge is to be more widely shared and more readily created and used, there is an implication that innovation in process and probably service or

products will also ensue and indeed should be sought. There are different types or levels of organizational KM systems: at the lower level expert practitioners simply make available their operating routines and information. At the second level, the new knowledge is used as a basis for a shift in the kind of services and products offered to customers. These different expectations should be clarified.

Finally, we should note that the concept of 'failure' (especially so from a knowledge management perspective) is somewhat problematical because it is possible that valuable lessons may be learned and/or that initiatives may be resuscitated at a later date. The latter already seems to be evident in the case of International Resources, the former is at present more open to question.

Acknowledgement

The research reported in this article derives from an ESRC-funded project: Award Number L125251053. This project was part of the ESRC's Programme on the management of innovation.

References

Argyres, N. (1996) 'Capabilities, technological diversification and divisionalization', *Strategic Management Journal*, Vol. 17, pp. 395–410.

Blackler, F. (1995) 'Knowledge, knowledge work and organisations: an overview and interpretation', *Organization Studies*, Vol. 16 No. 6, pp. 1021–47.

Bock, F. (1998) 'The intelligent organisation', *Prism* (Arthur D. Little) 2nd quarter, pp. 5–15.

Cheng, Y.T. and Van de Ven, A.H. (1996) 'Learning the innovation journey: order out of chaos?', *Organization Science*, Vol. 7, pp. 593–614.

Cohen, S. (1998) 'Knowledge management's killer applications', *Training and Development*, Vol. 52 No. 1, pp. 50–7.

Davenport, T. and Prusak, L. (1998) *Working Knowledge: How Organizations Manage What They Know*, Harvard Business School Press, Boston, MA.

Doz, Y., Angelmar, R. et al. (1987) 'Technological innovation and interdependence: a challenge for the large complex firm', *Technology in the Modern Corporation*, M. Horwitch, Pergamon Press, New York, NY.

Drucker, P. (1993) *Post-Capitalist Society*, HarperCollins, New York, NY.

DTI (1998) *The Competitiveness White Paper*, Department of Trade and Industry, London.

Edvinsson, L. and Sullivan, P. (1996) 'Developing a model for managing intellectual capital', *European Management Journal*, Vol. 14 No. 4, pp. 356–65.

Gibbons, M., Limoges, C. et al. (1994) *The New Production of Knowledge*, SAGE, London.

Grant, R.M. (1996) 'Toward a knowledge-based theory of the firm', *Strategic Management Journal*, Vol. 17, pp. 109–22.

Hamel, G. (1991) 'Competition for competence and interpartner learning within international strategic alliances', *Strategic Management Journal*, Vol. 12, pp. 83–103.

Hibbard, J. and Carillo, K.M. (1998) 'Knowledge revolution', *Informationweek*, Vol. 5 No. 663, pp. 49–54.

Huseman, R.C. and Goodman, J. (1998) *Leading with Knowledge: The Nature of Competition in the 21st Century*, SAGE, London.

Koffman, F. and Senge, P. (1993) 'Communities of commitment: the heart of the learning organization', *Organizational Dynamics*, Autumn, pp. 4–23.

KPMG, M.C. (1998) *Knowledge Management Research Report*, KPMG Website, London.

Lam, A. (1998) *Tacit Knowledge, Organizational Learning and Innovation: A Societal Perspective*, British Academy of Management, Nottingham.

Lucier, C. and Torsiliera, J. (1997) 'Why knowledge programs fail', *Strategy and Business*, 4th quarter, pp. 14–28.

Mintzberg, H. (1998) 'Covert leadership: notes on managing professionals', *Harvard Business Review*, November–December, pp. 140–7.

Mulhotra, Y. (1998) 'Tools@work: deciphering the knowledge management hype', *The Journal of Quality and Participation*, Vol. 21 No. 4, pp. 58–60.

Nelson, R.R. and Winter, S. (1982) *An Evolutionary Theory of Economic Change*, Cambridge University Press, Cambridge, MA.

Nonaka, I. (1994) 'A dynamic theory of organizational knowledge creation', *Organization Science*, Vol. 5 No. 1, pp.14–36.

Penrose, E. (1959) *The Theory of the Growth of the Firm*, Wiley, New York, NY.

Polanyi, M. (1962) *Personal Knowledge: Towards a Post-critical Philosophy*, University of Chicago Press, Chicago, IL.

Polanyi, M. (1966) *The Tacit Dimension*, Doubleday, New York, NY.

Prusak, L. (Ed.) (1997) *Knowledge in Organizations*, Butterworth-Heinemann, Boston, MA.

Quinn, J.B. (1992) 'The intelligent enterprise: a new paradigm', *The Academy of Management Executive*, Vol. 6 No. 4, pp. 48–64.

Reich, R. (1992) *The Work of Nations*, Vintage Press, New York, NY.

Ruggles, R. (1998) 'The state of the notion: knowledge management in practice', *California Management Review*, Vol. 40 No. 3, pp. 80–9.

Scarbrough, H. and Swan, J. (1999) *Case Studies in Knowledge Management*, IPD, New York, NY.

Scarbrough, H., Swan, J. et al. (1999) *Knowledge Management: A Literature Review*, IPD, London.

Schon, D.A. (1983) *The Reflective Practitioners: How Professionals Think in Action*, Arena, London.

Skyrme, D.J. and Amidon, D.M. (1998) 'New measures of success', *The Journal of Business Strategy*, Vol. 19 No. 1, pp. 20–4.

Spender, J.C. (1996a) 'Making knowledge the basis of a dynamic theory of the firm', *Strategic Management Journal*, Vol. 17, Winter (special issue), pp. 45–62.

Spender, J.C. (1996b) 'Organizational knowledge, learning and memory: three concepts in search of a theory', *Journal of Organizational Change Management*, Vol. 9 No. 1, pp. 63–78.

Stewart, T.A. (1991) 'Brainpower', *Fortune*, Vol. 123 No. 11, pp. 44–60.

Stewart, T.A. (1997) *Intellectual Capital: The New Wealth of Organizations*, Nicholas Brealy, London.

Swan, J. (1999) Introduction, *Case Studies in Knowledge Management*, in Scarbrough, H. and Swan, J., IPD, New York.

Tsoukas, H. (1996) 'The firm as a distributed knowledge system: a constructionist approach', *Strategic Management Journal*, Vol. 17, Winter (special issue), pp. 11–25.

Zack, M.H. (1999) 'Developing a knowledge strategy', *California Management Review*, Vol. 41 No. 3, pp. 125–45.

Further Reading

Cole-Gomolski, B. (1997) 'Users loathe to share their know-how', *Computerworld*, Vol. 31 No. 46, p. 6.

Fulmer, R. and Gibbs, P. (1998) 'The second generation learning organization: new tools for sustaining competitive advantage', *Organizational Dynamics*, Vol. 27 No. 2, pp. 6–20.

Green, K. et al. (1998) 'Differences in 'styles' of technological innovations; introduction to special issue', *Technology Analysis & Strategic Management*, Vol. 10 No. 1, pp. 403–7.

Hansen, M.T. and Nohria, N. (1999) 'What's your strategy for managing knowledge?', *Harvard Business Review*, March–April, pp. 106–16.

Holtshouse, D. (1998) 'Knowledge research issues', *California Management Review*, Vol. 40 No. 3, pp. 277–81.

Leonard, D. and Sensiper, S. (1998) 'The role of tacit knowledge in group innovation', *California Management Review*, Vol. 40 No. 3, pp. 112–33.

Lundvall, B. (1998) 'Why study national systems and national styles of innovation?', *Technology Analysis & Strategic Management*, Vol. 10 No. 4, pp. 407–22.

Lundvall, B.-A. (1992) *National Systems of Innovation: Towards a Theory of Innovation and Interactive Learning*, Pinter, London.

Nonaka, I. (1991) 'The knowledge creating company', *Harvard Business Review*, November–December, pp. 96–104.

Nonaka, I. and Takeuchi H. (1995) *The Knowledge-Creating Company: How Japanese Companies Create the Dynamics of Innovation*, Oxford University Press, Oxford.

von Krogh, G., Nonaka, I. and Ichijo, K. (1997) 'Develop knowledge activists', *European Management Journal*, Vol. 15 No. 5, pp. 475–83.

IC Valuation and Measurement: Classifying the State of the Art

Daniel Andriessen

In the past 10 years the intellectual capital (IC) community has produced an overwhelming amount of new methods for the valuation or measurement of intangibles. Andriessen (2004) identifies over 30 methods and analyses 25 of them. However, the IC community has now entered a phase of consolidation. Several authors have taken initial steps in this direction. Bontis (2001) complains that in the IC community many distinctions exist that are merely labeled differently. He suggests a standard definition and classification. Marr et al. (2003) analyze various motives for creating IC measurement methods and study empirical evidence for their effectiveness. Pike and Roos (2004) judge the rigor of these methods by assessing their compliance with measurement theory.

The time has come for the IC community to prove that its concepts can help in providing better understandings of the way organizations operate. More evidence is needed that shows that IC methods can help improve organizational performance. This consolidation requires three steps:

1   clarification by classification of existing concepts, motives and proposed methods;
2   separation of the corn from the chaff by assessing the rigor and effectiveness of the proposed methods; and
3   standardization and further development of the most promising methods.

This chapter contributes to the first step.

Clarification is needed with respect to three basic questions (Andriessen, 2004): what, why and how? This article focuses on the 'why' and the 'how' questions. 'Why' questions the motives found among influential writers for valuing or measuring IC. 'How' questions the approaches for valuing or measuring IC. The 'what' question is about the use of terminology and IC-classification schemes. This is beyond the scope of this chapter.

IC research has evolved primarily from the desires of practitioners (Bontis, 2002). Many of the leading authors in the field are more practitioners then academics. The field is dominated by a relatively small number of frequently quoted authors. Consolidation starts with analysing their work and clarifying their concepts, motives and methods.

Source: D. Andriessen (2004) 'IC valuation and measurement: classifying the state of the art', *Journal of Intellectual Capital*, 5(2): 230–42. Edited version.

Analysis of the 'why' of various methods shows that these methods are based on a wide variety of problem-definitions. These definitions are sometimes made explicit but often remain implicit. Many methods can be characterized as 'solutions in search of a cause'. It is often unclear what the organizational problem is that the methods intend to solve. In general, the field of IC measurement has paid little attention to organizational diagnosis. Generic methods have been proposed as a cure for all diseases.

The 'how' can also be problematic. Available methods use a broad array of approaches under various headings like valuation, financial valuation, measurement and assessment. However, there is a clear and distinct difference between valuation and measurement. This distinction is not yet recognized in the field and the concepts are being confused. For example, lack of insight into the value of IC is often used as a motive for creating IC reports, for example by Edvinsson and Malone (1997) and Roos et al. (1997). Yet, the methods these authors propose do not value intangibles; they merely measure them.

Based on a systematic and critical review of the most influential writers in the field of IC measurement and valuation, this chapter contributes to the field in three ways:

1 develop a taxonomy of expressed motives for IC valuation or measurement by influential authors;
2 clarify the concept of measurement and valuation from a theoretical point of view to be able to;
3 classify influential methods for IC measurement or valuation according to 'why' and 'how'.

This results in recommendations for the future research agenda.

Methodology

In order to analyze the motives and methods of influential authors, a literature review was undertaken. The selection of authors was based on their appearance in literature overviews by Bontis (2001), Bontis et al. (1999), Luthy (1998), Petty and Guthrie (2000), Pike and Roos (2004), Stewart (1997) and Sveiby (2002) that summarize the state of the art. Methods were selected that appear in at least four out of these seven publications. However, it became clear that these authors tend to overlook one important area of literature, the literature about the financial valuation of intangible assets (Reilly and Schweihs, 1999; Smith and Parr, 1994; Gröjer and Johanson, 2000). These authors were included in the review. This resulted in a sample of ten methods for valuing or measuring IC (see Table 11.1).

A systematic review of the work of the authors of these methods was undertaken in search of phrases that articulated the 'why' of the methods: the authors' motives

Table 11.1 Classification of methods

| Why | **How** | | |
	Financial valuation	**Value measurement**	**Value assessment**	**Measurement**
Improving internal management	Economic value added™ (Stewart, 1994) Market-to-book ratio (Stewart, 1997) Tobin's Q (Stewart, 1997)	Balanced scorecard (Kaplan and Norton, 1992, 1996a, b, 2001) Intellectual capital audit (Brooking, 1996)		Skandia navigator (Edvinsson and Malone, 1997) Intangible asset monitor (Sveiby, 1997) Intellectual capital index (Roos et al., 1997)
Improving external reporting	Economic value added™ (Stewart, 1994) Market-to-book ratio (Stewart, 1997) Tobin's Q (Stewart, 1997)			Skandia navigator (Edvinsson and Malone, 1997) Intangible asset monitor (Sveiby, 1997) Intellectual capital index (Roos et al., 1997)
Transactional and statutory motives	Calculated intangible value (Stewart, 1997) Cost, market and income approaches (Reilly and Schweihs, 1999; Smith and Parr, 1994)			

to value or measure IC. This resulted in 37 different quotes expressing the need for measurement or valuation (as reported in Andriessen, 2004). These 37 verbatim texts were used to create a classification of motives. First, they were grouped into 18 categories. Second, these categories were further grouped into three main problems.

In order to classify the 'how' of the methods, a theoretical framework was developed based on value theory. This framework provided four criteria that were used to assess the methods and determine what type of valuation or measurement they implied. Combining the motives and the types resulted in a classification of the methods into a 'why' by 'how' matrix, which was used to classify the state of the art (see Table 11.1).

Why Value or Measure IC?

Authors of IC valuation or measurement methods have a wide variety of motives. They have different ways to define the problem they intend to solve. On a more abstract level these problem definitions can be grouped into problems around improving internal management, improving external reporting, or statutory and transactional motives.

Improving Internal Management

The issue of improving internal management is a wide one. Various problem definitions fall into this category. The problem definitions found can be grouped into seven categories of problems:

1   What gets measured gets managed.
2   Improving the management of intangible resources.
3   Creating resource-based strategies.
4   Monitoring effects from actions.
5   Translating business strategy into action.
6   Weighing possible courses of action.
7   Enhancing the management of the business as a whole.

The first category of problem definitions is the popular notion that management requires measurement or that measurement leads to better management. Roos et al. (1997) phrase it in terms of what you can measure, you can manage and what you want to manage, you need to measure. However, measurement is neither a necessary nor a sufficient condition for management. Stewart (2001) calls the phrase 'you cannot manage what you cannot measure':

... one of the oldest clichés in management, and it's either false or meaningless. It's false in that companies have always managed things – people, morale, strategy, etc. – that are essentially unmeasured. It's meaningless in the sense that everything in business – including people, morale, strategy, etc. – eventually shows up in someone's ledger of costs or revenues. (Stewart, 2001, p. 291).

Therefore, we need a more detailed problem definition to justify the measurement of intangible resources.

A second, more valid group of problem definitions is based on the belief that intangible resources are not managed properly, that they deserve more management attention, and that they need to be managed differently than other resources. This has been the driving force of IC authors like Roos, Sveiby, and Edvinsson. Sveiby, for example, has made it his task to supply managers with a toolbox to help them in managing knowledge-based companies. Included in this second category are problems regarding the lack of awareness about the importance of intangible resources and the use of non-financial measures in managers' compensation plans (Marr et al., 2003).

Yet, improving the management of intangible resources is not a very specific problem. Kaplan and Norton (1992) are more concrete, and they identify a third category of problems. Their aim is to complement financial measures of company performance with operational measures to create a balanced view of results of action already taken and drivers of future financial performance. This means they want to create insight into the value drivers: the vital resources that determine future success. These resources are often intangible, and are the basis for creating resource-based strategies. Marr et al. (2003) call this motive 'strategy formulation'.

The second aim of the method of Kaplan and Norton (1996a) the balanced scorecard – is to measure performance in a balanced way as a feedback mechanism for management actions. This fourth category of problems lies at the core of the performance measurement community but also plays an important role in the IC community. Marr et al. (2003) call this motive 'strategy assessment and execution'.

After working with their method for a couple of years Kaplan and Norton (2001) found it addresses a more fundamental problem: how to link a company's long-term strategy with its short-term actions. Therefore, their problem definition shifted from measuring performance to strategy implementation:

But we learned that adopting companies used the Balanced Scorecard to solve a much more important problem than how to measure performance in the information era. That problem, of which we were frankly unaware when first proposing the Balanced Scorecard, was how to implement new strategies. (Kaplan and Norton, 2001, p. viii)

This leads to a fifth category of problems. Pike and Roos (2000) describe this category as translating strategic intent into actions.

The sixth category of problems is especially concerned with making trade-off decisions. This requires a method that consolidates different indicators into one measure of value. Roos has been one of the strongest advocates of methods that allow for making trade-off decisions. According to Roos et al. (1997), this is where the early IC models (which they referred to as first-generation models) fall short: 'Intellectual capital systems have long lists of indicators with no prioritization, thus making it impossible for managers to evaluate trade-off decisions' (Roos et al., 1997, p. 7). The last category of problems looks at the business as a whole. An example is the method of Economic Value Added™ (EVA, a trademark owned by Stern Stewart and Co). EVA is not a method specifically designed to measure the value of intangibles. Its aim is much wider. The problem EVA addresses is poor management decision making that destroys shareholder wealth. According to EVA advocates, poor decision making is often a result of using the wrong indicators of wealth creation, like return on investments or return on assets. The problem with most traditional indicators is that they are based on accounting-derived earnings instead of cash flow, and they do not include the cost of capital in the equation. EVA was developed to correct this.

Improving External Reporting

Within the accounting profession, the problem of intangibles is often described as one of 'relevance lost' (Johnson and Kaplan, 1987). This includes a loss of relevance of financial reporting to external stakeholders. An overview of problem definitions regarding external reporting can be clustered into five categories:

1   Closing the value gap between book and market value.
2   Improving information to stakeholders about the real value and future perfor-
    mance of the enterprise.
3   Reducing information asymmetry.
4   Increasing the ability to raise capital.
5   Enhancing corporate reputation and affecting stock price.

The first category has to do with the popular notion that we need to close the growing value gap between book and market value. However, it is not the objective of the balance sheet to approximate the market value of a company (Rutledge, 1997; White et al., 1997). Upton (2001) phrases this misunderstanding as follows:

> If accountants got all the assets and liabilities into financial statements, and they measure all those assets and liabilities at the right amounts, stockholders' equity would equal market capitalization. (Upton, 2001, p. 60)

This fallacy underlies the widespread statement that the difference between book value and market value represents intangibles or IC (see, for example, Edvinsson and Malone, 1997; Stewart, 1997, 2001; Sveiby, 1997; Roos et al., 1997). Not only is there no need to make book value equal market value, it is also impossible. Comparing the gap between market value and book value of companies with IC is like comparing the difference between an apple and an orange with a banana (Andriessen, 2001). Pike et al. (2001) add another argument by stressing the fact that all resources of a company combine and interact with each other. The equation market value = book value + intellectual capital is incorrect because the variables are not separable, as required by the equation.

A second and more accurate category of problems addresses disseminating poor information to stakeholders regarding the real value and future performance of the enterprise. Roos et al. (1997) want to give stakeholders a better understanding of the real value of a company. Sveiby (1997) questions how to describe the company as accurately as possible so stakeholders can assess the quality of management and the reliability of the company. Edvinsson and Malone (1997) state that traditional financial data as presented in the annual report are no longer leading indicators of future financial performance.

The third category of problems is concerned with the growing information asymmetry between the public and those who have access to information on investments and returns regarding intangibles. Edvinsson and Malone (1997) are looking for ways to provide nuanced, dynamic information to the small investor. They state that the asymmetry leads to a misallocation of capital:

> As a result, too many deserving companies are underoptimized and undercapitalized, and thus sometimes are unable to complete their destiny. Meanwhile, other, troubled firms are artificially propped up until they collapse, pulling down shareholders and investors with them. (Edvinsson and Malone, 1997, p. 8)

The misallocation of capital, in the end, produces social costs like unemployment, reduced productivity and even diminished national competitiveness.

The fourth category of problems focuses on the difficulty companies have in raising capital. A lack of transparency of intangibles makes it difficult for companies that lack tangible assets to raise money from investors or banks. Banking regulations may be biased against lending to companies with few tangible assets, which can be used as security. This may especially disadvantage young, high-tech companies with little record of accomplishment. Brooking (1996) wants her method to help create a basis for raising a loan. Pike et al. (2001) want to improve a company's ability to raise capital.

The fifth motive is enhancing external reputation and market valuation (Pike et al., 2001). At a recent meeting the author visited Edvinsson and stated that the Skandia navigator had saved Skandia about 1 percent in interest rate on external capital, just by improving the reputation of the company.

Statutory and Transactional Issues

Literature on methods for the valuation of intangibles (Reilly and Schweihs, 1999; Smith and Parr, 1994) provides additional statutory and transactional reasons for

Table 11.2   Statutory and transactional motives

Category	Type
1 Transaction pricing and structuring for the sale, purchase, or license of an intangible asset.	Discretionary
2 Financing securitization and collateralization for both cash flow-based financing and asset-based financing.	Mandatory
3 Taxation planning and compliance, with regard to all sorts of possible deductions, tax compliance, and estate planning.	Mandatory
4 Bankruptcy and reorganization, including the value of the estate in bankruptcy and the assessment of the impact of proposed reorganization plans.	Mandatory
5 Litigation support and dispute resolution, including infringement of intellectual property rights and breach of contract.	Mandatory and discretionary
6 Impairment testing of goodwill as required by FASB statement no. 142 (Financial Accounting Standard Board, 2001).	Mandatory

valuing IC. Statutory provision, administrative ruling or regulatory authority can mandate a valuation. Alternatively, valuation can be discretionary in the case of a transaction. Table 11.2 gives an overview of both types of motives.

The first category of motives focuses on transactions. Transactions involving IC include the purchase, sale, or license of an intellectual property right. Gröjer and Johanson (2000) call this the tradability motive. This category of problems also includes the sale, merger or acquisition of a business, of which IC is an important component. Marr et al. (2003) refer to this motive as 'Strategic development, diversification and expansion'. A valuation may be used to negotiate the transaction deal price.

The second category of motives covers the issue of financing securitization. Many financial institutions require an independent appraisal of IC that is pledged as collateral against loan commitments or lines of credit.

The third category looks at tax issues. Many tax jurisdictions allow for the periodic amortization of the cost of acquired intangible assets. Special tax regulations relate to the transfer of IC between subsidiaries of the same parent company. Many international conglomerates transfer IC and use IC royalty rates to shift taxable income into countries with lower income tax rates.

The fourth category of motives revolves around bankruptcy and reorganization. A valuation of the IC of a debtor in possession may be necessary for bankruptcy-related accounting and taxation considerations. Bankruptcy judges are empowered to authorize the sale of intellectual property rights to outside parties because of reorganization.

The fifth category looks at litigation support and dispute resolution. Litigation may require the quantification of economic damages related to breach of contract and intellectual property infringement.

Finally the valuation of IC became relevant for external reporting with the introduction of FASB statement no. 142 (Financial Accounting Standard Board, 2001). This statement from the FASB states that goodwill and intangible assets that have indefinite useful lives will no longer be amortized but instead will be tested annually for impairment. This means that their fair value must be compared with their recorded amounts. This requires estimating a fair value of certain types of intangible assets.

How to Value or Measure IC?

Available methods use a broad array of approaches under various headings like valuation, financial valuation, measurement and assessment. However, there is a clear and distinct difference between valuation and measurement. This distinction is not yet recognized in the field and the concepts are being confused. What is the nature of value, what do we mean by valuation and measurement, and what types of methods for valuation or measurement exist?

Value

Nowadays we think about money when we talk about value, but according to Crosby (1997), it was only during the Middle Ages that money developed as a means of quantifying value. Value closely relates to the concept of 'values'. According to Trompenaars and Hampden-Turner (1997), values determine the definition of good and bad, as opposed to norms that reflect the mutual sense a group has of what is right and wrong. A value reflects the concept an individual or group has regarding what is desired. It serves as a criterion to determine a choice from existing alternatives.

Following the *Longman Dictionary of Contemporary English* (Procter, 1978) as well as Trompenaars and Hampden-Turner (1997), value is defined as the degree of usefulness or desirability of something, especially in comparison with other things. The term usefulness is used to emphasize the utilitarian purpose of valuation. This is in line with Rescher's (1969) value theory. He states that values are inherently benefit oriented. People engage in valuation 'to determine the extent to which the benefits accruing from realization of some values are provided by the items at issue' (Rescher, 1969, pp. 61–2). However, usefulness is not the only aspect of value. Things can be valuable because they are beautiful, pleasing, or in other ways desirable, which is why the term desirability is included in the definition. Usefulness and desirability are not mutually exclusive. Things can be desirable because they are useful. Rescher (1969) states that value is not a property inherent in the item at issue. It depends on the subject's view of usefulness or desirability. In that respect, 'value is in the eye of the beholder'.

Valuation

Valuation requires implicit or explicit criteria, or yardsticks for usefulness or desirability. Rescher (1969, p. 61) describes valuation (he uses the term evaluation) as 'a comparative assessment or measurement of something with respect to its embodiment of a certain value'. Rescher (1969) describes the importance of values for valuation as follows:

> *Whenever valuation takes place, in any of its diverse forms ... values must enter in. It is true that when somebody is grading apples, say, or peaches, he may never make overt reference to any values. But if the procedure were not guided by the no doubt unspoken but nevertheless real involvement with such values as palatability and nourishment, we would be dealing with classification or measurement and not with grading and valuation. (Rescher, 1969, p. 71)*

Furthermore, he states that any valuation makes use of a value scale, reflecting the fact that this value is found to be present in a particular case to varying degrees. This value scale can be an ordinal scale that reflects the varying degrees of value but does not show us the interval between the positions on the scale. A value scale can also be a cardinal scale. Such a scale is of an interval or ratio level (Swanborn, 1981). With regard to an interval level, the interval between the varying degrees of value is known, whereas on a ratio level it is also known what constitutes zero value. We can represent cardinal scales numerically. The advantage of using money as the denominator of value is that it creates a value scale at the ratio level that allows for mathematical transformations.

Four Ways to Determine Value

So, valuation requires an object to be valued, a framework for valuation, and a criterion that reflects the usefulness or desirability of the object. Now we have several options.

- We can define the criterion of value in monetary terms, in which case the method to determine value is a financial valuation method.
- We can use a non-monetary criterion and translate it into observable phenomena, in which case the method is a value measurement method.
- If the criterion cannot be translated into observable phenomena but instead depends on personal judgment by the evaluator, then the method is a value assessment method.
- If the framework does not include a criterion for value but does involve a metrical scale that relates to an observable phenomenon, then the method is a measurement method.

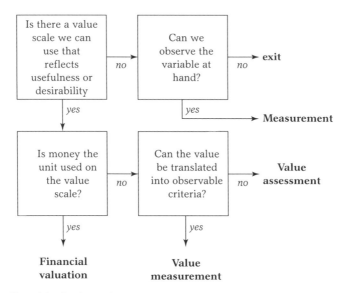

Figure 11.1   Financial valuation, value measurement, value assessment and measurement

So, a measurement method is not a method for valuation, yet this type of method is often used within the IC community. Swanborn (1981) defines measurement as the process of assigning scaled numbers to items in such a way that the relationships that exist in reality between the possible states of a variable are reflected in the relationships between the numbers on the scale. Measurement methods do not use value scales, but use measurement scales instead.

Figure 11.1 shows the relationship between financial valuation, value measurement, value assessment, and measurement. The decisive factors are the use of values as criteria, the use of money as the denominator of value, and the observability of the criteria or measured variable.

Classification of 10 Existing Methods

These categorizations of motives and approaches help us to classify the state of the art. Table 11.1 shows the position of ten influential models in the 'why' by 'how' matrix. Five models are financial valuation models that use money as unit of value. Economic Value Added™ is used for both improving internal management and external reporting. It is based on an analysis of the economic value that is added in a company, taking into account the cost of the capital needed to create that value. According to Bontis et al. (1999) and Strassmann (1998, 1999) EVA is a good representation of the financial value of IC. Market-to-book ratio and Tobin's Q are both based on an analysis of the difference between the market value and book value of companies. Stewart (1997) states that it could be useful for both improving internal management and external reporting. The calculated intangible value method is based on the assumption that the premium on a company's value is a result of its IC. It is used to acquire loans and for tax purposes (Stewart, 1997; Luthy, 1998). Cost, market and income approaches are more 'traditional' approaches to financial valuation that are used for various transactional and statutory purposes. The cost approach is based on the principle that an investor will pay no more for an investment than the cost to obtain an investment of equal utility. The market approach is based on the principle that in a free and unrestricted market, supply and demand factors will drive the price of any good to a point of equilibrium. In the income approach the value of IC is the value of the expected economic income generated by this capital.

Two out of the 10 methods can be labeled value measurement methods because they contain norms to act as yardsticks of value. The balanced scorecard groups financial and non-financial indicators and accompanying norms into four perspectives. It is predominantly used to improve internal management. The IC audit is a method to internally manage IC. It uses a range of indicators that have yardsticks attached that represent the optimal state of the indicator.

Among the ten methods no value assessment methods were found. However, they do exist. Viedma's Intellectual Capital Benchmarking System (Viedma, 2001) is a method of doing a value assessment that depends on expert judgment. Another example is Edvinsson's IC Rating™ (see www.intellectualcapital.se).

The Skandia navigator, the intangible asset monitor and the IC index do not use values, norms, or other yardsticks and we therefore cannot consider them valuation methods. They are merely measurement methods. They claim to have a purpose in both improving internal management and external reporting.

Reflection and Discussion

The classification of problems as described above shows that there are many different problems to solve. However, thorough diagnosis is needed to determine the specified problem of the situation at hand. This is especially essential when the intention is to improve the internal management of an organization. There can be many reasons why a company is performing sub-optimally or poorly. There can be many ways to optimize a company's performance. Valuation or measurement may or may not be the right solution. To check whether a valuation or measurement method is the right tool for the job the method should include a diagnosis phase. This phase is missing in all ten methods mentioned in Table 11.1. As a result there is a clear danger that the methods turn out to be 'solutions in search of a cause'.

The array of problems that is being addressed by many of the methods is so broad that it seems questionable whether they can all be solved using one method.

Yet this is what some authors claim. The problem definitions of Edvinsson and Malone (1997), Stewart (1997), Sveiby (1997) and Roos et al. (1997) cover a number of different problem categories within both the internal management and the external reporting domain. They claim their methods are a 'jack of all trades'. More empirical evidence is needed about the effectiveness of these methods to cover such a broad selection of problems.

Three well known methods, the Skandia navigator, the intangible asset monitor and the IC-index, do not measure value, despite their intentions. Edvinsson and Malone (1997, p. 70) state that their Skandia navigator fulfils the task to 'Look upward toward more sweeping measures of value'. Roos et al. (1997, p. 91) state that their IC index 'can help the company signify to the market its hidden value creation process, and thus help the market make a better assessment of the company's value'. Yet, both are merely measurement methods that do not provide a valuation.

Table 11.1 shows that when it comes to improving external reporting there is no value measurement method available among the ten methods studied. This is surprising as external stakeholders will have a strong need for yardsticks to help them judge the IC measures reported by companies. The absence of yardsticks may explain why Rylander et al. (2000) found that users in Sweden were not satisfied with the information on IC as it is presented in annual reports.

The link to value creation is unclear and the information is therefore perceived as difficult to interpret and does not provide deep enough insights to deliver any real value to users. (Rylander et al., 2000, p. 723)

Conclusion

The methods that have been proposed in the last decennium to value or measure IC address a wide array of problems. This chapter shows they address at least 18 different problems. IC research suffers from too much focus on solutions and a lack of focus on organizational problems. Within the IC community, not enough research has been done into the nature of the problems that valuation or measurement addresses. As part of the consolidation process more evidence needs to be generated about the problems that can be solved using valuation or measurement methods. The methods themselves can be improved by adding a diagnostic phase that will allow users to identify what the problem in their organization is and to judge whether a specific method can help in solving it.

Existing methods vary with respect to their approach. The language used is often not very consistent. This chapter shows that a distinction can be made between financial valuation methods, value measurement methods, value assessment methods and measurement methods. As part of the consolidation process within the IC community, more research is needed into the strengths and weaknesses of each of these approaches, related to the type of problems that need to be solved. This must lead to a more complete and empirically grounded 'why' by 'how' matrix that can help practitioners to choose the right tool for the job.

References

Andriessen, D. (2001) 'Weightless wealth; four modifications to standard IC theory', *Journal of Intellectual Capital*, Vol. 2 No. 3, pp. 204–14.

Andriessen, D. (2004) *Making Sense of Intellectual Capital*, Butterworth-Heinemann, Burlington, MA.

Bontis, N. (2001) 'Assessing knowledge assets: a review of the models used to measure intellectual capital', *International Journal of Management Reviews*, Vol. 3 No. 1, pp. 41–60.

Bontis, N. (2002) 'Managing organizational knowledge by diagnosing intellectual capital: framing and advancing the state of the field', in Bontis, N. (ed.), *World Congress on Intellectual Capital Readings*, Butterworth Heinemann, Boston, MA, pp. 621–42.

Bontis, N., Dragonetti, N.C., Jacobsen, K. and Roos, G. (1999) 'The knowledge toolbox: a review of the tools available to measure and manage intangible resources', *European Management Journal*, Vol. 17 No. 4, pp. 91–401.

Brooking, A. (1996) *Intellectual Capital: Core Asset For The Third Millennium*, International Thomson Business Press, London.

Crosby, A. (1997) *The Measure of Reality; Quantification and Western Society 1250–1600*, Cambridge University Press, Cambridge.

Edvinsson, L. and Malone, M.S. (1997) *Intellectual Capital: Realizing Your Company's True Value by Finding Its Hidden Brainpower*, HarperBusiness, New York, NY.

Financial Accounting Standard Board (2001) *Statement No. 142; Goodwill and Other Intangible Assets*, availble at: www.fasb.orgm

Gröjer, J.E. and Johanson, U. (2000) 'Accounting for intangibles at the accounting court', work in progress, available at: www.kunne.no/meritum/abstracts/court_a.pdf

Johnson, H.T. and Kaplan, R.S. (1987) *Relevance Lost*, Harvard Business School Press, Boston, MA.

Kaplan, R. and Norton, D. (1992) 'The balanced scorecard; measures that drive performance', *Harvard Business Review on Measuring Corporate Performance*, Harvard Business School Press, Boston, MA, pp. 123–45.

Kaplan, R. and Norton, D. (1996a) 'Using the balanced scorecard as a strategic management system', *Harvard Business Review on Measuring Corporate Performance*, Harvard Business School Press, Boston, MA, pp. 183–211.

Kaplan, R. and Norton, D. (1996b) *The Balanced Scorecard*, Harvard Business School Press, Boston, MA.

Kaplan, R. and Norton, D. (2001) *The Strategy Focused Organization*, Harvard Business School Press, Boston, MA.

Luthy, D.H. (1998) 'Intellectual capitial and its measurement', *Proceedings of the Asian Pacific Interdisciplinary Research in Accounting Conference (APIRA) Osaka, Japan*, available at: www3.bus.osaka-cu.ac.jp/apira98/archives/htmls/25.htm

Marr, B., Gray, D. and Neely, A. (2003) Why do firms measure their intellectual capital?', *Journal of Intellectual Capital*, Vol. 4 No. 4, pp. 441–64.

Petty, R. and Guthrie, J. (2000) 'Intellectual capital literature overview: measurement, reporting and management', *Journal of Intellectual Capital*, Vol. 1 No. 2, pp. 155–76.

Pike, S. and Roos, G. (2000) 'Intellectual capital measurement and holistic value approach (HVA)', *Works Institute Journal (Japan)*, Vol. 42 October/November.

Pike, S. and Roos, G. (2004) 'Mathematics and modern business management', paper presented at the 25th McMaster World Congress Managing Intellectual Capital, Hamilton.

Pike, S., Rylander, A. and Roos, G. (2001) 'Intellectual capital management and disclosure', paper presented at the 4th World Congress on Intellectual Capital, McMaster University, Hamilton.

Procter, P. (1978) *Longman Dictionary of Contemporary English*, Longman Group Ltd, Harlow.

Reilly, R. and Schweihs, R. (1999) *Valuing Intangible Assets*, McGraw-Hill, New York, NY.

Rescher, N. (1969) *Introduction to Value Theory*, Prentice-Hall, Englewood Cliffs, NJ.

Roos, G., Roos, J., Dragonetti, N. and Edvinsson, L. (1997) *Intellectual Capital; Navigating in the New Business Landscape*, New York University Press, New York, NY.

Rutledge, J. (1997) 'You are a fool if you buy into this', *Forbes ASAP*, April.

Rylander, A., Jacobsen, K. and Roos, G. (2000) 'Towards improved information disclosure on intellectual capital', *International Journal of Technology Management*, Vol. 20 No. 5/6/7/8, pp. 715–42.

Smith, G. and Parr, R. (1994) *Valuation of Intellectual Property and Intangible Assets*, John Wiley & Sons, New York, NY.

Stewart, G.B. III (1994) 'EVA: fact and fantasy', *Journal of Applied Corporate Finance*, Vol. 7, Summer, pp. 71–84.

Stewart, T.A. (1997) *Intellectual Capital; The New Wealth of Organizations*, Doubleday/Currency, New York, NY.

Stewart, T.A. (2001) *The Wealth of Knowledge: Intellectual Capital and the Twenty-first Century Organization*, Doubleday/Currency, New York, NY.

Strassmann, P.A. (1998) The value of knowledge capital', *American Programmer*, Vol. 11 No. 3, pp. 3–10.

Strassmann, P.A. (1999) 'Calculating knowledge capital', *Knowledge Management Magazine*, October, available at: files.strassmann.com/pubs/km/1999-10.php

Sveiby, K.E. (1997) *The New Organizational Wealth: Managing & Measuring Knowledge-Based Assets*, Berrett-Koehler Publishers, San Francisco, CA.

Sveiby, K.E. (2002) 'Methods for measuring intangible assets', available at: www.sveiby.com/articles/IntangibleMethods.htm

Swanborn, P.G. (1981) *Methoden van sociaal-wetenschappelijk onderzoek*, Boom Meppel, Amsterdam.

Trompenaars, F. and Hampden-Turner, C. (1997) *Riding The Waves Of Culture*, Nicholas Brealey Publishing, London.

Upton, W.S. (2001) *Business and Financial Reporting; Challenges from the New Economy*, FASB, Norwalk, CT.

Viedma, J.M. (2001) 'ICBS intellectual capital benchmarking system', *Journal of Intellectual Capital*, Vol. 2 No. 2, pp. 148–64.

White, G.I., Sondhi, A.C. and Fried, D. (1997) *The Analysis and Use of Financial Statements*, John Wiley & Sons, New York, NY.

12 Managing Knowledge and Innovation Across Boundaries

Paul Quintas

This chapter focuses on knowledge processes that cross organizational boundaries. Our interest is not in routine interactions but rather with those relating to the process of innovation. Innovation often involves cross-boundary working, whether it is between functional areas within organizations, or interactions with organizations in the external environment. Here our concern is with the latter: knowledge processes that occur across the external boundaries of the innovating organization.

Innovation depends on a number of knowledge capabilities, as for example the capability to generate novelty and variety in the knowledge available to the organization, and the ability to apply knowledge in practical contexts. Because innovation involves novelty and change, these knowledge capabilities must be continually developing; that is, they must be dynamic capabilities (Teece et al., 1997). However this presents a challenge, since organizations also need to maintain their core capabilities – the things they do well because they have accumulated knowledge through experience and engagement with practice in the past. A central knowledge dilemma for organizations seeking to innovate focuses on the need to cumulatively build and maintain the knowledge that underpins their core capabilities, while at the same time generating variety in their knowledge capabilities as the source of future novel developments.

For obvious reasons the greatest source of knowledge variety lies beyond the boundaries of the organization. However, accessing external knowledge requires the innovating organization to possess the capabilities to locate, understand, assimilate and internalize that external knowledge. Libraries and the Internet contain vast amounts of information, but turning that into useful knowledge for the firm requires effort and capability. Similarly, publicly-funded research-based knowledge is not a free good (Callon, 1994) since its acquisition requires significant investment in learning. Indeed, Cohen and Levinthal (1989) suggest that the reason why firms invest in research and development (R&D) has as much to do with maintaining the capability to track and understand external developments, as it is to do with pursuing internally-focused development.

It remains inconceivable, surely, that any organization could be isolated and self-contained in knowledge terms. Not least, each new recruit brings with them the knowledge they have acquired in their previous work, studies and personal life. Moreover, it has long been recognized that organizations are interconnected to external networks and cannot avoid cross-boundary transactions: 'Firms are not islands but are linked together in patterns of co-operation and affiliation' (Richardson, 1972: 895). Generally this means that organizations are linked to others that have complementary knowledge, as for example within their supply chain. A manufacturer's distributors know about their target markets, and its component suppliers know about their own manufacturing processes. Stigler (1951) observed that firms substitute inputs from external suppliers because these suppliers learn to provide these at lower cost than the vertically integrated firm can achieve. The superior performance of these external suppliers results from specialization, a theme that is central to this chapter. A further theme concerns the question of how far knowledge is created and shared in such cross-boundary contexts.

Whether knowledge is shared or created, at the boundaries between organizations in supply-chain relationships, depends on a range of factors, such as how far the different firms in the supply chain need to understand each other's processes, whether they work jointly on problem solving and to what extent they are concerned that their competitive advantage would be undermined by disclosure and so seek to protect their knowledge. Where innovation is being pursued across a network of organizations there are additional factors to consider, due to a large extent to the uncertainty and unpredictability of the innovation process. As innovation requires new knowledge to be created, knowledge issues are central to this unpredictability.

Nevertheless, the external network has increased in importance as a source of resources available to the innovating firm (Freeman, 1991). Indeed the network form of organization has been increasingly favoured by academics, business analysts and government policy-makers in the West, as a superior form of organization to the vertically integrated firm. The arguments are based primarily on flexibility and specialization (Piore and Sabel, 1984). The network enables specialist firms to configure into a coherent interdependent structure, but offers the opportunity for the network to reconfigure, changing the component organizations in response to shifting market conditions. Thus Miles and Snow (1986) refer to *dynamic networks* of large and small firms interacting in collaboration.

For economists the business network allows a configuration of resources that lies between markets and hierarchies (Williamson, 1975), where hierarchies refers to vertically integrated organizations. Between the extremes of market and hierarchy many kinds of formal and informal collaborative relationships between firms exist, from 'loosely coupled' to 'tightly coupled'. However the relative advantages of these forms of organization remain a highly contested debate, with the knowledge perspective introducing a key dichotomy:

> *Networks offer the benefit of both specialization and variety generation. ... The converse of this statement is that firms are superior vehicles for the accumulation of specialized learning. (Kogut, 2000: 407)*

The central theme of this chapter emerges from the above quotation. Organizations seeking to innovate may collaborate and participate in business networks comprising clusters of individual firms each creating and accumulating specialized knowledge. The aim is to benefit from the aggregate specialist knowledge of all the participating organizations, removing the need for each firm to know everything. For each participating firm, their partners bring different knowledge from their own – they bring variety. There is a *division of knowledge* (Hayek, 1937) between participating organizations, implying a lack of duplication. This reduction of duplication coupled with the cumulative advancement of knowledge in each participating organization, through specialization, suggests a high degree of efficiency. The central question is: how do these organizations then understand, access or assimilate knowledge from their partners, if they have no internal capability in the other's specialized area? This question applies not only to network relationships, but to any situation where an organization seeks to access knowledge from another organization in a knowledge domain in which they have no internal knowledge capability.

Knowledge Issues

Drawing on current understanding of knowledge processes, a number of issues need to be taken on board if we are to address this question. First, we perceive that knowledge cannot be regarded as a commodity that is easy to trade and share, and the process of acquiring knowledge requires learning and understanding, which pre-supposes some pre-existing capability. Second, knowledge is created through dynamic processes and is experiential. Knowing is an active process, resulting from action and engagement (Cook and Brown, 1999). Experiential knowledge is known to the individuals involved in specific activities, and is difficult if not impossible to communicate to others, since much of it remains irrevocably tacit. Third, knowledge is created in specific contexts and to an extent is dependent on that context to acquire meaning (Lave, 1993; Lave and Wenger, 1991; Nelson and Winter, 1982). Context specific knowledge (or *situated knowledge* in Lave and Wenger's terms) may be transient, and 'sticky' (von Hippel, 1994) and very difficult to share between contexts. Fourth, knowledge has a social dimension. Communities of practice, within which individuals share common work experiences and problem agendas, provide a social context where knowledge may be created and effectively shared (Brown and Duguid, 1998; Wenger, 1998). Within the community of practice knowledge may be mutually held in non-codified forms (Brown and Duguid, 1998; Wenger, 1998). Such communities have a degree of exclusivity – their knowledge is not readily available to outsiders who do not share similar practice-based experiences. It is clear that we cannot regard knowledge as a simple commodity that is easily 'transferred'.

All these factors reinforce the problem that is our central concern: how to bridge the division of knowledge that results from specialization. The term 'division of knowledge' intentionally links the central issues discussed here to their roots in the *division of labour*. 'Adam Smith explained the creation of wealth by emphasising the division of labour which led to the growth of differentiated knowledge' (Loasby, 1996: 299). The division of labour results in the division of knowledge, and specialization: 'knowledge grows by division; each of us can increase our knowledge only by accepting limits on what we can know' (Loasby, 1999: 135). In his seminal 1937 paper 'Economics and Knowledge' Friedrich Hayek (1937: 49) emphasized 'a problem of the *Division of Knowledge* which is quite analogous to, and at least as important as, the problem of the division of labour'. The use of the word 'analogous' is perhaps misplaced, since the division of knowledge is implicit in Adam Smith's focus on the division of labour as the basis of wealth creation. This occurs through the development of specialized skills, expertise and knowledge: 'Each individual becomes more expert in his own peculiar branch, more work is done upon the whole, and the quantity of science is considerably increased by it' (Smith, 1887: 12). Further, Smith presented empirical evidence that the division of labour leads through specialization to innovation: '... the invention of all those machines by which labour is so much facilitated and abridged, seems to have been originally owing to the division of labour' (Smith, 1887: 10).

The problem is that, the more effectively knowledge is specialized and divided between the different partners in a business network, the more the capacity for knowledge sharing is reduced. Grant (1996: 116) describes the core issue by analogy:

> ... *if two people have identical knowledge there is no gain from integration – yet, if the individuals have entirely separate knowledge bases, then integration cannot occur beyond the most primitive level.*

At the extreme, *perfect* specialization, where there are no overlapping knowledge capabilities, results in maximum barriers to knowledge sharing. If there is overlapping knowledge (or 'redundant' knowledge, as described by Nonaka and Takeuchi [1995]) between partners, advancement through specialization is retarded, the economic case for the network organizational form is reduced, and the benefits from having access to a wider variety of knowledge resources and capabilities are diminished.

Inter-organizational Knowledge and Innovation Processes

Given that there are finite limits to the knowledge resources within any organization, organizations increasingly need to access information, knowledge and expertise from outside in order to innovate. In large part this is driven by the increased complexity of products, services and processes, the pace and unpredictability of technological innovation, and the globalization and accelerated dynamism of markets. Even the largest firms have to collaborate with others (IBM-Sharp or Boeing-Mitsubishi) since it is impossible even for multinational corporations to grow and maintain capabilities in all relevant areas of current and emergent technology and markets. This extends to direct competitors who are forced to collaborate when they find they cannot innovate fast enough on their own, such as the December 2004 example of DaimlerChrysler announcing a collaboration with arch rivals General Motors in order to pool their resources to catch up with Toyota in hybrid vehicle technology (see Box 12.1).

Organizations of all sizes need to be able to access information from external sources, whether these are customers, suppliers, collaborators or partners, consultants, research institutions, regulatory bodies, publications or internet resources. Crucially, organizations require the internal capability to understand and make use of this external information, and turn it into useful knowledge. This capability is known as *absorptive capacity* (Cohen and Levinthal, 1990).

Box 12.1   GM and DaimlerChrysler collaboration

In December 2004 the world's largest motor vehicle manufacturer General Motors Corporation announced a partnership with their fourth largest competitor, DaimlerChrysler AG, to jointly develop hybrid petrol-electric power systems for cars and trucks. Both GM and DaimlerChrysler recognized the need to collaborate in order to catch up with Toyota Motor Corporation in the core technology of hybrid vehicles that are becoming increasingly popular. Minds are concentrated by the fact that in January 2004 Toyota overtook Ford to become the second largest motor manufacturer, with profits exceeding the combined profits of Ford, GM and DaimlerChrysler (Reuters, 2004). The growing popularity of hybrid vehicles is in part encouraged by government subsidies and tax breaks in some countries, and in part by consumer concerns over greenhouse gases, rising fuel costs and dependency on Middle East oil.

Despite DaimlerChrysler and GM spending respectively US$6.7 billion and US$5.7 billion on R&D (research and development) in 2004 (Technology Review, 2004) these giant corporations apparently do not individually have the knowledge and capabilities to develop advanced hybrid vehicles fast enough to compete with Toyota. Their previous R&D effort aimed at pursuing lower vehicle emissions and fuel efficiency had been largely focussed on fuel cells and, in the case of DaimlerChrysler, diesel technology, although GM have a basic petrol–electric system for trucks and buses. Pooling their R&D efforts will mean the two rivals can bring competitive hybrid vehicles to the market years earlier than they otherwise could. It also means shared costs and risks, and shared scarce resources – the skilled people with the knowledge to develop these complex systems.

There are other factors driving firms to collaborate in order to innovate. Collaboration has become especially important in innovation contexts where only one industry standard can succeed, such as in the example of the video cassette recorder (VCR). Having learned the cost of such 'standards wars', Philips formed a strategic alliance with Sony to develop the compact audio disk (CD). This also brought the benefits of pooled access to knowledge and technology, economies of scale and access to international markets (Tidd et al., 2001).

A further driver of cross-boundary interactions concerns what Teece (1988) refers to as complementary assets – those things that are required to be present in order to enable your innovation to be possible, but for which you depend on external sources. The interdependency of motor vehicle manufacturers and tyre, oil and electronic sub-assembly producers, or that between specialist software producers and computer hardware manufacturers are classic examples. Another factor is that many organizations have outsourced key functions such as IT, research and development and product design, so creating external cross-boundary transactions (Taylor et al., 2000).

The result of all these factors is that innovative processes are embedded in 'a dense network of external relationships' (Brusoni et al., 2001).

Case Studies

We now present some findings from two research projects. These cases shed light on the reasons driving inter-organizational knowledge processes in specific contexts, and the ways in which such knowledge processes are managed. The first project focused on R&D collaborations in the UK IT industry in the 1980s and unearthed a number of relevant issues. We then report on a series of case studies conducted in the late 1990s which looked at different types of innovating organizations involved in different forms of network relationships.

Collaborative R&D – The Alvey Programme

The Alvey Programme was a major programme of collaborative R&D focused on advanced information technology, orchestrated and part-funded by the UK government in the 1980s. Alvey spanned over five years and involved the majority of organizations with R&D capability in information technologies (hardware and software) in the UK. The programme supported 198 R&D collaborations, involving 115 firms, 68 academic institutions and 27 government research laboratories. For political reasons Alvey was restricted to 'pre-competitive' R&D; that is, R&D that is not geared to specific markets or short-term gains. Rather, the focus was on *enabling* technologies – those that might lead to a spread of downstream applications. Our research (Quintas and Guy, 1989, 1995) found that participating firms had a range of strategic objectives when entering into R&D collaborations:

- to acquire know-how and enhance their knowledge bases, primarily to exploit this knowledge in the subsequent in-house development of technology, but also to inform strategic decision-making regarding technological capabilities;
- to supplement their skills and expertise bases through sharing scarce skilled personnel;
- to reduce R&D costs and share risks;
- to participate in collaborative development of standards, and to track and learn about emergent standards;
- to develop a national base of collaboration upon which to develop international links.

We found that achievement of the first objective (acquisition of know-how and enhanced knowledge bases) depended on a number of factors:

- the capability and compatibility of collaborative partners in terms of expertise levels need to be roughly on a par at the start;
- the nature of the collaboration: that is, how work is divided, mechanisms for integration, the channels of communication;
- the nature of the technology or knowledge being generated and transferred (for example, codified knowledge such as software modules are easier to transfer than tacit knowledge);
- stability within participant organizations in terms of ownership, business and technology strategy, and continuity of personnel active in the collaboration;
- the ability of the recipient firm to understand and internalize the technology and know-how, that is their absorptive capacity or ability to learn. (Quintas and Guy, 1995: 341)

A lack of compatible knowledge and expertise in partner organizations was a key factor in many problematic collaborations. Participants would complain that they had lost significant amounts of time 'bringing their collaborators up to speed', or in some cases educating them up to a level where they could begin to communicate. Conversely, there were many examples of successful collaborations where the project teams, comprised of individuals and small groups from many organizations, formed an effective inter-organizational community of practice. Members of these teams commented that their working relationships with project colleagues based in external organizations were better than those within their own company. Colleagues in their own firm did not understand what they were working on, and they found they could not communicate easily on a technical level with people outside the project team. Non-technical barriers grew between themselves and fellow employees (and some managers) who became suspicious and sceptical about a project that involved close collaboration with outside organizations.

Collaboration enables firms to track developing and risky areas without the costs of building strong in-house capability, at least until it is clear that this has become a business imperative. Conversely, even where collaborations are focused on R&D trajectories that are central to participating firms' current business strategies, in the projects studied there were several costly examples of business strategies being changed and the reason for collaboration negated and routes to exploitation cut off.

A key question concerns the ability of participating organizations to exploit the outcomes of the collaboration. In those networks clustered around a systems integrator the satellite organizations are unlikely to have the capability to take things forward, other than spin-off outcomes in their own specialized areas. Also, as we have seen, the key issue concerns the major barriers to knowledge sharing between project teams and the rest of their organization. At the level of the individuals involved in inter-firm collaboration, their success in forming a community of practice with teams from other organizations contrasted sharply with the barriers that grew between themselves and their colleagues in their own firms.

Knowledge Management in Design and Innovation Networks

In 1996 the UK Design Council funded the three year research project Knowledge Management in Design and Innovation Networks (KAMDIN). The project stemmed from the understanding that product design and innovation increasingly take place across clusters or networks of organizations, which raises questions concerning the creation and management of knowledge across organizational boundaries. The KAMDIN project featured a number of case studies, two of which are described below in some detail, then three in brief form. The company names are disguised.

TeleMeter[1] The TeleMeter project aimed to develop the technology for remote meter-reading services, linking individual homes with various utilities (water, gas and electricity). The idea was to eliminate the need for human meter-readers. The TeleMeter innovation required the development of hardware and software connected to an existing telecommunications network, and linked to the utilities. Our research focused on the knowledge processes within and between the network of firms involved. Tel-Net was the systems integrator within a network of specialist software and hardware suppliers, and potential customers: gas, water and electricity utility companies.

The project required the integration of specialists from different knowledge domains, working for different companies, all contributing to the design of a complex system. The technical issues raised by different specialisms had to be integrated. However, understanding the different technical interfaces is only the start of the management problem, as the final design had to encompass the different political influences of this community of specialists. The innovation also had to cope with the constraints imposed by the legacies of existing telecommunications network, and the utilities' IT systems.

Significantly for our current focus, Tel-Net were keen to ensure that their own technical expertise was not being duplicated among the project network of firms. Financial considerations dictated that there should *not* be overlapping or redundant knowledge in the network. That is, external partners were only brought in if their expertise was lacking in the systems integrator.

Throughout the project there were no mechanisms by which the creation of knowledge within one specialist area would be of benefit to other specialists, so the communities remained compartmentalized, their outputs 'black-boxed'. The Tel-Net culture placed a great emphasis on formal, explicit processes, ignoring the informal and non-explicit elements of the project. It was assumed that, for example, the delivery of a commissioned report transferred the knowledge created. This was not necessarily believed by those who wrote the reports. Remarkably, although Tel-Net brought in a specialist software house to work on the project, with software engineers located at Tel-Net's own R&D department, no attempt was made by Tel-Net to learn from these people. Since the only communications with the specialists that were valued by Tel-Net were formal and codified, opportunities for peripheral knowledge creation and informal sharing of knowledge were lost.

Management of the project finally passed from Tel-Net's R&D department to a subsidiary systems integrator within the corporate group, with expertise in the development and management of large software systems. The subsidiary company sold a telemetry system into a different market – remotely read gaming machines, rather than utilities. This used telemetry in a different way from that originally envisaged.

The formal approach adopted by the systems integrator, with its emphasis on agreed deliverables and formal reports, with no attempt to learn from specialist partners, served to prevent any significant knowledge sharing, other than within the pre-conceived confines of the formal agreements. The rigid management of this complex innovation did not account for, and was not interested in, the potentially valuable by-products of knowledge created during the development across the network.

SouthTech SouthTech is a long established manufacturer of environmental monitoring equipment which it supplies to defence and security agencies throughout the world. The company's core technologies, developed to detect and identify chemical warfare agents, are a complex integration of electronics and chemical processes, miniaturized within a portable package. This very high technology continues to be refined for the protection of defence forces, while also expanding into commercial, law enforcement and scientific applications in international markets. SouthTech is now a subsidiary of a larger defence, medical and aerospace company. It is an R&D centred company, with marketing taking a subordinate role.

The case study focuses on the design, development and manufacture of portable chemical agent monitors. These developments became dependent on external sources of knowledge when a key individual left the company. The case is unusual in providing insights into military product developments and into the relationship between the company and the defence establishment, and detailed insight into the sources of knowledge and expertise in a highly technical and interdisciplinary science-based product development.

SouthTech's management state that new knowledge is introduced into the company by individuals, and through the literature, through licensed technology and through advanced tools such as computer aided design (CAD). The firm is conscious that its human resource policy must encourage staff to be receptive and to accumulate the knowledge breadth that will add robustness to the company's knowledge base.

Little knowledge is received from suppliers, indeed SouthTech routinely has to 'tell its suppliers what to do' – providing them with knowledge in order to enable them to meet its requirements. Materials supplied have to be further treated by SouthTech to achieve required performance. The firm has to maintain levels of knowledge capabilities that encompass and even exceed those of its suppliers in the fields that SouthTech and its suppliers span. It is an example of an innovative company that normally retains all the required knowledge in-house across all its activities. Exceptions to this have occurred however. In one key project the need to grow in-house knowledge about miniaturization was removed by substituting a modular product from elsewhere. This blackbox solution confined the need to learn to the acquisition of knowledge about the interfaces, but not of the internal workings of the module.

Attempts to capture and codify project knowledge are fundamental to defence contracts. All participants in defence projects are required to maintain detailed logbooks of all their activities. These are handed over as required deliverables. They are treated by contractors as a required hoop through which they must jump. However what is recorded meets the requirement for data without passing on anything of value: 'we don't ship understanding. Understanding is not for sale!'

The SouthTech case provides a further example of the limitations of codified knowledge, and a remarkable insight into a solution to the problem of systems integration in complex systems. A key individual, whom we will refer to as Dr Brown, left the firm during the product innovation process. He passed CAD drawings and assembled prototypes to his successors. However the successor team could not progress the development because even with these starting points they did not understand the lessons from the prototypes. These required interpretation in the light of the tacit knowledge accumulated in Dr Brown's head. Moreover they could not integrate all the complex component technologies conceptually. This task was exceptionally difficult because the component technologies spanned nuclear physics, electronics and chemistry. SouthTech were forced to re-hire Dr Brown as a consultant. They were well aware of his unique polymath capability, as expressed by a colleague:

> (Brown's) integration in one mind is also vortex-like. He pulls in knowledge from literature, from schoolboy recollection, from experiment. But he shuns teamwork for teamwork's sake. The team offers him nothing until he needs the aptitudes of an industrial designer to materialize his thoughts...

Dr Brown was aware of his own ability to conceptualize the whole product, and the lack of that ability elsewhere: 'I had remained in total control, and had short-circuited all the knowledge flow problems of a conventional design & manufacture company. (SouthTech) does not have the advantage of integration within one mind'.

The SouthTech case illustrates the limits of formal codified reporting as a means of communicating knowledge. The firm also exemplifies the 'need to know everything' solution to the problem of bridging between specialisms – SouthTech take the view that in most cases they need to know as much, if not more, than their specialist suppliers. However it seems that the severe challenge of integrating knowledge from disparate spheres is at times highly dependent on key individuals. The SouthTech example is remarkable in emphasizing the ability of Dr Brown to integrate the otherwise divided knowledge from three disparate fields. Whether such multi-disciplinary knowledge integration is often dependent on exceptional individuals is a question for further research.

Cellbase Cellbase is a UK-based world leader in the design and manufacture of specialist products and subsystems used in wireless (mobile) telecommunications systems. Their products are used exclusively in cellular-base stations around the world. Cellbase has design and manufacturing facilities in Europe, North America and Australia, and they collaborate with client companies and systems integrators (for example, Nokia, Ericsson, Motorola, Lucent, Cellnet, Northern Telecom) across the world. The fact that they are often the only non-US company in their field selected to work on advanced US military projects illustrates the level of their technology. They were among the fastest growing UK companies of the 1990s; internal growth augmented by a series of major international acquisitions. They are of particular interest because they represent a company with unique knowledge and technology. Also they have exploited military technology in a commercial environment.

Cellbase grow their knowledge base by recruitment of the best graduate engineers, and continual investment in R&D and innovation. Though they source information from the technical literature, they do not think they can learn anything from external organizations since they consider they are significantly ahead of the field. They collaborate and share knowledge with their customers, the telecommunications companies who put the base-stations together. However, Cellbase do not protect their technology with patents. This is because the technology moves so fast that what they supply today is already being replaced by the next generation in their R&D labs. This means that, should a customer pass on information gained from Cellbase to an alternative supplier in order to gain an alternative and cheaper source, Cellbase simply threatens to withhold the next generation of the technology.

Cellbase is an example of a specialist company that, having grown from military R&D roots, appears be largely self-sufficient in knowledge terms. Its customers treat Cellbase's products as blackboxes, and although some knowledge is shared with these customers, the knowledge that gives Cellbase its ability to innovate the next product generation is not shared. The case provides insights into the dynamics of knowledge and innovation in a specialist organization, and shows how the blackboxing of knowledge in technical systems can overcome the problems of bridging between specialisms, without actually sharing the vital knowledge driving innovation.

Artyfact This case focuses on the toy design company Artyfact. Artyfact is managed by designers, but changes in company ownership over the duration of the case study have resulted in major changes in working practices that have implications for knowledge management. Initially, Artyfact was a wholly owned subsidiary of a civil engineering company which took a hands-off approach to managing the firm. Artyfact existed as part of extensive collaborative networks that include external specialist designers, toolmakers and manufacturing companies in the UK and the Far East. This represented an established cross-boundary network that functioned successfully based on clear understanding of roles in the network coupled with good interpersonal relationships. Artyfact's takeover by a US firm removed its external network community, intending to replace its expertise with that in the US parent. Artyfact was almost destroyed by the transition as they lacked the capacity to manage the newly enforced processes for the communication of knowledge between the US parent organization and the UK outpost.

In this case study the level of technology was such that Artyfact and its original network were able to communicate between specialisms while maintaining a clear separation of specialist roles. The relationships and communication processes worked well, until the US takeover. Significantly, the need to establish new communication links with the US parent proved traumatic. The routines and personal relationships upon which previous communications depended had been destroyed, and could not be re-created without major effort.

F1 Grand Prix Engineering F1 Grand Prix Engineering manufacture and race Formula One racing cars. This is an extreme case of a complex system in which continuous technological innovation is an absolute requirement. Race by race, every car that competes is essentially a prototype – there are always differences from the previous race. Innovation is primarily focused on incremental painstaking improvement based on huge amounts of data (especially feedback from testing and racing). Periodically F1 or their rival teams develop more radical or step-change innovations. The latter are often associated with changes in the regulations (the 'formula') or inputs from different knowledge domains, for example orthogonal knowledge from computing, aerospace or new materials developments, allied to creative ideas of key engineers.

The quality and rapid availability of data and information, and rapid learning, are paramount. Knowledge sharing with tyre and brake manufacturers is vital. These are the main suppliers apart from the engine. Both tyres and brakes are, like the cars, in continuous development throughout a season. Their manufacturers depend on streams of accurate data from F1 GPE – there is a mutual dependency and relationship of trust since these partners are also working for rival teams. This means that the tyre and brake manufacturers must have 'Chinese walls' that isolate and protect the knowledge gained from different F1 teams. Like most Formula One teams F1 GPE do not produce their own engines. The relationship with the engine supplier is closer than customer–supplier, but collaboration is confined to close interaction on required engine output characteristics (primarily power and torque delivery), plus external packaging. How the engine manufacturer designs the engine to meet these requirements is not a matter for collaboration.

For their part F1 GPE have to maintain and develop their own absorptive capacity in tyre and brake technology in order to maximize the advantage they can gain from these ever-developing components. They have to maintain capabilities to continuously create competitive advantage which is difficult to replicate. Whereas the addition of an aerodynamic feature on a car may be seen and copied by other teams, many improvements are less visible, and indeed the capability to continuously innovate and stay ahead of the opposition is in large part due to tacit processes. Such capability is hard to copy, as is illustrated by another example, that of Chaparral Steel. The Chaparral CEO is happy to tour competitors through the Chaparral plant, showing them 'almost everything and we will be giving away nothing because they can't take it home with them' (Leonard, 1995: 7).

Discussion and Conclusion

The cases support the view that knowledge cannot be regarded as a commodity that is easy to 'transfer' between collaborating partners. Knowledge acquisition depends on the development of capability, although this may occur within the network community of practice without being internalized by the firms concerned, as the Alvey and Artyfact cases illustrated. The case studies confirm that knowledge sharing between specialisms becomes difficult if not impossible without specialization-bridging measures such as redundant or overlapping knowledge. This is especially notable in F1 GPE, Cellbase and SouthTech. In the latter two cases these firms usually have to know more than their supplier networks, in order to be able to gain the inputs they require. In the TeleMeter case the absence of knowledge duplication or overlap was insisted upon by the systems integrator for financial reasons, and became a barrier to knowledge sharing.

Specialists have their own knowledge domains, language and culture. These are some of the defining characteristics of 'communities of practice'. For a community of specialists to learn outside of their specialisms is very expensive, indeed in the Alvey study we found that the cultural divides between specialisms were greater than those between companies.

This observation also points up a significant negative side to communities of practice, currently regarded as fundamental structures supporting knowledge creation and sharing. While communication and knowledge sharing *within* communities of practice may be highly effective, we have to consider the resulting constraints on knowledge sharing *between* communities of practice. Certainly the success of some Alvey projects in developing inter-organizational communities of practice was counter-balanced by the distancing of the project teams from the rest of their own organization.

Sourcing knowledge from outside the boundaries of the organization requires considerable effort and capability. The findings from the cases suggest that the distinction between the possession of absorptive capacity and the development of in-house specialist knowledge capabilities is not clear-cut. The Cellbase and SouthTech cases accord with Granstrand et al. (1997), who found that large inno-vating firms not only maintain distinctive capabilities in core technology areas but also maintain a background capability in those technological fields in which firms in their network or supply chain are specialists. This enables them to be knowl-edgeable evaluators and purchasers as Granstrand et al. say, but unlike these authors' findings, Cellbase does not learn from its business network. In Cellbase's case there may be some justification for this approach in terms of the firm's high degree of specialization and internal-knowledge dynamic. The alternative reason for lack of learning, illustrated by the TeleMeter case, is rooted in a rigid approach to collaboration which emphasizes formal reporting and fulfilment of contracts. The approach ensures a systemic lack of learning, not only about what is inside the blackboxes, but also an ignorance of the knowledge being created during the innovation process.

There are a number of possible mechanisms to counter the *division of knowledge* problem. The first focuses on learning across specialisms, where organizations need to devote considerable time and effort into knowledge sharing across disciplines. We cannot expect all organizations to be populated by polymaths like Dr Brown in the SouthTech case, but we have to create cultures and frameworks that encourage and support cross-specialist learning. This requires specialists to alternate rôles between novice and expert, in order to share knowledge. This process may well be inhibited by individuals' unfamiliarity with the novice rôle, and within organizations' management regimes by the ways in which people's achievements are measured. It is, however, what appears to happen fairly naturally in many collaborative projects. We observed in the Alvey case that project teams from many different organiza-tions with different specialisms gelled as communities of practice engaged in joint learning.

The second (related) solution is that proposed by Nonaka and Takeuchi (1995) focused on ensuring the presence of redundant knowledge. The principle is that in order for specialists to share knowledge they require overlapping knowledge. One way to achieve this is for each team to contain representatives versed in the others' specializations. This redundant (or duplicated) knowledge enables communication, knowledge sharing and learning, but undermines the economic case for flexible specialization, and reduces potential for advancement within specialized fields.

A third solution offered by Leonard (1995) focuses on people who have func-tional or specialist skills but are also able to apply knowledge across a variety of situations. She refers to these as 'T-shaped' skills. This means having deep knowl-edge in one area, plus the ability to link to other areas of knowledge (Iansiti, 1995). When teams of people with T-shaped skills work together they are better at shar-ing knowledge than narrow functional specialists. Liedtka et al. (1997) report that the leading firms in the professional service sector benefit from having people with T-shaped skills because their teams can be smaller, and individuals can move easily between teams.

In all these solutions there is a requirement for joint activity, for working together and gaining shared experiential knowledge. It remains the case that without such close working practice, knowledge sharing will rely on codified knowledge and much tacit learning will be lost. In the context of innovation processes, where knowledge creation is certain but unpredictable, to miss out on these learning opportunities is to risk missing the point. This is particularly the case where the original goals are not met, as in the TeleMeter case. Such a project might be thought a complete failure by those who are not aware of the knowledge created. The systems integrator was also disadvantaged by its managerial culture which relied on formal communications, and on contractual transactions rather than trust. Both these prevented awareness of knowledge gains and indeed new business opportunities.

A further key question emerges from our knowledge focus: what is the nature of the knowledge division in any particular innovation network. What would constitute entirely separate knowledge domains, and indeed how disparate can knowledge domains be, before communication problems become insurmountable? Within the cases discussed above, it is notable that within Alvey collaborations, all focused on information technology, partners in collaborations often came from quite distinct knowledge areas, about which their partners knew little. Participants often referred to their collaborators having different vocabularies, and different ways of working. These divisions were also obvious in the TeleMeter case, and indeed were designed into the selection of partners, aimed at preventing duplication. Here the blackbox approach only worked up to a limited point. In the SouthTech case, the innovation brought together quite disparate knowledge domains which only one person was able to bridge, as was clearly shown by what happened when he left. For the rest of SouthTech the knowledge domain gap was insurmountable. For F1, the organization has no choice but to build internal capability to bridge the knowledge gaps between engineering, aerodynamics, electronics, new materials, tyre technology, and so on.

The above discussion is based on a very narrow set of case studies, and generalizability into wider contexts cannot be assumed. Further work is needed to explore the organizational and management processes that emerge as being crucial. High level (firm strategy and network level) studies are useful, but limited. There is a dearth of studies of knowledge processes at the level of the innovation practitioners. Only by engagement with practitioners do we begin to understand the nature of knowledge creation, sharing and application in innovation contexts. In particular we need to understand the conditions under which knowledge specialization will lead to severe communication problems, identify the costs of bridging these gaps, and explore the alternative solutions in a wide range of contexts.

A major methodological challenge remains in the area of tacit knowledge. Owing to the nature of such knowledge it is not available to researchers, in much the same way it is not available to collaborating partners. Avenues to explore include ethnographic studies relying on long-term observation and participation, and behaviourist approaches, which seek to identify the symptoms of knowledge that betray its existence – if a saxophonist can play, then we can assume he or she has internalized the knowledge.

There are also implications for policy makers. The network form of organization, collaborations and alliances, have all been encouraged by policies, and indeed by funded programmes, in Asia, North America and Europe. The issues raised here around the division of knowledge raise questions as to the assumed efficiency and effectiveness of the network form of organization in innovation contexts.

Note

1 This case draws on Demaid (1998).

References

Allen, T.J. (1977) *Managing the Flow of Technology*. Cambridge, MA: MIT Press.

Brown, J.S. and Duguid, P. (1998) 'Organizing knowledge', *California Management Review*, 40(3): 90–111.

Brusoni, S., Prencipe, A. and Pavitt, K. (2001) 'Knowledge specialization, organizational coupling, and the boundaries of the firm: why do firms know more than they make?', *Administrative Science Quarterly*, 46: 597–621.

Callon, M. (1994) 'Is science a public good?', *Science, Technology and Human Values*, 19: 395–424.

Cohen, W.M. and Levinthal, D.A. (1989) 'Innovation and learning: two faces of R&D', *Economic Journal*, 99: 569–96.

Cohen, W.M. and Levinthal, D.A. (1990) 'Absorptive capacity: a new perspective on learning and innovation', *Administrative Science Quarterly*, 35: 128–52.

Cook, S.D.N. and Brown, J.S. (1999) 'Bridging epistemologies: the generative dance between organizational knowledge and organizational knowing', *Organization Science*, 10(4): 381–400.

Demaid, A. (1998) 'Managing knowledge across the cultural divides', paper presented at the Movement of Knowledge and Innovation Research Unit (MKIRU) workshop, Open University/Design Council, 30 September, London.

Freeman, C. (1991) 'Networks of innovators: a synthesis of research issues', *Research Policy*, 20: 499–514.

Granstrand, O., Patel, P. and Pavitt, K. (1997) 'Multi-technology corporations: why they have "distributed" rather than "distinctive core" competencies', *California Management Review*, 39(4): 8–25.

Grant, R.M. (1996) 'Towards a knowledge-based theory of the firm', *Strategic Management Journal*, 17 (special winter Issue): 109–22.

Hayek (1937) 'Economics and knowledge', *Economica*, 4: 33–54.

Hippel, E., von (1994) '"Sticky information" and the locus of problem solving: implications for innovation', *Management Science*, 40(4): 429–39.

Iansiti, M. (1995) 'Shooting the rapids: managing product development in turbulent environments', *California Management Review*, 38: 37–58.

Kogut, B. (2000) 'The network as knowledge: generative rules and the emergence of structure', *Strategic Management Journal*, 21(3): 405–25.

Lave, J. (1993) 'The practice of learning', in S. Chaiklin and J. Lave (eds), *Understanding Practice. Perspectives on Activity and Context*. Cambridge: Cambridge University Press, pp. 3-32.

Lave, J. and Wenger, E. (1991) *Situated Learning: Legitimate Peripheral Participation*. Cambridge: Cambridge University Press.

Leonard, D. (1995) *Wellsprings of Knowledge: Building and Sustaining the Sources of Innovation*. Boston, MA: Harvard Business School Press.

Liedtka, J.M., Haskins, M.E., Rosenblum, J.W. and Weber, J. (1997) 'The generative cycle: linking knowledge and relationships', *Sloan Management Review*, Fall: 47-58.

Loasby, B.J. (1996) 'The division of labour', *History of Economic Ideas*, IV (1-2): 299-323.

Loasby, B.J. (1999) *Knowledge, Institutions and Evolution in Economics*. New York: Routledge.

Loasby, B.J. (2001) 'Industrial dynamics: why connections matter', *DRUID Academy Winter Conference*, Klarkovgaard, January, pp. 18-20.

Miles, R.E. and Snow, C.C. (1986) 'Network organisations, new concepts for new forms', *California Management Review*, 28: 62-73.

Nelson, R. and Winter, S. (1982) *An Evolutionary Theory of Economic Change*. Cambridge, MA: Belknap Press of Harvard University Press.

Nonaka, I. and Takeuchi, H. (1995) *The Knowledge-Creating Company*. Oxford: Oxford University Press.

Piore, M. and Sabel, C. (1984) *The Second Industrial Divide*. New York: Basic Books.

Quintas, P. and Guy, K. (1989) *Alvey in Industry: Corporate Strategy and the Alvey Programme*, Report to the Department of Trade and Industry, Science Policy Research Unit, Brighton: Falmer.

Quintas, P. and Guy, K. (1995) 'Collaborative, pre-competitive R&D and the firm', *Research Policy*, 24: 325-48.

Reuters (2004) 'Toyota overtakes Ford as No. 2 auto maker', *Reuters News*, January 25. Available at: http://www.reuters.com/

Richardson, G.B. (1972) 'The organization of industry', *Economic Journal*, 82: 883-96.

Smith, A. (1887) *An Inquiry into the Nature and Causes of the Wealth of Nations*. London: George Bell & Sons.

Stigler, G. (1951) 'The division of labour is limited by the extent of the market', *Journal of Political Economy*, June: 185-93.

Taylor, P., Quintas, P., Storey, J. and Fowle, W. (2000) 'Utilising internal and external resources for innovation: employment practices and inter-firm collaboration', Working Paper 2, MKIRU, Open University Business School.

Technology Review (2004) 'Corporate R&D Scorecard 2004', *Technology Review*. Available at: http://www.technologyreview.com/articles/04/12/scorecard 21204.pdf

Teece, D.J. (1988) 'Profiting from technological innovation: implications for integration, collaboration, licensing and public policy', *Research Policy*, 15: 285-305.

Teece, D.J., Pisano, G. and Shuen, A. (1997) 'Dynamic capabilities and strategic management', *Strategic Management Journal*, 18(7): 509-33.

Tidd, J., Bessant, J. and Pavitt, K. (2001) *Managing Innovation: Integrating Technological, Market and Organizational Change*, 2nd edn. Chichester: Wiley.

Wenger, E. (1998) *Communities of Practice*. Cambridge: Cambridge University Press.

Williamson, O.E. (1975) *Markets and Hierarchies: Analysis and Antitrust Implications*. London: The Free Press.

13

The Human Resource Architecture: Toward a theory of Human Capital Allocation and Development

David P. Lepak and Scott A. Snell

Given pressures for both efficiency and flexibility (Powell, 1990), firms are exploring the use of different employment modes to allocate work (Rousseau, 1995; Tsui et al., 1995). In addition to the use of internal full-time employees, many firms are depending increasingly on external workers, such as temporary employees, contract laborers, and the like. This shift highlights the fact that, as with other capital investments, the management of human capital often can be broken down into 'make-or-buy' decisions (Miles and Snow, 1984). On the one hand, firms may internalize employment and build the employee skill base through training and development initiatives. On the other, firms may externalize employment by outsourcing certain functions to market-based agents (Rousseau, 1995).

Although the make-or-buy distinction is admittedly simplistic, the growing number of subtle variations on this theme makes the effective management of employment at once more complicated and more directly related to organizational effectiveness. Some theorists have advocated the benefits of internal development of skills and capabilities (e.g. Bettis et al., 1992; Hamel and Prahalad, 1994; Lei and Hitt, 1995), whereas others have advocated externalization (e.g. Quinn, 1992; Snow et al., 1992).

The potential benefits of internal employment include greater stability and predictability of a firm's stock of skills and capabilities (Pfeffer and Baron, 1988), better coordination and control (Jones and Hill, 1988; Williamson, 1981), enhanced socialization (Edwards, 1979), and lower transaction costs (Mahoney, 1992; Williamson, 1975). Externalization, however, may enable firms to decrease overhead and administrative costs (Davis-Blake and Uzzi, 1993; von Hippel et al., 1997; Welch and Nayak, 1992), balance workforce requirements (Pfeffer, 1994), and enhance organizational flexibility (Miles and Snow, 1992; Snow et al., 1992). Externalizing employment may also provide organizations with more discretion in both the number and types of workers used (Davis-Blake and Uzzi, 1993; Pfeffer and Baron, 1988; Tsui et al., 1995) and allow them access to vendor innovations while focusing critical resources on the development of core capabilities (Quinn, 1992).

Despite the benefits of both internalization and externalization, each employment mode has its own associated costs. Internalization may increase the stability

Source: D.P. Lepak and S.A. Snell (1999) 'The human resource architecture: toward a theory of human capital allocation and development', *Academy of Management Review*, 24(1): 31–48.

of a firm's stock of human capital, but it also incurs bureaucratic costs stemming from administering the employment relationship (Jones and Wright, 1992; Rousseau, 1995). Moreover, internalization constrains a firm's ability to adapt to environmental changes, particularly those that influence the demand for labor. Externalization has its own set of costs. For example, since outsourcing involves the use of external skills and capabilities, an organization's continued reliance on it for short-term purposes may mitigate the development of core skills and capabilities – critical for long-term firm performance (Bettis et al., 1992; Lei and Hitt, 1995).

We argue that this discussion should not be reduced to an 'either/or' distinction of employment modes. In reality, organizations utilize a variety of approaches to allocate human capital and often use these forms simultaneously (Davis-Blake and Uzzi, 1993). In other words, firms often make *and* buy their human capital. Yet, the literature on how firms can manage their employment modes remains sparse. From the point of view of strategic human resource management (HRM), researchers need to investigate how various combinations of employment modes (i.e. internalization and externalization) lead to competitive advantage. Scholars also need to identify the configurations of staffing, training, appraisal and reward practices that are appropriate for the types of human capital embodied within those employment modes.

To date, most strategic HRM researchers have tended to take a holistic view of employment and human capital, focusing on the extent to which a set of practices is used across all employees of a firm as well as the consistency of these practices across firms (see Gerhart and Trevor, 1996; Huselid, 1995; Snell and Dean, 1992, for notable exceptions). By ignoring the possible existence of different employment practices for different employee groups within a firm, much of the strategic HRM literature may seem somewhat monolithic. For instance, many strategic HRM theorists (e.g. Arthur, 1992, 1994; Koch and McGrath, 1996; Kochan and Osterman, 1994; Lawler, 1992; Levine, 1995; Pfeffer, 1994) have advocated high commitment and other types of high-involvement work systems that focus on making large investments in human capital to foster sustainable competitive advantage. Although these suggestions are intuitively appealing, it may be inappropriate to simplify the nature of human capital investments and suggest that there exists a single 'optimal' HR architecture for managing all employees. Rather, we believe that the most appropriate mode of investment in human capital will vary for different types of human capital.

To address these issues, we draw upon several works in economics, organization theory, strategic management and HRM literature to develop the foundation of an HR architecture that aligns different employment modes, employment relationships, HR configurations, and criteria for competitive advantage. We use the term *architecture* to describe this framework because it is based on a set of fundamental parameters that, once established, allow us to draw inferences about both the form and function of the entire system (cf. Becker and Gerhart, 1996; Nadler et al., 1992). Although the notion of an HR architecture is consistent with the conceptualization of organizational configurations and the need to align strategic employment

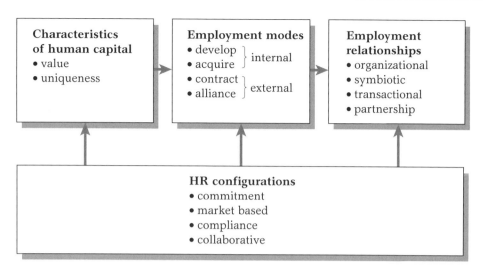

Figure 13.1 Theoretical model

and HR issues, the premise of our framework is that there may be different HR configurations within a single organization's architecture. Therefore, these HR configurations do not represent an entire organization but, rather, subgroupings within organizations.

The logic of the architecture is as follows. First, we discuss strategic considerations in terms of how they influence the employment mode used for various forms of human capital. Using the dimensions of value and uniqueness of human capital, we identify four different employment modes: 1 internal development; 2 acquisition; 3 contracting; and 4 alliance. Second, we view each employment mode as carrying with it an inherently different form of employment relationship. Rousseau (1995: 9) describes employment relationships as the 'psychological contract [of] individual beliefs, shaped by the organization, regarding terms of an exchange agreement between individuals and their organizations'. As employment modes differ, so too do the nature of the psychological contracts. Third, we view patterns of HR practices – or HR configurations – as helping to define the employment mode, maintain the employment relationship and support the strategic characteristics of human capital. Drawing on the Barnard–Simon notion of 'inducements-contributions exchange' (Barnard, 1938; March and Simon, 1958), we argue that HR configurations maintain equity between the employee and the organization in terms of what each contributes and receives. We depict the relationships among these elements of the human capital architecture in Figure 13.1. Theoretical and research implications that pertain to the static properties of the framework, as well as the dynamic properties occurring over time, are presented throughout the chapter.

The HR Architecture

In developing a theoretical foundation for this chapter, we have drawn primarily from transaction cost economics (e.g. Coase, 1937; Klein et al., 1978; Williamson, 1975), human capital theory (e.g. Becker, 1964; Flamholtz and Lacey, 1981; Schultz, 1961) and the resource-based view of the firm (e.g. Barney, 1991; Prahalad and Hamel, 1990; Wernerfelt, 1984) to discuss various employment modes. We have chosen these three theories for their explicit theoretical relevance concerning employment practices related to internalization and externalization. However, each theory offers only part of the underlying logic for understanding how firms can manage their workers to achieve competitive advantage.

As indicated in Table 13.1, each perspective offers a different lens for understanding how firms may manage their human capital. More important, perhaps, we offer each theory as evidence that two dimensions – value and uniqueness – are ubiquitous dimensions that differentiate most, if not all, human capital. Below, we briefly discuss each of the three theories and their interactions.

At a general level, much of the literature concerning both internalizing and outsourcing employment has its roots in the make-or-buy arguments elaborated within the transaction cost perspective. Teece (1984), for example, explicitly frames the make-or-buy decision as a special case of market failures. He (1984: 89) notes that 'arm's-length transactions in markets, such as when one firm purchases an input from another, and "in-house" production, as with vertical integration, can be thought of as alternatives'. In an effort to identify the most *efficient* form of organizing employment, firms either rely upon the market to govern a transaction, or they govern this process internally. Thus, according to transaction cost economics, internalization of employment is appropriate when it allows organizations to more effectively monitor employee performance and ensure that their skills are deployed correctly and efficiently (Williamson, 1975).

Related to this, human capital theorists suggest that organizations develop resources internally only when investments in employee skills are justifiable in terms of future productivity (Becker, 1964; Tsang et al., 1991). These theorists also raise the possibility that firms may internalize employment when they can do so without investing in employee development. However, if employee productivity is not expected to exceed investment costs, organizations likely will secure these skills from the labor market. Thus, the decision to internalize or externalize employment rests on a comparison of the expected returns of employee productivity.

Although many researchers have studied how firms make employment decisions based on traditional transactional or financial criteria, recent work suggests that attention should also be paid to strategic or resource-based factors (Welch and Nayak, 1992). Such scholars as Quinn (1992) and Venkatesan (1992) have argued that firms should base employment sourcing decisions on the degree to which skills contribute to the core capabilities of the firm. Rather than taking the transaction as the critical component in employment relations, the resource-based perspective encourages a shift in emphasis toward the inherent characteristics of

Table 13.1   Theoretical background for the HR architecture

Theoretical perspective	Implications for managing employment	Key constructs
Transaction cost economics	Market transactions and internal production can be viewed as alternatives; there are costs associated with managing employees through market arrangements (i.e. transaction costs) versus within hierarchical arrangements (i.e. bureaucratic costs); firms focus on securing the most *efficient* form of organizing employment; firm-specific investments incur costs of monitoring and securing compliance; firms strive to minimize ex ante and ex post costs associated with managing employment (Coase, 1937; Klein et al., 1978; Williamson, 1975).	Asset specificity, uncertainty, transaction versus bureaucratic costs
Human capital theory	Emphasizes the labor costs relative to the return on investment (i.e. future productivity) for developing employee skills and knowledge (i.e. education and training); employees own their own human capital; firms seek to protect themselves from the transfer of their human capital investments to other firms; investments in the development of generic skills are incurred by workers, whereas investments in firm-specific training are incurred by the firm (Becker, 1964; Flamholtz and Lacey, 1981; Schultz, 1961).	Generic versus specialized skills; transferability of skills
Resource-based view of the firm	Emphasizes the strategic relevance of knowledge-based competencies in terms of their direct link to achieving and sustaining a competitive advantage; core competencies should be developed internally while others may be outsourced; core competencies are those that are valuable, rare, inimitable, and non-transferable (Barney, 1991; Prahalad and Hamel, 1990; Wernerfelt, 1984).	Value, rareness, inimitability, nontransferability

employee skills and their relative contribution to value creation (Wright et al., 1995). This theory suggests that core employee skills (central to the firm's competitiveness) should be developed and maintained internally, whereas those of limited or peripheral value are candidates for outsourcing.

If we combine the arguments from transaction cost economics, human capital theory, and the resource-based view of the firm, we can gain a more complete perspective of how managers might make employment sourcing decisions. In our model of the HR architecture, the choice of employment modes depends on both strategic and cost/benefit considerations. Specifically, these decisions are based on the *value*-creating potential from various skills, as well as their *uniqueness* to a particular firm. These distinctions concerning value and uniqueness are consistent with existing theory regarding a firm's core resources. For instance, Porter (1985: 36) suggests that valuable activities are the primary components of a firm's competitive advantage, and 'differences among competitors value chains are a key source of competitive advantage'. Ulrich and Lake (1991) suggest that firms may create strategic, technological, financial, and/or organization value from human capabilities that are realized by consumers. They go on to note that the uniqueness of an employee's skills and capabilities is a critical requirement for gaining competitive advantage.

The Value of Human Capital

Those holding the resource-based view of the firm suggest that resources are valuable when they enable a firm to enact strategies that improve efficiency and effectiveness, exploit market opportunities, and/or neutralize potential threats (Barney, 1991; Porter, 1985; Ulrich and Lake, 1991; Wright and McMahan, 1992). Accordingly, the value of human capital is inherently dependent upon its potential to contribute to the competitive advantage or core competence of the firm.

Like other organizational assets, employee skills can be classified as core or peripheral assets (Barney, 1991; Quinn, 1992). Core assets, in particular, are vital to the competitive advantage of an organization (Porter, 1985) and often require continual internal development (Quinn, 1992). According to Bettis et al. (1992), outsourcing these kinds of skills might jeopardize the competitive advantage of the firm by eroding its stock of core skills. Further, because value 'is the amount that buyers are willing to pay for what a firm provides them' (Porter, 1985: 38), these skills must somehow contribute toward consumer-based perceptions of value (Snell et al., 1996). The value of human capital can be influenced by a multitude of sources, such as a firm's strategy and technologies (Arthur, 1992; Snell and Dean, 1992). Snell and Dean (1992), for example, note that an employee's potential contribution increases dramatically when firms implement advanced manufacturing technologies. They refer to this impact on the value of human capital as the transformation from touch labor to knowledge workers.

Yet, although internalization of human capital may enhance a firm's core capabilities and lower transaction costs, it also accrues managerial and bureaucratic costs (Jones and Hill, 1988; Jones and Wright, 1992). Expenses for staffing, training, compensation, benefits, and the like (Rousseau and Wade-Benzoni, 1994) may diminish the gains from internalization. These costs need to be entered into the value equation as well. Considering this, we define value as the ratio of strategic benefits to customers derived from skills relative to the costs incurred (Snell et al., 1996). Thus, employees can add value if they can help firms offer lower costs or provide increased benefits to customers. Because value has a direct impact on the performance of firms (Barney, 1991), we expect it to influence employment decisions.

The Uniqueness of Human Capital

Advocates of transaction cost economics and resource theory have argued convincingly that idiosyncratic resources are both essential and frequently occurring (Barney, 1991; Williamson, 1981). Because the degree of uniqueness – or firm specificity – of human capital impacts transaction costs, it can strongly influence the decision to internalize employment (Anderson and Schmittlein, 1984; Joskow, 1993; Monteverde and Teece, 1982; Mosakowski, 1991; Walker and Weber, 1984; Williamson, 1975, 1981). The uniqueness of an employee's skills may result from a variety of factors. For example, when employee skills are used in exceptional circumstances or possibly interdependent arrangements, they tend to require more tacit knowledge and expertise (Becker, 1964; Perrow, 1967). Specifically, such practices as team-based production and unique operational procedures that lead to enhanced social complexity, causal ambiguity and the development of tacit knowledge will enhance the uniqueness of a firm's human capital. Because these skills often involve idiosyncratic learning processes, firms are not likely to find these skills in the open labor market.

In addition to transaction costs, the degree to which assets are unique directly impacts their potential to serve as a source of competitive advantage (Wright and McMahan, 1992). As noted by Snell et al. (1996: 65):

> If the types and levels of skills are not equally distributed, such that some firms can acquire the talent they need and others cannot, then (ceteris paribus) that form of human capital can be a source of sustained competitive advantage.

Moreover, if an asset or skill cannot be duplicated or imitated by another firm, it provides a potential source of competitive advantage to the firm (Barney, 1991).

Combining these arguments, we can infer that as human capital becomes more idiosyncratic to a particular firm, externalization may prove infeasible and/or incur excessive costs. Furthermore, the development of unique or firm-specific human capital is often path dependent (Barney, 1991; Itami, 1987) and may require tacit skills and knowledge (Polanyi, 1966) that is acquired *in situ* (Williamson, 1975, 1981). Because of this, theorists have suggested that unique assets need to be developed internally (cf. Chiesa and Barbeschi, 1994).

In direct contrast, skills and capabilities that are generic and available to multiple firms may not justify the costs of internal development relative to the transaction costs incurred from relying on the external market to secure these skills. In these cases the external labor market may prove an efficient mechanism (Teece, 1984). In short, we can expect the degree to which employee skills are unique to a particular firm to influence the mode of employment for their development.

In summary, the value and uniqueness of human capital function as strategic determinants of alternative employment modes. When these dimensions are juxtaposed, we can begin to derive an architecture of four quadrants that simultaneously links the strategic characteristics of human capital, employment modes, employment relationships, and HR configurations. Figure 13.2 provides a summary of the HR architecture.

Quadrant 1: Developing Human Capital

In the top right-hand corner of the matrix (Quadrant 1), we find human capital that is both valuable and unique. As we noted earlier, firms are more likely to employ people internally when their skills are firm specific (Klein et al., 1978; Riordan and Williamson, 1985; Williamson, 1975, 1981). This makes intuitive sense when we consider that, by definition, firm-specific skills are not available in the labor market. With few alternative sources for unique skills, firms are likely to develop them internally. In addition to uniqueness, skills within this quadrant are valuable – that is, their strategic benefit exceeds the managerial and bureaucratic costs associated with their development and deployment.

Employment Mode: Internal Development   In these conditions firms have both financial and strategic incentives to *internally develop* (i.e. make) this particular form of human capital (Prahalad and Hamel, 1990; Reed and DeFillippi, 1990). From a strategic standpoint, employing and internally developing these employees offers firms a number of advantages.

Specifically, human capital theorists suggest that since firm-specific skills are not-transferable, the value of any employee's human capital will be less with any other firm, and internal development will be less likely to result in a capital loss (Becker, 1976). In addition, internally developing human capital helps firms realize the benefits of these employees in terms of their value-creating potential. Because employees in this skill group possess abilities that are both valuable and unique, we can view them as *core employees*, who may serve as a source of competitive advantage (Atchison, 1991; Barney, 1991; Stewart, 1997). For example, Intel's talented and creative engineers consistently develop new microprocessors, which create significant customer value and enable Intel to stay out in front of its competition.

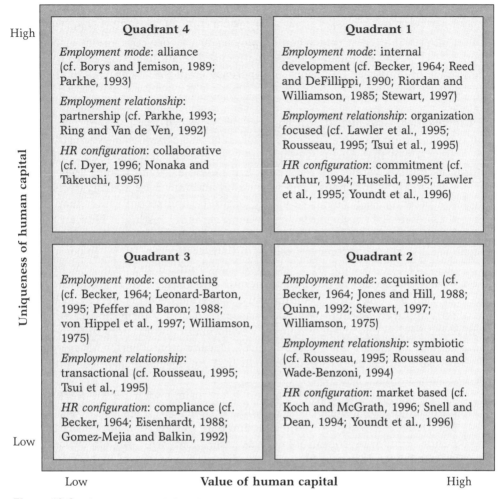

High

Quadrant 4

Employment mode: alliance (cf. Borys and Jemison, 1989; Parkhe, 1993)

Employment relationship: partnership (cf. Parkhe, 1993; Ring and Van de Ven, 1992)

HR configuration: collaborative (cf. Dyer, 1996; Nonaka and Takeuchi, 1995)

Quadrant 1

Employment mode: internal development (cf. Becker, 1964; Reed and DeFillippi, 1990; Riordan and Williamson, 1985; Stewart, 1997)

Employment relationship: organization focused (cf. Lawler et al., 1995; Rousseau, 1995; Tsui et al., 1995)

HR configuration: commitment (cf. Arthur, 1994; Huselid, 1995; Lawler et al., 1995; Youndt et al., 1996)

Quadrant 3

Employment mode: contracting (cf. Becker, 1964; Leonard-Barton, 1995; Pfeffer and Baron; 1988; von Hippel et al., 1997; Williamson, 1975)

Employment relationship: transactional (cf. Rousseau, 1995; Tsui et al., 1995)

HR configuration: compliance (cf. Becker, 1964; Eisenhardt, 1988; Gomez-Mejia and Balkin, 1992)

Quadrant 2

Employment mode: acquisition (cf. Becker, 1964; Jones and Hill, 1988; Quinn, 1992; Stewart, 1997; Williamson, 1975)

Employment relationship: symbiotic (cf. Rousseau, 1995; Rousseau and Wade-Benzoni, 1994)

HR configuration: market based (cf. Koch and McGrath, 1996; Snell and Dean, 1994; Youndt et al., 1996)

Low

Uniqueness of human capital

Low   **Value of human capital**   High

Figure 13.2   Summary of the HR architecture

Employment Relationship: Organization Focused   In terms of employment relationships for these employees, Tsui et al. (1995), as well as Rousseau (1995), have used the terms *organization focused* and *relational* to describe open-ended exchanges between employers and employees. Organization-focused employment relationships can be viewed as encouraging significant mutual investment on the part of employers and employees in developing critical firm skills. The notions of long-term involvement and investment are perhaps the key facets of this type of employment relationship. Theorists argue that by investing in employee development and allowing employees greater participation in decision making, organizations can foster a higher level of ongoing commitment from employees, which translates into exceptional performance (cf. Lawler et al., 1995). Indeed, both Rousseau (1995) and Tsui et al. (1995) suggest that when employees are a core component of competitiveness, firms may establish organization-focused relationships in order to elicit a wide range of employee behaviors and increase employee incentives to engage in firm-specific learning.

HR Configuration: Commitment To support or create an employment relationship that is organization focused, firms will likely rely on a *commitment-based* HR system (cf. Arthur, 1994) that nurtures employee involvement and maximizes the firms' return on human capital investments. For example, organizations may loosely define jobs to allow for change and adaptation and may base staffing decisions on employee potential (e.g. cognitive ability, aptitude, and so on) rather than simply current knowledge and skills (e.g. achievement testing). Human capital theorists suggest that firms will also invest significantly to develop unique (i.e. firm-specific) skills through extensive training initiatives (Becker, 1976). To complement training, organizations might sponsor career development and mentoring programs to encourage employees to build idiosyncratic knowledge that is more valuable to the firm than to competitors. Additionally, firms might structure pay systems to focus on employee learning (e.g. skill-based pay) and information sharing (e.g. team-based pay) to encourage employee development and mastery of firm-specific competencies (cf. Delany and Huselid, 1996). Developmental performance appraisal systems also may be used to make certain that employees receive continued and useful feedback (Snell and Dean, 1992).

Use of these practices in combination is consistent with recent work on HR configurations for high-performance work systems (cf. Huselid, 1995; Lawler et al., 1995). Arthur (1994), for example, found that, in steel minimills, an HR system emphasizing employee commitment was associated with higher productivity. Huselid (1995) extended these findings and showed the impact of high-performance work practices on employee turnover and corporate financial performance. Certainly, more research is needed, but a pattern is emerging that shows that high-performance work systems are instrumental for creating committed, long-term employment relationships, as well as firm-specific human capital vital for competitive advantage (Lawler et al., 1995; Rousseau, 1995; Tsui et al., 1995).

Quadrant 2: Acquiring Human Capital

Although Quadrant 1 contains core skills that are essential for competitive advantage, it by no means characterizes all forms of human capital needed or utilized by firms to function effectively. In this regard, a HR architecture also needs to address the ways in which other types of human capital are managed for maximum performance. Human capital in Quadrant 2 is valuable, yet widely available throughout the labor market. Because these skills are valuable, organizations have an incentive to internalize employment (Hamel and Prahalad, 1994). However, since skills in this quadrant are not unique or specific to a firm, human capital theorists would suggest that managers may be hesitant to invest in internal development (recall that employees with generic skills may leave and transfer the organization's investment to another firm).

Employment Mode: Acquisition Organizations may reconcile these conflicting pressures by *acquiring* (i.e. buying) from the market human capital that does not require further investment. An acquisition mode enables firms to reap the benefits of valuable skills that have been developed elsewhere while holding them internally. In so doing, the acquiring firm simply pays the value reflected in the market price and realizes immediate benefits vis-à-vis productivity (Becker, 1976). Selecting skilled employees directly from the market may also allow firms to realize significant savings in developmental expenditures while gaining instant access to a wide variety of capabilities that may incur positive returns on investment (Becker, 1964; Quinn, 1992).

For example, many firms hire CPAs who possess standardized accounting skills that are widely available to many firms. Although there exists a fairly large (but not exhaustive) supply of CPAs in the open labor market, each firm's return from their investment will depend on the productivity of these workers within their firm. The recent strike by the UPS drivers provides another example of this quadrant. These drivers have skills that are by no means unique to UPS, but without their valued contribution, UPS was essentially crippled. Moreover, because an acquisition mode involves internalization of employment, firms can exercise significant discretion regarding the deployment of these skills, without having to consult or revise contractual agreements with external actors (Jones and Hill, 1988; Tsui et al., 1995; Williamson, 1975).

Employment Relationship: Symbiotic The employment relationship for persons in Quadrant 2 reflects the conditions of an acquisition mode: these employees are valued contributors but not unique. To manage these employees, organizations may strive to establish a *symbiotic* employment relationship based on the utilitarian premise of mutual benefit (Etzioni, 1961; Tsui et al., 1995). In essence, a symbiotic relationship rests on the notion that both the employees and the organization are likely to continue the relationship as long as both continue to benefit.

In contrast to Quadrant 1, these types of employees are perhaps less committed to the organization and more focused on their career. Rousseau and Wade-Benzoni (e.g. Rousseau, 1995; Rousseau and Wade-Benzoni, 1994) note that careerists do not typically seek nor receive lifelong employment within a particular firm. Because these employees are often trained in a particular occupation or profession, they can effectively 'sell' their talents to a variety of organizations – wherever they can contribute and receive the highest returns on their human capital investment. In return for employment, organizations expect a certain degree of loyalty to the firm while the relationship exists (Rousseau and Parks, 1993). However, because each party has alternative options available to meet its needs, this symbiotic relationship may be terminated when either party believes that the costs of maintaining the relationship exceed the benefits it creates.

HR Configuration: Market Based   In situations where the employment mode focuses on human capital acquisition and the employment relationship is symbiotic, the HR configuration is likely to emphasize staffing and deploying skills for immediate contribution. Compared to workers in the commitment HR configuration within Quadrant 1, workers in this quadrant are not likely to receive as much training and development. Since these employees possess skills that are not unique to a particular firm, managers may not gain a return on any investments if employees leave. Instead, assuming that the market wage reflects the value of transferable human capital, the employee (rather than the firm) will likely accrue the returns on the firm's human capital investments. Given these risks to the firm, managers will be more likely to focus on recruiting and selecting employees who already possess the necessary skills.

Indeed, several researchers (e.g. Koch and McGrath, 1996; Snell and Dean, 1992) have suggested that a reliance on selective staffing procedures is logically related to an HR orientation that relies heavily on the external labor market for securing talent. Thus, a primary difference between the market and commitment HR configurations rests on the relative emphasis placed upon staffing versus training (i.e. buy versus make). In addition, the market-based HR configuration likely will focus on identifying workers with specific skills who can perform immediately (e.g. through achievement testing), whereas the commitment HR configuration more likely will emphasize identifying workers with future potential who could benefit from further training. Finally, a market configuration is likely to include externally equitable wages to focus attention on productivity concerns. Within their specified domains, Quadrant 2 employees might be given discretion and empowerment to make decisions that impact value.

Existing research in the strategic HRM literature provides some additional insight into these arguments. Youndt et al. (1996), for example, found that a HR system emphasizing staffing and equitable rewards was most appropriate for firms pursuing a strategy of low-cost production. Similarly, Delery and Doty (1996) found that the use of a market-type employment system for loan officers in banks was positively related to firm performance. Although these studies emphasized the linkage between firm strategy and HR systems, future research might focus on whether a *market-based* HR configuration – a system of selective staffing and rewards – is best for aligning valuable yet generic forms of human capital with the needs of the firm.

Quadrant 3: Contracting Human Capital

Although Quadrants 1 and 2 focus on human capital that is internalized within the firm, Quadrants 3 and 4 represent human capital that, technically speaking, may remain external to the firm. Quadrant 3, for example, contains human capital that is generic and of limited strategic value. Leonard-Barton (1995) describes this as 'public knowledge' skills that can be purchased easily on the open labor market and, therefore, can be treated essentially as a commodity. Like Quadrant 2, the limited uniqueness of these skills provides a disincentive for firms to invest significant resources toward employee development (Becker, 1964). In fact, because so many alternative sources for these skills exist, firms may decrease employment costs by contracting externally (Pfeffer and Baron, 1988; Williamson, 1975).

Employment mode: Contracting As the supply of qualified suppliers increases and the risk inherent in contractual arrangements decreases, organizations are able to contract work without jeopardizing their competitive position (Pfeffer and Baron, 1988; Rousseau, 1995; Von Hippel et al., 1997). Although many contractual relationships stipulate that the actual work be done off company premises (and only the product of those labors will be traded), it is increasingly common that contractual work is performed on site. Temporary employees, leasing arrangements, and other forms of contract work often fall within this category.

For example, firms are increasingly outsourcing administrative or lower-level jobs, such as clerical, support, and maintenance positions, which contribute little to the competitive position of the firm. The rapid growth of such companies as Aramark, which provides outsourcing services, furnishes further evidence of this trend. In these cases using outside workers enables organizations to reduce overhead costs and retain a significant degree of flexibility concerning the number of workers employed, as well as when they are employed. Such sourcing modes may actually improve the competitiveness of firms (Quinn, 1992) by enabling them to strategically focus their development expenses on those skills that may contribute to the firm's competitive advantage. As a result, *contractual* employment appears to be justified when skills are not unique to a firm and offer less potential for value creation.

Employment Relationship: Transactional In terms of employment relationships, Rousseau (1995) suggests that when employees have limited association with a firm and have explicit performance expectations, their psychological contract may be termed *transactional*, in that it focuses on short-term economic exchanges. Similarly, Tsui et al. (1995) use the term *job-focused employment relationships* to describe those situations in which individuals have specific performance requirements and limited organizational involvement. Although the terms differ, in both works the authors posit that arm's-length relationships focus on the work to be done, the results to be accomplished, the terms of the contract, and virtually nothing else.

Although the transactional relationship differs substantially from the organization-focused relationship of Quadrant 1, it is similar to the symbiotic approach of Quadrant 2. Their differences essentially come down to the scope of involvement and the expectations underlying the exchanges. With the symbiotic relationship, organizations seek continuity and loyalty from full-time employees, albeit on a limited basis. In contrast, with the transactional relationship, firms probably do not expect (and do not obtain) organizational commitment; the relationships simply focus on the economic nature of the contract (Rousseau and Parks, 1993).

HR Configuration: Compliance   As the transactional and symbiotic employment relationships are similar in nature, so too are their respective HR configurations. Perhaps the primary differences rest on the range of behaviors and expectations required of employees and their level of contribution permitted. Given the transactional nature of contract work, HR activities might need only focus on securing compliance with the terms and conditions of the contract versus executing broader responsibilities and assuming organizational roles (differences that would reflect the enhanced value of human capital in Quadrant 2). To ensure compliance, firms likely will concentrate on enforcing rules and regulations, upholding specific provisions regarding work protocols, and ensuring conformance to preset standards. This approach differs from the market-based orientation, which places greater emphasis on recruitment and selection to ensure that the right people are hired to do the work. Once hired, Quadrant 2 employees are likely to be permitted a greater degree of empowerment to carry out their organizational roles.

Organizations that rely on the external labor market to contract work rarely invest in training or development activities for those people (Becker, 1964). If training is done at all, it typically focuses on company policies, systems and procedures (cf. Rousseau and Parks, 1993). Similarly, performance appraisal and rewards are likely to be job based (Mahoney, 1989; Snell and Dean, 1994), focusing on prescribed procedures or specified results – or both. Researchers such as Gomez-Mejia and Balkin (1992) and Eisenhardt (1988) have studied the effectiveness of various reward systems and performance appraisals in agency situations. Their research might be expanded in the context of a broader HR architecture to address the fit among employment contracting, transactional relationships, and HR configurations based on *compliance*.

Quadrant 4: Creating Human Capital Alliances

Finally, Quadrant 4 contains human capital that is unique in some way but not directly instrumental for creating customer value. Given uniqueness, this form of human capital might, at first glance, appear to be optimized through internal development. Indeed, supporters of transaction cost economics would propose that firms internalize unique skills to lower transaction costs (Ouchi, 1980; Williamson, 1975, 1981). However, resource-based theorists suggest that given limited value-creating potential, minimal benefit may be gained from outright ownership of these types of skills. For example, an attorney has unique skills that require years of development to cultivate. Yet, particularly small firms may not be able to justify the expense of full-time internal employment (i.e. there is not enough value-creating potential).

Employment Mode: Alliance   It may be the case, as Leonard-Barton (1995) notes, that some unique forms of human capital are less codified and transferable than generic skills, yet more widely available than firm-specific skills. In these cases organizations face a paradox; they are simultaneously encouraged to use external and internal employment modes. If outright internalization is prohibitive from a cost–benefit standpoint and complete contracting involves risks of opportunism, some from of *alliance* between parties may provide a hybrid employment mode that blends internalization and externalization and overcomes these problems.

Researchers use the term *alliance* to refer to an external relationship where each party contributes to a jointly shared outcome (cf. Borys and Jemison, 1989; Parkhe, 1993). Frequently, this occurs through the creation of cospecialized assets – that is, assets that provide value only through the combined efforts of two or more parties (Teece, 1982). When organizations collaborate in the utilization of human capital, a synergistic value may be realized by both firms that exceeds the value either could generate independently. Engineers and scientists who do basic research with no direct customer-linked business application fit into this category. Such firms as IBM and AT&T recently have streamlined their research divisions, reducing or eliminating basic (versus applied) research, and have increased their reliance on external partners to provide this type of human capital. Since such specialized skills are only used occasionally or only pay off in the long run, they may not justify full-time employment. However, Microsoft recently announced that it was hiring hundreds of scientists and Ph.D.s to create a basic research unit like AT&T's former Bell Labs. Microsoft may have the necessary financial slack to justify internal employment of this form of human capital. Even so, experts or specialists, whether employed internally or externally, combine their knowledge with others in the organization to produce a cospecialized asset that has greater value (cf. Teece, 1982). Engineers, designers, programmers, and scientists are frequently used for just this purpose. By establishing an alliance, both parties can capitalize on the other's specialized knowledge – gaining value from the human capital as well as transferring knowledge – without incurring the entire costs of internal employment.

Employment Relationship: Partnership   Because of the nature of their exchange, alliances can create rather paradoxical employment relationships (cf. Parkhe, 1993; Pucik, 1988). At their root, alliances require information sharing and trust, engendering reciprocity and collaboration (Dyer, 1996). Without information sharing, partners can at best only pool their resources (Thompson, 1967; Van de Ven et al., 1978), and without trust, neither party is likely to give valuable information to the other nor act on the information they receive (cf. Ring and Van de Ven, 1992). Whenever two or more parties seek to engage in a collaborative action, such as in an alliance, there exists the possible threat that their idiosyncratic knowledge might be transferred to the other party (Parkhe, 1993). Awareness of this can lead to mistrust and exploitation of short-term contracts (cf. Williamson, 1975), which, unfortunately, is antithetical to a solid alliance. To minimize this risk, firms may create true *partnerships* that focus on mutual investment in the relationship and build trust among involved parties, while still protecting their investments and gaining access to each other's talents.

HR Configuration: Collaborative   Although alliances may involve structural arrangements in which employees from both parties work together, for synergistic benefits to be realized, HR systems that encourage and reward cooperation, collaboration and information sharing are also likely to be necessary. In the context of cospecialized rather than firm-specific assets, organizations will not be likely to expend resources for training and developing partners. A firm investing in the development of a partner's skills implies that it might justify the expense of internal employment (recall Quadrant 1). Instead of investing in the individuals per se, *collaborative* HR configurations tend to invest in the relationship and its effective functioning (cf. Dyer, 1996).

In this context, if training is done at all, it likely will focus on process facilitation and team building. Communication mechanisms, exchange programs, job rotations, mentoring relationships and the like may be established to facilitate information sharing and the transfer of knowledge necessary for joint decision making and productivity (Nonaka and Takeuchi, 1995). Organizations might also use group-based rewards and appraisal to encourage employees from both firms/parties to share and transfer information (cf. Quinn et al., 1996). In short, a collaborative HR configuration helps organizations invest in the partnership while improving trust and encouraging information sharing.

It would be a mistake to assume that the impact of human resources ends at the 'edge' of an organization. As firms engage in more innovative forms of work arrangements, such as alliances and networks, researchers might identify the most appropriate HR configurations to help develop and integrate those interdependencies. Such researchers as Ring and Van de Ven (1992), Parkhe (1993) and Snow and Thomas (1993) have examined the structures, processes, and systems that facilitate information exchange, trust, and collaboration. Their research might be expanded into the context of an HR architecture to see how alliances and other forms of collaborative endeavors may be managed to enhance a firm's competitive advantage.

Managing the HR Architecture

Up to this point, we have concentrated on each of the four quadrants of our framework to theorize how employment modes, employment relationships, and HR configurations might vary in concert with one another across different forms of human capital. From a configurational perspective, a greater fit or congruence among these three components logically would be associated with a more effective HR architecture. While this analysis of the HR architecture provides a number of potential ideas for further study, we believe that one of the primary benefits of adopting an architectural perspective is that it goes beyond the individual quadrants, as well as the individual components within each quadrant. In other words, we believe that this framework highlights the importance of managing the entire HR architecture, including the congruence of the individual components. From this level of analysis, the issues of complexity and dynamism become primary concerns.

The Complexity of the HR Architecture

Although most organizations develop and deploy human capital in each of the four quadrants, few researchers have examined HR issues across these boundaries. As we mentioned earlier, the preponderance of strategic HRM research implies that either 1 all employees should be managed in a manner appropriate for Quadrant 1 or 2 only those employees in Quadrant 1 are strategically important. In fact, many strategic HRM researchers have argued for a 'best practices' perspective to HR, suggesting that 'some HR practices are always better than others and that all organizations should adopt these best practices' (Delery and Doty, 1996: 803). Although other theoretical perspectives do exist (i.e. contingency and configurational approaches), the current status of strategic HRM research seems to support or advocate the best practices perspective (Becker and Gerhart, 1996).

Despite the practical appeal and theoretical parsimony of a 'one-size-fits-all' approach to HR management, employment modes in most organizations are not this homogeneous, and HR systems are rarely this monolithic. For example, researchers often make a distinction between the compensation practices used for exempt and nonexempt employees (e.g. Gerhart and Milkovich, 1990) and the training and development initiatives used for managers versus rank-and-file employees (e.g. Baldwin and Ford, 1988). Similarly, researchers are paying increasing attention to how employment relationships differ and how employees in different employment modes interact. Pearce (1993), for example, found that the presence of contract employees has a negative effect on the level of commitment and trust among permanent employees. Similarly, Barnett and Miner (1992) found that hiring temporary workers often delays promotions for lower-segment employees, while actually decreasing the time for promotion for advanced-segment employees. If these findings are indicative of organizational reality, it may be too simplistic to assume that one type of employment relationship or one set of HR practices will work for all employees.

Approaching this issue from the standpoint of an overall HR architecture, we adopt a contingent configurational view (cf. Delery and Doty, 1996; Meyer et al., 1993) and argue that HR systems are not likely to be appropriate in all conditions but, rather, depend upon the value and uniqueness of human capital. On viewing the entire HR architecture, it becomes clear that certain forms of human capital are more valuable to organizations and more available in the open labor market than others (cf. Wright et al., 1995). For example, firms will logically realize greater benefits by simply outsourcing generic work than relying upon internal development. Relatedly, because different HR configurations convey different meanings to employees and encourage different behaviors, they are likely to be appropriate under different employment modes (Guzzo and Noonan, 1994; Rousseau, 1995; Tsui et al., 1995). As a consequence, firms engaging in multiple sourcing modes are likely to require distinct configurations of HR practices that facilitate the utilization and deployment of human capital for each separate employment mode. In short, following Conant and Ashby's (1970) principle of requisite variety, competitive advantage may depend on the HR architecture being as complex as the organization in which it is used.

The Dynamics of the HR Architecture

The complexity of the HR architecture notwithstanding, the task of strategic HRM is made even more difficult when we consider that aligning the HR architecture to a firm's strategic posture may not prove viable in situations where competition is dynamic and evolves over time. Although HR systems may support a given advantage, there are a number of authors (e.g. D'Aveni, 1994; Prahalad and Hamel, 1990) who point out that a focus on *sustainability* per se may cause more harm than good. For example, committing resources to a core area (to achieve first mover advantages) may involve considerable risk, particularly in those industries in which competitive imitation is the norm rather than the exception. The extent of this risk, however, rests primarily on the degree to which a resource has natural and strategic barriers to imitation – that is, forces that protect the resource from imitation, duplication, or appropriation by competitors (Ghemawat, 1991; Lippman and Rumelt, 1982; Porter, 1985; Reed and DeFillippi, 1990; Wright and McMahan, 1992). Although some resources are more susceptible to imitation than others, every firm's competitive advantage is continually threatened (D'Aveni, 1994; Ghemawat, 1991; Reed and DeFillippi, 1990). As Barney (1995: 51) notes, 'Although a firm's resources and capabilities have added value in the past, changes in customer tastes, industry structure, or technology can render them less valuable in the future'.

Regarding a firm's HR architecture, if we assume that competitive situations change, we must also assume that value and uniqueness of human capital change and evolve. As the firm's environment changes and the nature of competition increases or shifts, barriers to imitation face greater threats, and the firm's existing stock of knowledge and skills may become obsolete (MacMillan et al., 1985). Dynamic competition may reduce the half-life of employee knowledge: the rate at which its relevance decays over time in comparison to prevailing standards (cf. Anderson, 1989).

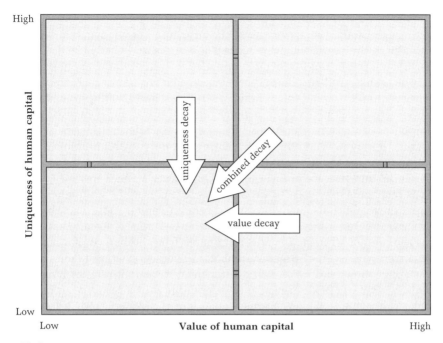

Figure 13.3 Dynamics of the HR architecture

For example, the value of an employee's knowledge of COBOL programming may diminish as competitors develop newer and more powerful computer languages. Given enough effort, competitors can often nurture and develop the same or functionally equivalent skills to mimic a firm's competitive advantage (Dierickx and Cool, 1989) or develop new skills that render existing advantages obsolete. As indicated in Figure 13.3, these pressures create a fundamental shift in human capital from high levels of value and uniqueness toward more generic and less valuable forms.

Although time and competition tend to erode the strategic positioning of human capital (cf. D'Aveni, 1994), firms may be able to counteract these natural forces. Researchers such as Amit and Schoemaker (1993), Barney (1991), Dierickx and Cool (1989) and Reed and DeFillippi (1990) have studied how firms maintain, enhance, or transform barriers to imitation. Porter (1985: 20), for example, suggests that firms try to sustain their competitive position by offering competitors a 'moving target' that is difficult to emulate by reinvesting in the skills and competencies that provide a source of advantage. As we show in Figure 13.3, firms may resist the decay of human capital by striving to make skills and capabilities more valuable and/or unique.

To make the deployment and value of human capital more firm specific, managers logically may try to enhance the degree of uniqueness of human capital by customizing or adjusting skills. For example, when organizations invest in human capital through on-the-job experiences, the resulting knowledge and skills may be idiosyncratic to the particular firm context (Dierickx and Cool, 1989). Those experiences that increase employee tacit knowledge (rather than explicit knowledge that can be transferred to competitors) especially are likely to increase the firm specificity of human capital (cf. Polanyi, 1966; Reed and DeFillippi, 1990). As these capabilities are developed within a particular organization, it may be impossible for competitors to either imitate or bid away these talents (Becker and Gerhart, 1996). Thus, it may be that employee training not only averts human capital decay (by continuously enhancing employee skills) but may also increase the uniqueness of human capital and move employees from Quadrants 2 and 3 toward Quadrant 1.

Just as managers may use HR investments to increase the uniqueness of human capital, so they might also strive to make human capital more valuable and shift employees from Quadrants 3 and 4 to Quadrants 1 and 2. Recall that if we view value as the ratio of strategic benefits obtainable from human capital relative to the costs incurred, we see that organizations can leverage existing talents across new business applications and, in so doing, alter the cost/benefit ratio of human capital. Prahalad and Hamel (1990) discuss the 'extendibility' of a resource in just this way and make the point that core competencies are developed from knowledge and skills that can be used repeatedly in different arenas. Similarly, researchers such as D'Aveni (1994) and Nonaka and Takeuchi (1995) have suggested that firms may also foster the creation of new talents that may prove to be the source of future core competencies. In the context of an HR architecture, if partners in an alliance (Quadrant 4) or contract workers (Quadrant 3) can be utilized on an increasing basis or in a fundamentally different way, their marginal product relative to labor costs – that is, their value – may increase to a point that justifies internal employment (Quadrants 1 and 2; Rousseau and Wade-Benzoni, 1994; Williamson, 1975). In response to these changes, organizations may shift their HR configurations (i.e. from collaborative- to commitment-based HR systems) in order to increase the value of human capital and support the changes in employment modes and employment relationships.

Of course, devoting the resources necessary to maintain and transform barriers to imitation may incur considerable risk, particularly in environments where sources of competitive success may change. As competition becomes more dynamic, firms may not have enough time to fully recoup their human capital investments. At the same time, without these investments, firms are likely to fall behind as barriers to imitation are challenged and overcome. Thus, it may be that firms succeeding in the long run are able to extend existing advantages while anticipating competitive shifts that require different sources of advantage (cf. deGues, 1988).

We encourage researchers to examine how firms integrate flexibility into an HR architecture to adapt to dynamic changes while maintaining congruence among the individual components to meet their existing needs (cf. Wright and Snell, 1998). In the context of a firm's HR architecture, this implies that researchers need to focus on how firms simultaneously develop and utilize both *current* as well as *future* forms of human capital for competitive advantage.

Conclusion

Our purpose in this article was to develop a framework for studying alternative employment arrangements used by firms in allocating work. Rather than simply categorizing various forms of employment (e.g. internalization or externalization), we have tried to make the argument that human capital theory, transaction cost economics, and the resource-based view of the firm all converge on two dimensions – the value and uniqueness of employee skills – as primary determinants of an HR architecture. We believe that this HR architecture raises a number of research issues worthy of further investigation.

First, as scholars proclaim the importance of employees as a critical resource for competitive advantage, it is important to note that not all employees possess skills that are equally unique and/or valuable to a particular firm (Stewart, 1997). Although it may be the case that some firms manage all employees the same way, regardless of their value and uniqueness, we anticipate that most firms make significant distinctions in the methods they use for different skill sets and that these are important determinants of firm performance. So, just as there may be no universally best set of HR practices for every firm, we argue that there may actually be no one best set of practices for every employee within a firm. We therefore encourage researchers to examine whether a firm's emphasis on one mode of employment for all employees versus the use of multiple modes for different groups of human capital impacts firm performance. If this framework reflects organizational reality, much of the current strategic HRM research may be overly simplistic, ignoring the possibility that firms may engage in more than one type of employment mode and rely upon different HR configurations to manage different employee groups.

Second, research is needed that transcends the individual quadrants of the framework and focuses on balancing the complexity and dynamics of the entire HR architecture. As environmental and competitive pressures may lead to the natural decay of human capital, we need to better understand how organizations make investments to compete through people over time. This type of research would focus on ways that organizations enhance or transform the value and uniqueness of human capital, as well as how the shifts in employment modes and relationships are supported by alternative HR configurations. Research that addresses the congruence or fit of all of the different components of the entire HR architecture, rather than focusing on the individual components, would prove particularly useful in this regard.

In conclusion, adopting an architectural perspective may help both academics and practitioners understand which forms of human capital have the potential to be a source of competitive advantage today and in the future, as well as those that do not. If that potential is identified, developed, and deployed strategically, firms may well be able to gain a competitive advantage. In fact, the ability to manage the HR architecture itself may actually become a core capability that other firms find difficult to replicate (cf. Becker and Gerhart, 1996). As Barney (1995), Ulrich and

Lake (1991), and others have pointed out, for organizations to utilize human capital strategically, they must be organized in a manner that enables them to do so.

References

Amit, R. and Schoemaker, P.J.H. (1993) Strategic assets and organizational rent. *Strategic Management Journal*, 14: 33–46.

Anderson, E. and Schmittlein, D. (1984) Integration of the sales force: An empirical examination. *Rand Journal of Economics*, 3: 385–95.

Anderson, G.M. (1989) The half-life of dead economists. *Canadian Journal of Economics*, 22: 174–83.

Arthur, J.B. (1992) The link between business strategy and industrial relations systems in American steel minimills. *Industrial and Labor Relations Review*, 45: 488–506.

Arthur, J.B. (1994) Effects of human resource systems on manufacturing performance and turnover. *Academy of Management Journal*, 37: 670–87.

Atchison, T.J. (1991) The employment relationship: Un-tied or re-tied? *Academy of Management Executive*, 5(4): 52–62.

Baldwin, T.T. and Ford, J.K. (1988) Transfer of training: A review and directions for future research. *Personnel Psychology*, 41: 63–105.

Barnard, C. (1938) *Functions of the executive*. Cambridge, MA: Harvard University Press.

Barnett, W.P. and Miner, A.S. (1992) Standing on the shoulders of others: Career interdependence in job mobility. *Administrative Science Quarterly*, 37: 262–81.

Barney, J. (1991) Firm resources and sustained competitive advantage. *Journal of Management*, 17: 99–120.

Barney, J. (1995) Firm resources and sustained competitive advantage. *Academy of Management Executive*, 9(4): 49–61.

Becker, B. and Gerhart, B. (1996) The impact of human resource management on organizational performance: Progress and prospects. *Academy of Management Journal*, 39: 779–801.

Becker, G.S. (1964) *Human capital*. New York: Columbia University Press.

Becker, G.S. (1976) *The economic approach to human behavior*. Chicago: University of Chicago Press.

Bettis, R.A., Bradley, S.P. and Hamel, G. (1992) Outsourcing and industrial decline. *Academy of Management Executive*, 6(1): 7–22.

Borys, B. and Jemison, D. (1989) Hybrid arrangements as strategic alliances: Theoretical issues in organizational combinations. *Academy of Management Review*, 14: 234–249.

Chiesa, V. and Barbeschi, M. (1994) Technology strategy in competence-based competition. In G. Hamel and A. Heene (eds), *Competence-based competition*: 293–314. Chichester: Wiley.

Coase, R.H. (1937) The nature of the firm. *Economica*, 4: 386–405.

Conant, R.C. and Ashby, W.R. (1970) Every good regulator of a system must be a model of that system. *International Journal of Systems Science*, 1(2): 89–97.

D'Aveni, R.A. (1994) *Hypercompetition: Managing the dynamics of strategic maneuvering*. New York: Free Press.

Davis-Blake, A. and Uzzi, B. (1993) Determinants of employment externalization: A study of temporary workers and independent contractors. *Administrative Science Quarterly*, 38: 195–223.

deGeus, A.P. (1988) Planning as learning. *Harvard Business Review*, 66(March–April): 70–4.

Delany, J.T. and Huselid, M.A. (1996) The impact of human resource management practices on perceptions of organizational performance. *Academy of Management Journal*, 39: 949–69.

Delery, J.E. and Doty, D.H. (1996) Modes of theorizing in strategic human resource management: Tests of universalistic, contingency, and configurational performance predictions. *Academy of Management Journal*, 39: 802–35.

Dierickx, I. and Cool, K. (1989) Asset stock accumulation and sustainability of competitive advantage. *Management Science*, 35: 1504–11.

Dyer, J.H. (1996) Does governance matter? Keiretsu alliances and asset specificity as sources of Japanese competitive advantage. *Organization Science*, 7: 649–66.

Edwards, R. (1979) *Contested terrain*. New York: Basic Books.

Eisenhardt, K.M. (1988) Agency- and institutional-theory explanations: The case of retail sales compensation. *Academy of Management Journal*, 31: 488–511.

Etzioni, A. (1961) *A comparative analysis of complex organizations*. New York: Free Press.

Flamholtz, E. and Lacey, J. (1981) *Personnel management: Human capital theory and human resource accounting*. Los Angeles: Institute of Industrial Relations, UCLA.

Gerhart, B. and Milkovich, G.T. (1990) Organizational differences in managerial compensation and firm performance. *Academy of Management Journal*, 33: 663–91.

Gerhart, B. and Trevor, C. (1996) Employment variability under different managerial compensation systems. *Academy of Management Journal*, 39: 1692–712.

Ghemawat, P. (1991) *Commitment: The dynamic of strategy*. New York: Free Press.

Gomez-Mejia, L.R. and Balkin, D.B. (1992) *Compensation, organizational strategy, and firm performance*. Cincinnati: South-Western Publishing.

Guzzo, R.A. and Noonan, K.A. (1994) Human resource practices as communications and the psychological contract. *Human Resources Management*, 33: 447–62.

Hamel, G. and Prahalad, C.K. (1994) *Competing for the future*. Boston: Harvard Business School Press.

Huselid, M.A. (1995) The impact of human resource management practices on turnover, productivity, and corporate financial performance. *Academy of Management Journal*, 38: 635–72.

Itami, H. (1987) *Mobilizing invisible assets*. Cambridge, MA: Harvard University Press.

Jones, G. and Hill, C. (1988) Transaction cost analysis of strategy-structure choice. *Strategic Management Journal*, 9: 159–72.

Jones, G. and Wright, P.M. (1992) An economic approach to conceptualizing the utility of human resource management practices. In G. Ferris and K. Rowland (eds), *Research in personnel and human resources*: 271–300. Greenwich, CT: JAI Press.

Joskow, P. (1993) Asset specificity and the structure of vertical relationships: Empirical evidence. In O.E. Williamson and S.G. Winter (eds), *The nature of the firm*: 117–37. New York: Oxford University Press.

Klein, B., Crawford, R. and Alchian, A. (1978) Vertical integration, appropriable rents and the competitive contracting process. *Journal of Law and Economics*, 21: 297–326.

Koch, M.J. and McGrath, R.G. (1996) Improving labor productivity: Human resource management policies do matter. *Strategic Management Journal*, 17: 335–54.

Kochan, T. and Osterman, P. (1994) *The mutual gains enterprise*. Boston: Harvard Business School Press.

Lawler, E.E. (1992) *The ultimate advantage: Creating the high-involvement organization*. San Francisco, CA: Jossey-Bass.

Lawler, E.E., Mohrman, S.A. and Ledford, G.E. (1995) *Creating high performance organizations: Practices and results of employee involvement and total quality management in Fortune 1000 companies*. San Francisco, CA: Jossey-Bass.

Lei, D. and Hitt, M.A. (1995) Strategic restructuring and outsourcing: The effect of mergers and acquisitions and LBOs on building firm skills and capabilities. *Journal of Management*, 21: 835–59.

Leonard-Barton, D. (1995) *Wellsprings of knowledge: Building and sustaining the sources of innovation*. Boston, MA: Harvard Business School Press.

Levine, D. (1995) *Reinventing the workplace: How business and employees can both win*. Washington, DC: Brookings Institution.

Lippman, S. and Rumelt, R. (1982) Uncertain imitability: An analysis of interfirm differences in efficiency under competition. *Bell Journal of Economics*, 13: 418–38.

MacMillan, I., McCafferty, M.L. and Van Wijk, G. (1985) Competitor's response to easily imitated new products – exploring commercial banking product introductions. *Strategic Management Journal*, 6: 75–86.

Mahoney, J. (1992) The choice of organizational form: vertical financial ownership versus other methods of vertical integration. *Strategic Management Journal*, 13: 559–84.

Mahoney, T.A. (1989) Employment compensation planning and strategy. In L.R. Gomez-Mejia (ed.), *Compensation and benefits*, ASPA/BNA Series, no. 3. Washington, DC: Bureau of National Affairs.

March, J.G. and Simon, H.A. (1958) *Organizations*. New York: Wiley.

Meyer, A.D., Tsui, A.S. and Hinings, C.R. (1993) Configurational approaches to organizational analysis. *Academy of Management Journal*, 36: 1175–95.

Miles, R. and Snow, C.C. (1984) Designing strategic human resource systems. *Organizational Dynamics*, 13: 36–52.

Miles, R. and Snow, C.C. (1992) Causes of failure in network organizations. *California Management Review*, 28: 62–73.

Monteverde, K. and Teece, D. (1982) Supplier switching costs and vertical integration in the automobile industry. *Bell Journal of Economics*, 12: 206–13.

Mosakowski, E. (1991) Organizational boundaries and economic performance: An empirical study of entrepreneurial computer firms. *Strategic Management Journal*, 12: 115–33.

Nadler, D.A., Gerstein, M.S. and Shaw, R.B. (1992) *Organizational architecture: Designing for changing organizations*. San Francisco, CA: Jossey-Bass.

Nonaka, I. and Takeuchi, H. (1995) *The knowledge-creating company: How Japanese companies create the dynamics of innovation*. New York: Oxford University Press.

Ouchi, W. (1980) Markets, bureaucracies, and clans. *Administrative Science Quarterly*, 25: 129–41.

Parkhe, A. (1993) Strategic alliance structuring: A game theoretic and transaction cost examination of interfirm cooperation. *Academy of Management Journal*, 36: 794–829.

Pearce, J.L. (1993) Toward an organizational behavior of contract laborers: Their psychological involvement and effects on employee co-workers. *Academy of Management Journal*, 36: 1082–96.

Perrow, C.B. (1967) A framework for the comparative analysis of organizations. *American Sociological Review*, 32: 194–208.

Pfeffer, J. (1994) *Competitive advantage through people: Unleashing the power of the work force*. Boston, MA: Harvard Business School Press.

Pfeffer, J. and Baron, J. (1988) Taking the workers back out: Recent trends in the structuring of employment. In L.L. Cummings and B.M. Staw (eds), *Research in organizational behavior*, vol. 10: 257–303. Greenwich, CT: JAI Press.

Polanyi, M. (1966) *The tacit dimension*. Garden City, NY: Doubleday.

Porter, M. (1985) *Competitive advantage: Creating and sustaining superior performance*. New York: Free Press.

Powell, W. (1990) Neither market nor hierarchy: Network forms of organizations. In L.L. Cummings and B.M. Staw (eds), *Research in organizational behavior*, vol. 12: 295–336. Greenwich, CT: JAI Press.

Prahalad, C.K. and Hamel, G. (1990) The core competence of the corporation. *Harvard Business Review*, 68(May–June): 79–91.

Pucik, V. (1988) Strategic alliances, organizational learning, and competitive advantage: The HRM agenda. *Human Resource Management*, 27: 77–93.

Quinn, J.B. (1992) *Intelligent enterprise*. New York: Free Press.

Quinn, J.B., Anderson, P. and Finkelstein, S. (1996) Managing professional intellect: Making the most of the best. *Harvard Business Review*, 74(March–April): 71–80.

Reed, R. and DeFillippi, R. (1990) Causal ambiguity, barriers to imitation, and sustainable competitive advantage. *Academy of Management Review*, 15: 88–102.

Ring, P.S. and Van de Ven, A.H. (1992) Structuring cooperative relationships between organizations. *Strategic Management Journal*, 13: 483–98.

Riordan, M. and Williamson, O. (1985) Asset specificity and economic organization. *International Journal of Industrial Organization*, 3: 365–78.

Rousseau, D.M. (1995) *Psychological contracts in organizations: Understanding written and unwritten agreements*. Thousand Oaks, CA: SAGE.

Rousseau, D.M. and Parks, J.M. (1993) The contracts of individuals and organizations. In L.L. Cummings and B.M. Staw (eds), *Research in organizational behavior*, vol. 15: 1–43. Greenwich, CT: JAI Press.

Rousseau, D.M. and Wade-Benzoni, K.A. (1994) Linking strategy and human resource practices: How employee and customer contracts are created. *Human Resources Management*, 33: 463–89.

Schultz, T.W. (1961) Investment in human capital. *American Economic Review*, 51(March): 1–17.

Snell, S.A. and Dean, J.W., Jr. (1992) Integrated manufacturing and human resources management: A human capital perspective. *Academy of Management Journal*, 35: 467–504.

Snell, S.A. and Dean, J.W., Jr. (1994) Strategic compensation for integrated manufacturing: The moderating effects of job and organizational inertia. *Academy of Management Journal*, 37: 1109–140.

Snell, S.A., Youndt, M.A. and Wright, P.M. (1996) Establishing a framework for research in strategic human resource management: Merging resource theory and organizational learning. In G.R. Ferris (ed.), *Research in personnel and human resources management*: 61–90. Greenwich, CT: JAI Press.

Snow, C.C., Miles, R. and Coleman, H. (1992) Managing 21st century network organizations. *Organizational Dynamics*, 20(3): 5–20.

Snow, C.C. and Thomas, J.B. (1993) Building networks: Broker roles and behaviors. In P. Lorange, B. Chakravarathy, J. Roos and A. Van de Ven (eds), *Implementing strategic processes: Change, learning and co-operation*: 217–38. Cambridge, MA: Blackwell.

Stewart, T. (1997) *Intellectual capital*. New York: Doubleday-Currency.

Teece, D.J. (1982) Towards an economic theory of the multiproduct firm. *Journal of Economic Behavior and Organization*, 3: 43–57.

Teece, D.J. (1984) Economic analysis and strategic management. In J.M. Pennings (ed.), *Strategy for decision making in complex organizations*: 78–101. San Francisco: Jossey-Bass.

Thompson, J.D. (1967) *Organizations in action*. New York: McGraw-Hill.

Tsang, M.C., Rumberger, R.W. and Levine, H.M. (1991) The impact of surplus schooling on worker productivity. *Industrial Relations*, 30: 209–28.

Tsui, A.S., Pearce, J.L., Porter, L.W. and Hite, J.P. (1995) Choice of employee-organization relationship: Influence of external and internal organizational factors. In G.R. Ferris (ed.), *Research in personnel and human resources management*: 117–51. Greenwich, CT: JAI Press.

Ulrich, D. and Lake, D. (1991) Organizational capability: Creating competitive advantage. *Academy of Management Executive*, 7(1): 77–92.

Van De Ven, A.J., Delbeq, A.L. and Koenig, R. (1978) Determinants of coordination modes within organizations. *American Sociological Review*, 41: 322–38.

Venkatesan, R. (1992) Strategic sourcing: To make or not to make. *Harvard Business Review*, 70(November–December): 98–107.

Von Hippel, C., Mangum, S.L., Greenberger, D.B., Heneman, R.L. and Skoglind, J.D. (1997) Temporary employees: Can organizations and employees both win? *Academy of Management Executive*, 10(1): 93–104.

Walker, G. and Weber, D. (1984) A transaction cost approach to make-or-buy decisions. *Administrative Science Quarterly*, 29: 373–91.

Welch, J.A. and Nayak, P.R. (1992) Strategic sourcing: A progressive approach to the make-or-buy decision. *Academy of Management Executive*, 6(1): 23–31.

Wernerfelt, B. (1984) A resource-based view of the firm. *Strategic Management Journal*, 5: 171–80.

Williamson, O.E. (1975) *Markets and hierarchies: Analysis and antitrust implications*. New York: Free Press.

Williamson, O.E. (1981) The economics of organization: The transaction cost approach. *American Journal of Sociology*, 87: 548–77.

Wright, P.M. and McMahan, G.C. (1992) Theoretical perspectives for strategic human resource management. *Journal of Management*, 18(2): 295–320.

Wright, P.M., Smart, D.L. and McMahan, G.C. (1995) Matches between human resources and strategy among NCAA basketball teams. *Academy of Management Journal*, 38: 1052–74.

Wright, P.M. and Snell, S.A. (1998) Toward a unifying framework for exploring fit and flexibility in strategic human resource management. *Academy of Management Review*, 23: 756–72.

Youndt, M.A., Snell, S.A., Dean, J.W., Jr. and Lepak, D.P. (1996) Human resource management, manufacturing strategy and firm performance. *Academy of Management Journal*, 39: 836–66.

HR's Role in Building Relationship Networks

14

Mark L. Lengnick-Hall and Cynthia A. Lengnick-Hall

Buckman Laboratories found that a customer who needed a solution to a problem in France was able to get one from an associate (i.e. employee) in Monaco after receiving input from US associates and locating previous solutions and presentations on the K'netix knowledge network.[1] Another Buckman associate had a microbiological control problem that was solved by a colleague halfway around the globe who had a hobby – micro brewing – that involved controlling a similar organism. In both cases, rapid knowledge sharing led to more productive people who solved customers' problems quickly. This capability resulted in big gains for the company.

Relationships are essential to getting things done. Formal relationships are typically documented with job descriptions and organizational charts. Every organization also has its informal networks – people who know each other and help each other regardless of rank, function or job title. Important relationships also occur between people in different organizations. Sales people establish relationships with customers, computer programmers have relationships with colleagues who work for competitors and executives develop relationships with politicians. In today's knowledge economy, social capital and relationships for the most effective firms extend well beyond conventional organizational boundaries. The intricate network of relationships both within and outside of the organization forms the circulation system that carries information and ideas to those who need it, when they need it. The purpose of this chapter is to show *why* there is a need for HR to restructure its role in organizations to enhance the development of social capital and to provide examples of *how* this can be done.

A reorientation of HR's role toward relationship building enables HR to contribute directly to the creation of competitive advantage. Relationships, which integrate human capital with other intangible aspects of a firm, leverage the human talent that falls within traditional HR responsibilities to create more powerful competencies. In addition, relationships limit the liability associated with the loss of a single individual since the entire relationship system must be duplicated to create the same organizational capabilities.[2] Thus, HR can contribute to creating sustained

Source: M.L. Lengnick-Hall and C.A. Lengnick-Hall (2003) 'HR's role in building relationship networks', *Academy of Management Executive*, 17(4): 53–63.

competitive advantage not only by enriching a firm's resource base but also by ensuring that these talents are embedded in networks of relationships that are difficult for competitors to observe, understand, or imitate.

While organizations invest in architectural designs that promote interaction, and design policies and procedures that stimulate discussions and communication, it is important to keep in mind that human networks involving trust, social links and personal commitment cannot be engineered or mandated; they can only be encouraged by nudges in the right direction.[3] These methods are similar to hanging a birdfeeder from a tree in your backyard and installing a birdbath in your garden. You cannot force birds to interact at a specific location, but you can create an appealing environment that attracts them to do so. Likewise, in the workplace HR cannot force people to interact and establish relationships, but HR can create conditions where those interactions are more likely to emerge.

Organizations consist of many types of relationships. Internal relationships (such as supervisor–employee, union–management, peer–peer) and external relationships (such as those with suppliers, customers, regulators, competitors) can lead to enhanced competitiveness. HR's ability to initiate, nurture, deploy, and extend relationships can create competitive value in ways that are difficult for competitors to duplicate and have few substitutes. Relationships, and the resulting organizational capabilities they create, can be an important source of sustained competitive advantage because they are heterogeneous, reflect individual differences, and are relatively immobile since they are embedded within a firm's culture and climate.[4] Moreover, high-involvement work practices that emphasize relationship-based systems enhance productivity, reduce turnover, increase innovation rates, improve operating performance, reduce cycle times, and enrich connections with customers and suppliers.[5] It is our intent to show that firms will benefit if HR takes a more active role in orchestrating an expanding range of relationships.

Adding Social Capital

Building richer, deeper and broader relationships can add social capital to the organization and the people in it. Social capital is the web of relationships among employees and groups (both inside and outside of the organization) that provides information, helps solve problems, expands customer bases, and does other things that add value and enhance strategic capability.

The importance of social capital to organizational effectiveness cannot be overestimated. Consider what happened to the Chrysler Corporation after it went through a major, largely successful reorganization in the 1990s.[6] The company had previously been organized around functional departments, such as emissions systems, body, steering, etc. After the reorganization, the company was focused on processes – platforms, or model types – instead of functions. This reorganization produced many immediate benefits (such as quicker new product introduction), but it also introduced a number of unexpected costs. Defects began cropping up in the new designs. And, disturbingly, many of these defects were caused by problems that had been solved successfully in the past. Why did this occur? The disbanded functional departments had been rich sources of relationships: senior engineers mentored new engineers and knowledge was shared widely. The reorganization disrupted these social networks that had taken years to develop, and nothing in the new system led to effective replacements. Key organizational memories were lost or disregarded because the social networks that made ideas easy to find, useful to store, comfortable to interpret, and natural to share were dismantled by the structural change.[7] Social capital may not be visible to the naked eye, but it can be a major factor in organizational success.

The Benefits of Social Capital

Social capital benefits an organizational in many ways.[8] It creates a richer pool of recruits when employees encourage friends and professional contacts to consider working for their organization. Research has shown that, in general, applicants hired from current-employee referrals tend to stay with an organization longer and perform better than applicants hired from more formal recruitment sources.[9] Social capital facilitates inter-unit resource exchange because employees are more likely to share what they have with people they know and care about. It enhances product innovation because few new products are the work of a single individual.

Social capital can improve cohesion within a group and lay the groundwork for collaborative effort. It helps create intellectual capital since people are more likely to share tacit knowledge (that which is undocumented) and take intellectual risks in a supportive social environment. It promotes cross-functional team effectiveness and enables firms to sense and respond to shifting market conditions since social capital enables people to see situations from perspectives that are different from their own. It reduces dysfunctional turnover (i.e. the loss of key or high-performing employees), since individuals are less likely to leave a firm if they have strong, positive social connections with their co-workers and supervisors. Likewise, employees who do not fit well with the organization are less likely to have good relationships with co-workers and supervisors and are more likely to leave or be terminated (i.e. functional turnover).[10]

For some firms, social capital is the keystone of their competitive strategy. For example, Skandia, the global insurance and savings firm, obtains its products through its relationships with financial services organizations and delivers its products through its relationships with institutional brokers – none of whom are direct employees of the firm.[11] Thus, social capital is built at the individual, group and organization levels.

HR's Role in Developing Social Capital

Human resource management responsibility for managing relationships has been rather narrowly conceived in the past – and often implied rather than explicit. From an operational perspective, HR attention typically has focused on relationships that are formal (e.g. between supervisor and subordinate), problematic (e.g. conflict between employees), introductory (e.g. orientation and socialization), and internal (e.g. between departments). Technical HRM activities (such as recruiting, selection, performance measurement, training, and the administration of compensation and benefits)[12] generally concentrate on formal relationships as captured in organization charts, reporting relationships, job descriptions, policies and procedures – the organization as documented, but not the organization as it oftentimes truly functions (e.g. workarounds). Informal networks/groups and relationships based on factors other than job or hierarchical position receive less attention and often are not actively orchestrated by HR. Yet it is these more fluid, non-specific, community-oriented relationships that are often the source of competitive gains. The relationships that Southwest Airlines employees develop with each other, with customers, and with members of other organizations operating out of the airport terminals they use are key to the fast turnaround of airplanes for which the company is known.

In contrast to technical HRM, the intent of strategic human resource management is to create business-related organizational capabilities and market effectiveness.[13] Through building and nurturing relationships, HR can facilitate the creation of organizational capabilities, such as the ability to locate and share knowledge rapidly and respond to market changes.

Developing and nurturing relationships requires a significant reorientation in HR's thinking about its own role within the firm. Effective relationship building means that HR must adopt a partnership perspective rather than a paternalistic, policing role.[14] Partners are jointly responsible for outcomes and for defining vision and purpose. To move toward a partnership orientation, HR needs to unlearn habits focused on imposing regulations or, conversely, on waiting for direction from corporate leadership. To build the depth and scope of relationships which the firm needs to succeed, HR should develop partnerships with line managers and employees. Through these partnerships HR can extend its involvement in the organization's work, and line managers and employees can collaborate to accomplish some things in the HR domain.

Effective partnerships are often characterized by: 1 teamwork based upon respect, trust, and mutual obligation for one another; 2 open communication with a sharing of inside information and resources; and 3 commitment to one another and the relationship. Partnerships are the building blocks of relationship communities. While HR will be responsible for initiating and nurturing some kinds of relationships directly, an equally important responsibility will be creating the culture, skills, and organizational capabilities that enable managers and other employees also to create the wide range of relationships needed to conduct the organization's work.

HR can contribute to the bottom line through increased involvement with the whole web of relationships that occur in and across organizations – those throughout the internal value-creation process and those in the supply chain that extend beyond the firm's borders; those that are informal as well as those that are formal. HR can tap into this web of relationships, observe what's going on, encourage and nurture some, discourage others, and manage them all for the organization's benefit.

HR can help a firm establish beneficial relationship priorities by conducting relationship analyses – diagnosing from whom employees get information and with whom they share it – that are similar to conventional job analyses. Using network analysis (a scientific tool for mapping social relationships), HR can identify employees who play important roles in their informal groups.[15] For example, *coordinators* or *connectors* are often outgoing and friendly people who spend time and effort making connections among informal group members. *Boundary spanners*, on the other hand, spread news about who knows what to different groups outside of the focal group, and sometimes even outside of the organization. *Mavens* share their specific expertise relative to the group's tasks or operations. *Evangelists* broadcast positive news about new ideas, people, and processes, spreading the word and generating excitement in others. And, finally, *gatekeepers* regulate the flow of information that enters and leaves from the outside world. HR can help identify individuals who play these important roles in their informal groups, then design incentives and provide mentoring for them.

For HR to assume the new role of relationship builder, an understanding of the anatomy of relationships and identification of relationships that are important to organizational success is required. This area will be discussed next.

Relationships that Matter and HR's Role in Managing Them

Relationships represent an ongoing association between two or more individuals, groups, or organizations. Five characteristics of relationships shape our ability to understand and manage them effectively.[16] First, relationships occur over time. They have a past history and an imagined future. Events in the past shape expectations and provide a context for evaluating the present. For example, an employee may interpret her supervisor's comments about her job performance differently depending upon whether she has developed a good or a poor working relationship over time. Expectations about the future are also shaped by the level of commitment and closeness between the partners in a relationship. Different kinds of relationships carry different expectations and require more or less time to develop. Work teams, which often remain intact for long periods, have time to develop trust and intimate knowledge of other team members that, in turn, leads to more predictable relationships.[17] Project teams, on the other hand, must be able to develop and adjust relationships quickly if they are to be effective.

Second, relationships often involve mutual influence. For example, worker A may agree to stay after working hours to clean the worksite to make it possible for worker B to leave early and watch his son play baseball. Worker A's willingness to do this may have emerged from his appreciation for the time that worker B spent teaching him how to use a new computer program the week before. Over the life of the relationship, the two co-workers balance out the favors asked of each.

Third, participants develop an understanding about the nature of the relationship and what each can expect from the other. A labor union and a company's management team develop an understanding about what will take place when they negotiate a contract and what to expect when the contract is administered. These expectations may reflect an adversarial or a cooperative relationship between the two parties.

Fourth, relationships usually are embedded in wider social networks. A worker may have several work relationships: with her supervisor, with her co-workers, with her union, and with her organization. She must balance the needs of one relationship with those of other relationships.

Fifth, relationships can range from unidimensional to multifaceted. For example, an employee may have only a work relationship (unidimensional) with a co-worker. She sees the co-worker only at work and has nothing to do with her outside of the work setting. Alternatively, an employee may have several relationships with a co-worker: a work relationship, a personal relationship as a friend outside of work, and the two also may be members of the same church.

Six Relationship Types

We believe there are six types of relationships that HR should actively manage (see Table 14.1). These relationships can occur between parties who are both within the same organization (internal-to-internal) or between parties who span organizational boundaries (internal-to-external). Internal-to-internal relationships are the traditional focus of HR interventions. While internal-to-external relationships are perhaps less familiar HR territory, they offer substantial potential for creating social-capital benefits throughout the value-creation chain. For example, an employee in the supply chain of an aircraft manufacturer may make an informal call to the materials manager at Boeing to alert him about a shipment delay because the two developed a relationship at a trade show. Each of these types of relationships requires specialized expertise and different kinds of interventions to build and manage effectively.

Individual-to-Individual

Greenhalgh identifies four dimensions that characterize individual relationships.[18] *Rapport* involves the comfort people have in dealing with each other and is based

Table 14.1 Types of relationships in organizations

	Individual	Group	Organization
Individual	Strong vs. weak	Inclusion vs. exclusion	Relational vs. transactional
Group		Cooperative vs. competitive	Facilitative vs. obstructive
Organization			Allies vs. rivals

upon trust, interpersonal disclosure, empathy, and acceptance. *Bonding* concerns the robustness of the relationship and is based upon a sense of alliance, cooperation, and a balance of economic exchange. *Breadth* of the relationship reflects differences in how relationships are experienced in terms of scope (from narrow to unlimited) and time (from transactional to ongoing). *Affinity* entails the degree to which people find each other intrinsically interesting and is based upon stimulation, sharing things in common, liking, and romantic interest.

HR can help employees forge productive individual relationships in a number of ways. For example, assigning buddies (current employees) to new employees during orientation provides an opportunity to create rapport between them which may lead to long-term relationships. Encouraging and supporting mentoring relationships between senior and junior employees facilitates relationship building. When participation in mentoring relationships is voluntary for both parties, all four relationship dimensions (rapport, bonding, breadth and affinity) may result. Conventional training programs provide an opportunity for HR to mix together employees from different parts of the company who do not normally interact with one another. Especially in training programs that are longer in duration, opportunities are created for employees to develop rapport and affinity for one another. Sponsored as well as informal social gatherings are like training programs in providing additional opportunities for employees to develop relationships with others in the organization with whom they do not normally interact.

All of the examples above represent traditional HR activities. What's different for HR is how those activities are perceived and managed from a relationship perspective. In the past, developing relationships was viewed more as a byproduct of those activities – not the main outcome to be achieved. Now, developing relationships is viewed as an important objective in its own right, and the bundle of HR activities is managed to enhance relationship building along with the other goals such as competence building or orientation.

By thinking creatively, HR can create additional opportunities to build individual relationships. For example, at Steelcase headquarters in Grand Rapids, Michigan, pictures of every employee from the CEO to the secretaries are displayed on the walls along with attached biographies and personal statements concerning hobbies, aspirations, philosophies, beliefs, and wishes, as well as information about current company projects.[19] In addition, whiteboards outside offices tell people about the work that employees are involved in. Employees can locate kindred spirits by just walking around. Using physical architecture to nurture relationship building offers another alternative. Considerable research demonstrates that physical architecture affects social networks and interaction patterns. For example, studies by Leon Festinger and colleagues in the 1950s showed that where people lived in university housing determined social interaction.[20] People developed friendships and social relations with those who were nearest to their own apartments. Members of social networks shared information and developed common attitudes.

How offices are assigned to employees may play a large role in how relationships develop in an organization. Many colleges assign office space to intentionally create opportunities for interaction across disciplines. A marketing professor may be next door to a finance professor who is also next door to an organizational behavior professor. Proximity facilitates interaction. A similar strategy can be used in any organization.

How offices are designed can also be viewed from the perspective of relationships. For example, Opticon, a Danish firm, built stairwells in a new building with wide landings, a coffee machine, and a place to sit.[21] This layout encourages employees to meet, have conversations and develop relationships.

While the physical architecture of an organization influences interaction patterns, the social architecture also plays an important role.[22] The social architecture includes the design of jobs, groups, and organization structures. HR can become more actively involved in managing interaction issues such as co-location, meetings, conferences, social events, employee roundtables, internal electronic communication networks and other means for bringing people together. HR professionals can become relationship brokers, using their social skills to help individuals forge powerful and enduring business relationships.

One route for doing this is to make the informal, interpersonal experiences that have often been reserved for special occasions a part of everyday business life. For example, PIPSA, one of Mexico's leading paper manufacturers, encourages inter-departmental meetings wherein members often rely on the Mexican tradition of oral and musical storytelling to share their ideas.[23] Rather than viewing organizationally sponsored social events as discretionary, HR can encourage them to be seen as invaluable sources of relationship building.

We believe there are three key elements in HR's role at the individual level. One, HR policies, programs, training, and counseling activities can enhance employees' personal relationship capabilities. Two, through facilitation, interventions, and the sharing of expertise, HR can create opportunities for relationships to form. Three, by adopting a partnership perspective with employees and managers, HR can encourage personal effort toward developing relationships that are important. Relationships that matter are those that make it possible for employees to improve their performance, create innovation, and help their organizations gain advantages over their competitors.

Developing relationships that matter is a challenging goal when economic conditions are favorable, and an even more difficult goal when economic conditions are unfavorable. In economic downturns, HR is often needed to restore individual relationships that have been lost or damaged due to downsizing and other disruptions. Helping individuals establish new relationships with other 'survivors' may become the paramount objective.

Individual-to-Group

The second type of relationship is between an individual and a group. This type of relationship can be within the same organization (e.g. between an individual and a work group or department) or between an individual employee and a group outside the firm (e.g. between an individual and a supplier's design–build team). The relationship may be one of inclusion or exclusion. Leaders play an important role in creating a climate of inclusion or exclusion among their followers. Research shows that leaders develop a separate relationship with each individual subordinate over time.[24] Individuals who feel a sense of inclusion have strong social ties to their leader in a people-oriented relationship noted for high mutual trust, exchange, loyalty and influence. In contrast, individuals who feel a sense of exclusion have few or no social ties to their leader and have only a task-oriented relationship characterized by lack of trust and loyalty, and top-down influence.

One important type of informal group of individuals in an organization is a community of practice. Communities of practice are defined as 'groups of people who share a concern, a set of problems, or a passion about a topic, and who deepen their knowledge and expertise in this area by interacting on an ongoing basis.'[25] Inclusion in these groups is usually voluntary and formed around common tasks, work interests, and contexts. Communities of practice are not constrained by geographic, business-unit, or functional boundaries. Etienne Wenger recommends that organizations identify strategically important competencies and then search for communities that have them.[26] HR can play an important role in this process by recognizing and understanding the various informal social relationships that are important for developing these communities as well as orchestrating the formal links. HR can be both a scout and a choreographer of effective communities of practice inside a firm and beyond its borders.

HR should be a source of support, advice, facilitation, and innovation for both formal and informal work groups, such as communities of practice. To do this effectively, HR has to balance between providing too much structure and influence, thereby stifling self-organization, and too little nurturance and attention, which would allow problems to fester unnecessarily. To paraphrase Thomas Stewart, organizations need to 'water the grass, don't mow, and wait for lightning to strike.'[27] Informal relationships are like grass – they are low to the ground, easily mowed down, and spread by dividing roots slowly to adjacent territory. Support, but not micromanagement, is necessary for nurturance. Too heavy an involvement and usurpation of the group may cause it to disband – to the detriment of the organization as well as the individuals. With HR's help, a number of strategies offered to support communities of practice, such as those bulleted below, could easily be extended to other types of informal groups in organizations:[28]

- Have a sponsoring board of senior managers who give legitimacy to communities of practice and keep them in the loop.
- Recognize participation in communities of practice through performance evaluations and promotion decisions.
- Remove barriers such as counterproductive policies.
- Provide budgets to cover such items as time, travel and teleconferences.

If HR creates a climate in which employees see customers, suppliers, and members of complementary firms as part of their own group, these relationships are much more likely to yield competitively valuable interactions. HR can provide 'insider' information to employees regarding external firms and groups that can increase awareness, shape expectations, and provide a foundation for mutual influence. Boeing offered a striking example of this insider approach during the development of its 777. Potential customers invited to examine plans for the new aircraft were adamantly against the location of the fuel tanks on the newly designed wings. Since the wings tilted upward, the fuel tanks were 10 feet above the ground. Refueling the new planes would require a fleet of new equipment. Because Boeing engineers viewed their customers as being on the same team, rather than as external troublemakers, the design change was implemented before manufacturing began, and as a result, customer loyalty was enhanced. HR can use its experience in managing group dynamics and its knowledge of team development processes to facilitate redrawing relevant group boundaries to include all those, like the Boeing 777 customers, who can make a contribution to organizational success.

HR can shape individual-to-group interactions within a firm through appraisal systems, selection criteria, work practices, and organizational culture. If employees are regularly assessed on their demonstrated interpersonal capabilities and accomplishments, they are more likely to pay attention to these aspects of their responsibilities. Many firms, from Southwest Airlines to Nucor Steel, incorporate attitudes toward teamwork, interpersonal adaptability, and similar criteria into their selection processes. Work practices that routinely blend both permanent and temporary team membership and foster opportunities to develop relationships ease the strain of entering and leaving groups. An organizational culture that celebrates diversity, promotes exposure to varied settings, and emphasizes collaboration creates a setting that facilitates healthy individual-to-group relationships.

Individual-to-Organization

The third type of relationship is between an individual and an organization. This relationship can be the traditional employment relationship, or it can occur between an individual and another organization (e.g. professional association). It can be either transactional (as in the case of the relationship between an independent contractor and an employee) or it can be relational (as in the case of an employee hired with the expectation of a long-term relationship). In addition to the familiar role that HR plays in the employment relationship, individual-to-organization relationships draw upon HR expertise regarding socialization, organizational citizenship, and culture fit.

At W.L. Gore and Associates, for example, relationships are the basis for employee connections and contributions to the firm.[29] No one is hired without a sponsor, and work assignments are developed out of each employee's diagnosis of how he or she can best contribute to the organization after trying out a number of different jobs and roles.

Viant, an Internet company, is an exemplar of HR relationship building in action.[30] Cultural fit is an important criterion in Viant's selection decisions. Most hiring decisions involve interviews with several people; as many as eight Viant employees who will work directly with the new hire interview candidates on the same day. If the employee group agrees to hire someone, assimilation of that new hire is initiated during the interview process. Throughout the hiring process, a network of connections (including potential advocates and mentors) is created that will help integrate the new person into the company.

Viant requires all employees to participate in a three-week orientation program to create social connections that, in turn, facilitate job performance long after the program is completed. Company veterans share their experience as new employees work through case studies and projects. Orientation is held at a single site in Boston so new hires from all eight of the company's offices can start forming personal relationships that will help them get things done when they return home. The training is intense, and the participants spend most of the days with each other. They also stay in the same apartment building at night. The CEO calls himself the chief cultural officer and believes that this approach creates lasting bonds among employees and between employees and the organization.

To foster the loyalty and commitment of those persons beyond the boundaries of the organization, HR can apply its expertise in a new arena. For example, many of the techniques that HR uses to help employees learn the ropes of the organization (i.e. orientation programs, handbooks, social events) can be used to help new customers become attuned to organizational practices that will, in turn, enable them to deal more effectively and efficiently with the firm.[31] Anyone who has recently purchased a new automobile probably has seen this approach in practice. Shortly after driving away in the new car, customers begin receiving invitations to return to the dealer to visit the service center, meet the managers, have a few refreshments and learn more about their purchase. These after-sale gatherings provide customers with the information needed to create long-term, productive relationships with the firm. HR can advise managers on how to design an agenda ensuring that customers know what to do, whom to see, how to work with the firm, and what to expect in the future. Likewise, HR can help a firm create a psychological contract with customers similar to the psychological contract it creates with employees.

Group-to-Group

The fourth type of relationship is between one group and another. This relationship can occur between two groups in the same organization (e.g. engineering and marketing, managers and plant workers) or between two groups, one of which is within the organization and one of which is outside (e.g. an engineering group in one organization with an engineering group in another organization, such as a supplier). A crucial dimension to manage is whether inter-group relationships are cooperative or competitive. Research has shown that even groups formed on the basis of arbitrary criteria will often behave in a competitive and aggressive manner toward each other. This can happen even when the reward structure permits noncompetitive behavior.[32] Sherif's famous Robber Cave's experiment demonstrated that a reward structure pitting one group against another led to strong intra-group cooperation and cohesion but also to strong inter-group aggressiveness, prejudice, and discrimination.[33]

HR can facilitate cooperative relations between groups in several ways.[34] One, if HR identifies a common enemy (e.g. a poor service reputation that must be improved), groups form alliances against the common problem rather than between themselves. Two, HR can develop problem-solving processes that minimize group differences and provide common goals, such as GE's 'Work Out!' program that encourages employees to find ways to overcome bureaucratic obstacles. Three, HR can encourage locating different groups together to promote informal interaction that reduces stereotypic perceptions. Four, HR can help a firm design cellular organization structures that routinely blend and reform sets of teams to ensure a broad array of units that are familiar and adept at working together.[35]

Managing different communities of practice is another way HR can influence group-to-group relationships. The World Bank, for example, has created over one hundred communities of practice that are geographically dispersed groups devoted to specific issues such as water infrastructure, urban poor, and rural transportation. These different communities of practice complement one another in the pursuit of organizational objectives. Each of these groups has a budget for network activities such as meetings and developing technologies. For HR to make a value-added contribution, it must understand the business relationships involved.

As organizations increasingly rely on relationships with other organizations to manage complexity, capitalize on technology advances and shape the marketplace, HR's contribution to managing group dynamics needs to extend to groups comprised of individuals that cut across organizational lines. Some communities of practice may be linked horizontally to different organizations through common or shared activities. These networks of practice (communities that extend beyond a single organization) broaden relationships outside of organization boundaries, bringing new knowledge and insight into the system. For example, Bristol-Meyers Squibb found that their oncology division had been extremely successful for a long time largely due to this group's rich networking outside of the organization's boundaries.[36] The number of people both inside and outside this group's network was substantially larger than for any other division in the company. The task for HR is to identify those communities of practice that have a direct impact on strategic objectives and invest in them, such as provide resources for face-to-face meetings, develop skills in cross-organizational communications, and so forth.

Group-to-Organization

The fifth type of relationship is between a group and an organization. These relationships can be characterized as facilitative and contributing or as obstructive.

Here, a group (e.g. a union) has a relationship with the larger organization of which it is a part. Through effective relationship building, HR can facilitate a cooperative effort between the union and the organization that benefits both parties. Kochan and Osterman suggest that a high-conflict, low-trust relationship is incompatible with the task of building and maintaining the psychological and social climate needed to produce and sustain mutual gains.[37] Therefore HR needs to anticipate the need for trust and common interests and design opportunities for creating productive relationships despite differing agendas. For example, HR can create a labor-management committee that provides an opportunity to work on a 'common enemy,' such as a problem confronting the entire organization.[38] A Delco plant in Indiana found many areas of common ground between union members and managers when General Motors indicated its intent to find another supplier if substantial cost savings could not be achieved.

HR does not need to wait for emergencies to extend the time for relationship building beyond a negotiation period. Collaboration on an issue that is not a source of contention between groups (such as Saturn's approach to product design) can offer a foundation for navigating other, more complicated relationships later on. Ongoing relationship building between potentially adversarial groups promotes awareness and shapes expectations, clarifies mutual dependencies, and provides an opportunity for the two units to view each other in a more multidimensional and interdependent manner.

Group-to-organization relationships also occur outside the firm. For example Harley-Davidson riders, Saturn drivers and Macintosh users have formed clubs that develop relationships with the company that sells the product they have in common. HR can design programs such as plant tours and employee sign-offs on products, through which customers can develop more personal relationships with the people that build their products. When firms allow customers to contact employees directly, employees take more pride in what they produce and customers have confidence in the products they purchase. Through training and socialization, HR can ensure that these interactions are beneficial and strengthen customer loyalty.

Organization-to-Organization

The sixth type of relationship is between (or among) organizations. These relationships can be characterized as allies (such as members of the supply chain) vs. rivals (such as producers of a competing product). Often relationships among firms change as the competitive landscape shifts. For example, competitors may form an alliance to create a new product application but still compete vigorously on their core products. Kale, Singh, and Perlmutter showed that when firms build relational capital (the result of close interaction at the personal level between alliance partners) coupled with an integrative approach to managing conflict, they are able both to learn know-how and capabilities from their alliance partners and to protect themselves from the opportunistic behavior of their partners in order to retain their own proprietary assets.[39] Furthermore, as many failed mergers and joint ventures attest, insufficient attention to integrating different corporate cultures can cause problems. HR can help firms avoid mistakes and achieve inter-organizational cooperation by orchestrating key relationships and by anticipating the consequences of blending diverse cultures.[40]

Relationships with other organizations can be either temporary or permanent. Permanent relationships (i.e. mergers) involve combining complementary resources and knowledge bases. One challenge for HR is to retain the key professionals and top-level executives of the acquired/merged firm. If relationships with key employees are developed before the merger/acquisition is finalized, costly turnover and loss of organizational memory that may have been the basis for the original transaction can be prevented. Temporary relationships, such as joint ventures, also benefit from ongoing relationship management. A joint venture provides the opportunity for partners' employees to have extended social interaction and increase the sharing of tacit knowledge.[41] Again, social capital plays an important role in the success of this type of partnership, and HR plays a crucial role in ensuring that social capital is created and nurtured.

HR can assist the organization in efforts to improve relationships across a variety of participants in the value-creation process (e.g. suppliers, distributors, and even with customers). Line managers often note the importance of effective supply chain management but overlook the importance of relationships in making that goal a reality. HR can be an effective partner in designing links between people serving in liaison roles, forging connections between groups that interact directly, and facilitating ties between the top-management groups of the supply-chain members.[42]

Intermingling employees (e.g. stationing workers from suppliers in an assembler's factories) from different parts of the value chain is one of the best ways to improve design-for-manufacturability-and-assembly (DFMA).[43] Cross-fertilization of employees provides new perspectives on problems and breaks down barriers at each organization's boundaries. HR can create the systems that make it possible to build these relationships across organizations.

As noted previously, building relationships with customers can lead to loyalty that results in competitive advantage. FedEx is one firm that has capitalized on this opportunity. Other companies have access to the operations of FedEx, and FedEx can also enter some of its customers' operational areas. Similar to intermingling employees between value chain partners, this strategy intermingles employees and processes between organizations and their customers. For customers to be effective co-producers, however, HR needs to ensure that customers know what to do, how to do it, and have the motivation to contribute.[44]

All six types of relationships contribute to the amount and quality of social capital that an organization possesses. By effectively managing all six types of relationships, organizations may be able to create a competitive advantage. When all six types of relationships are effectively managed, organizations may be able to respond more rapidly to new and emerging conditions in their environments.

The Right People with the Right Relationships

The creation of social capital that benefits an organization is a function of creating relationships between individuals, among groups and across organizations. The combination of high-quality human capital and high-quality social capital is key to competitive advantage in the knowledge economy. The best relationships – those in which individuals, groups or organizations work well together for mutual goals – can take a variety of forms. Individuals, groups, or organizations do only the minimum without effective relationships, or do not even get along well enough to work together.

While managing relationships is not the sole responsibility of any single business function, HR is in a unique position to facilitate, coordinate, and monitor an organization's management of relationships that matter. As noted at the outset, the knowledge economy requires a partnership orientation between HR and other members of the firm. Each employee is responsible for building relationships, both for personal survival and to benefit the organization. HR's role is that of facilitator and coach in identifying, encouraging, and supporting the establishment of relationships that are useful and valuable for the organization, and in putting formal and informal systems in place that nudge these relationships in the right direction. Leonard Greenhalgh describes the role of managing relationships as:

> *'tapping into relationship networks, learning who has a particular distinctive competency, earning trust, building commitment to long-term joint prosperity, forging bonds between people in different organizations, managing the conflicts that strain relationships, learning from others' strengths, building human capital and loyalty, and dealing with the relationship challenges that come with diverse workforces and global businesses.'[45]*

For most HR professionals, assuming this new role does not mean acquiring a new body of knowledge and skills. Instead, it more likely entails changing perspectives on how they view their responsibilities and how they view employees. Similar to changes that other professionals have made in relegating routine tasks to technology solutions and spending a greater proportion of time and effort on developing unique, unconventional, strategic capabilities, HR professionals will also need to restructure their allocation of energy. For years, HR professionals have prided themselves on being 'people oriented.' In the knowledge economy, HR can make a value-added contribution to competitive advantage by becoming 'relationship oriented.' Many firms state that people are their most important resource. If HR effectively reorients and extends its role within these organizations to emphasize building effective relationships, this rhetoric is more likely to become a reality.

Notes

Ideas in this chapter are adapted from Lengnick-Hall, M.L. and Lengnick-Hall, C.A. 2002. *Human resource management in the knowledge economy: New challenges, new roles, new capabilities*. San Francisco: Berrett-Koehler.

1 Hackett, B. 2000. *Beyond knowledge management: New ways to work and learn.* Research Report 1262-00-RR. New York: The Conference Board.

2 DeNisi, A., Hitt, M.A. and Jackson, S.E. 2003. The knowledge-based approach to sustained competitive advantage. In Jackson, S.E., Hitt, M.A. and DeNisi, A. (eds). *Managing knowledge for sustained competitive advantage: Designing strategies for effective human resource management.* San Francisco, CA: Jossey-Bass: 3–33.

3 Cohen, D. and Prusak, L. 2001. *In good company: How social capital makes organizations work.* Boston, MA: Harvard Business School Press.

4 Barney, J. 1991. Firm resources and sustained competitive advantage. *Journal of Management*, 17(1): 99–120.

5 See, for example, Becker, B.E. and Huselid, M.A. 1998. High performance work systems and firm performance: A synthesis of research and managerial implications. In G.R. Ferris (ed.). *Research in personnel and human resources management*, 16: 53–101. New York: JAI Press; Guthrie, J.P. 2001. High involvement work practices, turnover, and productivity: Evidence from New Zealand. *Academy of Management Journal*, 44(1): 180–90.

6 Cohen and Prusak, op. cit.

7 Huber, G.P. 1991. Organizational learning: The contributing processes and the literatures. *Organization Science*, 2(1): 88–115.

8 Adler, P.S. and Kwon, S. 2002. Social capital: Prospects for a new concept. *Academy of Management Review*, 27(1): 17–40.

9 Heneman, H.G., III and Berkley, R.A. 1999. Applicant attraction practices and outcomes among small businesses. *Journal of Small Business Management*, 27(1): 53–74; Kirnan, J.P., Farley, J.A. and Geisinger, K.F. 1989. The relationship between recruiting source, applicant quality, and hire performance: An analysis by sex, ethnicity, and age. *Personnel Psychology*, 42(2): 293–308.

10 Schneider, B., Goldstein, H.W. and Smith, D.B. 1996. The ASA framework: An update. *Personnel Psychology*, 48: 747–73; Dalton, D.R., Tudor, W.D. and Krackhardt, D.M. 1982. Turnover overstated: The functional taxonomy. *Academy of Management Review*, 7(1): 117–23.

11 Bartlett, C.A. 1998. *Skandia AFS: Developing intellectual capital globally.* Case #9-396-412. Harvard Business School Press.

12 Huselid, M.A., Jackson, S.E. and Schuler, R.A., 1997. Technical and strategic human resource management effectiveness as determinants of firm performance. *Academy of Management Journal*, 40(1): 171–88.

13 Huselid, M.A. et al., op. cit.

14 Lengnick-Hall and Lengnick-Hall, 2002, op. cit.

15 Cohen and Prusak, op. cit.

16 Browne, R. 1999. Relationships. In Manstead, A.S.R. and Hewstone, M. (eds), *The Blackwell Encyclopedia of Social Psychology*, 470–7. Oxford; Cambridge, MA: Blackwell Publishers.

17 Scott, S.G. and Einstein, W.O. 2001. Strategic performance appraisal in team-based organizations: One size does not fit all. *The Academy of Management Executive*, 15(2): 107–16.

18 Greenhalgh, L. 2001. *Managing strategic relationships: The key to business success.* New York: Free Press.

19 Cohen and Prusak, op. cit.

20 Festinger, L., Schachter, S. and Back, K. 1950. *Social pressure in informal groups: A study of human factors in housing.* Stanford, CA: Stanford University Press.

21 Cohen and Prusak, op. cit.

22 Baker, W. 2000. *Achieving success through social capital: Tapping the hidden resources in your personal and business networks.* San Francisco, CA: Jossey-Bass.

23 Matson, E. 1997. You can teach this old company new tricks. *Fast Company*, 11: 44–6.

24 Graen, G.B. and Uhl-Bien, M. 1995. Relationship-based approach to leadership: Development of leader member exchange (LMX) theory of leadership over 25 years: Applying a multi-level domain approach. *Leadership Quarterly*, 6(2): 219–47.

25 Wenger, E. 2000. Communities of practice. In E.L. Lesser, M.A. Fontaine, and J. Slusher (eds). *Knowledge and communities*. Boston, MA: Butterworth-Heinemann: 3–22.

26 Cohen and Prusak, op. cit.

27 Stewart, T.A. Water the grass, don't mow, and wait for lightning to strike. *Fortune*, 24 July 2000, 367–78.

28 Wenger, op. cit.

29 Lussier, R.N. and Achua, C.F. 2001. *Leadership: Theory, application, skill development.* Cincinnati, OH: South-Western College Publishing.

30 Cohen and Prusak, op. cit.

31 Lengnick-Hall, M.L. and Lengnick-Hall, C.A. 1999. Expanding customer orientation in the HR function. *Human Resource Management*, 38(3): 201–14.

32 Tajfel, H. and Turner, J.C. 1986. The social identity theory of intergroup behavior. In S. Worchel and W.G. Austin (eds), *Psychology of intergroup relations*. Chicago, IL: Nelson-Hall: 7–24.

33 Sherif, M. et al. 1961. *Intergroup conflict and cooperation: The Robber Cave's experiment.* Norman, OK: University of Oklahoma.

34 Greenhalgh, op. cit.

35 Miles, R.E. et al. 1997. Organizing in the knowledge age: Anticipating the cellular form. *The Academy of Management Executive*, 11(4): 7–25.

36 Cohen and Prusak, op. cit.

37 Kochan, T.A. and Osterman, P. 1994. *The mutual gains enterprise: Forging a winning partnership among labor, management, and government*, Boston MA: Harvard Business School.

38 Greenhalgh, op. cit.

39 Kale, P., Singh, H. and Perlmutter, H. 2000. Learning and protection of proprietary assets in strategic alliances: Building relational capital. *Strategic Management Journal*, 21: 217–37.

40 Nahavandi, A. and Malakzedah, A.R. 1988. Acculturation in mergers and acquisitions. *Academy of Management Review*, 23(1): 79–90.

41 Lane, P.J. and Lubatkin, M. 1985. Relative absorptive capacity and interorganizational learning. *Strategic Management Journal*, 19: 451–77.

42 Greenhalgh, op. cit.

43 Ibid.

44 Lengnick-Hall and Lengnick-Hall, 1999, op. cit.

45 Greenhalgh, op. cit., 122.

PART III: REVISING THE AGENDA

15

Tacit Knowing, Communication and Power: Lessons from Japan?

Tim Ray and Stewart Clegg

Not so long ago, Japan was on its knees: after the Second World War, much of its industry and many of its cities had been largely destroyed. In a September 1945 interview with the *New York Times*, the commander of the allied occupation of Japan (1945–52), General Douglas MacArthur, proclaimed that, 'Japan would never again become a world power'; and, five years later, his economic experts advised that, 'the Japanese economy's best course in the postwar era would be to make 'knickknacks' – their word – for underdeveloped countries' (Fingleton, 1997: 1–2). Although the occupation forces gave Japan an American-style constitution, which was intended to provide a foundation for American-style institutions, they did not anticipate that Japan would metamorphose into a technological and economic colossus.

Today, Japan is the world's second largest economy. Half a century ago, it did not have any entries in *Fortune* magazine's listing of the world's 50 largest corporations. By 1998, it had 100 entries in *Fortune*'s expanded compilation, which covered the global economy's 500 largest corporations. Japan was second only to the United States, which had a total of 185 listings and had more than double the number of entries for the next three countries: Germany at 42, France at 39 and Britain at 38 entries (Bergesen and Sonnett, 2001: 1607). However, as the 1990s unfolded, the growing perception that Japan's miracle economic growth had faltered coincided with increasing confidence in America's economic boom. Some of the Westerners, who had been so keen to learn-from-Japan a decade earlier, became triumphalist. Past concerns that Japan had developed a new and superior form of capitalism appeared to evaporate as US prosperity and globalization prompted the diagnosis that Japan's difficulties were a consequence of not adhering adequately to the 'universal' rules of free-market capitalism. By 2000, dot.com mania was at its height. Yet, the bubble burst a year later, while the aftermath of 9/11 prompted a new *Zeitgeist* that militated against taken-for-granted optimism. The publication of, *The Roaring Nineties: Why We're Paying the Price for the Greediest Decade in History*, by 2001 economics Nobel Laureate, Joseph Stiglitz (2004), for example, sounded a distinctly cautious note.

Celebrated in the 1980s and then spurned in the 1990s and since, Japan remains the most studied non-English-speaking-country in the Anglophone management and business canon. Yet, despite the waning interest in Japan, the second half of the 1990s saw, what may turn out to be, Japan's most significant intellectual export to world management: a widespread Western enthusiasm for knowledge management (KM), fuelled by Nonaka and Takeuchi's (1995) influential book, *The Knowledge-Creating Company: How Japanese Companies Create the Dynamics of Innovation*. Yet, there has not been a Western-style KM boom in Japan[1] and KM projects in Western contexts often fail to meet expectations. We will suggest that a significant reason for both the initial KM enthusiasm and its failure to deliver stem from two inter-related phenomena. First, a basic misunderstanding of the processes by which Japanese institutions enable and constrain Japanese organizational practices; and second, a Western willingness to accept a Japanese reinvention of Michael Polanyi's (1891–1976) concept of tacit knowing. Presenting Japan's knowledge-creating companies as models for the West glosses over the processes by which power, mediated by Japanese institutions, enables Japanese organizations to maintain disciplinary authority over their employees and exploit the benefits of highly aligned tacit knowing amongst organizational *insiders*. Within Japanese organizations, close community relationships lubricate communication among colleagues who, by virtue of knowing each other well, are able to coordinate their actions to a degree that might astonish even the most evangelical advocates of KM. However, the force of this point is often either overlooked or masked by siren voices that attract Western managers to the alluring prospect of 'managing knowledge'. Our contention is that KM could be more appropriately described as an illusion made possible by a subtle redefinition of Polanyi's concept of tacit knowing.

Whereas Polanyi argued that tacit knowing represented an inexpressible personal coefficient to every thought and action, Nonaka and Takeuchi (1995) have contributed to a craze in which KM practitioners seek to make tacit knowing explicit by finding a way to 'express the inexpressible' (Takeuchi and Nonaka, 2004: 36). There is more than a hint of ineffability to the notion. That it comes to the West replete with Eastern inscrutability only makes it more promotable. Oriental oracular mystique appears to have struck a chord with the Western willingness to waste large information-technology budgets in pursuit of miracles, in the hope of turning a trick. The KM trick turns on finding ways to communicate tacit knowledge by converting it into 'words or numbers that anybody can understand' (Nonaka and Takeuchi, 1995: 9). Moreover, these words or numbers are not merely mundane-sounding information, but are re-branded as 'explicit knowledge' – a commodity that is assumed to capture meaning and transfer it from one context to another. Against the background of dramatic advances in Information Communication Technologies (ICTs), it seemed as if KM was offering Anglophone managers *knowledge* served up in words or numbers 'that anybody could understand' and the capacity to control with the click of a mouse.

Although advances in ICTs have transformed information management, exploiting these new opportunities has conventionally been seen as an achievement of *knowers*: the people who 'know how to do things in practice'. In contrast, KM professes to be a tool that offers the manager 'knowledge' thereby raising fundamental questions about 'who knows what' and 'who is in charge of what'. Not surprisingly, competent knowers who perceive that their authority is being compromised by a KM initiative might doubt that 'words or numbers that anybody can understand' will be an effective substitute for judgements and 'deep smarts' (Leonard and Swap, 2004; Chapter 7 in this volume) evolved from many years of practical experience. Notwithstanding occasional attempts to draw attention to the idea that Polanyi was being misrepresented (Cook and Brown, 1999; Chapter 3; Tsoukas, 2003; Chapter 5; Clegg and Ray, 2003), the KM bandwagon rolled on. Yet, as Storey and Barnett (2000; Chapter 10) have argued, imposing a KM solution, without appropriate regard to how it might interact with established ways of doing things, can generate an opportunity to learn from failure. However, pausing to ponder what is claimed in the name of tacit–explicit knowledge-conversion might help to make the kernel of KM's improbability more apparent.

What is tacit knowing? A simple example is provided by Polanyi when he observed that we can recognize a person's face from one in a thousand, indeed one in a million, yet we cannot tell how we recognize the face that we know: *'we can know more than we can tell'* (Polanyi, 1983: 4, italics in the original). The gestalt tacit integration of subsidiary information 'clues' that make recognition possible is almost instantaneous – popularized recently as a 'blink' (Gladwell, 2005). We laugh before we know why a joke is funny, we brake when driving as much as 0.5 seconds before we are conscious of seeing the child run from in front of the car. Fortunately, from the point of view of accident statistics, ultra-rapid parallel processing means that people do not have to wait for the tacit perception to be 'converted' into explicit 'knowledge' before they start to brake. The Danish science writer Tor Nørretranders (1999: 125) argues that human senses are capable of assimilating more than 11 million bits of information per second (at least 10 million bits of which come from the eyes): gigantic amounts of brain-processing are accomplished in one of Gladwell's 'blinks', but Nørretranders suggests that our consciousness can only process 40 bits of information per second – at best. Tacit knowing enables consciousness, but it is not part of consciousness; rather the tacit dimension is a tool-of-knowing, in the way that spectacles might be represented as a tool-of-seeing. And, as Polanyi pointed out: 'You cannot use your spectacles to scrutinize your spectacles' (Polanyi and Prosch, 1977: 37). You cannot use the tacit dimension to 'see' the tacit dimension anymore than you can leave your body to see yourself as an object. Polanyi was clear that tacit knowing, which enabled every thought and action, could not be articulated by means of those thoughts and acts. In his valedictory book, *Meaning*, Polanyi stated: 'We can only point to the existence of tacit integration in our experience. We must be forever unable to give it an explicit specification' (Polanyi and Prosch, 1975: 62). Ironically, Nonaka and Takeuchi (1995) have propelled Polanyi's concept of tacit knowing into the KM limelight by opposing the thrust of his message.

As we will argue, communication depends on an alignment of tacit knowing that enables message senders and receivers to 'read' information signals in similar ways. People's sensitivity to what is communicated is influenced by how well they know each other. The American anthropologist, Edward T. Hall (1989: 91) approached differences in the context of communication by distinguishing between so-called 'low-context' cultures, such as those found in the United States and United Kingdom,

Germany, Switzerland and Scandinavia, where large amounts of background information are included with the message, and 'high-context' cultures, such as the Japanese, Chinese and Arab societies. In 'high-context' cultures, close community relationships generate *espirit de corps* associated with highly aligned tacit knowing among *insiders*, which mediates power in a way that creates significant discontinuities with *outsiders*.

For some, the position of the United States as today's sole superpower might confirm Nobel Laureate Douglass North's (1990: 46) view of history as a normative, unidirectional march (albeit lengthy and uneven) from unwritten traditions and customs, associated with less complex societies, to written laws, specialization and the division of labour, in more complex societies. North views the development of institutions, which he defines as the 'rules of the game', in terms of a progression from informal rules-of-practice (sanctions, taboos, customs, traditions, and codes of conduct) to formal rules (constitutions, laws and property rights). However, North's implicit view of history as a unidirectional march towards liberal individualism, impersonal market–rational entrepreneurship and the rule of law does not sit easily with Japan's position as a global leader in high-performance, high-technology, high-reliability products and production processes – despite exhibiting the characteristics of what North refers to as a 'less complex society'. In contrast to low-context cultures that can be atomized at the level of the individual, we argue that power mediated by Japan's institutions is such that workplace organizations provide a more relevant unit of analysis.

Informed commentators offer different opinions about the long-term viability of the Japanese approach to company-based working, learning, innovation and socializing (Fingleton, 1999; Gao, 2001; Hall, 2002; Johnson, 2004; Katz, 2003; Mikuni and Murphy, 2003; Terry, 2002) and the period since Japan's miracle growth faltered has seen notable changes and readjustments in the organizational landscape that would have been unimaginable in the era of miracle growth. However, behind the outward signs of adjustment and liberalization, the underlying status quo seems to be remarkably robust. Horizontal *keiretsu* continue to delineate family groups of top-tier organizations, while the governmental bureaucracy retains its connections with these top-tier groups. Meanwhile, vertical supply and distribution chains, which descend from top-tier organizations, provide tentacles of longitudinal authority. Fixed trading patterns institutionalize repeat transactions, thereby reducing the marginal cost of information transfer and fostering a coherent collective awareness of who is doing what. Accordingly, companies typically develop a highly nuanced sense of how hard they can lean on their suppliers, thereby facilitating the flow of authority into areas that go far beyond market-rational concerns with price. Similarly, company-as-family workplace organizations (which are sometimes referred to as the 'new *Gemeinschaft*' [Clegg and Kono, 2002: 278]) can lean heavily on the emotional dependency of their regular employees. In a Japanese company-as-family workplace organization, social learning is not an 'oxymoron' (Weick and Westley, 1996) but a taken-for-granted way of integrating working, learning, innovating and socializing – all of which might be regarded as separate, and possibly conflicting, activities in a US or UK organization.

While the ontological status of group activity is controversial, we take the view that *team spirit* cannot be usefully or meaningfully reduced to the atomized actions of individual team members. In Anglophone contexts, team spirit is often welcomed as an unexpected bonus, for example, when people collectively exceed their individual expectations. Conversely, the lack of coordination can become abruptly apparent when new people fail to 'read' the silent language associated with implicit expectations. Yet, the Anglophone management literature has often been more concerned with the responsibilities and rewards of individuals rather than teams. Our argument is that Japan's institutions effectively turn such expectations on their head. In Japan, team spirit disciplines and enables the individual but, ultimately, it is the collective that counts: individuals are of secondary importance. *Esprit de corps* embodies an ineffable, instantaneous capacity for 'tacit integrations' that enable the collective to think and act in an aligned way: this adaptive unconsciousness shapes what happens next and thereby mediates the practice of power.

In the sections that follow, we develop the *insider–outsider* concept of bounded contexts as a tool for critiquing KM and exposing the KM illusion. Ultimately, 'knowing' the facilitative and disciplinary power that is implied by membership of a tightly bounded community of *insiders* depends on the capacity to think and act in the manner of an *insider*. After reviewing aspects of Japan's institutionalized stability, we turn our attention to Nonaka and Takeuchi's (1995) concept of tacit–explicit knowledge-conversion and the nature of claims that have been made in the name of KM. We then consider tacit knowing, meaning and communication in some detail. On the basis of these arguments, we conclude that KM is a highly successful trick that turns on an illusion achieved by redefinition of Polanyi's concept of tacit knowing. Nevertheless, relating Polanyi's original concept of tacit knowing to the practice of power offers a useful way of developing an understanding of the nature and significance of *insider–outsider* divides, and this may offer a better basis for an understanding of the contexts that first generated KM. On that basis, we might have a shrewder idea of how to manage the people who know things.

Japan's Specificity

According to Lewin et al. (1999), the dominant features of contemporary nation-state capitalism in industrialized countries reflect the 'imprinting conditions' – social movements and macro-environmental forces – that framed the transition from the craft to the industrial age (Lewin et al., 1999). In Japan's case, its imprinting conditions were forged during more than two centuries of self-imposed international isolation. When Commodore Matthew Perry delivered US demands to open trade-relations in 1853, accompanied by the military threat of his now infamous 'Black Ships', he precipitated the end of 250 years of unbroken rule by the Tokugawa Shogunate's military government. While calls to 'repel the barbarians' precipitated shifts in prevailing power practices, the realignment reflected in the 1868 Meiji Restoration was neither a Norman Conquest nor a French Revolution (Mason and

Caiger, 1973: 217). Under the slogan 'rich nation, strong army' (*fukoku kyôhei*) the new Meiji government sought to establish a prosperous nation that remained free from Western colonization. From the outset, the Meiji rulers established a plan-rational developmental state: instead of simply setting the rules of play (as in market-rational Anglo-Saxon economies), the Japanese government has been intimately involved with shaping the structure of industry and setting goals for innovation (Johnson, 1992: 19). Japan's centralized government possessed the capacity to direct the process of learning from the West; exploiting the fruits of learning according to the Japanese spirit (*wakon yôsai*) – thereby maintaining the purity of the Japanese *insiders'* world.

In the feudal era, members of the warrior class (*bushi*) were paid a salary (in rice) but unlike the upper strata of pre-modern England, continental Europe, India and China, they were neither landed gentry nor merchants – rather the *bushi's* status resembled that of bureaucrat, albeit a hereditary bureaucrat (Nakane, 1972: 142). Although the military government backed its *bushi*, the *bushi's* authority in the local community depended upon being intimately involved with that community's affairs: there was a strong expectation of mutual obligation. The castes descended from the *bushi* to the lower tiers of farmer, artisan and merchant. Below these four castes, were two outcasts: the 'amply polluted' or 'heavily contaminated' ones (*eta*) and the 'inhuman' or 'non-humans' (*hinin*) – whose descendents collectively form today's *burakumin* underclass (Sugimoto, 2003: 189–93). Although many aspects of Japan changed beyond recognition during its 150-year transition from late-feudalism to technological and economic superpower, the institutional fabric of Japanese society is remarkably effective at disciplining each successive generation in a highly aligned understanding of what is and what is not acceptable.

Consider, for example, the case of the *burakumin* underclass. In open societies that foster public debate and change, one might expect such discrimination to have melted into history. Today's Australians, who celebrate being descended from convict families, illustrate the point. However, according to Yoshio Sugimoto, Japan's *burakumin*, which he estimates number three million, might have rather less to celebrate:

> *A wide range of nasty discriminatory practices against burakumin reflect an invisible caste system in Japanese society. ...*
>
> *Prejudice exists against burakumin in marriage, employment, education, and many other areas. The marriage patterns of burakumin give an indication of persistent discrimination against them. A government survey of buraku communities shows that two out of three marriages in the sample are between those who were born in these communities. Inter-community marriages between burakumin and non-burakumin are in the minority, and marriages between a buraku male and a non-buraku female are much more frequent than between a buraku female and a non-buraku male. There are numerous examples of non-buraku parents or relatives opposing marriages with burakumin, refusing to attend marriage ceremonies, or declining to associate with a couple after marriage. Discriminatory practices in marriage sometimes involve private detective agencies called kôshinjo. At the request of conservative parents, these agencies investigate the family backgrounds, friends, political orientation and other private and personal details of a prospective bride or groom. (Sugimoto, 2003: 189–90).*

Notwithstanding the effects of atomic bombs, an American-style constitution that apparently guarantees individual rights (introduced by the Allied Occupation), previously undreamt of economic prosperity, 'friction-free' information transactions across cyberspace and 21st century globalization, minority groups, such as the *burakumin* or children who are born in Japan, but have Korean or Chinese parents, can experience significant discrimination in their quest to be treated as 'first-class' Japanese *insiders*. It is no easy thing to become a Japanese *insider*.

Even those who are born 'first-class' Japanese citizens discover that unwarranted absence from Japan can jeopardize their *insiderness*. Dr Masao Miyamoto (1995), who has been described as one of the most trenchant *insider* commentators on Japan, provides a graphic account of his painful readjustment to Japanese society after 11 years of practising and teaching psychiatry in the United States. Close alignment with group-norms is fundamental to being accepted as an *insider* within a Japanese organization and Miyamoto's heroic individualism was not without consequences. Certainly, the pressure to conform to peer-group expectations contrasted sharply with his experience of liberal individualism in US society; somewhat bravely (if not perversely) he persisted in testing the differences and succeeded spectacularly in marginalizing himself from his colleagues, while acquiring celebrity status among many Japan commentators.

One of the principal acts of faith in working for a Japanese organization rests on emotional involvement with the activities of colleagues: not going home before one's boss and taking few holidays. Being away from the action is a crime against commitment and working abroad for 11 years might have been rather too much of a crime for those who had fought continuously to tend the home fires. Spending time with colleagues, after-hours socializing and weekend excursions with colleagues are important demonstrations of loyalty: continuous involvement with group activities is an essential part of knowing what it means to be an *insider*. Miyamoto's overseas experience and ability to speak fluent English cut little ice with his Japanese colleagues. Although his skills with the English language did win him some sympathy when he spoke with mothers of children who had returned to Japan after accompanying their parents on overseas postings:

One of the mothers replied, 'Dr. Miyamoto, don't you know? Children who've come back from overseas have to try as hard as they can to speak English poorly at school.'

'That's only common sense,' agreed another.

'Yes, if they speak too well, the other children pick on them,' chimed in a third. I was further taken aback to hear that the children's teachers often took the lead in such bullying.

The trials of returnee children are a relatively recent phenomenon. What happens to children who study overseas and then return to Japan? They are criticized for things like stating their opinions too clearly, questioning what the teacher says, chattering during lunchtime instead of eating in silence, and lacking in the spirit of cooperation. They are urged to go along with the group, and those who do not are made the targets of bullying. That in nutshell is exactly what happened to me in the bureaucracy [where he worked]. (Miyamoto, 1995: 142)

While those who are schooled in the traditions of formal rules might seek recourse to the law in the face of unfair or discriminatory practices, discipline at school is a matter for teachers (although occasional cases of 'over-disciplining' resulting in the death of pupils have attracted outspoken media attention). Compared to its Western counterparts, Japan has comparatively few lawyers;[2] recourse to the law is rare as are robberies and violent crimes that blight other advanced industrial societies.

Although disciplinary power mediated by aligned tacit knowing is effective in shaping what does not happen, aligned tacit knowing about potentially advantageous change can ease the introduction of novelty. Whereas the female contraceptive pill was resisted for three-decades, six-months of debate amongst Japan's male-dominated legislature was sufficient to authorize the marketing of the impotence drug, Viagra. Yet, laws that might be expected to change the status quo are routinely eclipsed by the power of established practice. For example, a law to allow equal opportunities for women employees (enacted in 1985) and the Child-care Leave Law (enacted in 1992) have done little to change expectations in Japan's male-dominated workplace; neither law caries any penalty clause (Sugimoto, 2003: 158). Unlike Schumpeter's (1976: 84) famous image of capitalism advancing by the 'perennial gale of creative destruction', Japan represents what might be seen as steady state stability.

Along with other industrial societies, Japan is subject to centrifugal forces that tend to diversify its structural arrangements, lifestyles and value orientations (Sugimoto, 2003: 271). However, the dramatic increase in the rate of change that appears to make Japan look more like a liberal market-rational economy is offset by centripetal forces that drive Japanese society toward perpetuation of the status quo. In contrast to the American aphorism that, 'the squeaky wheel gets oiled', in Japan, gratuitous individualism is countered by what psychologists call adaptive unconsciousness: instantaneous tacit integrations of the type that enable a soccer team to score the winning goal enable un-specifiable judgments, feelings, emotions and so on to be delivered in microseconds as choreographed disapproval of the offender – 'the nail that sticks out gets hammered down'. Dancing to the right tune is essential. Power mediated by highly aligned tacit knowing acts in the manner of an unseen gyroscope that maintains the same angle of spin despite constant changes in the façade offered to the international community. It represents a significant but frequently overlooked centripetal force.

Can Aligned Tacit Knowing Discipline a Nation?

After noting the difficulties of developing a working definition of 'nation', Benedict Anderson suggested an approach based on imagined communities:

In an anthropological spirit, then, I propose the following definition of the nation: it is an imagined political community – and imagined as both inherently limited and sovereign.

It is imagined because the members of even the smallest nation will never know most of their fellow-members, meet them or even hear them, yet in the minds of each lives the image of their communion. (Anderson, 1991: 5–6, emphasis in original)

Anderson goes on to explain that the nation is imagined as limited because, 'even the largest of them, encompassing perhaps a billion living human beings, has finite elastic, boundaries, beyond which lie other nations. No nation imagines itself coterminous with mankind' (Anderson, 1991: 7). Sovereign nations have come to be aligned with geographical spaces, although the boundaries of these spaces might be subject to dispute. Lastly, a nation is, 'imagined as a *community*, because, regardless of the actual inequality and exploitation that may prevail in each, the nation is always conceived as a deep, horizontal comradeship' (Anderson, 1991: 7, italics in original). On occasions, this sense of imagined alliance among people of the same imagined community of nationhood can drive people to heroic sacrifices – including the willingness to die – in struggles with nations based on different imaginings.

Compared to the ethnic diversity of multicultural societies such as the United States and the United Kingdom, Japan's imagined community of insiders appears to have a much more aligned and highly disciplined sense of what it means to be an *insider*. Literary genres, such as *Nihonjinron*, theorize about the unique qualities of being Japanese: a race set apart from the rest of humanity. And, as Dr Miyamoto discovered, redoubtable disciplinary forces preserve the status quo. Romantic images of *bushidô* ('the way of the warrior' or 'the warrior's code' [Cleary, 1999]) are regularly reconstructed as an appeal to the feudal warrior's ideals of service, honour, loyalty, discipline and absolute dedication. The concept of death before dishonour has, for example, inspired *kamikaze* pilots and post-1945 economic warriors, with subsequent media interest in *karôshi* (death from overwork) among hitherto fit men in their prime years, adding poignancy.

Even in low-context cultures, communication relies on many taken-for-granted expectations about who should communicate with whom, in what manner and to what effect. Yet, these are often overlooked unless somebody does something that tests the bounds of acceptability. As Granovetter (1985: 490) argued, there is much less malfeasance than formal theories would suggest – and malfeasance tends to be reduced where repeat transactions generate reliable relationships. Japan is distinguished from other nations by a sharp *insider–outsider* distinction: as an imagined community, the Japanese nation has highly aligned tacit knowing that automatically guides (in the manner of an unseen choreographer) the way any given type of social event unfolds on any given occasion – and *insiders* are rarely surprised by what happens next. At the micro level, the institutionalization of repeat transactions in company-as-family workplace organizations hammers down nails that stick out in ways that escape consciousness of those who wield the hammers. People are in each other's minds and the level of coordination and 'automatic' management that this enables is quite simply breathtaking.

Knowledge Management: *Yamato-damashii* or Category Mistake?

Yamato-damashii is the 'spirit of Japan' – an alignment of Japanese *insider*-emotions that has been nurtured over centuries and more recently celebrated as a causal link in Japanese economic success (see the discussion in Clegg [1990]). In *Japanese Society*, the Japanese anthropologist Chie Nakane described how Japanese organizations form a distinct social entity that is separate from other groups:

> *In an extreme case, a company may have a common grave for its employees, similar to the household grave. With group-consciousness so highly developed there is almost no social life outside the particular [workplace] group on which an individual's major economic life depends. The individual's every problem must be solved within this frame. Thus group participation is simple and unitary. It follows then that each group or institution develops a high degree of independence and closeness, with its own internal law which is totally binding on members. (Nakane, 1972: 10)*

While many Japanese are quick to dismiss Nakane's influential account as stereotypical and dated, the expectations that situate Japanese workplace organization and legitimate its practices are embedded in highly aligned tacit knowing that shapes how the rules of practice are interpreted in situ; explicit 'etiquette guides' for visitors might detail some informal rules but their interpretation depends on judgments that evolve over a lifetime of disciplined *insider* experience. A rich account of life in a lower-tier organization is provided by the Japanese American, Dorinne Kondo, in her ethnographic study (supervised by Nakane) of working in a small family owned factory that is far removed from the top-tier corporation that is normally viewed as the model for Japanese management (Kondo, 1990).

In the 1980s, the study of Japanese management became a growth industry (Kono and Clegg, 2001). Despite Japan's faltering growth, KM afforded a new lease on life to the well-established tradition of trying to learn secrets from Japan. Here was another source for translation of inscrutable Orientalism into a marketable product. KM resonated with the spirit of globalization by bridging the divide between local knowing and 'universal' knowledge. As a measure of KM's impact outside Japan, Carla O'Dell and Jackson Grayson (1998: ix) open their popular book, *If only we Knew what we Know* with telling comments from two captains of US business:

> *If TI only knew what it knows.*
> *– Jerry Junkins, ex-CEO of Texas Instruments*
> *I wish we knew what we knew at HP.*
> *– Lew Platt, Hewlett-Packard*

However, the above complaints hardly fit with expectations in Japan's company-as-family organizations where organizational *insiders* most certainly 'know what they know' or, to be more precise, have a clear sense of what might be achieved in practice; but the *esprit de corps* that underpins Japanese practice depends on Japanese institutions: it cannot be converted into information and 'managed'.

O'Dell and Grayson argue that, whereas cave dwellers once froze to death on unseen beds of coal that were right underneath them, today's organizations are feeling the chill despite sitting on 'beds of knowledge'. Sticking with their mechanical metaphor, O'Dell and Grayson contend that companies can save themselves from being frozen out by mining knowledge with machinery called 'knowledge management'. While the authors note the contributions to the knowledge debate from Plato, Aristotle, Daniel Bell and Peter Drucker, two names are singled out as founding fathers of the KM paradigm: Michael Polanyi and, Japanese academic, Ikujiro Nonaka:

> *Polanyi and Nonaka both point out that knowledge comes in two basic varieties: tacit and explicit, also known as informal/uncodified and formal/codified. Explicit knowledge comes in the form of books and documents, white papers, databases, and policy manuals. The tacit/uncodified variety, in contrast, can be found in the heads of employees, the experience of customers, the memories of past vendors. Tacit knowledge is hard to catalogue, highly experiential, difficult to document in detail, ephemeral and transitory. Both types of knowledge are important. (O'Dell and Grayson, 1998: 3)*

Although the above quotation reflects a view that has become institutionalized, it reflects a fundamental misunderstanding of Michael Polanyi's concept of tacit knowing.

Arguably, KM's attempt to learn from Japan is an example of what the British philosopher Gilbert Ryle (1900–76) called a 'category-mistake': an example of misunderstanding arising from the application of apparently competent rational thinking:

> *A foreigner watching his first game of cricket learns what are the functions of the bowlers, the batsman, the fielders, the umpire and the scorers. He then says 'But there is no one left on the field to contribute the famous element of team-spirit. I see who does the bowling, the batting and the wicket-keeping; but I do not see whose role it is to exercise* esprit de corps.' *(Ryle, 2000: 18)*

Outsiders who are unable to think and act in the manner of Japanese *insiders* are apt to suffer from the same problem. Even if they take the trouble to spend time in a Japanese organization, they will not be able to 'see' disciplinary authority and facilitative power that enables Japanese organizational *insiders* to 'know what they know' and 'do what they do'.

Tacit–Explicit Knowledge Conversion

For many years, Nonaka et al. (2000: 6; Chapter 2 in this volume) resisted the term 'knowledge management':

The 'knowledge management' that academics and business people talk about often means just 'information management'. In the long tradition of Western management, the organization has been viewed as an information processing machine that takes and processes information from the environment to solve a problem and adapts to the environment based on a given goal.

To their credit, Nonaka and Takeuchi (1995: 58) confronted the difference between knowledge and information head-on, making the point that knowledge involves beliefs and commitments; it is directed towards action, and embodies context-specific meaning. We agree wholeheartedly. However, contradictory implications flow from other parts of their message – and, specifically, from their proposal for tacit–explicit knowledge-conversion.

For tacit knowledge to be communicated or shared within the organization, it has to be converted into words or numbers that anybody can understand. It is precisely during the time this conversion takes place – from tacit to explicit, and, as we shall see, back again into tacit – that organizational knowledge is created. (Nonaka and Takeuchi, 1995: 9)

Nonaka and Takeuchi (1995: 72) argue that a 'knowledge spiral' starts at the individual level and moves up through expanding communities of interaction, within and then beyond the organization. Ultimately, the process might lead to 'universal' understanding, as the book's closing sentences proclaim:

Japanese companies have taught us that innovation can be achieved by continuously creating new knowledge, disseminating it widely through the organization, and embodying it quickly in new technologies, products, and systems. This knowledge-creating process is no longer an enigma. This process is also no longer endemic to Japanese companies. It is universal. (Nonaka and Takeuchi, 1995: 246)

Whereas the Anglophone management and business literature had long regarded knowledge as a subject 'too slippery to handle with even a moderate degree of precision' (Penrose, 1995: 77), Nonaka and Takeuchi confronted knowledge head-on and provoked a response. Scarbrough and Swann (2001: 6) report that KM started to eclipse previous interest in its close relative, the Learning Organization (LO), noting that there were more references to KM in the first six months of 1998 than there were cumulatively to the LO over the previous five years. Mainstream KM has come to resemble a scientific paradigm, based on the 'commitment and apparent consensus' (Kuhn, 1970: 11) of *normal science*, replete with its own agenda and specialist vocabulary. Nonaka and Takeuchi (1995) became widely cited and Peter Ducker described their book as a 'classic' (Takeuchi and Nonaka, 2004: ix). A fad had been born.

Fads create waves and it would be an unusual management academic who deliberately sought to miss an opportunity to surf a wave and gain momentum. Despite earlier misgivings, Nonaka and Takeuchi embraced knowledge management in the title of their subsequent book, *Hitotsubashi on Knowledge Management* (Takeuchi and Nonaka, 2004: ix): 'We contend that knowledge management is now at the very center of what management has to do in today's fast-changing environment.'

However, the philosophical implications of tacit–explicit knowledge-conversion involve a degree of syncretism that undermines KM's viability. The next two sections will consider Polanyi's concept of tacit knowing, first with regard to meaning, and second with regard to communication. We will then propose that KM occupies a space that is incompatible with its own assumptions; in short, it is based on an illusion.

Tacit Knowing and Meaning

Throughout the history of occidental epistemology, a substantial body of opinion has portrayed knowledge as the capacity to represent a knowable reality 'out there'. To be taken seriously, knowledge had to be independent of the knowing subject and represent the world of objects in a more or less veridical fashion. However, as founding figures in radical constructivism, such as Ernst von Glasersfeld (2002) note, sceptics of all ages have offered persuasive arguments that explain why these requisites are unattainable: from the constructivist point of view the subject cannot transcend the limits of human experience or speculations based on that experience – all that we have is our experiential knowing as it appears to us in a given time and place. Einstein also expressed a similar view of knowing: 'the whole of science is nothing more than a refinement of everyday thinking' – as he goes on to explain:

> *I believe that the first step in the setting of a 'real external world' is the formation of the concept of bodily objects and of bodily objects of various kinds. Out of the multitude of our sense experiences we take, mentally and arbitrarily, certain repeatedly occurring complexes of sense impressions (partly in conjunction with sense impressions which are interpreted as signs for sense experiences of others), and we correlate to them a concept – the concept of the bodily object. Considered logically this concept is not identical with the totality of sense impressions referred to; but it is a free creation of the human (or animal) mind. On the other hand, this concept owes its meaning and its justification exclusively to the totality of the sense impressions which we associate with it. (Einstein, 1982: 291)*

Our sense perceptions comprise the basis on which we come to know things and, unless we claim some form of direct mystical revelation of an eternal truth (such as a message from the gods), all of human knowing – including scientific information about a supposedly independent reality – is constructed. Radical constructivism replaces the notion of 'truth' (as a true correct representation of an independent reality) with 'viability' within the subject's experiential world (von Glasersfeld, 2002: 22). This is not to deny that information derived from the pursuit of science cannot enable extremely viable constructions (at least among scientists and others who can interpret that information in a meaningful way), but rather to refute the idea that science corresponds to an absolute and eternal metaphysical conception of truth that transcends human experience.

Science generates information that can be expressed in an orderly and coherent way that is accepted as viable by the scientific community. Einstein expressed amazement that the human mind was able to construct order among sense perceptions and render them comprehensible, using the term 'comprehensibility' in its most modest sense – as he explains:

> It implies: the production of some sort of order amongst sense impressions, this order being produced by the creation of general concepts, relations between these concepts, and by definite relations of some kind between the concepts and sense experience. It is in this sense that our world of experiences is comprehensible. The fact that it is comprehensible is a miracle. (Einstein, 1982: 292)

For Einstein, the connection between sense perceptions and thinking cannot be fixed scientifically; it could only be comprehended intuitively.

The American philosopher, C.S. Peirce (1839–1914), made a similar point in his work on 'abduction' (Jha, 2002: 182), which (as Peirce himself was gracious enough to point out) might be paraphrased as 'an inspired guess'. The illogicality, implied by using 'what you know' to express 'what you do not know', was also recognized by Plato (c.427 – c.347 BC) and noted by Polanyi (1983: 22). In his Socratic dialogue, *The Meno*, Plato's character, Meno (Plato never appeared as himself), quizzed Socrates about an obstacle in the search for 'virtue' (Williams, 2001: 62–3). This revealed a paradox: the search for the solution to a problem is an absurdity; for either you know what you are looking for and so do not have a problem; or you do not know what you are looking for, in which case you cannot expect to find anything – yet, problems do exist and answers are offered.

Michael Polanyi pointed out that, while Plato's solution that all of discovery is a remembering of past lives, is hardly ever accepted, there had been a lack of alternative solutions. His theory of tacit knowing is developed from the idea that: 'we can know things, and important things that we cannot tell' (Polanyi, 1983: 22). We might recognize our friend from a face in a thousand or indeed a million, but we cannot say how we do this – and neither can you: it is an instantaneous gestalt integration of subsidiary information 'clues' that takes place in an instant. Although none of us can observe the 'causal connections' that enable people to recognize each other, we might be happy to accept that recognition takes place. For example, you have the power to recognize your friend that is denied to us: in this sense, we are *outsiders*. However, the brain processing that enabled you to recognize your friend is beyond your consciousness and beyond the objectivist paradigm. By virtue of being beyond consciousness, the tacit dimension is beyond observation and scientific comprehension – as, indeed, Einstein noted.

Suppose that you are standing among a group of people who suddenly burst out laughing when you have no idea why – you're an *outsider* who lacks the degree of aligned tacit knowing to read events in a way that causes you to laugh: there is an *insider–outsider* divide, which might range from the trivial to the highly significant. Possibly, friendly insiders will try to explain what they found funny, but this can only be a partial explanation and might not even sound particularly funny. The meaning that made the people laugh was, in terms of brain processing, already history by the time that the people were conscious of laughing (literally millions of bits of information will be processed by the tacit dimension in the half second or so that it takes to become conscious of laughing). Friendly *insiders* might start to construct explanations, but the tacit dimension's high-speed parallel processing will have been eclipsed by new arrangements of sense perceptions – and the meaning associated with the moment of laughter will be, in comparative terms, history.

The Greek philosopher Heraclitus (c.535–475) observed: 'No man can cross the same river twice, because neither the man nor the river are the same' – and so it is with meaning. Attention and intention are similarly 'of the moment' and might be reconstructed in different ways as time passes. In a similar vein, the Italian philosopher Giambattista Vico (1668–1744) remarked that we cannot reconstruct the past exactly as it was, because we cannot avoid framing and understanding our recollections in terms of the concepts we have at present – and, two centuries later, Jean Piaget came to the same conclusion (Glasersfeld, 2002: 2). If we bear in mind the sheer speed of a cognitive 'blink', it is clear that the instantaneous impulses, for example, that cause a driver to initiate an emergency stop, embody scope for meaningful thoughts and actions (reflected in the response of braking) that run in advance of consciousness. Similarly, we might suddenly strike others as looking guilty or shifty before we are conscious of having something to hide.

We can talk about what we thought, but not about how we thought it – for that lies in the tacit dimension: it is beyond consciousness. Although we can speak, we cannot plan our arguments before constructing them; as Ryle (2000: 31) noted, the plan would need a plan and we could never break into the loop. Accomplished debaters are able to develop complex and coherent arguments in a confident manner without being conscious of quite where the next sentence is coming from: tacit knowing does that for them. Most of the time it works in tandem with consciousness, although we occasionally say things that we regret, as consciousness, so to speak, catches-up with us a moment or two later.

Figure 15.1 illustrates the idea that sense perceptions are delivered to the brain at more than 11 million bits per second (according to Nørretranders's numbers), where they intermingle with re-presentations of past experience to generate mental 'blinks' (here-and-now gestalt tacit integrations) that might be associated with meaning, intention and attention; but these are of the moment; they precede the subsequent evolution of consciousness half-a-second or so later. Although we cannot reconstruct the past exactly as it was, we can 're-present' traces of experience. The hyphen in 're-present' indicates the sense of 'repeat' (Glasersfeld 2002: 195), which occurs when mental traces are fused with the here-and-now input of sensory perceptions – as indicated at the centre of the circle in Figure 15.1. Thus, the driver's preconscious braking when a child steps in front of the car's path might be seen as a re-presentation of traces from past experience. A nervous front-seat passenger, who is also a driver, might simultaneously push a non-existent brake pedal as the

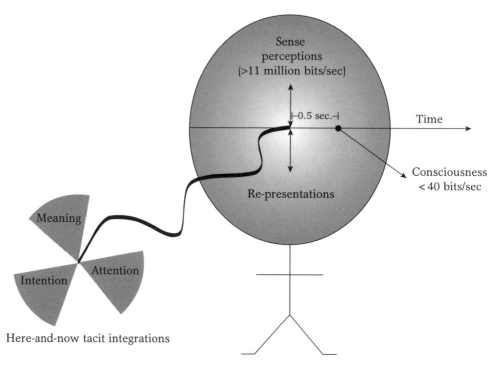

Figure 15.1 Sense perceptions and consciousness

car speeds towards a possible collision – whereas a passenger who has no idea how to drive and is ignorant of the function of a brake pedal would not, one assumes, engage in pre-conscious sympathetic braking. The information flow of sense perceptions to the unseen tacit 'mental butler' is astounding: consciousness is only fast enough to sample a brutally edited and belated summary. Any explicit statement about meaning is always a reconstruction and per force out-of-date. Similarly, the *attention* of knowing subjects (for example, what drivers were attending to when they initiate an emergency stop) and what they were *intending*, at any given instant, is lost in the moment. Meaning, intention and attention are all lost in the moment; thinking is a process that links traces of these moments together. Accordingly, free will is not an object of thinking but part of the thinking process: it is enabled by the mental butler's arrangements, although we can exercise a conscious veto that feeds back into the tacit dimension. (Not always though, as the person who eats an entire box of chocolates *without intending to* might acknowledge.)

In Nonaka and Takeuchi's model of knowledge creation, the conversion of the tacit dimension into 'words or numbers that anybody can understand' effectively could be read as a claim to objectify meaning. Understanding is no longer a construction on the part of the knowing subject but universal: capable of conveying the same meaning to anybody. Thus, knowledge is commodified and communication is presented as a conveyance. Yet this blindingly simplistic assumption masks many problems. As the philosopher Ludwig Wittgenstein (1889–1951) demonstrated in his *Philosophical Investigations*, no *message* could account for its own interpretation: any attempt to include an explanation of how signs should be interpreted would itself require an interpretation – and the specification of what was signified would regress into infinite explanation. Making a similar point, Polanyi pointed out that: 'No map can read itself. Neither can the most explicit possible thesis on map-reading read a map' (Polanyi and Prosch, 1977: 30). Or, to take another example, consider the explicit 'knowledge' that something is 'red'. Would this be red also for somebody who is colour-blind? And how would this red appear when the light fades? As Wittgenstein (2001: 119) pondered, would a red rose be red in the dark, too? If we say that this is positively a red rose, might you see it as such in pitch-blackness? Perhaps you can imagine the red as clear as if it were day? Now, if we offer you a white rose, can you imagine that it is also white in the dark? Now can you tell us, which rose is which colour, or can you, after all, not see anything in the dark?

The temptation to see red as an independent thing-in-itself is often compelling. Yet, as optical illusions demonstrate, there is no necessary correlation between, what we see and the objects we believe that we are seeing. Gestalt tacit integrations lead us to interpret films as moving pictures rather than a sequence of individual frames. The perception of colour or anything else is a property of the brain rather than the object. However, Nonaka and Takeuchi's concept of 'explicit knowledge' overrides this distinction: the knowing subject's tacit integration capacity that constructs 'red' is 'externalized' as an 'explicit knowledge' object. Hence, the object red becomes a *thing-in-itself* rather than a *thing-for-us*. The explicit 'knowledge' that something is red denies the idea that red is constructed in the mind of the knowing subject.

Consider another example. So-called 'explicit knowledge' detailing America's global war against terror comprises ceaseless detail about the latest 'victories' and 'advances' that criss-cross the world through television, the Internet, radio, print and other media; but the interpretation of what is a 'victory' or a 'defeat' is shaped by one's mental 'frame of reference', what one watches, where one watches it and with whom one watches it. Different people interpret the same information signal in different ways.

If you tell us something, we might learn. Yet we might not. Or we might learn something wholly different from the meaning that was intended. Communication requires that sender and a receiver construct signals in broadly similar ways: receivers are not an extension of the sender's imagination. Should you, the sender, sense that we, the receivers, have misinterpreted your words, you might offer us more words. Yet, no matter how many words you provide, ultimately the interpretation of what you said is a construction in our minds, using our sensemaking tools – not the tools that you might imagine we use. People who know each other well tend to communicate easily and rely heavily on their 'silent language' (Hall, 1990), but when they are visited by a stranger, who is unfamiliar with their context of communication, huge amounts of information may fail to get the message across. So what differentiates *insiders* from *outsiders*?

Aligned Tacit Knowing and Communication

There was once an Australian trade minister who was a bit of a clown: a nice bloke, but folksy, keen on jokes. One time when speaking to a Visiting Chinese Trade Delegation, the translator translated his remarks by saying: 'The Minister has just made a joke – please laugh.' Laughter can be revealing. Although there is no record of whether the laughter was spontaneous there is every reason that it might have been because the joke that resides in the instruction is quite subtle. When hitherto unknown tribes are occasionally discovered, the capacity to make them laugh is typically regarded as a sign that something or other has been 'read' in an amusing way – indeed, it might be taken as a good sign: but what are the strangers really laughing about? As in the case of the Chinese Trade Delegation, the minister's sense of the received communication might differ markedly from that of the translator and receivers.

Sometimes *outsiders* will have little jokes played on them. Malinowski's (1932) seemingly strange questioning of the sexual knowledge of the Trobriand Islanders, prompted them to pretend that they did not know that sexual intercourse created babies. Insistent questioning from strangers about what everyone knows can produce these little jokes. On other occasions, *insiders* can be genuinely baffled by the failure of *outsiders* to see why their joke is funny or their approach to a particular problem is reasonable.

Occasionally, animals can be the butt of jokes – even though it is generally conceded that they are non-linguistic beings in the sense that they might understand those who have human linguistic capacity. Nonetheless, it is sometimes said that animals 'understand' what they are instructed to do. Consider the case of the horse, Clever Hans, and his apparent capacity to respond coherently to words and numbers.

> *This horse was trained to 'answer' simple questions of arithmetic. Numbers on a blackboard were successively pointed to, and the horse gave correct answers by stamping its foot until the right number was reached. Critical observers could find no fault in the horse's performance until they asked the question to which they themselves did not know the reply. The horse went on stamping away senselessly. This led to the discovery that the horse had been able to stop at the right point previously because observers had unwittingly, by small gestures, signalled to the horse their expectation that he would stop at that point. Since he was rewarded when he stopped at these signals, the animal learnt to stop at these signals. This shows how well animals can rival and even surpass man's native capacity to establish regularities inductively. Animals can also identify members of a species, that is, establish what functions as a conception of the species. Their restlessness in sleep indicates that they can dream. This shows that they also possess imagination.*
>
> *In the case of man, evolution has added to these gifts the surpassing powers of language. Language makes thinking possible; i.e., we are enabled by language to 'look before and after.' (Polanyi and Prosch, 1977: 120)*

To a point, it was possible to communicate with Clever Hans and exercise some facilitative and disciplinary authority over his foot stamping. Yet, this did not occur in quite the way that onlookers first imagined. It was the onlookers, not Hans, who did the arithmetic. Hans's triumph was in mastering the tacit 'blink' necessary to stop stamping and be rewarded. Tacit re-presentations of mental traces from past experience of the trick were sufficient to enable the onlookers and Hans to 'communicate'.

We might see a stranger, whereas you recognize your friend and your friend appears to recognize you. You and your friend might laugh uproariously, while we cannot conceive what is funny. In this respect, mutual recognition is a sign that experience of shared interaction between you and your friend is allowing re-presentations of past experience to facilitate a dimension of *insiderness* from which we, as strangers, are excluded. An apparent alignment in tacit knowing between you and your friend acts as an unperceived choreographer in the communicative 'dance' between you and your friend (Hall, 1989: 71). If asked, *insiders* might struggle to explain what they expect in the communicative dance; but they can notice those who are not synchronized in an instant.

Although much of the communication between friends who know each other well appears to take place without words, explicit language is essential to the process of conscious thinking that joins traces of momentary tacit integrations together. In *Personal Knowledge*, Polanyi (1974: 69) opens his chapter on articulation by quoting an experiment conducted in the 1930s in which a baby, Donald Kellogg, was raised, from the age of five months, in the company of a chimpanzee called Gua, then aged seven-and-a-half months. For nine months, the two infants were brought up in exactly the same way and subjected to identical tests. Although Donald had an edge, the chimpanzee was not far behind until, at the age of 15–18 months, the chimpanzee's mental development neared completion, just as Donald started to speak. By this single trick, Donald's development soared above the animal's achievements. He acquired the capacity for sustained thought and access to the cultural heritage of his ancestors: learning had entered a new dimension.

The high density of repeat transactions among *insiders* (of the types that are common in Japan and other high-context cultures), might be propagated in any close relationship. Identical twins that grow up together, for example, might evolve a highly aligned *insider* sense of tacit knowing that shapes their sense of information signals in ways that *outsiders* might not appreciate. A striking example of minimal information conveying a significant message is evident in Victor Hugo's correspondence with his publisher:

> *Victor Hugo – famous for writing* The Hunchback of Notre Dame *– had gone on holiday following the publication of his great novel* Les Misérables. *But Hugo could not restrain himself from asking how the book was doing. So he wrote the following letter to his publisher: '?'*
>
> *His publisher was not to be outdone and replied fully in keeping with the truth: '!'*
> (Nørretranders, 1999: 91)

For Hugo, the meaning was unmistakeable – and the popular novel *Les Misérables* later enjoyed success as a musical and movie. The question and exclamation marks were explicit but they did not externalize meaning in the way KM suggests. Aligned tacit knowing enabled Hugo and his publisher to coherent interpretations of meanings from the minimum of information.

Clearly, the use of language is an invaluable tool for arranging conscious thought, as Wittgenstein's famous arguments against the viability of a private language demonstrate. If a language was understood only by one person it would, effectively, be no language at all because it could not begin to communicate. Communication is the form of life of language. It is what it exists to do. Language is a social achievement created by the alignment of tacit knowing amongst communicating subjects. Although Wittgenstein died in 1951, some of his observations appear consistent with Polanyi's subsequent development of tacit knowing. 'If language is to be a means of communication there must be agreement not only in definitions but also (queer as this may sound) in judgments' (Wittgenstein, 2001: 75).

Judgements are an achievement of the tacit dimension, which – as Figure 15.1 illustrated – fuses re-presentations of mental traces from the past with here-and-now *intention*, *attention* and *meaning*: thinking is the process that joins these momentary tacit integrations together.

Wittgenstein makes the point that *talking* and *thinking* are not concepts of the same kind (even though they are intimately connected) and then ponders the possibility of unconscious *intention* that arises when two people think of the same person at the mention of a single word:

> *'At that word we both thought of him.' Let us assume that each of us said the same words to himself – and how can it mean MORE than that? – But wouldn't even those words be only a germ? They must surely belong to a language and to a context, in order really to be the expression of the thought of that man.*
>
> *If God had looked into our minds he would not have been able to see there whom we were speaking of. (Wittgenstein, 2001: 185)*

For those who might prefer to remain agnostic about divine intervention in the construction of such an argument, bear in mind the following: the real implication is that no such meta-being exists to demonstrably do as God might. If two people thought of the same person's name at the mention of a given word, we can take it as a sign that their sense perceptions of the here-and-now fused in some aligned way with their respective re-presentations of past experience. Their adaptive unconsciousness was aligned. Short of mystical revelation, the tacit knowing that facilitated this alignment cannot be converted into 'explicit knowledge' (i.e. information) and 'managed'.

The KM Illusion

The history of Western philosophy has tended to treat the subject and object as discontinuous entities. On the one hand, the mainstream management and business community has tried to be as objectivist as possible and fix the problems that arise (for example, through 'critical realism' [Archer et al., 1998; Danermark et al., 2002]); on the other hand, constructivism and related positions have stressed that knowing subjects – people – are essential to the process of knowing.

Noting that a focus on scientific approach necessarily excluded the importance of people and context-specific know-how, the economist (and from 1974, Nobel Laureate in Economics), Friedrich von Hayek, lamented in 1945 that:

> *Today it is almost heresy to suggest that scientific knowledge is not the sum of all knowledge. But a little reflection will show that there is beyond question a body of very important but unorganised knowledge which cannot possibly be called scientific in the sense of knowledge of general rules: the knowledge of the particular circumstances of time and place. It is with respect to this that practically every individual has some advantage over all others in that he possesses unique information of which beneficial use might be made, but of which use can be made only if the decisions depending on it are left to him or are made with his active cooperation. (Hayek, 1945: 521)*

After the Second World War, it seemed as if investing in science would provide the discoveries from which wealth would flow. However, the rapid economic growth of countries such as Japan, which spent a relatively low proportion of GDP on basic research, prompted research into the causes of technological innovation and pointed to 'needs' associated with the 'particular circumstances of time and place' to which Hayek referred. Major studies such as *Wealth from Knowledge* (Langrish et al., 1972) revealed that, while the exploitation of scientific discoveries was occasionally responsible for establishing new trajectories of development, context-specific necessities were more often the parents of improvement innovations and novel ways of exploiting past practice. Gibbons et al. (1994) and Nowotny et al. (2001) later coined the terms Mode 1 and Mode 2 knowledge production to differentiate the generation of scientific information (Mode 1) from generating the capacity to do things 'in the context of application' (Mode 2).

From the point of view of managers, KM offered the alluring possibility of extending the coherence of Mode 1 knowledge production to Mode 2 knowledge production. The subjective would be 'raised' to the level of the objective, while common sense and other context-specific know-how would become a resource – 'best practice' would be cut from the cake of experience and served up on a platter, wherever it was required.

Nonaka and Takeuchi's proposals for converting tacit know-how into explicit 'knowledge' provided a technique for aligning the capacity of individuals to make a difference – the practice of power – with objective knowledge that transcended power and human experience. This sleight-of-hand is evident in the caveat added to their definition of knowledge as 'justified true belief':

> *[W]e adopt the traditional definition of knowledge as 'justified true belief'. It should be noted, however, that while traditional Western epistemology has focused on 'truthfulness' as the essential attribute of knowledge, we highlight the nature of knowledge*

as 'justified belief'. This difference in focus introduces another critical distinction between the view of knowledge of traditional Western epistemology and that of our theory of knowledge creation. While traditional epistemology emphasises the absolute, static, and nonhuman nature of knowledge, typically expressed in propositions and formal logic, we consider knowledge as a dynamic human process of justifying personal belief toward the 'truth'. (Nonaka and Takeuchi, 1995: 58, emphasis in the original)

Nonaka and Takeuchi appear to be saying contradictory things. If knowledge is based on experience and justified according to belief in its viability (as advanced by radical constructivism outlined in this chapter), the concept of 'truth' as something that transcends human experience is inadmissible. Conversely, if a metaphysical notion of transcendental 'truth' is accepted as the goal that knowledge-creation moves towards, personal belief becomes an inadmissible part of the objective knowledge being sought. The tension is between anchoring faith in human experience or absolute 'truth'. So how does the KM illusion manage to do both things at the same time?

KM sales-pitches tend to avoid using the verb 'to know', its gerund 'knowing' and adjectival uses of 'knowing'. Instead, the noun 'knowledge' is often used as if it were an adjective: one that qualifies a commodity, which can be moved around, for example, through *knowledge sharing* or *knowledge flows*. But what exactly is *shared* and what *flows*? If you tell us something, we might *learn*, yet your knowledge will not be diminished or 'converted' into something else. As we have argued, the capability to know is possessed by people: short of brain transplant, it stays with the knowing subject. Yet, reflecting this idea in management plans might be counterproductive. Who would give a second glance to fads based on *knowing sharing, knowing flows* and *knowing management? Knowing workers* hardly has the ring of *knowledge workers*. Even a dedicated follower of management fashion might ask for clarification.

Trying to construct a comparative theory of abstracted things without a basis for comparison can be a frustrating business:

There once was a man who aspired to be the author of the general theory of holes. When asked 'What kind of hole – holes dug by children in the sand for amusement, holes dug by gardeners to plant lettuce seedlings, tank traps, holes made by road-makers?' he would reply indignantly that he wished for a general theory that would explain all of these. He rejected ab initio the – as he saw it – pathetically common-sense view that of the digging of different kinds of holes there are quite different kinds of explanations to be given; why then he would ask do we have the concept of a hole? Lacking the explanations to which he originally aspired, he then fell to discovering statistically significant correlations; he found for example that there is a correlation between the aggregate hole-digging achievement of a society as measured, or at least one day to be measured, by econometric techniques, and its degree of technological development. The United States surpasses both Paraguay and Upper Volta in hole-digging. He also discovered that war accelerates hole-digging; there are more holes in Vietnam than there were. These observations, he would always insist, were neutral

and value-free. This man's achievement has passed totally unnoticed except by me.
(MacIntyre, 1978: 260)

Had he turned his talents to a general theory of abstracted knowledge and its management, there are signs that our erstwhile fool in a hole might have achieved high office and influence.

Some time after co-authoring *The Knowledge-Creating Company* with Ikujiro Nonaka, Hirotaka Takeuchi teamed up with Michael Porter to answer the question *'Can Japan Compete?'* In a list of the *Top Two Hundred Business Gurus*, Harvard Business School professor, Michael Porter, is rated number one[3] (Davenport and Prusak, 2003: 219). In remarkable contrast to the centre-of-stage role afforded to knowledge in Takeuchi's work with Nonaka, his collaboration with Michael Porter produced a book whose index does not have an entry for knowledge, let alone tacit knowledge; but it does include a robust testimony to what the authors believe to be 'universally true'.

> *Our study of Japan's competitive and uncompetitive industries has generated findings that are consistent with what we know to be universally true about the competitiveness of nations: vigorous competition in a supportive business environment, free of government direction, is the only path to economic vitality. Japan is not a special case after all. (Porter et al., 2000: 100)*

Even so, the universalism becomes more qualified by the book's conclusion, where the authors offer their view about Japan's capacity to compete. They argue that, in the more successful parts of Japan's economy, Japan has already demonstrated its ability to move from 'a stability-based system to a competition-based system' (Porter et al., 2000: 188) and the challenge is to remove obstacles to further progress. Thus, Japan will need to embrace some elements of the Western approach, as in the past. Nevertheless, the result: 'will not be a clone of American capitalism but a new and distinctly Japanese conception of competition'. Hence, the authors pose the question: 'Where will the uniqueness lie?' It seems odd to want it both ways: either local people in specific contexts can make local differences – our argument – or situational determination should bow to universal pressures, which seems to be Porter et al.'s (2000: 100) argument.

Conclusion

We are not opposed to the idea that knowledge and knowing provide valuable tools for better understanding practice and supporting the search for new and different approaches to management. On the contrary, we have argued that such tools are essential to appreciating the active process of 'knowing how to do things' in the here-and-now of any given specific. However, tacit knowledge cannot be objectified: it is a tool of knowing in the way that spectacles are a tool of seeing and, as

Polanyi noted, he could not use his spectacles to scrutinize his spectacles. Any quest for objectivity embraces the delusion that observations could be made without an observer. Accordingly, objective knowledge is presumed to transcend the complexities of practice to represent a universal 'truth' – yet, by its very nature, such knowledge would be divorced from the knowing subject and the practice of power.

To the extent that 'explicit knowledge' aligns itself with the assumed virtues of trying to be 'as objective as possible', it is divorced from the knowing subject's capacity to 'imagine a difference' and the processes by which this is aligned with the capacity to 'make a difference': the practice of power. Whereas tacit–explicit knowledge-conversation provides the basis for Nonaka and Takeuchi's (1995: 246) claim that the Japanese knowledge-creating process is no longer an enigma but 'universal', somebody who had never been to Japan could read their book over and over again and still be unable to think and act in the manner of a Japanese *insider*. Explicit knowledge *is* information – and no information signal can account for its own interpretation by the reflexively automatic actions of *insiders* acting in situ. Information is no substitute for the tacit knowing that evolves as a result of dwelling in a particular context. Reading an etiquette guide for visitors to Japan or a book of hints about how to tackle mathematical puzzles or play chess is no substitute for the tacit knowing that evolves as consequence of practical experience. Insight, intuition and judgement depend on a journey that other people cannot make on your behalf. To be sure they can help, but ultimately such qualities depend on the knowing subject's capacity to know.

Edward T. Hall (who coined the terms 'high-context' and 'low-context' cultures introduced earlier) suggests that, 'even Sherlock Holmes would be helpless in a country so different as Japan': as an *outsider*, Holmes would lack the *insider's* capacity to 'read' and interpret clues – thus, 'only his Japanese counterpart could play such a role' (1990: 35). In perhaps his most subtle and famous analysis, *The Adventure of Silver Blaze*, Sherlock Holmes investigated the murder of John Straker and the disappearance of the famous racehorse Silver Blaze. When the police inspector asked Holmes if there was any point to which his attention should be drawn, Holmes replied:

> 'To the curious incident of the dog in the night-time.'
> [Inspector] 'The dog did nothing in the night-time.'
> 'That was the curious incident,' remarked Sherlock Holmes.[4]

Holmes deduced that the midnight visitor was someone whom the dog knew well: but how might KM capture this capacity for insight? Simply concluding that people should pay attention to the significance of what does happen is not particularly helpful. Holmes's insight derived from his gestalt tacit integration of information clues; his companion, Dr Watson, could tell the story of what happened, but Watson lacked Holmes's capacity for tacitly integrating the clues.

In Japan and other high-context cultures, much of communication resembles interaction among networks of people who develop highly aligned Holmesian capacities for 'reading' the silent language of information signals that might be overlooked by *outsiders*. Of course, these *insiders* might construct stories about how they knew whatever it was they know, whether for their own consumption, as in the case of *Nihonjinron* (theorizing about being Japanese), or for amusement (as we saw with the case of the Trobriand Islanders) or the entertainment of distinguished visitors who play the role of Dr Watson. Hence, a Japanese Sherlock Holmes might find it polite or expedient to present a 'public face' that goes along with Western approaches based on 'universal truth', but his or her 'true feelings' might not be commensurate with such a view – even if it was presented by a very distinguished Dr Watson.

Our argument has been that close community relationships within Japanese organizations mediate disciplinary and facilitative power through highly aligned tacit knowing – the *insider's esprit de corps* – that *outsiders* cannot 'see', still less objectify. *Insiders* themselves cannot articulate their adaptive unconsciousness, yet it enables and constrains their practices. The power mediated by the tacit dimension cannot be reduced to presumptions of cause and effect: tacit integrations cannot be articulated and any attempt to propose that an ineffable X causes an objectified Y is constructed on ontological quicksand. The capacity to know *insider* practice is only implied by the capacity to read events in a manner that seems to be aligned with *insider* practice. Although some Western academics might have their questionnaires translated into Japanese and trumpet their responses as signs of North's unidirectional march to market-rational specialization and the division of labour, such questionnaires and surveys are blind to the power that is mediated by aligned tacit knowing – unless, of course, their authors believe in Nonaka and Takeuchi's (1995) concept of tacit–explicit knowledge-conversion. Although the believers are legion and include some very distinguished people, this does not in itself render tacit–explicit knowledge-conversion viable. Ample evidence exists to suggest that all sorts of distinguished people are capable of holding beliefs that are implausible.

Many US or UK organizations rely heavily on explicit communication, along with formal rules and contracts. Nowadays, even quite important matters, which would once have demanded a face-to-face meeting, are often dealt with by email and mobile communications. Expectations about innovation and change are often coupled to the extensive 'horizontal' movement of people and ideas, as traditional notions of organizational boundaries are recognized to be ambiguous. The interaction between ICTs and accepted working practices has, for example, generated new opportunities and constraints. Informal networks, communities of practice and the recent recognition of virtual teams, which work across cyberspace – which were almost unheard of a decade or so ago, have helped to focus attention on the relationship between the organization and its context. However, the question of who is *inside* and *outside* any given organization is often ambiguous: 'hot ideas' might be clicked across the globe but fail to find their way into the adjoining office (Brown and Duguid, 2001). To the extent that KM projects purport to offer 'explicit knowledge' as a product that is superior to information, they are likely to fall short of expectations precisely because 'explicit knowledge' *is* information. Noting KM's lack of philosophical foundations, Brown and Duguid (2002: 118) cautioned that people might be 'trying to lift a gun too heavy to handle to aim at a target too insubstantial to matter'. Indeed, it could be worse if, for example, shots from the KM gun hit the judgement of experienced knowers and their 'deep smarts'.

Japan's institutional rules-of-practice sustain a highly developed sense of who belongs to which organization. The practice of power produces a degree of coordination that renders KM superfluous. An individual cannot get far without an organizational affiliation and breaking the *insiders'* implicit code is a recipe for ostracism and unpalatable if not unbearable unpleasantness – short of going to work for a foreign organization, his or her employment prospects within Japan would become 'difficult'. In Japan, organizational affiliation, connections and introductions are essential to effective practice. The individual is not a 'free agent' in the sense of being able to make 'rational' choices without regard to obligations to the groups on which he or she depends. Japan's institutions act as a lens that focuses the merits of social learning and story telling, of the type that is evident in Anglophone literature about communities of practice, on the integrated working, learning, innovation and social practices of organizational *insiders*. In Anglophone terms, we might find something similar to Japanese social learning at work in deeply integrated professional communities (Perrow, 1986). Loyalty to a professional vocation is a fast-disappearing concept in Western organizations and it is often undermined by remorseless economic rationalism, efficiency-drives and the rhetoric of value above all else – nevertheless, professional loyalty represents an important example of how the benefits of Japanese-style knowing might be exploited in low-context cultures.

The symbolism implied by those Japanese companies that have a graveyard for their employees, with the implication that the employee's soul and corporate destiny are journeys that should be made together, might appear wholly incongruent with market-rational concerns that couple liberal individualism to efficiency and price. Yet, it is an embedded part of the power relations that bind Japanese employers and their senior cadre together – and power mediated by highly aligned tacit knowing among organizational insiders is an essential part of the process that makes this possible. As Foucault (1991: 27) argued, we should not talk merely about either 'power' or 'knowledge', rather: 'power and knowledge directly imply one another ... there is no power relation without the correlative constitution of a field of knowledge, nor any knowledge that does not presuppose and constitute at the same time power relations'. Of course, as Western management and organization theory largely marginalizes and trivializes any concern with power it is perhaps not surprising that it can get knowledge and knowing so wrong (Clegg et al., 2005).

Notes

1 The basis for this observation includes seven years of first-hand experience derived from working in Japan for a Japanese organization (1992–9). See also: Hirotaka Takeuchi (1998) 'Beyond Knowledge Management: Lessons from Japan'. Available at: http://www.sveiby.com/articles/LessonsJapan.htm

2 According to comparative data provided by Japan's Ministry of Justice (quoted in *Nikkei Weekly*, 25 November 2002: 3), in 2001 Japan had 18,851 lawyers (or 14.8 per hundred thousand of population). In 1999, France had 32,036 (54.7 per hundred thousand) lawyers. Figures for 2000 indicate that there were 116,282 (141.4 per hundred thousand) lawyers in Germany, compared to 89,341 (168.8 per hundred thousand) in the UK and 972,722 (352.1 per hundred thousand) in the United States.

3 For the record, Ikujiro Nonaka is rated number 57 and the co-author of this chapter, Stewart Clegg is number 130.

4 http://www.ongoing-tales.com/SERIALS/mystery/DOYLE/Blaze.html

References

Anderson, B. (1991) *Imagined Communities: Reflections on the Origin and Spread of Nationalism.* New York: Verso. [Originally published by Verso 1983.]

Archer, M., Bhaskar, R., Collier, A., Lawson, A. and Norrie, A. (1998) *Critical Realism: Essential Readings.* London: Routledge.

Bergesen, A.J. and Sonnett, J. (2001) 'The global 500: mapping the world economy at century's end', *American Behavioral Scientist*, 44(10): 1602–15.

Brown, J.S. and Duguid, P. (2001) 'Knowledge and organization: a social-practice perspective', *Organization Science*, 12(2): 198–213.

Brown, J.S. and Duguid, P. (2002) *The Social Life of Information.* Boston, MA: Harvard Business School Press.

Clegg, S.R. (1990) *Modern Organizations.* London: SAGE Publications.

Clegg, S. and Kono, T. (2002) 'Trends in Japanese management: an overview of embedded continuities and disembedded discontinuities', *Asia Pacific Journal of Management*, 19: 269–85.

Clegg, S.R., Kornberger, M. and Pitsis, T. (2005) *Managing and Organizations.* London: SAGE Publications.

Clegg, S. and Ray, T. (2003) 'Power, rules of the game and the limits to knowledge management: lessons from Japan and Anglo-Saxon alarms', *Prometheus*, 21(1): 23–40.

Cook, S.D. and Brown, J.S. (1999) 'Bridging epistemologies: the generative dance between organizational knowledge and organizational knowing', *Organization Science*, 10(4): 381–400.

Cleary, T. (1999) *Code of the Samurai.* Tokyo: Tuttle.

Danermark, B., Ekström, M., Jakobsen, L. and Karsson, J. (2002) *Explaining Society: Critical Realism in the Social Sciences.* London: Routledge. [Originally published in Swedish by Studentlitteratur, 1997.]

Davenport, T.H. and Prusak, L. (2003) *What's the Big Idea? Creating and Capitalizing on the Best Management Thinking.* Boston, MA: Harvard Business School Press.

Einstein, A. (1982) *Ideas and Opinions.* New York: Three Rivers Press. [Originally published by Crown 1954.]

Fingleton, E. (1997) *Blindside: Why Japan is Still on Track to Overtake the US by the Year 2000.* Tokyo: Kodansha International. [Originally published in the US by Houghton Mifflin, 1995.]

Fingleton, E. (1999) *In Praise of Hard Industries: Why Manufacturing, Not the New Economy is the Key to Future Prosperity.* London: Orion.

Foucault, M. (1991) *Discipline and Punish.* London: Penguin. [Originally published in French as *Surveiller et punir*, 1975; first English translation by Allen Lane, 1977.]

Gao, B. (2001) *Japan's Economic Dilemma: Prosperity and Stagnation.* Cambridge: Cambridge University Press.

Gibbons, M., Limoges, C., Nowotny, H., Schwartsman, S., Scott, P. and Trow, M. (1994) *The New Production of Knowledge*. London: SAGE Publications.

Gladwell, M. (2005) *Blink: The Power of Thinking without Thinking*. New York: Little, Brown.

Glasersfeld, E., von (2002) *Radical Constructivism: A Way of Knowing and Learning*. London, RoutledgeFalmer. [Originally published 1995.]

Granovetter, M. (1985) 'Economic action and social structure: the problem of embeddedness', *The American Journal of Sociology*, 91(3): 481–510.

Hall, Edward T. (1989) *Beyond Culture*. Garden City, NY: Anchor Press/Doubleday. [Originally published 1976.]

Hall, Edward T. (1990) *The Silent Language*. New York: Anchor Press. [Originally published by Doubleday, 1959.]

Hall, I. (2002) *Bamboozled! How America Loses the Intellectual Game with Japan and its Implications for Our Future in Asia*. New York: M.E. Sharpe.

Hayek, F.A. (1945) 'The use of knowledge in society', *The American Economic Review*, 35(4): 519–30.

Jha, S. (2002) *Reconsidering Michael Polanyi's Philosophy*. Pittsburgh: University of Pittsburgh Press.

Johnson, C. (1992) *MITI and the Japanese Miracle: The Growth of Industrial Policy 1925–1975*. Tokyo: Charles E. Tuttle. [Originally published in US by Stanford University Press, 1982.]

Johnson, C. (2004) *Blowback: The Costs and Consequences of American Empire*. New York: Holt and Company.

Katz, R. (2003) *Japanese Phoenix: The Long Road to Economic Revival*. New York: M.E. Sharpe.

Kondo, D. (1990) *Crafting Selves: Power, Gender, and Discourses of Identity in a Japanese Workplace*. Chicago, IL: University of Chicago Press.

Kono, T. and Clegg, S. (2001) *Trends in Japanese Management*. London: Palgrave.

Kuhn, T.S. (1970) *The Structure of Scientific Revolutions*, 2nd edn. Chicago: University of Chicago Press.

Langrish, J., Gibbons, M., Evans, W.G. and Jevons, F.R. (1972) *Wealth from Knowledge*. Basingstoke: Macmillan.

Leonard, D. and Swap, W. (2004) 'Deep smarts', *Harvard Business Review*, September: 88–97.

Lewin, A., Long, C. and Carroll, T. (1999) 'The coevolution of new organizational forms', *Organization Science*, 10(5): 535–50.

MacIntyre, A. (1978) *Against the Self-Images of the Age: Essays on Ideology*. Notre Dame, Indiana: University of Notre Dame Press. [Originally published by Gerald Duckworth and Company, 1971.]

Malinowski, B. (1932) *The sexual life of savages in north-western Melanesia: an ethnographic account of courtship, marriage, and family life among the natives of the Trobriand Islands, British New Guinea, with a preface by Havelock Ellis*. London: Routledge & Kegan Paul.

Mason, R.H.P. and Caiger, J.G. (1973) *A History of Japan*. Rutland, Vermont and Tokyo, Japan: Charles E. Tuttle Company.

Mikuni, A. and Murphy, T. (2003) *Japan's Policy Trap: Dollars, Deflation and the Crisis of Japanese Finance*. Washington, DC: Bookings Institution Press.

Miyamoto, M. (1995) *Straightjacket Society: An Insider's Irreverent View of Bureaucratic Japan*, Tokyo. [Originally published in Japanese as Oyakusho no Okite by Kodansha International 1993.]

Nakane, C. (1972) *Japanese Society*. Berkeley, CA: University of California Press. [Originally published by University of California Press, 1970.]

Nonaka, I. and Takeuchi, H. (1995) *The Knowledge-Creating Company: How Japanese Companies Create the Dynamics of Innovation*. Oxford: Oxford University Press.

Nonaka, I., Toyama, R. and Konno, N. (2000) SECI, *Ba* and leadership: a unified model of dynamic knowledge creation, *Long Range Planning*, 33: 5–34.

Nørretranders, T. (1999) *The User Illusion: Cutting Consciousness Down to Size*. London: Penguin Books. [Originally published in Danish as *Maerk verden* by Gyldedendalske Boghandel, 1991.]

North, D. (1990) *Institutions, Institutional Change and Economic Performance*. Cambridge. Cambridge University Press.

Nowotny, H., Scott, P. and Gibbons, M. (2001) *Re-thinking science: Knowledge and Public in an Age of Uncertainty*. Cambridge: Polity.

O'Dell, C. and Grayson, C.J. (1998) *If Only We Knew What We Know*. New York: Free Press.

Penrose, E.T. (1995) *Theory of the Growth of the Firm*. Oxford: Oxford University Press. (Originally published in 1959.]

Perrow, C. (1986) *Complex Organizations: A Critical Essay*. New York: Random House.

Polanyi, M. (1969) *Essays by Michael Polanyi*, ed. M. Greene Chicago, IL: University of Chicago Press.

Polanyi, M. (1974) *Personal Knowledge: Towards a Post-Critical Philosophy*. Chicago, IL: University of Chicago Press. [Originally published 1958.]

Polanyi, M. (1983) *The Tacit Dimension*. Gloucester, MA: Peter Smith. [Originally published by Doubleday, 1966.]

Polanyi, M. and Prosch, H. (1977) *Meaning*. Chicago: University of Chicago Press. [Originally published 1975.]

Porter, M., Takeuchi, H. and Sakakibara, M. (2000) *Can Japan Compete?* Basingstoke: Macmillan.

Ryle, G. (2000) *The Concept of Mind*. London: Penguin Books. [Originally published by Hutchinson, 1949.]

Scarbrough, H. and Swann, J. (2001) 'Explaining the diffusion of knowledge management: the role of fashion', *British Journal of Management*, 12(1): 1–12.

Schumpeter, J. (1976) *Capitalism, Socialism and Democracy*. London: George Allen & Unwin. [Originally published in the USA, first UK publication 1943.]

Stiglitz, J. (2004) *The Roaring Nineties: Why We're Paying the Price for the Greediest Decade in History*. London: Penguin Books.

Storey, J. and Barnett, E. (2000) 'Knowledge management initiatives: learning from failure', *Journal of Knowledge Management*, 4(2): 145–56.

Sugimoto, Y. (2003) *An Introduction to Japanese Society: Second Edition*. Cambridge: Cambridge University Press.

Takeuchi, H. and Nonaka, I. (2004) *Hitotsubashi on Knowledge Management*. Singapore City, Singapore: John Wiley and Sons.

Terry, E. (2002) *How Asia Got Rich: Japan, China and the Asian Miracle*. New York: M.E. Sharpe.

Tsoukas, H. (2003) 'Do we really understand tacit knowledge?', in M. Easterby-Smith and M. Lyles (eds), *The Blackwell Handbook of Organizational Learning and Knowledge Management*. Oxford: Blackwell. pp. 410–27.

Weick, K. and Westley, F. (1996). 'Organizational learning: affirming an oxymoron', in S. Clegg, C. Hardy and W. Nord (eds), *Handbook of Organization Studies*. London: SAGE Publications, pp. 440–58.

Williams, B. (2001) 'Plato', in R. Mong and F. Raphael (eds), *The Great Philosophers: From Socrates to Turing*. London: Weidenfeld & Nicolson, pp. 47–92.

Wittgenstein, L. (2001) *Philosophical Investigations*. Oxford: Blackwell. [Originally published by Blackwell, 1953.]

Index

'abduction' 28, 332
absorptive capacity 131, 259
Ackoff, R.L. 135
action
    connection with knowledge 24–5, 53,
        60, 85, 115
    distinguished from practice 60
    knowing as 12, 60–1, 109, 112, 257
    Pragmatist focus on 61–2
    preceded by cognition 136
ActivePhoto 168
'adaptive unconsciousness' 5, 323, 326
'affordance' 64–5
Alvesson, M. 176, 190–1
Alvey Programme 260–2, 267, 268, 269
American Girl Place 167
Anderson, B. 326–7
Anderson, Brad 158
'anti-representationalism' 145
apprenticeship 26, 32, 58, 75, 76, 120, 167–8, 169
Aramark 285
architecture
    physical 305–6
    social 306
Arthur, J.B. 282
Artyfact 265–6, 267
autonomy 42
    knowledge workers 186–7
'autopoietic system' 42
Awad, E.M. 130

ba (shared context in motion) 25–6, 30–6
    building, connecting and energizing 41–4
    dialoguing 33–4
    exercising 34
    originating 33
    plurality of 35–6
    systemitizing 34

Bacdayan, P. 52
Bailey, T. 189
balanced scorecard 241, 243, 250
Bales, R.F. 138
Bank of America 169
Barnes, B. 92–3
Barnett, E. 1, 3, 321
Barnett, W.P. 289
Bell, D. 88, 91, 94, 100, 107
Bergeron, B. 129
Best Buy 158–9, 166–7, 169
'best practices' 16, 289
Bettis, R.A. 278
bicycle riding example 13, 56–7, 59, 62–3, 66,
        110–11, 142, 144
Blackler, F. 224
blind man example 321
'blinks' 5, 321, 333
Bock, F. 230
Boeing 304, 308
Bontis, N. 239, 249
'bounded rationality' 141, 147–8
bread-making machine example 72–4, 116–22
Bristol-Meyers Squibb 310
Brooking, A. 245
Brown, J.S. 9, 12–13, 98, 215, 343–4
Buckmann Laboratories 299
buddies 305
burakumin 324–5
bushi 324
bushidô 327
business networks 256–7

calculated intangible value 241, 250
Campbell, Bill 159–60
Campbell, J.P. 211
car driving examples 57, 114–15
care 33, 44

Carlile, P.R. 148
Cartesian view 54–5, 57–8, 85
'category mistakes' 61, 329
Cellbase 265, 267, 268
Center Parcs 210
Chrysler Corporation 201, 300–1
Clark, K.B. 133
Claxton, G. 5
Clever Hans 336–7
cognition
    information receptors 161–2
    and language 89–90
    preceding action 136
cognitive science 133
Cohen, W.M. 255
coherence 142, 146
    among *ba* 36
combination *see* explicit-explicit
        knowledge conversion
commitment 33, 44
    human resource configuration 282
    organizational and occupational, knowledge
        workers 171–98
communication
    and aligned tacit knowing 321–2, 336–8
    informal 98
communities of practice 13–14, 58, 148, 213,
        227, 228, 257
    application of rules 92
    ba compared 32
    inter-organizational 261, 267
    role of human resources 307, 310
    telephone operators 99
conceptual knowledge assets 38
consciousness
    Piaget/Vygotsky debate 137
    sense perceptions preceding 5, 321, 333–4
    redefinition 138
    and tacit knowing 114, 321, 333
constructive controversy 215
context 24, 64, 88, 91, 115, 257
    importance to knowledge workers
        175–6, 179–82
    see also *ba*
Cook, S.D.N. 9, 12–13, 215
core capabilities
    as 'core rigidities' 41
    and innovation 255
core competencies
    'extendibility' 292
    rethinking 78, 79
    in teams 58
core employees 280
'corporate culture' 207, 223, 225

cost, market and income approaches 250
creative chaos 42–3
Crick, F. 10–12

DaimlerChrysler/General Motors
        collaboration 259
data
    distinction from meaning and practice
        127, 130, 135–8, 141, 146, 147
    management of 133, 139–40
    vs. information 131–4
data-information-knowledge continuum
        88, 100
data-information-knowledge-wisdom (DIKW)
        model 135
Davenport, T.H. 85–6
Dean, J.W. 278
deep smarts 15–16, 157–69, 321
    cost 169
    creating receptors 161–2
    and experience 160–1, 163
    managerial 159–60
    technical 159
    transfer techniques 162–9
Delco 311
Delery, J.E. 284
dentist example 113
Deutsche Bank 207
Dewey, J. 61–2, 88
distinction drawing 88–90
division of knowledge 257–8
    countering 268–9
    nature in particular networks 269
DNA structure 10–12
domain of action 88, 90
Doty, D.H. 284
Drucker, P. 4, 127, 201, 330
Duguid, P. 1–2, 98, 343–4
dynamic affordance 65–7, 73

Economic Value Added (EVA) 241, 244, 249
Edvinsson, L. 240, 243, 245, 251
Einstein, A. 10, 144, 331, 332
employment modes 273–4
    acquisition 282
    alliance 287
    contracting 285
    internal development 280
    theoretical perspectives 276–8
    and value/uniqueness of human capital 278–80
employment relationships 275
    dualistic model 176–7, 191–2, 193–4
    market model 172, 173–4, 193
    organization focused 281–2

employment relationships *cont.*
  partnership 287–8, 302, 306
  symbiotic 283–4
  transactional (job-focused) 285–6
enclaves 176–7, 182–5
experience 10
  and deep smarts 160–1, 163
experiential knowledge assets 37–8
experimentation, guided 168–9
explicit-explicit knowledge conversion
    (combination) 27, 28, 30, 34, 116
explicit knowledge 2, 25, 51, 224
  conceptual knowledge assets 38
  privileged over tacit knowledge 52, 54–5
  relationship with tacit knowledge 55–7,
    108, 122, 135
  synonymous with information
    342, 343
  systemic knowledge assets 38
explicit-tacit knowledge conversion
    (internalization) 27, 28, 30, 34, 116
  non-viability 57, 77
externalization *see* tacit-explicit
  knowledge conversion

F1 Grand Prix Engineering 266–7, 269
FedEx 312
Festinger, L. 305
Fiol, C.M. 212, 213
first line management (FLM) 209
flutemakers 74–7
Flyvbjerg, B. 17
Ford, Henry 200
Foucault, M. 344

Gadamer, H.-G. 101
Gaver, W.W. 64, 65
GE healthcare 162
General Motors 201, 311
  DaimlerChrysler collaboration 259
generative dance 12–13, 54, 70–2
  examples 73–4, 76
genres 67–9
Ghazari, H.M. 130
Gibbons, M. 175, 182, 339
Gibson, J.J. 64, 65
Gladwell, M. 5
Glaserfeld, E. von 10, 331, 333
Granovetter, M. 327
Granstrand, O. 268
Grant, R.M. 31, 258
Grayson, C.J. 328, 329
Greenhalgh, L. 304–5, 313
Groff, T.R. 129

group (collective) knowledge 51
  all knowledge as 87, 92–3
  as domain of action 90
  effect on thinking 137
  as 'free resource' 9
  individual knowledge privileged 52,
    54–5, 57–8
  informal 98
  relationship with individual knowledge 8–9,
    12–13, 57–9
group explicit knowledge (stories) 67
group tacit knowledge (genres) 9, 13, 67–9
group-to-group relationships 309–10
group-to-organization relationships 310–11

Hall, E.T. 321–2, 342
Hamel, G. 292
hammer and nail example 111–12
Hampden-Turner, C. 247
Hayek, F. von 258, 339
Henderson, R.M. 133
Heraclitus 333
heuristic knowledge/heuristics 101, 102,
    103–4, 140–1, 149
Hill, S. 176
Holmes, Sherlock 342–3
Horibe, F. 200
Hugo, Victor 337–8
human capital
  distinguished from structural capital 200
  importance 210
  see also human resource architecture
human capital theory 276, 277
human resource (HR) architecture 15, 273–98
  acquiring human capital 282–4
  contracting human capital 284–6
  creating human capital alliances 286–8
  developing human capital 280–2
  'make or buy' 273–4, 276
  managing complexity of 289–90
  managing dynamics of 290–2
  uniqueness of human capital 279–80
  value of human capital 278–9
human resource configurations 275
  collaboration 288
  commitment-based 282
  compliance 284
  market-based 284
human resources (HR) 3, 199–219
  conceptual framework for knowledge
    work policies 204–16
  implications of knowledge work 201–2
  individual/systems perspectives 199–200
  lack of formal policies 185

human resources (HR) *cont.*
  management compared with personnel
    management 202–4
  need for change 217
  role in relationship building 299–315
Huselid, M.A. 282
Hutchins, E. 52

idealism 136, 145
imagination
  constraints on 131–2, 133, 138, 146, 147–8
  and management of uncertainty 134,
    140–3, 147
imagined communities 326–7
improvisation 45, 100–1
individual knowledge 51, 85
  privileged over group knowledge 52,
    54–5, 57–8
  relationship with group knowledge 8–9,
    12–13, 57–9
  see also personal knowledge
individual explicit knowledge (concepts) 67
individual tacit knowledge (skills) 67
individual-to-individual relationships 304–6
individual-to-group relationships 306–8
individual-to-organization relationships 308–9
indwelling 25, 95, 109, 114
information 2
  vs. data 131–4
  data-meaning meld 132–3, 139–40
  knowledge compared 24–5, 85, 88, 100–1, 330
  synonymous with explicit knowledge 342, 343
  synonymous with organizational
    knowledge 86
  see also explicit knowledge
Information Technology/Systems (IT/IS) 2, 103,
    128, 129–31, 223–5, 320
  and systemitizing *ba* 34
innovation
  deep smarts about 158
  and the generative dance 71–2
  inter-organizational 255–71
  managers' attitudes to 207–9
insider-outsider divide 7, 14, 323, 325–6, 327,
    332–3, 336–8, 342–3
intangible asset monitor 250, 251
Intel 280
intellectual capital (IC) 79
  benefits of social capital for 301
  indispensability 222
  see also knowledge assets
intellectual capital (IC) audit 250
Intellectual Capital Benchmarking System 250
intellectual capital (IC) index 250, 251

intellectual capital (IC) rating 250
intellectual capital (IC) valuation and
    measurement 2, 239–253
  classification of existing methods 249–50
  improving external reporting 244–5
  improving internal management 242–4
  literature review 240–2
  measurement/valuation distinction 240, 247
  statutory and transactional issue 245–7
  value and valuation 247–9
inter-organizational knowledge and innovation
    15, 29, 255–7
  case studies 260–7
  factors driving collaboration 258–60
  knowledge issues 257–8
inter-organizational networks 213
inter-organizational relationships 311–12
interaction with the world 25, 31, 63–4, 91
  and constraints on imagination 146
  'facilities' and 'frustrations' 64
  paper handling example 77–9
  two dimensions of 33
internalization *see* explicit-tacit
    knowledge conversion
Intuit 159–60

James, W. 135
Japan 3, 6–8, 319–47
  aligned tacit knowing and nation 327
  economic performance 6, 319, 322, 339, 341
  esprit de corps 7, 8–9, 322, 323, 339, 343
  insiderness 7, 320, 325–6, 327, 328–9,
    342–3, 344
  institutional and organizational power 6–8,
    14, 320, 322, 323, 326, 343, 344
  specificity 323–6
  yamato-damashii 328–9
Jet Propulsion Laboratory 158
job design 212
Jones, T.P. 129

Kale, P. 311–12
Kant, I. 137
Kao Corporation 44
Kaplan, R. 243
Katz, A.M. 121
Kay, J. 86
Kellogg, Donald 337
knowing
  as action (active process) 12, 60–1, 109,
    112, 257
  distinction from knowledge 53, 59,
    60–2, 62–3
  epistemology of practice 53, 59–67

knowing *cont.*
  interplay with knowledge 53-4, 69-72
  role of the body 110
knowing-as-a skill 94, 110-12
knowledge 257-8
  adjectival use of term 340
  as 'all of a piece' 51, 52, 134-5
  change in character over time 107-8
  collective nature 87, 92-3
  and competitive advantage 23, 128,
      199, 201, 222
  connection with action 24-5, 53, 60,
      85, 115
  and context 24, 64, 88, 91, 115, 257
  definitions 24, 85-6, 90, 339-40
  distinction from knowing 53, 59,
      60-2, 62-3
  division of 257-8, 268-9
  and economic development 107
  epistemology of possession 53, 54-9
  idealist position 136
  information compared 24-5, 85, 88,
      100-1, 330
  interplay with knowing 53-4, 69-72
  managers' 208-9
  personal nature 87, 93-4, 109-10, 112, 119
  and power 23, 344
  problematical nature of concept 135-6
  realist position 9, 136, 331
  as a tool 94-5, 114, 120
knowledge-as-data 127-8, 133
knowledge-as-meaning 127-8, 133
knowledge-as-practice 127-8, 135-8
knowledge assets 25-6, 36-8, 128
  developing and promoting sharing of 40-1
knowledge coaches 163, 166, 167, 169
knowledge conversion 9-10, 26-30
  'generation' preferred 74
  SECI process 25-6, 26-30
  see also explicit-explicit knowledge
      conversion; explicit-tacit knowledge
      conversion; tacit-explicit
      knowledge conversion; tacit-tacit
      knowledge conversion
'knowledge economy' 107-8, 171, 222,
    299, 313
knowledge intensive firms (KIFs) 201
knowledge management (KM) 127-54, 222-6
  for certainty/uncertainty 134, 140-3, 149
  data, meaning and practice 128-9, 138-40
  explosive growth 1, 127
  'fad' 1-2, 127, 330
  and generation of reflective
      practice 102-3

knowledge management (KM) *cont.*
  heuristic knowledge 103-4
  as illusion 320, 323, 338-41
  as information management 23, 330
  and IT/IS 103, 128, 129-31, 223-4
  Nonaka's change in attitude 329-30, 330-1
  optimistic claims 222, 234
  pipeline/river metaphors 212
  reasons for attention 222-3
  yamato-damashii or category mistake 328-9
Knowledge Management in Design and
    Innovation Networks (KAMDIN) 262-7
knowledge management initiatives, failure 1, 3,
    221-37, 320-1
  International Resources case 226-32
  lessons from 234-5
  problems and barriers 223-6, 232-4
knowledge producers 39, 40, 41, 44-5, 46
knowledge production
  Mode 1 339
  Mode 2 175-6, 182, 339
knowledge 'spiral' 9, 24, 26, 29-30, 45, 52,
    58, 116, 330
knowledge vision 39-40
knowledge work 199-219
  developing for 214-15
  implications for human resources 201-2
  integrated approach to 204-5
  management style 209
  organizational values, culture and
      climate 206-9
  performance management 215-16
  requirements 205-6
  staffing 210-11
  work and organization design 211-14
knowledge workers 14-15, 171-98, 225
  control relations 186-8
  dual dependent relationship 176-7,
      191-2, 192-3
  empirical cases 177-88
  enclaves 176-7, 182-5
  importance of contextual knowledge
      175-6, 179-82
  importance of management strategy 175
  job expectations 188
  marketization strategy 172, 173-4
  organizational/occupational commitment
      171-2, 174, 177, 188-92
  recruitment and selection 210-11
  reward systems 185-6, 216
Kochan, T.A. 311
Kogut, B. 52
Kondo, D. 8, 328
Kuhn, T.S. 133, 134, 136, 141, 144

Lake, D. 278
language
  and communication 338
  and distinction drawing 89
  and knowledge conversion 45
  and meaning 131–2
  as reminder of things known 122
Lave, J. 148
learning
  'accretion' model 133
  'by doing' 27, 163, 164
Learning Organization (LO) 223, 234, 330
legitimate peripheral participation 58
Leonard, D. 15–16, 268
Leonard-Barton, D. 285, 287
Lepak, D.A. 15, 210
Lewin, A. 323
Liedtka, J.M. 268
love 33, 44
low-context/high-context cultures 321–2
Lucier, Charles 221

MacArthur, Douglas 319
McCarthy, T. 91
McGowan, J. 102
machine design *see* bread-making machine
Maekawa Seisakusho 36, 43
Malinowski, B. 336
Malone, M.S. 240, 245, 251
'management knowledge' 208–9
management strategy, importance for
    knowledge workers 175
management style 209
managerial deep smarts 159–60
map example 109, 110
March, J.G. 144
market-to-book ratio 241, 249–50
Marr, B. 239, 243, 246
meaning
  and data vs. information 131–4
  distinction from data and practice 127, 130,
    135–8, 141, 146, 147
  management of 132, 133, 139
  tacit knowing and 331–5
Meiji Restoration 323–4
mentoring 305
Mercer, N. 90
Merrill Lynch 207
Microsoft 287
Miers, D. 91
Miner, A.S. 289
Mintzberg, H. 225
mission statements 69, 132
Miyamoto, M. 325–6, 327

Mohrman, S.A. 213
Mowday, R.T. 188

Nakane, C. 328
NEC 42
networks of practice 310
Newton's laws 109–10
Nietzsche, F. 31
Nishada, K. 31
Nonaka, I. 3–4, 8–10, 14, 52, 55, 72–4, 77, 85,
    87, 108, 109, 116, 118–19, 121, 122, 222,
    268, 292, 320, 321, 323, 329–30, 330–1,
    334–5, 339–40, 342, 343
Nord, Toby 167
Nørretranders, T. 5, 321, 333
Nortel (Europe) 212
North, D. 6, 322
Norton, D. 243

O'Dell, C. 328, 329
Oakeshott, M. 118, 119, 121
observation, guided 166–7
Opticon 306
Oracle Computers 207
organization-as-theory 92
organizational genres 68–9
organizational knowledge 58, 85–106
  case study 95–101
  collectivist understanding 86, 93
  as essence of firm 86
  ownership of 148
  and personal knowledge 88–95
  synonymous with information 86
organizational knowledge creation 8–12, 23–49
  bread-making machine example 72–4, 116–22
  leading the process 38–45
  process of 25–38
organizational relationships 300
  analyses 302
  five characteristics 303–4
  human resources role 15, 299–315
  types of 304–11
organizational structures 213
organizations
  cognitive limitations 162
  Japan 6–8, 8–9, 14, 320, 322, 325–6,
    328–9, 343, 344
  values, culture and climate 206–9
Orlikowski, W.J. 101
Ortega y Gasset, J. 64
Osterman, P. 311

Panafon Customer Care Department 87, 95–101
paper handling 77–9

Pearce, J.L. 289
peer learning 182–3
Peirce, C.S. 332
Penrose, E. 9, 93
performance management 215–16
Perlmutter, H. 311–12
Perry, Matthew 323
personal knowledge
  all knowledge as 87, 93–4, 109–10, 112, 119
  and organizational knowledge 88–95
  see also individual knowledge
Philips/Sony collaboration 260
Piaget, J. 137, 138, 333
Pickering, A. 145
Pike, S. 239, 243, 245
PIPSA 306
Plato 332
Polanyi, M. 3, 4, 6, 8, 10, 13, 56, 86–7, 89, 93–5,
  100, 108–9, 109–16, 119–20, 120–1, 135
  143, 144, 320, 321, 323, 329, 332, 335, 337,
  338, 342
Popper, K. 146
Porter, M. 278, 291, 341
power
  and choice of meaning 132
  of Japanese institutions and organizations 6–8,
    14, 320, 322, 323, 326, 343, 344
  and knowledge 23, 344
  and making a difference 3, 339, 342
  mediated by aligned tacit knowing 6, 7,
    326, 328, 343
  and operation of collectives 14
practice 59–60
  connection with tacit knowledge 143
  distinction from data and meaning 127, 130,
    135–8, 141, 146, 147
  epistemology of 53, 59–67
  goal-oriented vs. explorative 144
  guided 163–6
  inherent creativity 142
  irreducible to rules 17
  management of 139–40
  and thinking 144–6
Pragmatism 53, 61–2
Prahalad, C.K. 292
problem solving, guided 167–8
productive inquiry 62
prospect theory 133
Prusak, L. 85–6
Pulakos, E.D. 211

R&D 41, 255
  centralized 176
  collaborative 259, 260–2

radical constructivism 10, 142, 143–7,
  148, 331–2
realism 136, 145
'redundant' (overlapping) knowledge 43, 258,
  267, 268
Reed, M.I. 172, 173–4, 175, 192
reflective practice 45, 102–3, 163–6, 224
relationships see employment relationships;
  organizational relationships
requisite variety 43–4, 290
Rescher, N. 247, 248
resource-based view of the firm 222,
  276–8, 279
reward systems 185–6, 216, 282
Roberts, K.H. 52
Roos, G. 239, 240, 242, 243–4, 245, 251
Rorty, R. 145
Rousseau, D.M. 275, 281, 282, 283, 285
routine knowledge assets 38
Roy, D. 137
Ruggles, R. 223
rules
  vs. guided experience 164
  organizational 91–3
  practice irreducible to 17
Rylander, A. 251
Ryle, G. 118, 135, 329, 333

SAIC 166, 169
Salaman, G. 212
Scarbrough, H. 330
Schon, D.A. 45, 224
Schumpeter, J. 326
science 10, 55, 136, 331–2
'scientific management' 200–1, 212
Scribner, S. 148
SECI process 25–6, 26–30
  promoting 44–5
sense perceptions 110
  preceding consciousness 5, 321, 333–4
  and thinking 331–2
Seven-Eleven Japan 34–5
sexism 207
Sharp 42
Sherif, M. 310
Shotter, J. 121
Simon, H. 8, 31, 52, 55, 58, 140,
  141, 147–8
Singh, H. 311–12
Skandia 301
Skandia navigator 241, 245, 250, 251
Skinner, B.F. 138
Smith, A. 138, 258
Snell, S.A. 15, 210, 278, 279

social capital
  benefits 301
  human resource's role in developing 302-12
  importance 300-1
  and team learning 215
socialization *see* tacit-tacit
    knowledge conversion
Sony/Philips collaboration 260
SouthTech 263-5, 267, 268, 269
Southwest Airlines 302
staffing 210-11
Steelcase 305
Stewart, T.A. 222, 223, 242-3, 250,
    251, 307
Stigler, G. 256
Stiglitz, J. 319
Storey, J. 1, 3, 209, 212, 321
stories and storytelling 3, 67, 98, 132,
    163, 306
Strassman, P.A. 249
Strategos 158, 166, 169
Strawson, P.F. 102-3
Sugimoto, Y. 324-5
Sveiby, K.E. 243, 245, 251
Swanborn, P.G. 249
Swann, J. 330
Swap, W. 15-16
Swart, J. 201
systemic knowledge assets 38

T-shaped skills 268
tacit-explicit knowledge conversion
    (externalization) 4, 8, 9-10, 27, 28, 30,
    31, 33, 44, 45, 52, 72-3, 116, 122, 320,
    323, 329-31
  bread-making example 72-4, 116-22
  non-viability 5, 12, 57, 77, 87, 120, 334-5,
    339-40, 341-2, 343
tacit knowledge/tacit knowing 25, 51, 107-25
  communication and aligned
    321-2, 336-8
  connection with practice 17, 142
  customer care operators 99-100
  development 214
  distinction from knowing 62-3
  as evidence of imagination 142-3
  exceptional individuals 264
  experiential knowledge assets 37-8
  explicit knowledge privileged over
    52, 54-5
  functional aspects 112-13
  ineffability 5, 6, 8, 120-1, 321
  and meaning 331-5

tacit knowledge/tacit knowing *cont.*
  methodological challenge 269
  misunderstanding 3, 4-5, 108, 116-17,
    122, 329
  national discipline and aligned 326-7
  neglect in IT-driven approaches 224
  phenomenal aspects 112-13
  Polanyi's conception 4, 10, 13, 56, 109-16,
    135, 320, 321, 323, 329, 332-3
  power mediated by aligned 6, 7, 326, 328, 343
  relationship with explicit knowledge 55-7,
    108, 122, 135
  routine knowledge assets 38
  semantic aspects 112-13
  significance for organizations 108
  understanding 118-22
  and uniqueness of human capital 279, 292
  see also deep smarts
tacit-tacit knowledge conversion (socialization)
    26-7, 28, 30, 116
Takeuchi, H. 3-4, 8, 9, 52, 72-4, 77, 85, 87,
    108, 109, 116, 118-19, 121, 122, 268, 292,
    320, 321, 323, 330-1, 334-5, 339-40,
    341, 342, 343
Taylor, F.W. 200
team spirit 323
Teece, D.J. 260, 276
TeleMeter 262-3, 267, 268, 269
theoretical (codified) knowledge 107-8
  importance for knowledge workers 181-3
  refraction through the 'lifeworld' 115-16
  synthesis with contextual knowledge 175-6
theory
  organization as 92
  and personal knowledge 91
Thiétart, R.-A. 148
Tobin's Q. 249-50
Toffler, A. 23
Toyota 41, 43, 169, 259
transaction cost economics 276, 277, 279
Trobriand Islanders 336
Trompenaars, F. 247
trust 33, 36, 44
Tsoukas, H. 4-5, 136
Tsui, A.S. 281, 282, 285
Twining, W. 91

Ulrich, D. 278
Upton, W.S. 244

Viant 308-9
Vickers, G. 59
Vico, G. 145, 333

von Foerster, H. 90
Vygotsky, L.S. 137, 138, 145

W.L. Gore and Associates 308
Wade-Benzoni, K.A. 283
Watson, J. 10–12
Weick, K.E. 52, 98
Wenger, E. 13–14, 98, 307
Whirlpool 168, 169
Whitehead, A.N. 25

Wittgenstein, L. 2, 87, 122, 142, 335, 338
work design 211–14
World Bank 310
X-ray example 89–90, 113–14
Xerox 77–9

yamato-damashii 328
Youndt, M.A. 284

Zander, U. 52